D1190000

"This book takes us a long [illegible] s credibility will be lost unles[illegible] recognizes [illegible] celibacy as a privileged participation in the virginal heart of Christ. In Christ, there burned such an ardent love that He did not hesitate to sacrifice Himself for His Bride, the Church. St. John Paul II affirmed that priestly celibacy is a 'nuptial reality' when advancing his renewal of priestly formation called for by the Second Vatican Council. Bishop Cozzens offers a solid and thorough theological exploration of this nuptial reality and how it is lived out in excellence through the evangelical counsels."

Archbishop Allen H. Vigneron
Archbishop of Detroit, Michigan

"True to form, Bishop Cozzens presents with depth, faith, and insight the beauty of the Church's tradition on the fittingness of the evangelical counsels in the life of priests who follow Christ, the Bridegroom of the Church. Clergy in every stage of life and ministry will glean beautiful truths and be confirmed in their particular calling to follow Christ, as I have been through reading this wonderful book. May this book inspire priests to live with greater given-ness for the Bride of Christ, the holy people of God."

Most Reverend David L. Toups, S.Th.D.
Bishop of the Diocese of Beaumont, Texas
Former Rector, St Vincent DePaul Seminary, and author of
Reclaiming Our Priestly Character

"This book is a rich theological study and a prayerful meditation on a principal element in the vocation of every priest: he is irrevocably united to Christ the Bridegroom of the Church. Explaining how living the evangelical counsels, making a total gift of himself, brings profound freedom to the priest, Bishop Cozzens invites us to enter more deeply into a life of prayer—'being with' Christ the Bridegroom —so that with and in Christ, we will be even more deeply 'for' his Bride, the Church. I have no doubt that this book will help every priest who reads it to grow in his desire to be a living image of Christ."

Archbishop Peter Sartain
Archbishop Emeritus of Seattle, Washington

A LIVING IMAGE OF THE BRIDEGROOM
THE PRIESTHOOD AND THE EVANGELICAL COUNSELS

BISHOP ANDREW H. COZZENS, S.T.D., D.D.

INSTITUTE FOR PRIESTLY FORMATION
IPF PUBLICATIONS

INSTITUTE FOR PRIESTLY FORMATION
IPF Publications
2500 California Plaza
Omaha, Nebraska 68178-0415
www.IPFPublications.com

Copyright © October 19, 2020 by
Institute for Priestly Formation, Inc.

All Rights Reserved. No part of this book may be
reproduced, stored in a retrieval system, or transmitted by any
means, electronic, mechanical, photocopying, recording, or
otherwise, without the written permission of the Institute for
Priestly Formation.

Printed in the United States of America
ISBN-13: 978-1-7342831-3-6

Scripture texts in this work are taken from the *New American
Bible, revised edition* © 2010, 1991, 1986, 1970 Confraternity
of Christian Doctrine, Washington, D.C. and are used by
permission of the copyright owner. All Rights Reserved.
No part of the New American Bible may be reproduced
in any form without permission in writing from the
copyright owner.

Cover design by Timothy D. Boatright
Vistra Communications
Tampa, Florida

INSTITUTE FOR PRIESTLY FORMATION
MISSION STATEMENT

In collaboration with Catholic seminaries and dioceses,
we form seminarians, priests, and bishops in holiness and
accompany them in their ongoing spiritual growth, so they
can more effectively lead others to Christ.

INSTITUTE FOR PRIESTLY FORMATION
Creighton University
2500 California Plaza
Omaha, Nebraska 68178-0415
www.priestlyformation.org
ipf@creighton.edu

To Saint John Paul II who inspired a generation of priests
to try and live the total self-gift of their calling.
Saint John Paul II, pray for us.

TABLE OF CONTENTS

INTRODUCTION

"The priest is called to be the living image of Jesus Christ, the bridegroom of the Church."[1]

In what way is a priest a bridegroom? What does marriage have to teach us about the Catholic priesthood? If the priest, through his ordination, is in a spousal relationship with the Church, how is he to understand this relationship? What does it mean for his life? Many of those involved in the pastoral care of the young know the creative theological revolution Pope St. John Paul II has caused with his *Theology of the Body*, especially how he opened up with new spiritual depth the beauty of the Sacrament of Marriage. However, St. John Paul II also applied his nuptial theology to priests. In his most important document on the priesthood, *Pastores Dabo Vobis*,[2] St. John Paul II invited priests to understand their priesthood through the profound supernatural reality of marriage. He used the nuptial image, so present in the mystery of redemption, to reveal who the priest is for the Church and how the priest should live. In fact, through the use of this image, St. John Paul II gave the Church a new and deeper understanding of the ministerial priesthood.

St. John Paul II was not the first to try to use the nuptial image to understand the priesthood; the Fathers of the

1

Church did it long before he did. But his *Theology of the Body* allowed him to bring this understanding to a new depth for the priest. It is likely his greatest contribution to the theology of the priesthood. As Archbishop Allen Vigneron has commented:

> I read Pope John Paul II's teaching [in PDV] that priestly celibacy is a nuptial reality, that something of the essence of marriage is essential to the celibacy of a priest, as just the "break-through" insight that is capable of yielding that renewal of priestly celibacy hoped for by the Council, so that now revitalized, this element of the Church's life and teaching—far from being an encumbrance—will be part of that store of resources she can draw upon in her efforts to evangelize the contemporary world.[3]

This book aims to study and explain the fundamental insight of St. John Paul II—that the priest is called to be a living image of Jesus Christ, the Bridegroom of the Church. St. John Paul II wants to use this image to inspire priests to make a more profound gift of themselves so they can live in deeper union with Christ for the salvation of their people. To serve this goal, we will study the nuptial image in the whole Tradition, starting with the Scriptures and paying special attention to the Fathers of the Church. We will see the nuptial nature of the Sacrament of Holy Orders and come to understand how this image inspires the priest to total self-gift.

The identity of the priest, like that of every Christian, is fundamentally relational. Christians come to know who they are in relationship because everything in Christianity flows from and leads to the communion of the Trinity. As St. John Paul II said in *Pastores Dabo Vobis*, "It is within the Church's mystery, as a mystery of Trinitarian communion in missionary tension, that every Christian identity is revealed, and likewise the specific identity of the priest and his ministry."[4] For the priest to understand his identity, he must understand two central relations: his relationship with Christ and his relationship with the Church. The primary point of reference for priestly identity is Christ Himself: "The priest finds the full truth of his identity in being a derivation, a specific participation in and continuation of Christ himself, the one high priest of the new and eternal covenant. The priest is the living and transparent image of Christ the priest."[5] The second point of reference for priestly identity is Christ's relationship to the Church: "Reference to the Church is therefore necessary, even if it is not primary, in defining the identity of the priest. As a mystery, the Church is essentially related to Jesus Christ. She is his fullness, his body, his spouse."[6]

Thus, to understand who he is and, therefore, how he should live, the priest must understand himself in relationship with the Trinity through his relationship with Christ and the Church. Since Jesus Christ is the Bridegroom of the Church, understanding this nuptial image, which is deeply rooted in the Scriptures and patristic theology, will help the priest understand his fundamentally relational identity. From this, he will understand more deeply his own path to union with God, living in imitation of Christ the Bridegroom. Although this book seeks to explore theology in depth, it also provides provide some intellectual food for the priest's prayer life. It is in prayer that the priest more deeply understands who he is in relationship with Christ and receives the spiritual motivation and grace needed to live that identity. For this reason, some reflection questions for prayer have been placed at the end of every chapter for the priest to use to spur interior conversation with God. The goal of this book is to invite priests to embrace Christ's own nuptial love so that they might be led to the deeper freedom and joy in giving their lives in union with Christ for the Church.

We might ask from where St. John Paul II got this idea of the priest as an image of Christ the Bridegroom? Of course, one has to see the origins in St. John Paul II's own thought, and we will explore these origins further[7] But it is interesting to note that at the 1990 Synod on the Formation of Priests, which led to the document *Pastores Dabo Vobis*, only one of the synod fathers connected the priesthood to Christ the Bridegroom of the Church in his *relatio* given in the synod hall. Bishop Robert Brom of San Diego, California, stated that "a deeper understanding and appreciation" of the priesthood could be gained if it was understood that priests are not only ordained "to represent and act *in persona Christi, capitis Ecclesiae*," but also "*sponsi Ecclesiae*."[8] He said, "Through the imposition of the hands and the outpouring of the Holy Spirit, priests are assimilated and configured to Christ, bridegroom of the Church, to be for her in love after the manner of Jesus in the pattern of his paschal activity."[9] This insight apparently found a warm reception among the synod fathers since the main theme of it was included in their post-synodal *propositiones* submitted to the Holy Father.[10]

Bishop Brom argues that this understanding of the priesthood flows from a proper Christology: "The image of Jesus as head of his body the Church is enhanced when he is further seen to be Son in the spousal imagery of a bridegroom in relation to his bride."[11] He points out how this understanding of Christ is derived from the Scriptures, both in the Old and New Testaments, and is the primary lens through which many prophets, evangelists, and St. Paul himself understood the covenantal relationship of Christ with His Church. Brom argues that it is also important for a proper ecclesial understanding of the priesthood: "Priestly identity must be seen primarily in essential terms—in terms of communion—first, as identification with Christ, the bridegroom of the Church, and consequently, as a new way of being in the Church and for the Church as stand-ins for the Bridegroom."[12] When one reads *Pastores Dabo Vobis*, one sees that St. John Paul II took this exhortation to heart, perhaps because it had such a deep accord with his own *Theology of the Body*.

Yet Bishop Brom takes St. John Paul II's insight even deeper. He goes on to show that the bridegroom image applied to the priest has practical ramifications for how the priest should live. As Bishop Brom describes:

> Pastoral poverty, celibate chastity and mature obedience can only be understood and appreciated as evangelical ways of being like the bridegroom in behalf of the Bride. It is the bridegroom who out of love for the Bride "emptied himself, taking the nature of a slave" (Phil 2:7) and "being rich, became poor" (2 Cor 8:9); it is the bridegroom who "humbled himself, obediently accepting even death, death on a cross" (Phil 2:8), in order to demonstrate the depth of his love for the Bride that she might be the spotless spouse of the spotless lamb.[13]

This is a profound insight. Since Vatican II, the Magisterium has consistently called for the priest to embrace the evangelical counsels of obedience, celibacy, and poverty. Bishop Brom argues that understanding the priest as an image of the bridegroom helps us understand why the priest should live the evangelical counsels. He argues that when one fully understands the nature of Christ's spousal love as the bridegroom of the Church, and how the priest is called to be a living image of the bridegroom, one finds a reason for the priest to live obedience, celibacy, and poverty. This is a doctrinal reason, rooted in the sacramental identity of the priest, to show how the evangelical counsels fit with the very nature of the priesthood. Bishop Brom argues that the priest's sacramental configuration to Christ the Bridegroom of the Church reveals why the priest is meant to live the evangelical counsels. St. John Paul II adopted this insight in *Pastores Dabo Vobis*, and this book will show its depth and importance by explaining the bridegroom image in Scripture and the Tradition.

The Relationship Between the Priesthood and the Evangelical Counsels

Most of the discussion of the priestly life in the twentieth century, especially since Vatican II, has been dedicated to the topic of priestly celibacy. Rivers of ink have been poured out about celibacy, and a few of these works have even explored celibacy as a nuptial reality. Notably, St. Pope Paul VI briefly expounded the nuptial nature of celibacy in his encyclical *Sacerdotalis Caelibatus*.[14] However, it is with the work of St. John Paul II that this motivation for celibacy begins to be fully explored.[15] This book is not another book on priestly celibacy, although its conclusions have profound ramifications for why priests should be celibate. This book is an exploration of the spousal self-gift of Christ that included more than just His celibacy, rather it included His whole life. Christ's life was a life lived in total dedication to the Father, completely poured out for the Church, His bride. He made His life a total gift of self through obedience, celibacy, and poverty, which reached their fulfillment in His self-gift on the Cross. In fact, the evangelical counsels only really make sense when they are lived as a unity; to live celibacy without poverty or obedience does not make sense. Only together are they a total self-gift.

To come to this deeper understanding of the priesthood and priestly way of life, we will begin with a scriptural study of the nuptial nature of redemption so that we may understand fully Christ as the Bridegroom of the Church and His nuptial self-gift on the Cross. Then, we will show how this nuptial self-gift is lived concretely by Christ through the evangelical counsels, which make His self-gift total. In this, we explore how and why Christ lived obedience, celibacy, and poverty as an expression of His nuptial self-gift. It is this connection between Christ's evangelical way of life and His spousal self-gift that allows us to see the connection between the evangelical counsels and the priesthood. To become a living image of the bridegroom, the priest must imitate this total self-gift of Christ by living all the evangelical counsels and not only celibacy.

As Vatican II made clear, the life of the priesthood is a life of pastoral charity.[16] St. John Paul II explains in *Pastores Dabo Vobis* that pastoral charity is not only the love of the shepherd for his sheep but also the love of the bridegroom for his bride.[17] To live the pastoral charity of Christ, the priest is invited to the total self-gift of the bridegroom for the bride. This is expressed best through a life according to the evangelical counsels.

Brief Historical Background

Priests have always been invited to live the evangelical counsels in some way, since the first Apostles were called to leave everything and share Christ's own way of life. A history of the evangelical counsels and the priesthood through the centuries is too much to be accomplished here,[18] but it is worth pointing out the current distinctions between diocesan priests and religious were not always as clear as they are today. In the second half of the first millennium, it was generally seen that there were three groups of people living completely consecrated to God: the monks, the virgins, and the clerics; all were seen as different expressions of consecrated life. Each of them had their own version of a profession or consecration. Ludwig Hertling has shown that "all three [types of profession] meant a commendation of the person to God and an irrevocable adoption of holy obligations, that all three contained something that we would today theologically describe as vows."[19] Both the monks and the priests lived according to the rule. The "canons," as Church discipline called them at the time, were a rule for the life of the clergy; they served the clergy in the same way that the rule served monks.[20]

This sheds light on some priestly reform movements like the Canons Regular in the eleventh and twelfth centuries. Many historians see these movements as diocesan priests being asked to live like monks for the sake of pursuing holiness. In fact, these were renewals of the discipline that had often been practiced in the first millennium which legislated that priests should live together under a set of rules for holiness of life. As Hertling explains:

The origin of the regular canons in the second half of the 11th century should not be imagined as if at this time secular clerics had congregated into an order to make vows in the manner of monks. There were no "secular clerics" at the time, at least not according to the law. Every cleric was "a man having been devoted to God, a religious, living under sacred profession." The intention of the reform of the clergy in the 11th century was not to create something new, but to highlight the old interpretation of the status of the clerics, in its complete circumference, as a holy status, especially through the revival of the old "canons."[21]

These origins are especially interesting when one considers that the first explicit formula for profession of the three evangelical counsels of poverty, chastity, and obedience as vows was in the 1148 edition of the Canons of St. Genevieve.[22] These canons certainly lived a lot like monks, but they began as a reform movement for diocesan priests. It was not until after this time that the strict distinctions began to develop between the secular and religious clerics.[23] It was also about this time when the Church stopped ordaining married men who had promised a vow of continence and started ordaining only those who were not married and promised perpetual celibacy.[24] What we see in the history of the priesthood is that all the important reform movements for priests pushed them toward things we would probably today consider the domain of the religious: the life of poverty, chastity, obedience, and community life.[25]

It is no wonder, then, that today the Magisterium is pushing diocesan priests in the same direction. Since Vatican II, and even before,[26] there has been a consistent call from the

Magisterium for priests to live the three evangelical counsels. *Presbyterorum Ordinis*, although it never directly mentions the "evangelical counsels," speaks of the need for priests to live obedience, celibacy, and voluntary poverty (15-17).[27] In *Pastores Dabo Vobis*, St. John Paul II states explicitly that priests are called to live the evangelical counsels in accord with their priestly identity,[28] and both the 1994 and 2012 Directory on the Ministry and Life of Priests dedicate a section to each of the three counsels. The current teaching of the Church seems to argue that the evangelical counsels, rather than being a point of distinction between the religious life and the priesthood, are actually a point of unity:

> As PDV and the Directory so strongly advise, the character-shaping qualities of the evangelical counsels of obedience, chastity and poverty are essential to the identity of every priest. . . . Far from being any mark of disparity between diocesan and religious priests, the evangelical counsels lived by both are a basis of profound unity.[29]

What, Precisely, Are We Advocating?

This book proposes that the reasons for a priestly life according to the evangelical counsels can be found in the sacramental identity of the priest—that is, in an understanding of the priest as a living image of Jesus Christ the Bridegroom of the Church. Since Vatican II, several other authors have explored the correlation between the priestly way of life and the evangelical counsels.[30] In explaining the importance of the counsels for priesthood, these authors do not argue that there should be no distinction between priests and religious, or that priests should take vows as religious do. There are important distinctions in theology and canon law between the priesthood and the consecrated life,[31] and because of these distinctions, there will be a different way of living the counsels for priests than for religious. In fact, we will demonstrate that priests have a distinct motivation for living the counsels, which will result in unique ways of living obedience, celibacy, and poverty. Rather than trying to turn all priests into religious, we want to show that through the nuptial nature of the Sacrament of Holy Orders, one can discover the priest's call to a life of total self-gift. This total self-gift is best expressed by the priest through a life of obedience, celibacy, and poverty, just as Christ Himself lived it. The counsels are a means—in fact, the best means—for a man to respond subjectively to the sacramental consecration that he receives in ordination. The counsels are the expression in the life of the priest of what he is for Christ and for the Church—a living image of the bridegroom.

We will demonstrate about the evangelical counsels what many authors have already stated about the Church's discipline of celibacy for her priests. The Second Vatican Council made it clear that celibacy "is not demanded by the very nature of the priesthood,"[32] even as the same council fathers argued that "celibacy has a many-faceted suitability (multimodam convenientiam) for the priesthood."[33] As we will see, this idea that celibacy, or the evangelical counsels, is "suitable" for the priesthood is more than saying that it is a nice fit, or that there are lots of good reasons for priests to be celibate. This fittingness of celibacy means that the priest better images Christ through celibacy. As Jean Galot, S.J., points out:

Celibacy enables the priest to better actualize his consecration to Christ with undivided love. It affords greater freedom and availability to serve his kingdom and to practice the perfect charity that consists in being all things to all. It bears witness to the mysterious marriage established between Christ and the Church, and to the dedication that encourages Christians to wed themselves to this one spouse as a chaste virgin to be presented to Christ (2 Cor 11:2). It gives access to a more extended spiritual fatherhood, thus enabling the priest to contribute more efficaciously to the work of regeneration from on high. It posits "a vivid sign of that future world which is already present through faith and charity, and in which the children of the resurrection will neither marry nor take wives" (PO 16; OT 10).[34]

From the very beginnings of the priesthood, when the Apostles were asked to leave everything to follow Christ, priests have always been invited, in various ways, to make a subjective response to the call of Christ—that is, to make a gift of their lives. As the tradition has developed from the beginning, this has involved a closer and closer link between the priesthood and celibacy. As St. John Paul II said, "On the basis of her experience and reflection, the church has discerned, with growing clarity through the ages, that priestly celibacy is not just a legal requirement imposed as a condition for ordination. It is profoundly connected with a man's configuration to Christ, the Good shepherd and Spouse of the Church."[35]

This book will demonstrate that this close connection between priesthood and celibacy is because the consecration of the priest in ordination calls forth from him a subjective response, the response of total self-gift of his life. And this call to a total self-gift is the reason for the "multimodam convenientiam" between all the evangelical counsels and the priesthood, not only celibacy. The evangelical counsels become the most suitable way for the priest to live because they are the way he imitates Christ's self-giving love for his bride. Of course, it is true that no subjective response can be absolutely required by the Sacrament of Holy Orders. This is because the only specifically human response required for the sacrament to be valid is intention. There can be no absolute requirement for celibacy or the evangelical counsels for the validity of the Sacrament of Holy Orders, just as holiness is not absolutely required. Yet who would argue that holiness is not essential to the priesthood? Jean Galot helps explain these distinctions when he speaks about celibacy and the priesthood:

> We must speak of a bond through suitability rather than necessity. It is an essential bond since celibacy conforms to the very nature of the priesthood. It is a bond of conformity since celibacy is absolutely necessary neither for the validity of the priesthood nor for the valid and fruitful accomplishment of priestly functions.[36]

Rather, what we would say is that celibacy is "so well adapted to the state as to illuminate its very nature."[37] This same argument must be made about all three evangelical counsels. Through living the evangelical counsels, the priest is better able to be a living image of Christ. This is because the evangelical counsels are co-natural with the priesthood. That is, when a priest lives obedience, celibacy, and poverty, it reveals more deeply the very nature of his priesthood, a life of total self-gift for the bride.

The Importance of the Bridegroom Image for Understanding the Priesthood

The 1990 Synod on the formation of priests was called together precisely to handle what the Holy Father called a "crisis in priestly identity."[38] It is well known that in the period following the Second Vatican Council, when many priests left active ministry, there was wide-spread confusion and even dissent from the Church's teaching about the nature and identity of the priesthood.[39] Through the use of the bridegroom image, St. John Paul II has opened up a deeper understanding of the identity of the priest, especially the relational dimension of this identity. Before Vatican II, there was almost no mention of the priest as representing Christ the Bridegroom of the Church in magisterial documents, and the Second Vatican Council made only a brief reference to the priest representing Christ as Bridegroom when it was reconfirming the Church's teaching on the importance of celibacy.[40] No magisterial teaching has gone as far as St. John Paul II in *Pastores Dabo Vobis*, when he says the priest "represents Christ the head, shepherd and spouse of the Church."[41] This is an expansion of the use of the traditional notion that the priest stands in the person of Christ (*in persona Christi*), which Vatican II had expanded to say in the person of Christ the head (*in persona Christi capitis*).[42]

In persona Christi capitis reveals a central aspect of the relational identity of the priest: he represents Christ, the head to His Body, the Church. But Christ is not only the head of the Church; He is also her bridegroom, and as St. John Paul

II says, "sacred ordination . . . configures the priest to Jesus
Christ the head and spouse of the Church."[43] To be faithful to the tradition, and a proper ecclesiology, we must also
see the Church as the bride of Christ, not only the body of
Christ. As we will demonstrate in chapter 2, an emphasis on
Christ as the head of the Church without an understanding
that he is also the bridegroom of the Church can reduce the
primacy of Christ in the relationship to the Church. Christ
could be seen as part of the Church, but not as the one who
stands before her and gives life to her. Thus, we will demonstrate that for a balanced ecclesiology, the priest must also be
seen as a representative of Christ the Bridegroom toward the
bride; as *Pastores Dabo Vobis* says, "Inasmuch as he represents
Christ the head, shepherd and spouse of the Church, the
priest is placed not only in the Church but also in the forefront of the Church."[44]

What is important is that by applying the bridegroom
image to the priesthood, the priest can come to a deeper
understanding of his own life lived in relationship with
Christ and the Church. Here is the real power of St. John
Paul II's application of the nuptial image to the Sacrament of
Holy Orders:

> Christ stands "before" the Church, and "nourishes and
> cherishes her" (Eph 5:29), giving his life for her. The
> priest is called to be the living image of Jesus Christ, the
> Spouse of the Church. . . . In virtue of his configuration
> to Christ, the Head and Shepherd, the priest stands in
> this spousal relationship with regard to the community.
> "Inasmuch as he represents Christ, the Head, Shepherd
> and Spouse of the Church, the priest is placed not only
> in the Church but also in the forefront of the Church"

("Propositio" 7). In his spiritual life, therefore, he is called
to live out Christ's spousal love towards the Church, his
Bride. Therefore, the priest's life ought to radiate this
spousal character which demands that he be a witness
to Christ's spousal love, and thus be capable of loving
people with a heart which is new, generous and pure,
with genuine self-detachment, with full, constant and
faithful dedication and at the same time with a kind
of "divine jealousy" (cf. 2 Cor 11:2), and even with a
kind of maternal tenderness, capable of bearing "the
pangs of birth" until "Christ be formed" in the faithful
(cf. Gal 4:19).[45]

The Holy Father is inviting us to see that we come to
a deeper understanding of how the priest is configured to
Christ *in persona Christi capitis* when it is understood that this
also includes his being *in persona Christi sponsi Ecclesiae*, in the
person of Christ the Bridegroom of the Church. Through
this image, the priest is seen both in his relationship with
Christ, configured to Christ the Bridegroom, and in his
relationship with the Church, standing in the forefront of
the Church representing the bridegroom. We will argue that
the priestly motivation to live the evangelical counsels comes
from his relationship with Christ in and for the Church. We
find here a motivation for a priestly life that is both Christological and ecclesiological.

The Power of Symbols

Twentieth-century theology saw a return to the more
patristic method of theology animated by the use of symbol
to help us capture theological truth.[46] A symbol is a complex sign that is rich in its power to convey meaning, evoke

memory, and stir up feelings. Symbols help us to grasp truths that cannot be adequately explained only through a purely discursive or abstract explanation.[47] Symbols are the way the Bible speaks to us, and symbols have the power to open us up more directly to the experience of God. One needs only to look at the sacraments to see the power of symbol in the Christian life. The sacraments, by virtue of the supernatural power given to the signs by Christ, put us into direct contact with God. In the sacraments, "signs and symbols taken from the social life of man: washing and anointing, breaking bread and sharing the cup, can express the sanctifying presence of God and man's gratitude toward his Creator."[48]

The nuptial symbol, which is also a sacramental reality, must be called an archetypal symbol because of its foundation in creation and universality in every culture and religion. It is especially important for Christians (and Jews), since it is the central image used to explain the covenantal relationship of God with His people. The power of this symbol is seen in how it is able to disclose the human relationship with God in terms that come from human experience:

> The symbolizing of the divine-human covenant in spousal imagery gives us a natural, human context for understanding a supernatural, divine reality. This imagery, furthermore, has the capacity to endure throughout the ages because mankind continues to marry, and it has the capacity to transcend cultural barriers because all peoples marry. The use of the spousal imagery for symbolizing the divine-human covenant is as temporally and spatially universal as the use of bread for symbolizing the Eucharistic Body of Christ. The ordinary, everyday stuff of humanity becomes the image for symbolizing

the extraordinary, supramundane divine reality that has embraced human existence and transformed it.[49]

Because of its centrality and universality, the marriage symbol can help us to understand the priesthood better. One could view the priesthood through many lenses, but seeing the priest in his relationship with Christ and the Church through the spousal image reveals new insights about the priestly life. These insights, while new, are also deeply rooted in the tradition, since the Scriptures and patristic theology are heavily imbued with a spousal understanding of the covenant and the Church.[50]

If the crisis in priestly identity is to be overcome, priests need the power of symbols to facilitate a deeper grasp of their life and ministry.[51] Because these can connect to the priest at the level of his identity, the spousal image is able to put the priest existentially in touch with the real roots of his priesthood: the covenantal, sacramental, and sacrificial life that he is called to live. This symbol can provide a powerful antidote to the problematic understandings of priesthood in today's world. As Dermot Power states strongly:

> The significance of this model of the Church and its powerful symbolism for the ministerial priesthood cannot be underestimated at a time when the emphasis in ministry tends towards the appropriation of functions and professional skills which in themselves, however valuable, cannot substitute for the miracle of grace which is the mystery of the Church and the priesthood which exists to serve and protect that nuptial mystery.[52]

If the marriage image applied to the priesthood is fully understood, it will provide not only new intellectual insights but new insights at the level of praxis in the life of the priest.[53] The marriage image, thus, gives a real explanation and motivation for the daily self-giving life of the priest. The symbol of marriage can fire his imagination to help him understand and embrace the life of total self-gift to which he is called.

One of the most important reasons for properly understanding the nuptial image is that it can feed the priest's prayer life. Deep down, every priest knows that to sustain his sacrificial way of life, he must be rooted in prayerful union with Christ. Thus, understanding Christ's own nuptial way of life, a way that is so deeply rooted in the Scripture, will deepen the priest's prayerful union with Christ and allow him to make his life a gift in, with, and through Christ. It is no accident that the mystical tradition of our Church prefers the nuptial image to describe the relationship with God. The mystics all know the power of this image, and the priest must come to know it too.

John Paul II and the Nuptial Image in Theology

Perhaps no one saw the importance of the nuptial image in theology more than St. John Paul II.[54] Through his *Theology of the Body*, the Holy Father taught the Church about the nuptial reality that is at the heart of both creation and redemption. He sought to give deeper insight and clarification to the Church's teaching on human sexuality, including both the Sacrament of Marriage and celibacy for the sake of the kingdom. St. John Paul II explained what he calls the "nuptial meaning" of the body: that written by God into the very body of every person is the capacity for expressing nuptial love. The Holy Father defined nuptial love as "that love in which the human person becomes a gift and—through this gift—fulfills the very meaning of his being and existence."[55] For St. John Paul II, this is what it means to be made in the image and likeness of God. It means to be made for union through self-giving love and, of all the loves a human being is capable of, it is nuptial love that leads to union through a person making a total gift of themselves. This is why for St. John Paul II, celibacy and virginity must be seen as nuptial because through them, one makes a total gift of oneself for union with God. To his mind, celibacy is no less nuptial than the physical love between two married people. As St. John Paul II wrote almost twenty years before he was pope:

> It is not sexuality which creates in a man and a woman the need to give themselves to each other, but, on the contrary, it is the need to give oneself, latent in every human person, which finds its outlet, in the conditions of existence in the body, and on the basis of the sexual urge, in physical and sexual union, in matrimony. But the need for betrothed love, the need to give oneself to and unite with another person is deeper and connected with the spiritual existence of the person. It is not finally and completely satisfied simply by union with another human being. Considered in the perspective of the person's eternal existence, marriage is only a tentative solution of the problem of union of persons through love. . . . Spiritual virginity, in the perspective of eternal life, is another attempt to solve the problem."[56]

Those who choose celibacy do so because they are convinced of the "possibility of betrothed and requited love between God and man: the human soul, which is betrothed to God, gives itself to Him alone."[57]

This is also why Christ's redemption must be understood as a nuptial gift (just as the Scriptures portray it). Because in redeeming us, Christ gives us Himself; He shares with us His own life, and He becomes one with us; this is properly nuptial love. As St. John Paul II says in *Mulieris Dignitatem*:

> We find ourselves at the very heart of the Paschal Mystery, which completely reveals the spousal love of God. Christ is the bridegroom because "he has given himself": his body has been "given," his blood has been "poured out" (Lk 22:19-20). In this way "he loved them to the end" (Jn 13:1). The "sincere gift" contained in the Sacrifice of the Cross gives definitive prominence to the spousal meaning of God's love. As the Redeemer of the world, Christ is the bridegroom of the Church.[58]

In redeeming us, Christ has revealed the heart of spousal love in God by His total self-gift; and in this love, he has also revealed the true heart of every human vocation, the call to self-gift that leads to union. It is this same understanding of love as total self-gift that St. John Paul II applies to the priest in his definition of pastoral charity:

> The essential content of this pastoral charity is the gift of self, the total gift of self to the Church, following the example of Christ. Pastoral charity is the virtue by which we imitate Christ in his self-giving service. It is not just what we do, but our gift of self, which manifests Christ's love for his flock. Pastoral charity determines our way of thinking and acting, our way of relating to people. It makes special demands on us.[59]

This understanding of pastoral charity as spousal love, as total self-gift, is what will allow us to see the connection between the evangelical counsels and Christ's spousal love. We will fully explain what Bishop Brom stated, that the priest's living of obedience, celibacy, and poverty unites him to Christ as a living image of the bridegroom and has a particularly pastoral character, imitating Christ's self-gift in pastoral charity. Following the insights of St. John Paul II and Bishop Brom, we will explain this insight of St. John Paul II in *Pastores Dabo Vobis*, which brings together spousal love, pastoral charity, and the evangelical counsels:

> Jesus Christ, who brought his pastoral charity to perfection on the cross with a complete exterior and interior emptying of self, is both the model and source of the virtues of obedience, chastity and poverty which the priest is called to live out as an expression of his pastoral charity for his brothers and sisters. In accordance with St. Paul's words to the Christians at Philippi, the priest should have "the mind which was in Christ Jesus," emptying himself of his own "self," so as to discover, in a charity which is obedient, chaste and poor, the royal road of union with God and unity with his brothers and sisters (cf. Phil. 2:5).[60]

Questions for Discussion, Reflection, and Prayer

1. How does your understanding of the priesthood change when you begin to see the priest as a bridegroom? Why is it not enough to see the priest as head and shepherd of the Church? Why does St. John Paul II think we also need the image of the bridegroom?

2. As you pray and ponder, what does using the nuptial image contribute to an understanding of the relationships of Christ, the priest, and the Church?

3. Do you know the desire for total self-gift through the evangelical counsels? Do you desire to say with St. Paul, "I even consider everything as loss because of the supreme good of knowing Christ Jesus my Lord. For his sake I have accepted the loss of all things and I consider them so much rubbish, that I may gain Christ and be found in him" (Phil 3:8-9)?

NOTES

1. John Paul II, *Pastores Dabo Vobis* (1992), sec. 22.

2. *Pastores Dabo Vobis* (PDV) was published in 1992 following the Eighth Ordinary Synod of Bishops, which gathered in 1990 to discuss the Formation of Priests in the Circumstances of the Present Day.

3. Allen Vigneron, "Renewed Celibate Living for Heralds of the New Evangelization," in *Chaste Celibacy: Living Christ's Own Spousal Love; Proceedings of the First Annual Symposium on the Spirituality and Identity of the Diocesan Priest*, March 15-18, 2001, by the Institute for Priestly Formation and Sacred Heart Major Seminary, ed. Edward G. Matthews, Jr. (Omaha, NE: privately printed, 2001), 13-14.

4. *Pastores Dabo Vobis*, sec. 12.

5. Ibid.

6. Ibid.

7. In the Holy Father's writings, the priest as a representative of the bridegroom first shows up explicitly in *Mulieris Dignitatem* (15 August 1988 in *Acta Apostolicae Sedis* [AAS] 80 [1988]: sec. 26), although, as we will explore below, the roots are clearly seen in the collection of four sets of Wednesday audiences given between September 1979 and November 1984 which have come to be known as the "Theology of the Body" (published together as: *Man and Woman He Created Them: A Theology of the Body* [Boston: Pauline Books and Media, 2006]).

8. Robert Brom, "Understanding the Ordained Priesthood through Biblical Imagery," *Relatio in Aulam*, 3 October 1990 (Eighth Ordinary Synod of Bishops, 1990): 2. Our quotations come from a personal copy of the transcript of the *relatio* given at the synod; however, a published summary is available in Italian: Mons. Robert H. Brom, vesc. di San Diego (USA) Relatio n. 6, Interventi in Aula, 3 Oct. 1990, in Giovanni Caprile, S.J., "Il Sinodo dei Vescovi 1990" (Roma: *La Civiltà Cattolica*, 1990), 87.

9. Ibid.

10. The official *Propositiones* of the Synod are the summary of the important themes given to the Holy Father when the Synod is finished. They were not published, but St. John Paul II quotes them at several points in *Pastores Dabo Vobis*, and from this, we see that the synod fathers applied the spousal image to the priesthood in sec. 7.

11. Brom, *Relatio in Aulam*, 1.

12. Ibid., 2.

13. Ibid., 3.

14. *Sacerdotalis Caelibatus* (1967), in AAS, 59 (1967): n. 26.

15. John Paul II develops the nuptial nature of priestly celibacy in his *Theology of the Body* (see *Man and Woman He Created Them*, 412-462) and applies it directly to the priesthood in *Pastores Dabo Vobis* (sec. 29; see also

sec. 22 and 23). The most thorough work on the nuptial nature of priestly celibacy has been done by Laurent Touze, *Célibat sacerdotal et théologie nuptiale de l'ordre*, Thesis ad Doctoratum in Theologia totaliter edita (Roma: Pontificia Universitas Sanctae Crucis, 2002). Touze points out that the use of the spousal image to justify celibacy is found frequently in different parts of the tradition, although it was not often the primary reason given for celibacy; that reason tended to focus on other ecclesiological, spiritual, or moral reasons. Yet he says the nuptial nature of Holy Orders has been cited more and more as a reason for celibacy during the last fifty years, yet without being fully explained (see Touze, 6).

16. "Hence, as they fulfill the role of the Good Shepherd, in the very exercise of their pastoral charity, they will discover a bond of priestly perfection which draws their life and activity to unity and coordination" (*Presbyterorum Ordinis*, sec. 14).

17. See *Pastores Dabo Vobis*, sec. 22.

18. In fact, this author is not aware of any comprehensive history on the subject although much can be learned from the important historical study of the common life of secular clergy by Jerome Bertram, *Vita Communis: The Common Life of the Secular Clergy* (Leominster, UK: Gracewing, 2009).

19. Ludwig Hertling, S.J., "Die Professio der kleriker und die entstehung der drei gelübde," Zeitschrift für Katholische Theologie 56 (1932): 153.

20. Ibid., 163.

21. Ibid., 164-165. Jerome Bertram makes it clear that one of the main distinctions between the monks and the secular clergy had to do with the vow of poverty. In the first millennium, secular clergy most often lived in community with a superior, a rule, and a common way of life; but they were often allowed to keep their property. One reason for this was that some of them were married, and even though upon ordination they took a vow of continence and moved into the common house, property could be maintained to care for their wives and families (see chapters 1-7, *Vita Communis: The Common Life of the Secular Clergy*).

22. Basil Cole, O.P., and Paul Conner, O.P., *Christian Totality: Theology of the Consecrated Life*, revised edition (Mumbai, India: St. Paul's, 1997), 60. Even though poverty, chastity, and obedience do not show up explicitly until the twelfth century, they, of course, existed since the beginning in the life of Jesus and the evangelical way of life to which He called His apostles. These counsels were always at least implicitly expressed in the various forms of consecrated life in the Church which existed since the beginning; see Hans Urs von Balthasar, *The Christian State of Life*, trans. Sister Mary Frances McCarthy (San Francisco: Ignatius Press, 1983), 14ff.

23. As Balthasar says, "The Middle Ages also opened up for the first time a deep and tangible gulf between the secular clergy and the religious clergy, which in fact first allowed these states of life to come into being

and confront one another consciously in their difference" (Balthasar, *The Laity and the Life of the Counsels*, trans. Brian McNeil, C.R.V., with D.C. Schindler [San Francisco: Ignatius Press, 2003], 86).

24.   Many authors cite the fact that the absolute requirement of celibacy for all clerics—that is, not ordaining any married men—can only be traced to the eleventh century. But it is important to point out that although married clergy existed in the first millennium, perpetual continence was required of them by law from at least the fourth century, and several important studies in the last three decades have argued that the vow of perpetual continence for married clergy was widespread in the Church long before the fourth century; see Christian Cochini, S.J., *The Apostolic Origins of Priestly Celibacy*, trans. Nelly Marans (San Francisco: Ignatius Press, 1990); Stefan Heid, *Celibacy in the Early Church: the Beginnings of a Discipline of Obligatory Celibacy for Clerics in the East and West*, trans. Michael Miller (San Francisco: Ignatius Press, 2000); Alfons Maria Stickler, S.D.B., *The Case for Clerical Celibacy*, trans. Brian Ferme (San Francisco: Ignatius Press, 1995). These opinions have not been without their critics, but seem to have been given some magisterial approval in the *Directory on the Ministry and Life of Priests*, which says, "the Church, *from apostolic times*, has wished to conserve the gift of perpetual continence on the part of the clergy and choose the candidates for Holy Orders from among the celibate faithful (see 2 *Thes* 2:15; 1 *Cor* 7:5; 9:5; 1 *Tim* 3:2-12; 5:9; *Tit* 1:6-8)" (81, emphasis added).

25.   This implicit relationship between the priestly state of life and the life of the evangelical counsels is one of the main points of von Balthasar's book, *The Christian State of Life*, see especially pp. 266-329, entitled, "The Priestly State and the State of the Counsels." To see how the Church has consistently encouraged common life for the renewal of the priesthood, see the work by Jerome Bertram, *Vita Communis: The Common Life of the Secular Clergy*.

26.   See John XXIII, *Sacerdotii Nostri Primordia*, (1 August 1959) in AAS 51(1959): sec. 14-35.

27.   Heidi Böhler (*I consigli evangelici in prospettiva trinitaria: Sintesi dottrinale* [Milano: San Paolo, 1993], 85-86) theorizes that council fathers did not refer to the "evangelical counsels" as such because in the mentality at the time, the counsels were too strictly associated with the religious life, and it would have seemed like imposing religious life on the priesthood. This was true even though *Lumen Gentium* (sec. 39) had already mentioned the counsels as means of sanctification for all Christians.

28.   "A particularly significant expression of the radicalism of the Gospel is seen in the different 'evangelical counsels' which Jesus proposes in the Sermon on the Mount (cf. Mt. 5-7), and among them the intimately related counsels of obedience, chastity and poverty. The priest is called to live these counsels in accordance with those ways and, more specifically,

those goals and that basic meaning which derive from and express his own priestly identity" (*Pastores Dabo Vobis*, sec. 27).

29. Cole and Conner, 329. As we will see, although both religious and priests are called in some way to embrace the counsels, there is certainly a distinction in the motivation for the priest and religious to live the counsels, as well as in the way they express them.

30. Among the more important works in this area are: Hans Urs von Balthasar, *The Christian State of Life*, trans. Sister Mary Frances McCarthy (San Francisco: Ignatius Press, 1983), esp. 251-364; Cole and Conner, esp. chap. 9, "Consecrated Life and the Ministerial Priesthood: Mystery of Complementary Configuration to Christ"; Gisbert Greshake, *The Meaning of Christian Priesthood*, trans. Peadar MacSeumais, S.J. (Westminster, MD: Christian Classics, 1989), esp. 120-143; Dermot Power, *A Spiritual Theology of the Priesthood: The Mystery of Christ and the Mission of the Priest* (Washington, DC: Catholic University of America Press, 1998), esp. chap. 5, "Priesthood as a State of Life: The Evangelical Counsels and the Radicalism of the Gospel."

31. According to Canon Law, one enters consecrated life by means of vows or other sacred bonds which explicitly bind the person to live the evangelical counsels (CIC 573), although Canon Law does admit that through secular institutes diocesan clergy can enter consecrated life (CIC 713 and 715).

32. Paul VI, *Presbyterorum Ordinis* (1965), sec. 16. Of course, this would rule out the married priesthood that continues to exist in the Orthodox Churches and in the Eastern Rite Catholic Churches, not to mention the pastoral provision which has been made for married ministers of other denominations who have become Catholic priests in recent decades.

33. Ibid.

34. Jean Galot, S.J., *Theology of the Priesthood*, trans. Reverend Roger Balducelli, O.S.F.S. (San Francisco: Ignatius Press, 1984), 244.

35. John Paul II, "Priests: Granted the Gift of Celibacy through Humble Prayer," *Ad limina* Address to the Bishops of Eastern Canada (8 November 1993), in *Priesthood in the Third Millennium* (Princeton, N.J.: Scepter Publishers, 1994), 146.

36. Galot, "The Priesthood and Celibacy," 950. Galot explains that celibacy conforms to the nature of the priesthood because it is connected with the consecration of the priest through the priestly character: "Character means consecration and conformity to Christ the Shepherd. When consecration reaches the depth of personal being, it calls for an expression of itself in the way the person lives, or at least in the general orientation of one's life. True, consecration does not include absolute determinations in this respect, nor does it, as such, impose precise and detailed obligations, but it does seek to concretize itself by letting God exercise an ever more total dominance of the self" (*Theology of the Priesthood*, 244). St. John Paul II also explains the reason for priestly celibacy

based on how the priest is configured to Christ: "The will of the church finds its ultimate motivation in the *link between celibacy and sacred Ordination*, which configures the priest to Jesus Christ the Head and Spouse of the Church" (*Pastores Dabo Vobis*, sec. 29; see also 50, emphasis in original).

37.   Galot, "The Priesthood and Celibacy," 938.

38.   *Pastores Dabo Vobis*, sec. 11.

39.   For a good analysis with examples from this period, see David L. Toups, *Reclaiming Our Priestly Character* (Omaha: IPF Publications, 2008), especially chapter 2. An excellent diagnosis of the problem with some prescriptions for fixing it can be found in the opening address given at the 1990 Synod by Cardinal Ratzinger: "The Formation of Priests in the Circumstances of the Present Day," *Communio*, 17.4 (1990): 616-627.

40.   Priests are asked "to show themselves as a chaste virgin for Christ, and thus to evoke the mysterious marriage established by Christ, and fully to be manifested in the future, in which the Church has Christ as her only Spouse" (*Presbyterorum Ordinis*, sec. 16). The Sacred Congregation on the Doctrine of the Faith, in *Inter Insigniores* (1976), develops the image of the priest representing the bridegroom with the purpose of defending the constant teaching of the Church that only men can be ordained to the priesthood (Part 5, par. 29).

41.   *Pastores Dabo Vobis*, sec. 16. This language is picked up by the *Ratio Fundamentalis* published in 2016, which says that Priests "are configured to Christ, Head and Shepherd, Servant and Spouse" (Congregation for the Clergy: The Gift of the Priestly Vocation, *Ratio Fundamentalis Institutionis Sacerdotalis* (Vatican City: *L'Osservatore Romano*, 8 Dec. 2016).

42.   See *Lumen Gentium*, sec. 10; *Presbyterorum Ordinis* 1, 2, 12; Optatum Totius, sec. 8.

43.   *Pastores Dabo Vobis*, sec. 29.

44.   Ibid., sec. 16.

45.   Ibid., sec. 22.

46.   See Marie-Josèphe Rondeau, "Jean Daniélou, Henri-Irénée Marrou et le renouveau des etudes patristiques," in *Les Pérès de l'Église au XXe siècle. Histoire-Littérature-Théologie. L'aventure des Sources Chrétiennes,* Patrimoines-Christianisme (Paris: Les Éditions du Cerf, 1997), 351-378. Henri de Lubac, one of the promoters of this patristic revival in theology before the council, defended this more symbolic method of theology against some critics who said it abandoned the scientific and rational method of theology inherited at the beginning of the 20th century. De Lubac argued that he was attempting to regain some of the fruits of patristic theology and release some of the strength of the patristic theological vision without simplistically abandoning the theology of the time (*Corpus Mysticum: The Eucharist and the Church in the Middle Ages*, trans. Gemma Simmonds CJ, ed. Laurence Paul Hemming and Susan Frank Parsons, [Notre Dame, Indiana: Univ. of Notre Dame Pres, 2006], xxiii-xxiv).

47.   Avery Dulles, S.J., "Symbol in Revelation," *New Catholic Encyclopedia,* 2nd ed., vol. 13 (Detroit: Gale, 2003) 662. For other works on the importance of symbol in theology see: Michael Girard, *Les symboles dans la Bible* (Montréal-Paris: Bellarmin-Cerf, 1991), esp. 31-99; Julien Ries, "Symbole, Symbolisme," in *Catholicisme: hier, aujourd'hui, demain,* vol. 14, ed. G. Mathon and G-H. Baudry (Paris: Letouzey et Ané, 1996), 636-654; James M. Somerville, "Symbol," *New Catholic Encyclopedia,* 2nd ed., vol. 13 (Detroit: Gale, 2003), 660-662.

48.   *Catechism of the Catholic Church,* sec. 1148.

49.   Susan Mathews, "Called to the Wedding Feast of the Lamb: Covenantal Spousal Imagery from Genesis to Revelation," in Chaste Celibacy: Living Christ's Own Spousal Love. Proceedings of the First Annual Symposium on the Spirituality and Identity of the Diocesan Priest, March 15-18, 2001, by the Institute for Priestly Formation and Sacred Heart Major Seminary, ed. Edward Matthews [Omaha, Nebr.: privately printed, 2001], 47.

50.   Many of these patristic references will be explored in chap. 6.

51.   Dermot Power argues that there is "a growing perception among commentators that the resolution to the present crisis facing the ministerial priesthood cannot remain solely at the level of spiritual or developmental issues, but *must rediscover archetypes and original models of vocation and identity* if the process of trial and dysfunction is to become a journey towards transformation and integrity" (Ibid., 6, emphasis added).

52.   Power, 156.

53.   What Bishop Vigneron says about the nuptial understanding of celibacy can be applied to the priest's whole life: "the deepened understanding of the nature of priestly celibacy is, to use the terminology of the Ancients, an achievement of *theoria*. It can, I believe, be 'cashed out' on the level of *praxis*, the level of living and acting in history" (Vigneron, "Renewed Celibate Living," 14).

54.   For an explanation of the contribution of John Paul II's use of the nuptial image to theology which attempts to draw out many of the ramifications see Angelo Scola, *The Nuptial Mystery,* trans. Michelle Borras, (Grand Rapids, Michigan: Eerdmans, 2005).

55.   John Paul II, *Man and Woman He Created Them,* 186. The Pope references *Gaudium et spes,* which says that man "can fully discover his true self only in a sincere giving of himself" (24).

56.   Karol Wojtyla, *Love and Responsibility* (San Francisco: Ignatius Press, 1993), 253-4.

57.   Ibid., 251.

58.   *Mulieris Dignitatem,* sec. 26.

59.   *Pastores Dabo Vobis,* sec. 23.

60.   Ibid., sec. 30.

CHAPTER 1

THE SPOUSAL NATURE OF GOD'S COVENANT WITH US IN THE SCRIPTURES

Salvation history is the story of God's entering into a covenant with His people. As *Lumen Gentium* says:

> [God] therefore chose the race of Israel as a people unto himself. With it he set up a covenant. Step by step he taught and prepared his people, making known in its history both himself and the decree of his will and making it holy unto himself. All these things, however, were done by way of preparation and as a figure of that new and perfect covenant, which was to be ratified in Christ.[1]

The Scriptures can be described as the history of God's covenant with us. A covenant in its most basic biblical form is "a solemn promise made binding by an oath, which may be either a verbal formula or a symbolic oath."[2] In an attempt to understand the meaning of scriptural covenants, scholars analyze many different kinds of covenants, like the treaties between a king and his vassals, grants of privileges and power by a king, and even familial relationships. However, the image most frequently used by the Scriptures themselves to describe the covenant between God and His people is marriage. "From the beginning to the end, from the very first prophets up to the Book of Revelation, this covenant is described under the image of marriage."[3] In fact, the marriage image is so central to the Scriptures "that one cannot properly grasp the biblical revelation regarding God's relationship to His people without understanding this particular image and what it symbolizes."[4] In the Old Covenant, the Lord appears as the bridegroom of Israel, His chosen people; and in the New Covenant, Christ is the bridegroom and the Church is the bride.

The Old Testament

God enters into a covenant with His people at Mount Sinai.[5] This covenant, which is sealed in the covenant ceremony of Exodus 24, is the foundational covenant for the Israelite people. It is what some scholars call a kinship-type covenant—that is, the covenant makes family.[6] The covenant that God makes with His people Israel goes far beyond a simple legal contract; rather, it is an expression of love: "you will be my treasured possession among all peoples" (Ex 19:5). This phrase, which could be said to express the essence of the covenant, is used often in the Pentateuch and the Prophets: "I will take you as my own people, and I will be your God" (Ex 6:7).[7] The covenantal relationship demands from the people their recognition of God's absolute sovereignty over them, but also requires that the Lord will provide for all the needs of His people.[8] Also, God's love will not tolerate rivals, since Yahweh is a jealous God.[9] From the beginning of the covenant, we find that God describes infidelity in terms of harlotry.[10] This foundational covenant of Israel with God already has the seeds of the marriage imagery, as Pierre Grelot, S.J., points out:

> The covenant made on Sinai, while in essence a contract, goes far beyond the merely legal requirements: on God's side it presupposes love, fidelity, *hesed* (Ex 34:6-7; Deut 7:7-8); on Israel's side, it also demands love, fidelity, *hesed* (Deut 6:4; Hos 4:1, 6:6). To gain a clear and accurate picture of the relationship between God and his people, as it is laid down by the covenant on Sinai, it is not sufficient to compare it to the treaties between lord and vassal, which provide the legal model for the contract. It is essential to bear in mind, too, the comparison with the relationship established between a man and woman at the time of their marriage.[11]

It is this depth of love in the covenantal relationship between God and Israel upon which all the prophets will draw to call the people Israel to fidelity. It is because "Israel and her God are bound by ties of the heart and not only by those of law"[12] that the prophets will find the marriage imagery so useful for describing Israel's relationship with God.

In one of the earliest Prophetic books, Hosea, we find a fully developed understanding of the covenant as a marriage between the divine husband, Yahweh, and Israel, His bride. In the first three chapters of Hosea, the relationship between Yahweh and Israel is presented as a matrimonial union in which the bride, Israel, is unfaithful because she is chasing after false gods (baals). The story tells how Hosea is asked to represent this relationship between God and the people in his own conjugal life by taking a "woman of prostitution" (Hos

1:2).[13] Hans Urs von Balthasar notes the almost scandalous realism this gives to the spousal image of the Bible:

> This shows that God wants to give his relationship with his people an incredibly vivid reality. It is no longer the legal relationship of the earthly wife with her heavenly Lord. It is the relationship of love of a God humiliated by the woman's adultery, a God who in his wrath discloses more his own "shame," a God who, by taking back the harlot, by betrothing her in justice and changing the names of her sons, shows the "weakness" of his love.[14]

The meaning of this marriage image for the covenant of God with Israel is clearly seen in chapter 2 of Hosea, which demonstrates two fundamental aspects of the marriage image in the covenant. First, God lists the infidelity of Israel to the Mosaic covenant, specifically worship of false gods, an action he sees as adultery.[15] Grelot comments, "At this stage the experience of love as far as humanity (the wife) is concerned resembles that of human love as it actually is: impaired and subject to the set-backs and failures of adultery and prostitution."[16] Yet, it is precisely here that we see the second and more important aspect: God's understanding of the marriage covenant is different because God promises fidelity and restoration in spite of the infidelities of Israel. Yahweh's spousal love is rarely more tenderly expressed than it is in these verses:

> Therefore, I will allure her now; I will lead her into the wilderness and speak persuasively to her. Then I will give her the vineyards she had, and the valley of Achor as a door of hope. There she will respond as in the days of her youth, as on the day when she came up from the

land of Egypt. On that day—oracle of the Lord—You shall call me "My husband," and you shall never again call me "My baal." I will remove from her mouth the names of the Baals; they shall no longer be mentioned by their name. . . . I will betroth you to me forever: I will betroth you to me with justice and with judgment, with loyalty and with compassion; I will betroth you to me with fidelity, and you shall know the Lord. (Hos 2:16-22)

The scandal of this kind of love in a society where adultery was punishable by death should not be underestimated. As Grelot says, "the parable of the prodigal son and the forgiving father (Lk 15) is scarcely more telling in this aspect than the story of the husband who takes back his wanton wife."[17] Pope Benedict XVI comments on this love of God expressed by the prophet Hosea:

> God's passionate love for his people—for humanity—is at the same time a forgiving love. It is so great that it turns God against himself, his love against his justice. Here Christians can see a dim prefigurement of the mystery of the Cross: so great is God's love for man that by becoming man he follows him even into death, and so reconciles justice and love.[18]

It is also in Hosea that God begins to speak about an eschatological fulfillment of His marriage with Israel. He speaks about a time in the future when He will overcome the infidelities of His people. Later prophets will develop this eschatological vision more clearly, but here we see already that God intends to make for Himself a faithful bride and unite her to Himself in an unbreakable covenant. Claude

Chavasse points out, however, that this purification happens through sacrifice:

> In Hosea . . . the union between Yahweh the Divine
> Husband and Israel the Bride is consummated in sacrifice.
> Thus, in the parable of his family life, a part of the
> discipline to which Hosea submitted his unfaithful wife,
> after he had redeemed her from her paramour, was that
> she was to remain for a season as if unmarried.[19]

This idea of purification through sacrifice in preparing
for eschatological fulfillment of marriage will be a constant
theme of the covenant. This theme will be picked up in the
New Testament where we will see that the Cross is the place
of the marriage between God and His people.

The Prophet Ezekiel's treatment of the marriage image
is of special importance because he speaks of the whole
development of the covenant in terms of a marriage. Chapter
16 is one long analogy of a marriage.[20] The prophet describes
how Yahweh finds Israel as a young woman, marries her, and
bestows on her precious gifts[21]; Israel is unfaithful and given
to harlotry, even sacrificing the children born of the marriage
to false gods.[22] This results first in divine judgment,[23] but ultimately it leads to forgiveness and restoration through a new
and eternal covenant.[24]

Gordon Hugenberger, in his work *Marriage as Covenant*,
argues that chapter 16 of Ezekiel is one of only two places in
the Old Testament where marriage is directly referred to as a
covenant.[25] The reference is found in Ezekiel 16:8. Yahweh
says: "I passed by you again and saw that you were now old
enough for love. So I spread the corner of my cloak over you
to cover your nakedness; I swore an oath to you and entered

into covenant with you—oracle of the Lord GOD—and
you became mine." This is obviously a clear reference to the
covenant of Sinai, but it becomes explicitly a reference to
marriage when we understand that "I spread the corner of
my cloak over you to cover your nakedness," according to
Hugenberger, "refers to a literal act of covering which was
typically performed in the contraction of marriage."[26] This is
the most explicit reference to describing the Sinai covenant as
an actual marriage.

In the prophecies of Isaiah to the people in exile, we
find the fullest development of the eschatological vision of
marriage. The book interprets the exile as punishment for the
sins of the people, and chapter 40 begins to speak about the
restoration of the people from exile. In chapter 50, through
the prophet, the Lord addresses His marriage relationship
with the people: "Where is the bill of divorce with which I
dismissed your mother? Or to which of my creditors have I
sold you? It was for your sins you were sold, for your rebel-
lions your mother was dismissed" (Is 50:1). The point of the
rhetorical question is to clarify that God has *not* divorced His
people. In fact, He intends to call them back from exile, taking them back again as a wife:

> For your husband is your Maker; the Lord of hosts is
> his name, Your redeemer, the Holy One of Israel, called
> God of all the earth. The Lord calls you back, like a wife
> forsaken and grieved in spirit, A wife married in youth
> and then cast off, says your God. For a brief moment I
> abandoned you, but with great tenderness I will take you
> back. (Is 54:5-7)

This re-betrothal depicted by the prophet reveals the depth of God's love for His people, a love so paradoxical in nature that the creator becomes the husband:

> From a transcendent relationship he seems to condescend to an intimate relationship. The one who acts external to his creation, takes her in a relationship of surrender. As if he were alone and searching out company, he created her not for service, but for love. By means of the symbol of matrimony the poet is able to transmit a profound and convincing emotion. By means of this human symbol God wants to reveal his mysterious love.[27]

St. John Paul II uses this passage to explain how and why God uses the analogy of marriage for the covenant. Because we are made in God's image, the reality of marriage can speak of the mystery of divine love:

> Since the human being—man and woman—has been created in God's image and likeness, God can speak about himself through the lips of the Prophet using language which is essentially human. In the text of Isaiah quoted above, the expression of God's love is *"human,"* but the love itself is *divine*. Since it is God's love, its spousal character is properly divine, even though it is expressed by the analogy of a man's love for a woman. The woman-bride is Israel, God's Chosen People, and this choice originates exclusively in God's gratuitous love. It is precisely this love which explains the Covenant, a Covenant often presented as a marriage covenant which God always renews with his Chosen People. On the part of God the Covenant is a lasting "commitment," he remains faithful to his spousal love even if the bride often shows herself to be unfaithful.[28]

The last chapters of the Book of Isaiah go so far as to describe an eschatological wedding between Yahweh and Israel. Isaiah presents the Lord as the victor returning to celebrate His wedding with Jerusalem whom He claims as His bride in a passage that contains all the characteristics of the wedding of a king:[29]

No more shall you be called "Forsaken," nor your land called "Desolate," But you shall be called "My Delight is in her," and your land "Espoused." For the Lord delights in you, and your land shall be espoused. For as a young man marries a virgin, your Builder shall marry you; and as a bridegroom rejoices in his bride, so shall your God rejoice in you. (Is 62:4-5)

Here we have a profound transformation. Jerusalem is the city-spouse which will be made like a new bride, "From the prostitute that she was (Isa 1:21), she has become both virgin (Isa 62:5) and mother of many children. This return to original innocence after God's triumph over sin is a miracle of grace, and it is this which is at the heart of the prophetical promises."[30]

There is one more development important to see in the Old Testament about how the covenant with God is understood as a marriage. The idea gets so deeply embedded in the prophetic mindset that, in fact, human marriage as an institution begins to be seen in terms of the covenant with God. In the book of Malachi, the prophet refers to human marriage as a divine covenant.[31] In Ezekiel 16, God called the divine covenant a marriage; here, we see the reverse: Malachi appears to offer the first of many "reverse applications" of the marriage analogy. In other words, while the marriage analogy was originally intended to elucidate Yahweh's relationship to Israel, it is now being reapplied to serve as a paradigm for marriage itself.[32]

This is an important development because it shows what we will see even more clearly in the New Testament—namely, that the marriage covenant of God with His people is, in fact, the model for human marriages.[33]

The New Testament

The marriage image provides a key to the intrinsic link between the Old and New Testaments. In the Old Covenant, God promises to espouse Israel to Himself in virginal purity and fidelity; and in the New Covenant in Christ, this image becomes a reality with the coming of the Messiah-Bridegroom. Christ, in His relationship with the Church, "is the perfection of the Old Testament marriage relationship between Yahweh and the people."[34] Because of the Incarnation, "the divine archetype of the couple is no longer a dream or even a promise; it is a reality which has entered the realm of human experience."[35] As Pope Emeritus Benedict XVI said in his first encyclical, "The real novelty of the New Testament lies not so much in new ideas as in the figure of Christ himself, who gives flesh and blood to those concepts—an unprecedented realism."[36] The marriage image takes on this unprecedented realism in the relationship between Christ and the Church.

The Synoptic Gospels

Jesus enters into a world that expects the Messiah to come as the bridegroom and applies these images to Himself.[37] He refers to Himself as the bridegroom quite openly: "Jesus said to them, 'The wedding guests cannot fast while the bridegroom is with them, can they? As long as they have the bridegroom with them, they cannot fast. The days will come when the bridegroom is taken away from them, and then they will fast on that day.' (Mk 2:19)"[38] In light of the contemporary understanding, we can see clearly that Jesus' response to the Pharisees is meant to be a sign that the messianic age has come.

The text also points to a tension seen throughout Jesus' use of the bridegroom image: His disciples will fast when He is taken away, (i.e., although the messianic age has dawned, there is still a final fulfillment to be awaited). As Grelot says, "Christ, the bridegroom, will only be restored to his friends on the day of his return in glory."[39] In the Gospels, this eschatological fulfillment is also often put in terms of a wedding banquet with the return of the Messiah-bridegroom. For example, in the parable of the ten virgins, often translated as "bridesmaids,"[40] the focus is usually interpreted as an eschatological return of the bridegroom and the need for the disciples to be prepared (Mt 25:1-13).[41]

Perhaps the clearest reference to the kingdom as a wedding banquet and Jesus as the bridegroom in the synoptic gospels is Matthew 22:1-14. Jesus says, "The kingdom of heaven may be likened to a king who gave a wedding feast for his son" (Mt 22:2). We know from the Old Testament that it was customary to offer a banquet on the wedding day,[42] and comparing the kingdom to this wedding banquet emphasizes the celebration of eschatological joy at the presence of the Messiah.[43] It was customary to send two invitations: the first, to announce the coming celebration and the second, as an immediate summons when the banquet was ready.[44] In this parable, we have record only of the summons, which happens twice, emphasizing the urgency of the King who wants the invited guests to come, since the banquet is completely prepared. The rejection of the summons with the mistreatment and the killing of the slaves[45] can only be an allusion to the rejection of the prophets by Israel, which has already been made explicit in the previous parable of the wicked tenants.[46] It also follows that the son killed in the previous parable and the son who is the bridegroom in this wedding banquet should both be identified with Jesus.[47] Clearly, Jesus is speaking about the invitation made to the Jews to come to the eschatological wedding banquet; and when they reject this call, shaming the king's honor, he sends his troops to kill them, and he determines to fill his wedding hall with the outcasts. The message is clear to the Jewish audience: all are invited to the eschatological wedding banquet, even the outcasts. However, we see at the end of the parable that showing up at the wedding banquet also does not suffice for acceptance into the kingdom. One must be properly attired, which Joachim Jeremias sees as a reference to repentance needed to enter the kingdom.[48] When the whole parable is taken into account, then the analogy is very clear: "the conclusion is inescapable that the parable of the wedding-feast compares the kingdom, in its deepest and most profound sense, to the nuptial mystery in which Christ is the bridegroom."[49]

The Gospel of John

The Gospel of John, more than any other book of the New Testament, draws upon the image of the spousal relationship to present the mission of Jesus in terms of His role as the messianic bridegroom. This is seen especially from two events in the first three chapters: the announcements of John the Baptist and the wedding feast at Cana.

When one looks at the four central announcements of John the Baptist concerning his relationship to Jesus in the first three chapters of John,[50] one finds them "perfectly linked by thematic unity—the relationship between John and Jesus."[51] The fourth declaration provides the key to under-standing the Baptist's clear emphasis on the priority of Jesus over himself in these three chapters. Here, Jesus is clearly called the "bridegroom" by John the Baptist when John's dis-ciples report that Jesus is baptizing. It is the nuptial image that distinguishes John the Baptist from Jesus, as John says, "The one who has the bride is the bridegroom; the best man, who stands and listens to him, rejoices greatly at the bridegroom's voice. So this joy of mine has been made complete. He must increase; I must decrease" (Jn 3:29-30).[52] We know that there was in Jewish society a role played by intermediaries in the betrothal and wedding of a couple:

> Two men played an important role in the formation of a Jewish marriage. One, known as "the friend of the bridegroom," took the groom's part, and the other represented the bride. They had a number of duties. They acted as liaisons between the bride and groom. To all intents and purposes, the representatives conducted the couple's wooing, and when the matter was settled, it was the "friends" who arranged the wedding and sent out the invitations.[53]

By calling himself the "friend of the bridegroom," John the Baptist is making clear his role and demonstrating the priority of Jesus: "The Messiah is not another prophet that comes to preach conversion, but he is the bridegroom that, with full rights, comes to renew the matrimonial alliance with Israel."[54]

Seeing Jesus as the Messiah-bridegroom in John's eyes provides the key to help us understand a very important patristic exegesis of John 1:27 where John the Baptist says of Jesus: "whose sandal strap I am not worthy to untie." Luis Alonso-Schökel and Pierre Proulx believe that this phrase can only be understood properly in terms of the levirate law explained in Deuteronomy 25:8-10.[55] According to this law, when a brother died without leaving offspring, the next brother was required to marry his deceased brother's wife, as Judah said to Onan in Genesis 38:8: "Have intercourse with your brother's wife, in fulfillment of your duty as brother-in-law, and thus preserve your brother's line."[56] If the next brother refused to take up his duty, the wife was to remove his sandal and spit in his face[57]; this was considered an act to shame the brother for not doing his duty. However, by the time of the book of Ruth, this ceremony seems to have become a ritual symbolizing the passing on of the juridical right to inheritance and marriage. For when Boaz seeks to marry Ruth, since he is not the "next-of-kin," he presents the proposal to the next-of-kin who, in refusing, takes off his sandal and gives it to Boaz.[58] This figure helps us understand John the Baptist, who by saying that he is not worthy to untie the strap of his sandal, is claiming, in reference to this law, that he does not have any right to be considered worthy of being the bridegroom himself: "*The enigmatic phrase about the sandals refers to the law of the levirate,* formulated in Deuteronomy 25:5-10 and exemplified in the book of Ruth. John would never have thought to take the place of the groom; he does not have the right to take off the ritual sandals, being only the friend of the groom."[59]

Alonso-Schökel and Proulx argue that this is the "traditional" patristic exegesis of the passage.[60] For example, St. Jerome sees in this phrase about the sandal strap a deeper mystery, what he calls "a sacramentum" in his commentary on the parallel passage in Mark (1:7):

> It is certainly seen to be an indication of humility; almost as if he says, "I am not worthy to be his servant." But in these simple words is revealed something of a sacrament. We read in Exodus, we read in Deuteronomy, and we read in the book of Ruth if someone was related, and he was coming to her not wanting to take her as a wife who was of his relation, another was coming, second in order of relation, and in the presence of the judges and the elders it was said . . . John himself says: He who has the bride is the bridegroom. He has the Church his bride, I however am the friend of the bridegroom: I am not able to untie the thong of his sandal.[61]

The Fathers found this image used by John the Baptist able to provide rich connotations pointing to the preeminence of Jesus as the bridegroom. For example, both St. Cyprian and St. Ambrose connect the text in John 3:29 with Moses and Joshua, whom the Fathers argue must "take off their sandals" in the presence of God because neither Moses nor Joshua is the bridegroom. St. Cyprian says:

> He who is the bridegroom of the Church has the spouse, from him the spiritual children are born. The mystery of these things is revealed by Joshua, when he is commanded to take off his sandals, namely he is not the

bridegroom. It was in the law that whoever refused the marriage should take off the sandal, but he who will be the bridegroom should have the sandals put on. Similarly in Exodus Moses is commanded to take off his sandals because he is not the bridegroom [Ex 3:2-6].[62]

Alonso-Schökel and Proulx argue that this passage inspired St. Ambrose:

"After me will come the man whose sandal I am not worthy to remove" . . . this pertains to the incarnation, that he would send among men before him a mystical type of the sandal. For according to the law the bond with one's wife should be deferred to a neighbor or brother of the deceased, in order that the seed of the brother or neighbor should raise up children for the deceased . . . Moses is not the bridegroom, nor is Joshua the bridegroom, there is no other bridegroom, but only Christ is the bridegroom, about whom John said, "he who has the bride is the bridegroom." Therefore these ones took off their sandals (Ex 3,5; Josh 5:15), and this one was not able to remove the sandal, as John said, "I am not worthy to untie the strap of his sandal."[63]

This use of the levirate law will also be important for our study later, as the Fathers will use this image to speak about the nuptial nature of the apostolic ministry carried on after Jesus ascends to heaven. Many fathers will see in St. Paul's words, "For I became your father in Christ Jesus through the gospel" (1 Cor 4:15) another application of the levirate law. St. Paul steps into a spousal relationship with the Church for the "dead brother," (i.e., Jesus, who has ascended into heaven); and St. Paul raises up children, not in his own name, but on behalf of his brother.

These announcements of John the Baptist are not, however, the most important references to Jesus as the bridegroom in the Gospel of John. Rather, in the wedding feast at Cana,[64] we ought to see a symbolic portrayal that reveals Jesus' mission as the messianic bridegroom. "In a real way, this pericope is not about an ordinary wedding at all, but rather about the New Covenant in Christ."[65] At Cana, Jesus does this "first of his signs" by providing the new wine at a wedding feast; the messianic symbolism of this cannot be accidental.

First, we should notice the very generalized details of this wedding mentioned by John. We know that it is a wedding, but no bride is mentioned; and the bridegroom gets mentioned only once.[66] "This already indicates that John's interest is orientated in a totally different direction than the external circumstances of the wedding."[67] Rather, the scene focuses clearly on Jesus, His Mother, the wine, and His hour. We have already seen that wedding banquets in Scripture can have an eschatological symbolism, thus Jesus' providing wine in this story points to the fact that He is the Messiah.[68] As Susan Mathews points out, what we see here is the Johannine technique of revealing a deeper meaning beneath ordinary events:

> Typical in John is the technique of misunderstanding, so that what is happening on a literal level is symbolic of what is really taking place on the spiritual plane. Thus the real groom is Jesus, not the man getting married, in the same way Jesus is the real water in John 4, not the substance the Samaritan seeks from the well.[69]

However, when Mary asks Jesus to provide the wine, what is meant by His strange response? If we were to translate it literally, it would be: "What is this to me and to you, woman? My hour has not yet come."[70] Some see hostility or annoyance in the first part of Jesus' response, but it is possible to see that Jesus is trying to shift the focus of Mary to the deeper meaning of the event. Édouard Delebecque argues that "What" (Tí) refers directly to the wine, and Jesus is saying something like this: "Do you know what it means for me and you if I create wine at a wedding feast?"[71] As Ignace de la Potterie, S.J., comments:

> Scarcely having heard the word "wine" Jesus thinks of the symbolism of wine in the biblical tradition. Without refusing to interest himself in the present situation, since he will perform the miracle, Jesus, at once, wishes to make it understood what this *signifies*, by raising the conversation to the level of his mission to the world. He has in mind the messianic benefits which he wishes to bring and which are precisely designated here in the symbols of the wedding feast and the wine; this wine which he will give in profusion is the "sign," the symbol of his mission.[72]

To grasp the full meaning of the symbolism of Cana we must see its connection with the whole mission of Jesus as described in the Gospel of John, especially His Death upon the Cross. This connection becomes clear in an analysis of the "hour of Jesus" and the Mother of Jesus, whom both at Cana and the Cross Jesus calls "woman."

His "hour," which Jesus first mentions at Cana, is the "high point" toward which "the whole life of Jesus is tending."[73] Jesus' reference to His hour at Cana is usually translated, "My hour has not yet come" (Jn 2:4). But it is possible to read the negative statement about His hour in terms of a question: "Has not my hour come?"[74] Reading it this way might allow us to see a fuller meaning of Jesus' hour in this passage:

> The "hour" of Jesus which *begins* here, is the hour of the messianic revelation, that which Israel aspired to from the time of the prophets. It begins now, but it continues during the whole public life of Jesus and it will attain its total accomplishment in the mystery of the Cross and of the Resurrection.[75]

Jesus' hour begins when He reveals His glory at the wedding feast of Cana and summarizes His whole life and mission. After Cana, He will refer to it as the hour that "is coming, *and* is now here," (Jn 4:23, emphasis added) when He speaks to the Samaritan woman (Jn 4:5-29),[76] and also when He speaks about the resurrection of the dead.[77] It is finally in the introduction to the Last Supper when Jesus will solemnly state, "The *hour* has come for the Son of Man to be glorified" (Jn 12:23, emphasis added).

In that final hour, as Jesus is hanging on the Cross, our attention is drawn back again to Cana when He calls His mother "Woman," as He entrusts to her the Beloved Disciple (Jn 19:26). Since these "two scenes are the only places in the Gospel that the mother of Jesus appears; [and] in each she is addressed as 'Woman,'" John is inviting us to see the messianic wedding feast of Cana being fulfilled at Calvary.[78]

Why does Jesus refer to His mother as "Woman" in both places? Although scholars disagree about how to interpret this unusual way for Jesus to address His mother, they all agree that the title has an important symbolic meaning. Raymond Brown explains:

> What is peculiar is the use of "woman" alone (without an accompanying title or a qualifying adjective) by a *son* in addressing his *mother*—there is no precedent for this in Hebrew nor, to the best of our knowledge, in Greek. Certainly it is not an attempt to reject or devalue the mother-son relationship, for Mary is called the "mother of Jesus" four times in chap. 2:1-12 (twice after Jesus has addressed her as "Woman"). All of this leads us to suspect that there is symbolic import in the title, "Woman."[79]

Some Scripture scholars argue that Jesus' calling His mother "Woman" at Cana and Calvary should be understood in terms of her role as representing the New Eve. Raymond Brown argues for a connection between these passages and the woman of Revelation 12:

> In Rev 12 there is a mysterious, symbolic figure of "a woman" who is a key figure in the drama of salvation. There can be no doubt that Revelation is giving the Christian enactment of the drama foreshadowed in Gen 3:15 where enmity is placed between the serpent and *the woman*, between the serpent's seed and her seed, and the seed of the woman enters into conflict with the serpent. In Revelation the woman in birth pangs brings forth a male child who is the Messiah (12:5; Ps 2:9) and is taken up to heaven.[80]

Other scholars will argue that the title "Woman" used here refers to Mary as "Daughter of Zion":

In this perspective, the definite woman Mary, the Mother of Jesus, is in a certain way the historical realization of this symbolic figure who is called in the prophets—depending on the context—the "Daughter of Zion," the "Mother-Zion," or the "Virgin Israel." All of Israel's expectation of salvation was projected upon this symbolic figure of the "Messianic Daughter of Zion."[81]

What is common in both interpretations is that the Mother of Jesus takes on a symbolic role. Although she is only one person, whether she represents all humanity and the Church as the New Eve, or the hope of Israel's salvation as the "Daughter of Zion," in both cases, she clearly represents *the bride of Jesus the bridegroom.*[82] This becomes even clearer when we investigate more specifically Mary's role at Calvary, where she seems to represent both mother and bride.[83] When Jesus, looking down from the Cross, gives His Mother to the Beloved Disciple and the Beloved Disciple to His Mother, He is revealing a new relationship that comes about because of His Cross. As de la Potterie says, "The scene of Mary and the disciple, viewed on the messianic level, can no longer be limited to a simple moral example of filial piety. What takes place between the three persons is the highest revelation of Christ's love for his own."[84] Mary, in this moment, becomes the mother of all Jesus' disciples and fulfills her role both as the Mother of Zion and the New Eve by taking part with Jesus in giving birth to the people of God:

> In becoming the mother of the Beloved Disciple (the Christian), Mary is symbolically evocative of the Lady Zion who, after the birth pangs, brings forth a new people in joy (Jn 16:21; Isa 49:20-22, 54:1, 66:7-11). . . .

Her natural son is the firstborn of the dead (Col 1:18), the one who has the keys of death (Rev 1:18); and those who believe in him are born anew in his image. As his brothers, they have her as mother. Jesus' mother is the New Eve who, in imitation of her prototype, the "woman" of Gen 2-4, can say: "With the help of the Lord I have begotten a man."[85]

In this way Mary also represents Christ's Bride, the Church:

Mary constitutes precisely the transition, the passage between the ancient and the new people of God. In this unique person the whole of the Old Covenant converges, but also, typologically, the new Israel arises, the Church. . . . Mary really symbolizes the Church, she is its "beginning"; but considered from another, complementary, point of view, she is also its mother, since she became the mother of the disciple. For he, from another point of view, is an image of all Christ's disciples, of whom Mary is the mother."[86]

Understanding the role of the Mother of Jesus at this final hour on the Cross, in the light of its connections with the wedding feast at Cana, points to the spousal nature of the Cross itself. Jesus' self-gift on the Cross is the fulfillment of the hour that was foreshadowed at Cana. The Cross is the final consummation of the marriage. As Alonso-Schökel says, "In Cana, in a wedding, the first sign of Jesus announces that the messianic era has arrived. The spouse is present, but the wedding is postponed, because there will be a wedding of blood (cf. Ex 4:25) when the hour arrives."[87] This explains why, after Jesus gives His Mother to the Beloved Disciple,

He will say, "It is finished" (Jn 19:30); "the action of Jesus in relation to his mother and the Beloved Disciple completes the work that the Father has given Jesus to do and fulfills the Scripture."[88] In this way, perhaps, the marital connotations of St. Jerome's translation of John 19:30 are not so far off: Jesus says, "*consummatum est*,"—that is, the messianic wedding is consummated; Christ has become the bridegroom by the total gift of Himself on the Cross for the Church, His Bride.

Thus, at the beginning and the end of the Gospel of John, Jesus is revealed as the Divine Bridegroom. Cana, the first of Jesus' signs, encourages us to interpret His whole mission in terms of His role as bridegroom: "The Miracle which he performed was a sign, a symbol wherein Jesus manifests himself as the divine Bridegroom of the new people of God, with whom he wishes to conclude a new and definitive covenant, which finds its final achievement in the paschal mystery."[89]

The Book of Revelation

The book of Revelation brings together almost all the aspects of the Old and New Testament marriage imagery in the consummation of the whole of salvation history in the "wedding feast of the Lamb" (19:9): "All the movement of the Apocalypse, its cycles and series, its dramatic moments, its battles and victories, tend towards this definitive resolution: the wedding feast of the Lamb with the heavenly Jerusalem, the Church."[90] The marriage between Christ and the Church is explicitly seen in two passages:

> Then I heard something like the sound of a great multitude or the sound of rushing water or mighty peals of thunder, as they said: "Alleluia! The Lord has

established his reign, [our] God, the almighty. Let us rejoice and be glad and give him glory. For the wedding day of the Lamb has come, his bride has made herself ready. She was allowed to wear a bright, clean linen garment." (The linen represents the righteous deeds of the holy ones.) Then the angel said to me, "Write this: Blessed are those who have been called to the wedding feast of the Lamb." And he said to me, "These words are true; they come from God." (Rev 19:6-9)

"Then I saw a new heaven and a new earth. The former heaven and the former earth had passed away, and the sea was no more. I also saw the holy city, a new Jerusalem, coming down out of heaven from God, prepared as a bride adorned for her husband" (Rev 21:1-2).

Here, just as the Prophets and the Gospels foretold, the end of time is presented as a wedding feast. As Isaiah had done in Chapter 62, the author of Revelation identifies the bride as Jerusalem, as well; however, this time, we see an even clearer eschatological sense as the city descends from heaven. The bride is a corporate reality. She is the saints who are clothed in "righteous deeds"; she is "the holy city, a new Jerusalem." The reference to the bride being prepared for her bridegroom with special clothing is important.[91] This "bright, clean" clothing is a symbol of the bridal purity bestowed by the bridegroom through the eschatological battle. How does the lamb who wins the victory confer this bridal purity? Elsewhere, Revelation tells us the victory of the Lamb happens through His Cross. The elders then sing to the Lamb in 5:9-10:

Worthy are you to receive the scroll and to break open
its seals, for you were slain and with your blood you
purchased for God those from every tribe and tongue,
and people and nation. You made them a kingdom and
priests for our God, and they will reign on earth.

The faithful, then, who make up the corporate bride can
be connected with those who have come out of the great trial
and "have washed their robes and made them white in the
blood of the Lamb" (Rv 7:14). Thus, the Cross that confers
holiness and bridal purity can be seen as the central moment
of the espousal.[92]

Connected to this is the reference to the bridegroom
as "lamb." The title reveals the sacrificial nature of Christ's
spousal love because it connects to the Gospel of John,
which portrays Jesus as the new Passover lamb.[93] In the
beginning of John's Gospel, John the Baptist refers to Jesus
as the "Lamb of God, who takes away the sin of the world"
(Jn 1:29).[94] Also, the Gospel of John places the condemnation
to death of Jesus at the very moment the priests begin to
slaughter the paschal lambs at the temple[95]; and the Gospel
mentions the hyssop branch, which is the type of branch
specified for use to spread the blood of the Passover lamb,
being used to raise a sponge of wine to Jesus.[96] The identification of Jesus with the Passover lamb becomes even clearer
in the solemn description of the Death of Jesus on the Cross
in John's Gospel. The description of the blood and water
flowing out of the side of Christ on the Cross is followed
by a solemn guarantee of the words of the evangelist unique
in the Gospel of John: "An eyewitness has testified, and his
testimony is true; he knows that he is speaking the truth" (Jn

19:35). Then, this Passover Lamb who was slain on the Cross
shows up again in Revelation:

> The Lamb of Rev 5:6 is a slain lamb. In Rev 15:3 the
> Song of Moses is the song of the Lamb. In Rev 7:17
> and 22:1 the Lamb is seen as the source of living water,
> and this may be another connection with Moses who
> brought forth water from the rock. Rev 5:9 mentions the
> ransoming blood of the Lamb, a reference particularly
> appropriate to the paschal motif where the mark of the
> lamb's blood spared the houses of the Israelites.[97]

Thus, when Revelation speaks of the end of time as the
"wedding feast of the Lamb," it brings together the Passover,
the sacrifice of the Cross, and the marriage covenant, through
the Bridegroom, the Lamb that was slain.

Furthermore, following the tradition of the Old and New
Testaments, the virgin nature of the bride is emphasized even
more clearly in Revelation. The heavenly Jerusalem, the bride
of the lamb, is contrasted with the corrupt and adulterous
Babylon.[98] Babylon is to be given to the beast and the dragon;
the virgin, Jerusalem, will be wed to the lamb. Babylon has
"sovereignty over the kings of the earth" (17:18), while Jerusalem belongs solely to the "King of kings and the Lord of
lords" (19:16). Babylon's end will be the cup of punishment,[99]
while the virgin, Jerusalem, will celebrate the wedding banquet of the lamb.[100]

What we see is that the Book of Revelation brings
together two central elements in our study. First, as we saw
in the Gospel of John and will see in St. Paul, in Revelation,
the sacrifice of the Cross is interpreted as the central moment
of the wedding covenant. Second, as in the Old Testament,

though, there is an eschatological tension with the marriage covenant. The marriage is consummated at the Cross but will not be fulfilled until the "bride has made herself ready" (Rv 19:7)—that is, when the elect have "washed their robes and made them white in the blood of the Lamb" (Rv 7:14). This is the moment when heaven will be fully wed to earth in the New Jerusalem where God will dwell with us.[101]

St. Paul—2 Corinthians 11:2

There are two important passages where St. Paul refers to the Church as the bride of Christ: 2 Corinthians 11:2 and Ephesians 5:21-33.[102] In the first, St. Paul makes a clear reference to the Church as the Bride of Christ: "For I am jealous of you with the jealousy of God, since I betrothed you to one husband to present you as a chaste virgin to Christ." St. Paul, in this passage, is defending himself against his opponents who seem to have been accusing him of being jealous for the Corinthian church. St. Paul vindicates himself by saying he feels a divine jealousy for the people, feeling in himself Christ's own love for the bride. Here, he makes a key distinction, reminding us of the words of St. John the Baptist. St. Paul has a role to play in the spousal relationship as the apostle, but he is not the bridegroom. He is the one who espoused the Church to the true bridegroom, who is Christ:

> Paul cannot claim to be unique in adopting the spousal metaphor to describe and defend his apostolic mission. In this respect it seems possible to make a parallel with the figure of John the Baptist, who speaking of his ministry affirms: "The one who has the bride is the bridegroom" (Jn 3:29). John therefore considers himself the friend of the bridegroom. This would lead one to think that in the

period of the New Testament there circulated commonly the idea that the apostles are not the ones who possess the community (cf. 2 Cor 1:24; 4:5); but they could consider themselves ministers of the nuptial relationship between Christ and the community.[103]

This image will be important for us later as we explore how the priest fits into this spousal relationship of Christ with the Church.

St. Paul is picking up two central themes we saw in the Old Testament. Yahweh, in the Old Testament, reacted jealously against the infidelities of His spouse; in the New Covenant, Christ loves jealously, which is why the apostle demands "sincere and [pure] commitment to Christ" (2 Cor 11:3). Also, St. Paul speaks of presenting the Church as a "chaste virgin." This is surely a reference to the adultery that Paul sees in their accepting "another Jesus," "a different spirit," or "a different gospel" (2 Cor 11:4). Yet, this phrase "chaste virgin" may have a deeper connection to the Old Testament. According to de la Potterie, "This is a reference to the Daughter of Zion, sometimes called 'virgin Zion', 'virgin Israel' by the prophets, especially when she is invited, after past infidelities, once more to be true to the covenant, to her marriage relationship with her only Bridegroom."[104] We have already seen Mary representing this collective person, Daughter of Zion, at Cana and at the Cross. Here, the chaste virgin is contrasted with Eve, who was "deceived" by the serpent and "led astray from a sincere and [pure] commitment to Christ" (2 Cor 11:3). St. Paul's application of the "chaste virgin" to the Church makes clear that he sees the Church as the Bride of Christ in the New Covenant. This becomes even more explicit in the most important passage in the New Testament for understanding the spousal relationship between Christ and the Church.

Ephesians 5:21-33

It is in chapter 5 of the Letter to the Ephesians that we reach the zenith of the expression of the marriage image in Scripture, when St. Paul holds up the image of Christ and the Church as a model for all marriages. As St. John Paul II says, "this *image of spousal love,* together with the figure of the divine Bridegroom—a very clear image in the texts of the Prophets—finds crowning confirmation in the Letter to the Ephesians."[105] The passage speaks on two levels; Jules Cambier calls them "the parenetic level and the profound level."[106] What starts as a practical teaching to spouses about love (i.e., the parenetic level) becomes the forum to reveal the profound depth of the spousal relationship between Christ and the Church—the relationship that is, in fact, the "great mystery" of which the letter ultimately speaks.[107] In Ephesians, the Cross is revealed as the heart of Christ's spousal love, a love that purifies the Church to make her both bride and body of Christ.

The center of the passage is found in verses 25-30, where St. Paul is encouraging husbands to love their wives as Christ loved the Church. In this instruction, he explains by analogy that the Paschal Mystery is a marriage between Christ and the Church. Verse 25 reads: "Husbands, love your wives, even as Christ loved the church and handed himself over for her." The verbs ἠγάπησεν ("loved") and παρέδωκεν ("gave over") taken together in this verse are a reference to Christ's sacrificial Death on the Cross.[108] This becomes even clearer when one considers the parallels between Ephesians 5:25 and

5:2 where the same two verbs are used: "Christ loved us and handed himself over for us as a sacrificial offering to God for a fragrant aroma."[109] In both verses, Christ is clearly described as embracing death in love for the sake of the Church. This reveals the Cross as the heart of Christ's spousal love. As St. John Paul II comments:

> We find ourselves at the very heart of the Paschal Mystery, which completely reveals the spousal love of God. Christ is the Bridegroom because "he has handed himself over": His body has been given, his blood has been "shed" (cf. Lk 22:19-20). In this way, "he loved them to the end" (Jn 13:1). The "sincere gift" contained in the Sacrifice of the Cross gives definitive prominence to the spousal meaning of God's love.[110]

St. Paul defines the spousal love of Christ as the self-giving love of the Cross. This shows us the truth behind what we will see in the next chapter: the Fathers of the Church often referred to the Cross as the marriage bed between Christ and the Church.

Verse 26 describes the result of the love of Christ poured out for the Church "to sanctify her, cleansing her by the bath of water with the word." We already saw in the Old Testament (in chapter 2 of Hosea) the idea of purification of the bride through sacrifice. However, there, Yahweh submitted the bride to purification through making her sacrifice. Here, the roles are reversed, the bridegroom, Christ, actually sacrifices Himself in order that the bride might be pure. He purifies His bride through His sacrificial love. This verse reflects aspects of actual marriage cleansing rituals which were present in the Old Testament. The most immediate connection can be made with Ezekiel 16:9-13 where Yahweh is described as bathing His bride in water to prepare her for marriage.[111] We must ask what precisely is meant by the means of purification, "the bath of water by the word"? The Fathers of the Church saw this washing as a reference to the Sacrament of Baptism.[112] In fact, St. Augustine used this passage from Ephesians to speak about the nuptial nature of the Sacrament of Baptism. For Augustine, verses 26 and 27 symbolized the members of the baptized, (i.e., the bride is washed clean by the blood of Christ poured out on the Cross and then united with Him as the Bride of Christ "in splendor, without spot or wrinkle or any such thing—that she might be holy and without blemish" [Eph 5:27]). Augustine describes the beauty and purity of Jesus' bride won through the sacrifice of the bridegroom: "Sweet scents come from your garments. His garments are his saints, his elect, the whole Church which he presents to himself, without spot or wrinkle; For the spot has been washed away in his blood, and the wrinkle has been stretched out on the cross."[113]

If the Cross is the moment of the marriage, and the bride is prepared through a cleansing of water and the Word, then this passage can easily be seen to reveal, not only the marriage of the Church, but also the birth of the Church. Hence, the connection the Fathers often made between this passage and the blood and water flowing from the side of Christ on the Cross (see Jn 19:34):

> There is also occasion to compare the teaching of Ephesians about the Church, washed by the love that gushed forth from the Cross, with the vision of John that evokes the presence of the faithful community, at the foot

of the Cross, under the figure of Mary, the Woman par excellence, and that shows how the sacraments gush forth from the wound of the pierced heart (Jn 19:25-37).[114]

Through this connection, Mary once again represents the Church bride, as the exemplum of the *ecclesia immaculata* in Ephesians 5.

The result of this washing of the Church is a "consecration" or "sanctification" (ἁγιάσῃ) of the Church. The bride is made holy, set apart for her bridegroom: "This consecration makes [the Church] participate in the holiness of God, to enter into the divine sphere as something that belongs there."[115] It is worth noting a change in verse 27 from 2 Corinthians 11:2. There, St. Paul spoke about presenting the Church to Christ as a chaste virgin. The same verb παρίστημι ("to present") is used in both verses, but here in Ephesians, Christ actually presents the Church to Himself, without an intermediary. This emphasizes the fact that in Ephesians, Christ Himself is the source of the Church's holiness. We already pointed out in the Old Testament the almost scandalous nature of the spousal love of Yahweh, who takes back His adulterous bride and makes her holy. In the New Testament, God in Christ goes even further by giving up His own life to renew and purify His bride and unite her to Himself: "Christ, going beyond what God in the Old Testament does in the covenant with Israel, is the Bridegroom who has entirely given himself up for her."[116] This is the depth of Christ's spousal love for His bride.

In verses 28-31, returning more directly to exhorting husbands, the author continues to base his analogy on the way Christ loves the Church:

So [also] husbands should love their wives as they do their own bodies. He who loves his wife loves himself. For no one hates his own flesh but rather nourishes and cherishes it, even as Christ does the church, because we are members of his body. "For this reason a man shall leave [his] father and [his] mother and be joined to his wife, and the two shall become one flesh" (Eph 5:28-31).

Many readers miss the important development St. Paul makes here. We saw in the Old Testament that Israel was often referred to as the bride, but Israel is never referred to as the body of God. St. Paul brings a new depth to the marriage image in Ephesians. He sees the union between Christ and the Church as so real that we become members of Christ's body. To support his thesis, St. Paul quotes Genesis 2:24: "the two shall become one flesh." The union between Christ and the Church reaches a depth never imagined in the Old Covenant.[117] Here, you see what we will explore later, that the important Pauline image of the Church as the Body of Christ is actually rooted in the marriage image where Christ and the Church become one flesh.

In light of this union, we come to understand the description of Christ's care for the Church: "he nourishes and cherishes it" (v. 29). This speaks of how the Church's power to grow and develop comes from Christ. It is not too much of a stretch to see here a reference to the Eucharist, where Christ nourishes the Church sacramentally and she becomes "one flesh" with him.[118]

The quotation of Genesis in this passage is very important. St. Paul quotes Genesis 2:24 entirely, but places it in a new light: "For this reason a man shall leave [his] father and [his] mother and be joined to his wife, and the two shall become one flesh" (Eph 5:31). By quoting this passage here, St. Paul shows that marriage, created by God in the beginning is fulfilled in Christ and the Church: "Paul for his part does not deny that marriage can and must be explained on the ground of this text [Gen 2:24]. However, he asserts that at its deepest level this key text speaks of 'Christ and the church.' Marriage does not exist in its own right."[119] It as if he is saying that marriage from the beginning has always implicitly been pointing to the relationship of Christ and the Church. This becomes even more clear in the conclusion of the passage.

St. Paul concludes the passage with the pregnant theological statement in verse 32: "This is a great mystery, but I speak in reference to Christ and the church." To interpret this verse correctly, we must know to what "this" refers, in other words, what is the great mystery? Jules Cambier, in his extensive study of this passage argues that "this is a great mystery" refers directly to the union of Christ with His Church. Cambier sees verse 32 as a theological summary of the profound level of the whole passage. Cambier would translate it this way: "This is a profound mystery; I want to speak about the mystery concerning Christ and His Church."[120] This is a great mystery because understanding Christ as the bridegroom of the Church captures the essence of the covenantal relationship:

> Paul returns, in his conclusion, to the explanation which, in fact, had become the essential part of 5:22-33: in effect, he was returning to describe once again, in the end of the epistle, the mystery of Christ in his perfect realization, in the heavenly Church which he has founded in his love, which he has sanctified, and to which he

is intimately united. 5:32 is, in one sense, a summit of the Epistle.[121]

Thus, as was stated in the beginning of this chapter, the whole passage must be read in light of the profound revelation of the nature of the spousal relationship of Christ with the Church. Ephesians 5 begins by giving practical marital advice based on Christ's spousal relationship with the Church, but it ends having surpassed this practical realm to expound the centrality of marriage for understanding the covenantal relationship of Christ to the Church. The passage shows us how Jesus, the messianic bridegroom, is the fulfillment of the spousal love prophesied in the Old Testament. The heart of Christ's spousal love is the Cross; and through His self-gift on the Cross, Christ sanctifies the Church, His bride, and unites her to Himself so completely that she becomes one flesh with Him, sharing His very life. According to St. Paul, the eschatological marriage prophesied throughout the Old Testament is fulfilled in Christ and the Church. This marriage is the "great mystery" that is at the heart of God's plan to redeem us through making us one with Him. This scriptural mystery will also have profound ramifications on the sacramental economy of the Church.

Conclusions from the Scriptures

In the Old Testament, the marriage image is used to understand the covenant in the Scriptures with increasing frequency and detail. Yahweh is the transcendent God who seeks to draw His people into this intimate, exclusive, covenantal relationship. He loves His bride with a jealous love and refuses to admit infidelity, which the prophets always describe as adultery. Starting with Hosea, but becoming increasingly clear in Jeremiah, Ezekiel, and Isaiah, we see the divine nature of God's spousal love revealed: a love that amazes because it goes completely beyond what could be expected of human love.

In the latter half of the Old Testament, because of the consistent infidelity of the people, the prophets begin to focus on the eschatological marriage as the time of the full restoration of this virginal purity of the bride. The spousal image becomes a means to express the eschatological hope of God's union with His people, despite their unfaithfulness. Israel will be made worthy of Him by the love of the bridegroom who will unite her to Himself in a new covenant where she will never be unfaithful again. In fact, in later Israel, especially approaching the time of Jesus, the image of the bridegroom began to be applied not directly to Yahweh, but to the Messiah who will come: "The final renewal of the covenant between God and the people, intimated by the prophets, was expected by the Rabbis in the days of the Messiah. Thus we often find the view that in these days there will take place the true marriage feast."[122] It is also to this period almost contemporary with Jesus that scholars trace the interpretation of Psalm 45 as a hymn about the coming of the Messiah as bridegroom and also the Song of Songs as an allegory of the love of God or the Messiah for Israel.[123] It is the nuptial nature of the covenant described in the Old Testament, combined with the messianic hope of Israel, which provides the necessary context for us to understand the Gospel's description of Jesus as the Messianic bridegroom. The nuptial image, so deeply rooted in the Old Testament, is the basis for the New Testament revelation of Christ as the bridegroom of His Church.

In the New Testament, Christ is presented as the Bride-groom of the Church in the Synoptic Gospels, in the Gospel of John, the Book of Revelation, and in two of St. Paul's epistles. These texts reveal the centrality of the Cross for the spousal covenant. In the Gospel of John, the wedding feast of Cana proposes viewing the whole of Jesus' life and min-istry through the lens of His role as messianic bridegroom. Thus, the hour of the messianic nuptials foreshadowed at Cana is fulfilled on the Cross, where with the consent of the "woman" Mary, the new wine of salvation, Christ's own blood, pours forth from His side. As Pope Benedict XVI said about Cana and the Cross:

> In a situation laden with symbols of the Covenant, such as the wedding feast, the Virgin Mother intercedes and provokes, so to speak, a sign of superabundant grace: the 'good wine' that refers to the mystery of Christ's Blood. This leads us directly to Calvary, where Mary stands beneath the Cross together with the other women and with the Apostle John. The Mother and the disciple receive spiritually the testament of Jesus: his last words and his last breath, in which he begins to pour out the Spirit; and they receive the silent cry of his Blood, poured out entirely for us (cf. Jn 19:25-34).[124]

The Book of Revelation shows us how the Cross begins and foreshadows the wedding feast of the lamb that is fulfilled at the end of time, and that it is through the Cross that the bride is prepared for this wedding feast. Most particularly in the letter to the Ephesians, Christ's spousal love is defined in terms that refer directly to His self-gift on the Cross through which His bride is purified and prepared for union. As Angelo Amato demonstrates, the sacrificial aspect of Christ's spousal love is present throughout the New Testament:

> The Bridegroom will be taken from his friends (Mk 2:20). The lamb will be "slain" (Rev 5:6) in order to purify his bride (Rev 21:9) and make her as the "blessed who are called to the wedding feast of the lamb" (Rev 19:9). In his intense spousal love Christ "has loved the Church and has given himself for her" (Eph 5:25). His covenant is made in his blood: "This is my blood, the blood of the covenant" (Mk 14:24; Mt 26:28)."[125]

It is possible to say that to understand Christ's spousal love, one must understand "the sacrifice of his life consumed on the cross" because this is the "decisive act by which Jesus gave his life to the Church, by which he gave birth to her as his Bride and his Body and celebrated with her the spiritual marriage."[126]

Admittedly, the graphic use of the marriage image in the Scriptures tends to make us a little uncomfortable. Phrases like the "jealousy" of God can seem to anthropomorphize God too much. In fact, this shows how well the marriage image captures the heart of the understanding of the Covenant. A proper jealousy that a husband ought to have for his wife (or vice versa) is understood. It is a love that is rightly offended by infidelity because of the depth and intimacy of the love. This is exactly the kind of love the Prophets and the Pentateuch ascribe to God when they ascribe the jealousy of marital love to God[127] or every time they speak about the adultery of the people. As Pope Emeritus Benedict XVI points out, the Scriptures do not hesitate to describe "God's

passion for his people using boldly erotic images."[128] This
is the real newness of the biblical vision of God and brings
home the intensely personal nature of the love of God for
man in the Scriptures:

> The one God in whom Israel believes, on the other hand,
> loves with a personal love. His love, moreover, is an
> elective love: among all the nations he chooses Israel and
> loves her—but he does so precisely with a view to healing
> the whole human race. God loves, and his love may
> certainly be called *eros*, yet it is also totally *agape*.[129]

Scriptural study has shown the centrality of the spousal
image for understanding God's relationship with us. This covenant that began in the Old Testament and is fulfilled in the
Paschal Mystery is best understood through the analogy of
marriage. The next chapter will look more closely at how this
analogy is used in theology, but its centrality for understanding redemption is already inescapable. This is why St. John
Paul II has argued so much for its importance and ultimately,
why he applies this image to the priesthood. As he said:

> The analogy of spousal love contains a characteristic of
> the mystery that is not directly emphasized by the analogy
> of merciful love, nor by the analogy of fatherly love (nor
> by any other analogy used in the Bible to which we could
> have appealed).

> The gift given by God to man in Christ is a "total" or
> "radical" gift, which is precisely what the analogy of
> spousal love indicates: it is in some sense "all" that God
> "could" give of himself to man, considering the limited
> faculties of man as a creature. In this way the analogy of

spousal love indicates the "radical" character of grace: of the whole order of created grace.[130]

Questions for Discussion, Reflection, and Prayer

1. What surprises you the most about the use of the marriage image in the Scriptures? What draws you to meditate more?

2. Using the Scripture verses from the Old Testament, prayerfully ponder the aspects of God's love for His people, for you. Note the reality of His fidelity to the marriage covenant despite the infidelity of the people. Can you apply this faithful love of God to yourself? Do you experience God's jealous love for you, God's desire for the "virgin Israel," the "weakness" of His love[131] as He draws near to you in your infidelity?

3. What does the priest learn by witnessing that Christ's love for His bride is expressed through the marriage of the Cross? (See Hosea 2; John 19; Ephesians 5:25; Revelation 19:6-9).

4. What is the role of Mary in the Marriage covenant of the New Testament? What is her role in your life? (See John 2:1-12; John 19:26-27).

5. What does St. Paul's "divine jealousy" for the bride (2 Cor. 11:2), teach us about the heart of a priest?

NOTES

1. Paul VI, *Lumen Gentium* (1964), sec. 9.

2. George E. Mendenhall, "Covenant," in *Interpreter's Dictionary of the Bible*, ed. G. A. Buttrick, et al., vol. 1 (Nashville: Abingdon, 1962), 714.

3. Ignace de la Potterie, S.J., *Mary in the Mystery of the New Covenant*, trans. Bertrand Buby, S.M. (New York: Alba House, 1992), xxiv.

4. Susan Mathews, "Called to the Wedding Feast of the Lamb: Covenantal Spousal Imagery from Genesis to Revelation," in *Chaste Celibacy: Living Christ's Own Spousal Love. Proceedings of the First Annual Symposium on the Spirituality and Identity of the Diocesan Priest, March 15-18, 2001*, by the Institute for Priestly Formation and Sacred Heart Major Seminary, ed. Edward Matthews [Omaha, NE: privately printed, 2001], 39.

5. See Exodus 19-24.

6. Scott Hahn, "Kinship by Covenant: A Biblical Theological Study of Covenant Types and Texts in the Old and New Testaments" (Ph.D. diss., Marquette University, 1995), 41.

7. See also: Leviticus 26:12; Deuteronomy 26:17-19; Jeremiah 31:31-34; Ezekiel 36:24-28.

8. See Exodus 19:4.

9. Exodus 20:5, 34:14; Deuteronomy 4:24, 5:9, 6:15, 32:21. See also Jean Danielou, S.J., "La jalousie de Dieu," in *Dieu vivant* 16 (1950): 61-73.

10. See, for example, Exodus 34:14-16 or Deuteronomy 31:16.

11. Pierre Grelot, *Man and Wife in Scripture* (New York: Herder and Herder, 1964), 57-58.

12. Ibid., 58.

13. See also Hosea 3:1-5.

14. Hans Urs von Balthasar, *Explorations in Theology*, Vol. 2: *Spouse of the Word*, trans. A.V. Littledale (San Francisco: Ignatius Press, 1991), 199.

15. See Hosea 2:4-17.

16. Grelot, *Man and Wife in Scripture*, 67.

17. Ibid., 61.

18. Benedict XVI, *Deus Caritas Est* (2005), sec. 10.

19. Claude Chavasse, *The Bride of Christ: An Enquiry into the Nuptial Element in Early Christianity* (London: Faber and Faber, 1940), 106, emphasis in original.

20. Ezekiel 16 is a favorite passage of Pope Francis in helping us understand God's Mercy [See Pope Francis, *The Name of God is Mercy* (New York: Random House, 2016)].

21. See Ezekiel 16:8-14.

22. See Ezekiel 16:14-58.

23. See Ezekiel 16:59.

24. See Ezekiel 16:60-63.

25.   Gordon Hugenberger, *Marriage as Covenant: A Study of Biblical Law and Ethics Governing Marriage, Developed from the Perspective of Malachi* (New York: Brill, 1994), 304. The other is Malachi 2:14-16; see below.

26.   Ibid.

27.   Luis Alonso-Schökel, "Levirato," *Símbolos matrimoniales en la Biblia.* (Navarre: Editorial Verbo Divino, 1997), 176.

28.   John Paul II, *Mulieris Dignitatem* (1988), sec. 23.

29.   Alonso-Schökel (73-74) points out that many of the characteristics contained here are found in the descriptions of the wedding of a king in Psalm 45 and in Song 3 and 6.

30.   Grelot, *Man and Wife in Scripture*, 67.

31.   See Malachi 2:14-16. There is considerable controversy about how to interpret whether this passage is referring to a literal marriage or to a symbolic marriage (that is, between God and His people). Hugenberger argues convincingly that Malachi 2:14 refers to a covenant that exists between a husband and his wife (30).

32.   Hugenberger, 30.

33.   See Ephesians 5:21-33, below.

34.   Hans Urs von Balthasar, *The Glory of the Lord: A Theological Aesthetics*, Vol I: *Seeing the Form*, trans. Erasmo Leiva-Merikakis (San Francisco: Ignatius Press, 1982; reprint, 1989), 577.

35.   Grelot, *Man and Wife in Scripture*, 84.

36.   Benedict XVI, *Deus Caritas Est* (2005), sec. 7.

37.   "Jesus moves wholly within the circle of ideas of his contemporaries when he expresses the meaning and glory of the Messianic period in the images of the wedding and wedding feast" (Ethelbert Stauffer, "ἀγαπάω, ἀγωπη, ἀγαπητός" s.v., in *Theological Dictionary of the New Testament*, ed. Gerhard Kittel [Grand Rapids: Eerdmans, 1968], 654). This is why Jesus' statements about Himself as the bridegroom must be interpreted in light of the prophets, especially the nuptial imagery they used to explain the eschatological salvation. "He presupposes the prophets; the New Testament cannot be interpreted without the Old. He takes the prophets up in such a way that the great political events and the great rhetorical diatribes 'become human' on the stage of his own life" (Balthasar, *Spouse of the Word*, 205). See also pages 19-28 of Brant Pitre's *Jesus the Bridegroom: The Greatest Love Story Ever Told* (New York: Image, 2014).

38.   Parallels: Matthew 9:15; Luke 5:34.

39.   *Man and Wife in Scripture*, 103.

40.   In Greek: παρθένος.

41.   See Luke 12:36. Chavasse (57) points out that Matthew's placing of this parable in the last week of Jesus' ministry adds to the eschatological expectation that He is the bridegroom whom the virgins are waiting to escort. Chavasse also sees echoes of Psalm 45 in this Gospel passage where the bride is ready to meet her groom. Stauffer (654) cites several

examples of rabbinical writings from the time of Jesus that mention
torch-lit processions of the groom to the wedding banquet and show us
the clear reference to the eschatological wedding banquet. Grelot adds,
"the fact that, in the interplay of symbols, those who are waiting for the
bridegroom and who go into the wedding-feast are described as virgins is
doubtless far from accidental" *(Man and Wife in Scripture*, 105).

42. For example, Genesis 29:22, Tobit 7:14.

43. The Old Testament prophets spoke of a so-called "messianic banquet" at which the messiah was present, about which Isaiah writes in 25:6-
8. This parable picks up and expands on that tradition; see Dennis Smith,
"Messianic Banquet," in *The Anchor Bible Dictionary*, vol. 4, ed. David N.
Freedman (New York: Doubleday, 1992), 789.

44. See Pheme Perkins, *Hearing the Parables of Jesus* (New York: Paulist
Press, 1981), 97; Joachim Jeremias, *The Parables of Jesus* (New York: Scrib-
ner, 1954), 33.

45. See Matthew 22:6.

46. See Matthew 21:35-46.

47. Alonso-Schökel, 78.

48. Jeremias (131) says we should not dwell on the lack of some
special garment that was worn at weddings, but rather on the offense
given by coming in a soiled garment, and he adds that there is a possible
connection with the garments washed clean by the blood of the Lamb in
Revelation 19:8 and 22:14.

49. Grelot, *Man and Wife in Scripture*, 104.

50. See John 1:15; 1:26-27; 1:29-30; 3:27-30.

51. Alonso-Schökel, 111.

52. As Richard Batey says, "As far back as one can go in the tradition preserved by the Gospel writers, nuptial imagery was employed to
distinguish the role and ministry of Jesus from that of John the Baptist"
(Nuptial Imagery, 59).

53. David J. Williams, *Paul's Metaphors: Their Context and Character* (Pea-
body, MA: Hendrickson Publishers, 1999), 54.

54. Alonso-Schökel, 113.

55. For the exegesis of this phrase, we follow Alonso-Schökel in his
chapter entitled "Levirato" from his book *Símbolos Matrimoniales*, 109-130.
This chapter is a reworking of the more technical article by Luis Alonso
Schökel and Pierre Proulx, "Las Sandalias del Mesías Esposo," *Biblica*
59 (1978): 1-37, where they argue strongly that this is not just a "moral"
phrase pointing to the priority of Jesus over John but a "juridical statement" where John does not have the legal "right" to do this action of
untying the thong of the sandal. Alonso-Schökel and Proulx argue for a
connection among all five places that this peculiar and oft-misunderstood
phrase shows up in the Scriptures: (Matthew 3:11; Mark 1:7; Luke 3:15b-
16; John 1:25-27; Acts 13:24f). This interpretation, which was common
among the Fathers of the Church, has also been taken up by others in

modern scholarship: see Renzo Infante, "Lo sposo e la sposa. Contributo per l'ecclesiologia del quarto Vangelo," *Rassegna di Teologia* 37 (1996): 451-481, especially 453-55.

56.   Richard Kalmin defines a levirate marriage: "According to Deuteronomy, when a man dies without leaving a son, his widow is forbidden to marry outside the family. Her husband's brother 'takes her as his wife and performs the levir's duty. The first son that she bears shall be accounted to the dead brother.' Should the levir refuse, the ceremony of *ḥăliṣâh* (removal of the sandal) is performed and the widow is free to marry outside the family" ("Levirate Law," in *The Anchor Bible Dictionary*, vol. 4, ed. David N. Freedman [New York: Doubleday, 1992], 296).

57.   See Deuteronomy 25:9.

58.   See Ruth 4:7-8.

59.   Alonso-Schökel and Proulx, "Sandalias del Mesías Esposo," 12, emphasis in original.

60.   Alonso-Schökel and Proulx, 12. Among the Fathers, there were different streams of interpretation: Origen proposed a symbolic, allegorical interpretation of the sandal representing the mystery of the Incarnation (*Comment. in Joannis*, Tom. IV, [PG 14, 257ff]). Augustine and Chrysostom both proposed a moral interpretation that focused on the humility of John (see St. Augustine, *De Consensu Evangelistarum*, 2,12,26 and 29 [CSEL 43, 126, 129], and *In Ioh. Evang.*, 4 [CCSL 36, 35-36]; St. John Chrysostom, ΟΜΙΛΙΑΙ ΕΙΣ ΤΟΝ ΑΓΙΟΝ ΙΩΑΝΝΗΝ, 29 [in *Corona Patrum Salesiana, Series Graeca*, vol. 13 (Turin: Società Editrice Internazionale, 1948), 143-145]). However, there was a strong tradition among the Fathers of connecting this passage with the levirate law, an interpretation that was common up through the Middle Ages: in addition to Jerome, Cyprian, and Ambrose quoted below, one can see this interpretation in Pseudo-Jerome (*Comment. in Marc.*, Cap. I,7 [PL 30, 613]), Gregory the Great (*Hom. in Evang.*, Lib. I, Hom. VII [PL 76, 1101]), Bede (*In Marc.*, I,3-7, CCSL 120, 441]), Pseudo Bede (*In Matt.*, Lib. I, [PL 92,17]), and Rabin Mauro (*Comment. in Matt.*, Lib. I [PL 107, 773]). Thomas Aquinas, in his *Catena Aurea* on Matthew 3:11 notes the two main streams of interpretation: first, the humility of John and second, the connection with the levirate law of Deuteronomy 25:10 (see *Catena Aurea in Quator Evangelia: Expositio in Mattheum*, ed. P. Angelici Guarienti, O.P. [Roma: Marietti, 1953], 51).

61.   St. Jerome, *In Marci evangelium*, CCSL 78, 456. See also St. Jerome's commentary on Matthew 3:11 where he relates it to John 1:27: "Here [Mt 3:11] humility, there [Jn 1:27] is demonstrated the mystery that Christ is the Bridegroom; John is not worthy to remove the sandal of the bridegroom because his house is not called the house of the discalced, according to the law of Moses and the example of Ruth" (CCSL 77, 18).

62.   *Testimonia ad Quirinum* II, XVIII: CCSL 3, 55-56.

63. *De fide*, III, 10: CSEL 78, 134-35, Alonso-Schökel and Proulx, 14. See also St. Caesarius of Arles (†543) in his sermon *De rubo et corrigia calciamenti*, 4 (CCSL 103, 394-395).

64. See John 2:1-11.

65. Mathews, 43. See Birgur Olsson: "The Cana narrative [is] a symbolic narrative text, i.e., a narrative which seeks to convey a message apart from the actual events described. Such a characterization is in agreement with the majority of modern exegetes" (*Structure and Meaning in the Fourth Gospel. A Text-linguistic Analysis of John 2:1-11 and 4:1-42*, in *Coniectanea Biblica New Testament Series, 6*, trans. Jean Gray [Lund ,Sweden: CWK Gleerup, 1974], 95).

66. See John 2:9.

67. La Potterie, *Mary*, 159.

68. Schnackenburg (*John*, 338) says that the wine, which is mentioned five times in the passage, should be seen as an "eschatological gift of the messiah," and he points out that in the Old Testament (Amos 9:13; Hosea 2:24; Joel 4:18; Isaiah 29:17; Jeremiah 31:5) wine in abundance (along with oil or milk) is a sign of the age of salvation; in the ancient blessing of Jacob, it is a characteristic of the Messiah from Judah (Gen 49:11 f.).

69. Mathews 43: note 14.

70. "Τί ἐμοὶ καὶ σοί, γύναι; οὔπω ἥκει ἡ ὥρα μου" (John 2:4). Scholars all point to the difficulty of translating this phrase.

71. Édouard Delebecque, "Les deux vins de Cana," in *Revue Thomiste* 85 (1985): 250. La Potterie, in *Mary*, 184, argues that a rebuke does not fit the scene.

72. La Potterie, *Mary*, 185-86.

73. Idem, *The Hour of Jesus: The Passion and the Resurrection of Jesus According to John: Text and Spirit*, trans. Dom Gregory Murray, O.S.B. (Middlegreen, England: St. Paul Publications, 1989), 22.

74. Albert Vanhoye, S.J., has made a precise study in "Interrogation johannique et éxègese de Cana (Jn 2:4)," *Biblica*, 55 (1974): 160, which claims that this passage should be read in the affirmative.

75. La Potterie, *Mary*, 188.

76. It is not difficult to see the nuptial imagery also present in the story of the Samaritan woman (John 4:5-29) who represents her whole people. She has had five husbands and is still awaiting the messiah, the true bridegroom. See Balthasar, *Spouse of the Word*, 205. Alonso-Schökel (179-185) connects the story of the Samaritan woman with Hosea 2.

77. See John 5:25, 5:28.

78. See La Potterie, *Hour of Jesus*, 134-36. See also Brown, *The Gospel According to John XIII-XXI*, The Anchor Bible, vol. 29a (New York: Doubleday, 1966), 925.

79. *John*, vol. 29, 99.

80. Brown, *John, Vol. 29*, 107-8. De la Potterie lists several other scholars (Gächter, Braun, Hoskyns, Dubarle, Michaud) who take this position,

which he calls "totally traditional," but with which he disagrees because he holds that "neither at Cana nor the Cross is there the slightest hint of the Genesis account" (*Mary*, 203).

81.   La Potterie, *Mary*, 203.

82.   See Mathews, 43-44. De la Potterie explains that contemporary exegesis has shown "that John has his characters function as personifications of a group, and, in a certain sense, as symbols, as 'types.' He does not do this so that his characters vanish into a mythological vacuum, but rather to have them stand as representatives of a definitive group" (*Mary*, 218).

83.   According to Brown, there is no problem in seeing Mary, the Mother of Jesus, also representing the Church, His Bride, at Calvary, because "symbolism is very plastic especially in different contexts: in Hos 2:18 (16) Israel is the wife of Yahweh, while in 11:1 Israel is the son of Yahweh" (Brown, *John*, Vol. 29a, 927).

84.   *Hour of Jesus*, 138-9.

85.   Brown, *John*, Vol 29a, 925.

86.   La Potterie, *Hour of Jesus*, 144-46.

87.   Alonso-Schökel, 81.

88.   Brown, *John*, Vol. 29a, 923.

89.   La Potterie, *Mary*, 200.

90.   Alonso-Schökel, 97. Stauffer adds, "The image of the bride is most powerfully used in the final visions of the Apocalypse, which brings together all the varied imagery of the Messianic banquet" (655).

91.   See Psalms 45; Isaiah 61:10 and 62:5; Ephesians 5:27.

92.   As Miller comments, "It seems that the Lamb's victory can even be called divine victory, and that the Lamb communicates to the members of the churches who become his bride a share in that victory as he redeems them by the blood he sheds when slain" ("The Nuptial Eschatology of Revelation 19-22," *Catholic Biblical Quarterly* 60 [1998]: 312).

93.   That the identification of Jesus as the Passover lamb was common among the early Christians is clear from the other places where it shows up in the Bible: see 1 Corinthians 5:7 and 1 Peter 1:18-19. For the full explanation of this identification see Brown, *John*, Vol. 29, 62.

94.   See also John 1:36.

95.   John 19:14.

96.   See John 19:19. Hyssop was used to apply the blood of the paschal lamb to the doorposts of the Israelites, see Exodus 12:22.

97.   Brown, *John*, Vol. 29, 62.

98.   Revelation 18:3.

99.   Revelation 18:6.

100.   As Grelot says, "Opposite the Virgin-Bride, the logic of the symbols puts another city: Babylon, the prostitute with whom all the kings of the earth fornicate (Rev 17). Prostitution is here a symbol of idolatry (cf. Hos 1-2). But whereas the Virgin-Bride is mother of the elect, the great

harlot is merely the seductress of the reprobate (cf. 18:3). The ambivalence of woman for man is here reproduced symbolically: on the one hand, Virgin, Bride and Mother; on the other hand, the "strange woman" (cf. Prov 7) who draws man into her clutches and sets him on the road to death" (*Man and Wife in Scripture*, 109).

101.   See Revelation 21:3.

102.   There are other passages that make reference to a spousal relationship between Christ and an individual Christian: for example, Romans 7:3-4 and 1 Corinthians 6:12-20. Chavasse (67) also argues that Galations 4:21-31 should be seen as an example of St. Paul's describing the relationship of Christ with the Church, but this passage does not directly mention Christ's marriage to the Church.

103.   Giuseppe Baldanza, *La metafora sponsale in S. Paolo e nella tradizione liturgica siriaca*, Bibliotheca "Ephemerides Liturgicae," no. 114, ed. A. Pistoia, C.M. and A.M. Triacca, S.D.B. (Roma: Centro Liturgico Vincenziano——Edizione Liturgiche, 2001): 32.

104.   Ignace de la Potterie, S.J., "The Biblical Foundation of Priestly Celibacy," in *For Love Alone: Reflections on Priestly Celibacy* (Maynooth, Ireland: St. Pauls, 1993), 23.

105.   *Mulieris dignitatem*, 23, emphasis in orginal.

106.   "Le grand mystère concernant le Christ et son Église. Éphésiens 5, 22-33," *Biblica* 47 [1966]: 88.

107.   As Alonso-Schökel says, "From the exhortation to the spouses, [the author] soars to a theological vision which founds and completes the institution of marriage" (86).

108.   Edouard Cothenet explains: "The two verbs are aorist, and they point us to a precise moment in time, which is the death of Christ upon the cross. (cf. Eph 2:14-16)" ("L'Église, épouse du Christ: Éph 5; Apoc 19 et 21." In *L'Église dans la liturgie: conférences Saint-Serge XXVIe semaine d'études liturgiques*, Paris, 26-29 Juin 1979, ed. A. Pistoia, C.M. and A.M. Triacca, S.D.B. [Roma: Centro Liturgico Vincenziano, 1980],88).

109.   J. Paul Sampley points out the technical meaning of this phrase: "The combination of the verb παραδίδωμι and the preposition ὑπέρ with some pronominal object was very early formalized as a way of speaking of the death of Jesus. There is no question that the occurrences in Eph. 5:2b and 5:25b likewise refer to Jesus' death by means of this traditional formula" (36).

110.   *Mulieris Dignitatem*, sec. 26.

111.   Alonso-Schöckel (87) will also point to places in the Old Testament that reflect this nuptial bath of sanctification, for example, Ruth 3:3 and Judith 10:1-3. Sampley demonstrates that the use of Old Testament marriage references in these two verses (26 and 27) reveals that the author of Ephesians wants to root the marriage of Christ with the Church in the whole Old Testament understanding of the marriage of Yahweh with Israel: "It is ultimately possible to see the milieu of the Ephesian hieros

gamos in that elusive portrait of YHWH's marriage to Israel. There are, to be sure, reflections of such an understanding already to be found in Hosea, Ezekiel, Jeremiah and other writings in the OT" (37-38).

112.   Ernest Best, (*Ephesians: The International Critical Commentary*, ed. J.A. Emerton, C.E.B. Cranfield and G.N. Stanton [Edinburgh: T & T Clark, 1998], 543-44) lists all the possible meanings of this phrase and says "the great majority of modern commentators" prefer the explanation attributed to St. John Chrysostom: i.e., "ἐν ῥήματι" refers to "the words of the baptismal formula, 'in the name of Christ', spoken over the candidate at the moment of baptism."

113.   St. Augustine, *Enarrationes in Psalmos* 44, 22 [CCSL 38, 509]). See also *En. in ps.*, 132, 10 (CCSL 38, 10); *Sermones ad populum*, 95, 4 (PL 38, 582); 181, 2 and 5; 341, 11.

114.   Cothenet, 92-93. This teaching in the Fathers will be explored later.

115.   Alonso-Schökel, 88.

116.   Mathews, 45.

117.   As Giuseppe Baldanza points out: "The Author of the letter knows the spousal symbolism of the Old Testament is used to express the spousal love of YHWH towards Israel. But there Israel is considered as partner and not the body of YHWH. The physical relationship is characteristic of the letter to the Ephesians, and when this is pointed out, it underlines the fact that the body and bride the Church is vivified by the Spirit" (27-28).

118.   See Cambier (79) who argues strongly that this is the case.

119.   Markus Barth, *Ephesians: Translation and Commentary on Chapters 4-6*, The Anchor Bible (New York: Doubleday, 1974), 64.

120.   Cambier, 86.

121.   Ibid., 88.

122.   Stauffer, 654.

123.   Godefridus N. Vollebregt, O. Praem., *The Bible on Marriage* (London: Sheed and Ward, 1965), 93.

124.   "Marian Vigil for the Conclusion of the Month of May," 30 May 2009.

125.   Angelo Amato, S.D.B., *Gesù il Signore. Saggio de cristologia*, Corso di teologia sistematica, 4 (Bologna: Edizioni Dehoniane, 1999), 504.

126.   Vincenzo Battaglia, "Gesù Cristo Crocifisso Sposo della Chiesa: Prospettive di recerca e traiettorie tematiche per lélaborazione di una critologia sponsale," *Antonianum* 74.3 (1999): 437.

127.   See Exodus 20:5, 34:14; Deuteronomy 4:24, 5:9, 6:15; Ezekiel 16:34, 42.

128.   *Deus Caritas Est*, 9.

129.   Ibid.

130.   John Paul II, *Man and Woman He Created Them: A Theology of the Body* (Boston: Pauline Books and Media, 2006), 501.

131.   Balthasar, *Explorations in Theology*, 199.

CHAPTER 2

NUPTIAL THEOLOGY

Having studied the marriage image in the Scriptures, we can begin to understand some of its ramifications for theology within the Catholic tradition. To understand the nuptial meaning of the Sacrament of Holy Orders will require that we understand some foundational aspects of what might be called "nuptial theology." Nuptial theology explores the mystery of redemption through the lens of the divine marriage presented in the covenant of the Scriptures. It seeks deeper insights into soteriology and ecclesiology through the understanding of Christ as the bridegroom and the Church as bride. Of course, to understand Christ and the Church we need many images,[1] but given the prominence of marriage image in the Scriptures, we cannot avoid the theological truths the nuptial image reveals to us.

The Power of Scriptural Analogy

Philosophy being the handmaid of theology, the first step to understanding nuptial theology requires us to answer a philosophical question: When Scripture uses the bridegroom image to speak about Christ in His relationship with the

Church, what does it actually tell us? Does it tell us anything about God, per se, Himself? Is it just an analogy? This is an area in which we find considerable debate among modern theologians because it enters into one of the central questions of theology: what is the relationship of our human language and our understanding of God? Many modern scholars argue that biblical images are helpful but are limited in that they are only metaphors. These scholars argue that human language and images do not actually tell us anything about God Himself. Proponents of this "negative" view argue that biblical images like the mystical marriage are useful but they are very limited. For example, Elizabeth Johnson says:

> Whether expressed by metaphorical, symbolic, or analogical theology, there is basic agreement that the mystery of God is fundamentally unlike anything else we know of, and so is beyond the grasp of all our naming. . . . We have seen that God dwells in unapproachable light so that no name or image or concept that human beings use to speak of the divine mystery ever arrives at its goal: God is essentially incomprehensible.[2]

The agreement Johnson speaks of among theologians may not be so universal. In fact, taken to an extreme, her understanding would make real theology impossible. If our words when applied to God are only metaphors, that is, they do not really tell us anything about God in Himself, then our theological language would be too limited. We could never actually assert anything positively about God. As the Thomistic Scholar George Peter Klubertanz points out:

Knowledge through symbol and myth is direct, profound, and vitally moving, but it is not a grasp of the intrinsic reality of the thing known. . . . A being that is known only through symbol, myth or metaphor is not known in itself; hence we can never make any statement about that being in itself, but only statements about ourselves and objects of direct experience.[3]

Catholic theology seeks to know something about the essence of God, and since God has revealed Himself, we believe that we can express in human language real truths about who He is. This was one of the main points that St. John Paul II wanted to affirm in his encyclical *Fides et Ratio*: human language is capable of saying something about the nature of God; God is not completely beyond naming. This is possible through the use of analogy:

Faith clearly presupposes that human language is capable of expressing divine and transcendent reality in a universal way—analogically, it is true, but no less meaningfully for that. Were this not so, the word of God, which is always a divine word in human language, would not be capable of saying anything about God.[4]

The Holy Father, in this context, cites the Fourth Lateran Council, which makes the key point: "Between the Creator and the creature there cannot be a likeness so great that the unlikeness is not greater."[5] Thus, it is true that we can never fully comprehend the essence of God through our human language, since He is so unlike us. Yet, the Catholic Tradition has always affirmed that theological and scriptural analogies do tell us something about the essence of God. As St. John Paul II pointed out, Catholic philosophy must be able "to vindicate the human being's capacity to know this transcendent and metaphysical dimension in a way that is true and certain, albeit imperfect and analogical."[6]

St. Thomas, in the beginning of his *Summa Theologicae*, asks "whether any name can be applied to God substantially?"[7] He points out that since God is completely different from humans (not just in degree but in essence), concepts cannot be predicated of God in the same way they are predicated of humans. If we will say anything substantial of God, we must have another way of predication. For example, to say that the adjective "living" means the same thing when applied to God ("God is living,") that it means when applied to a person ("John is living") would be an equivocation. God lives in a completely different way than any human being. Yet because of the likeness between God and humans, especially since we know that God created humans in His image and likeness, we know it is true that God is living. We can apply the term "life" to God substantially, even though it is only analogous to the way we use it for humans.

However, not all terms can be applied to God in this same way—that is, some terms are metaphorical not analogical. When the Scriptures say that God is a rock, or Jesus says that He is the gate, it means something different than when Jesus says, "I am the way and the truth and the life" (Jn 14:6). The first examples are metaphors; the second ones are analogies. God cannot really be a rock, although He has some attributes that are rock-like since He is firm, secure, and unmovable. Yet, understood properly, we must say that Jesus really is the way, the truth, and the life. This is the important distinction that classical theology has made between a metaphor and an analogy. Metaphors are applied to two subjects based on similarities that are extrinsic to the essence of the things, and analogies are applied to two subjects based on similarities that are intrinsic to the essence of the things.[8] Benedict Ashley makes this distinction between metaphor and analogy clear in some biblical examples:

> Thus when the Bible calls God "my Rock" (Ps 18:3), "Rock" is taken metaphorically, because the point of comparison is "solidity," but "solidity" is not the very nature of a rock, nor of God, so that the comparison is very superficial. But when we call God "Light" (1 Jn 1:5) the analogy is proper and essential, since it is based on the comparison of what is essential and intrinsic to both "light" and "God," i.e., as it is the very nature of light to reveal the visible, material world to us, so it is very nature of God to know and to reveal the truth of all things, visible and invisible, to us.[9]

Metaphorical language falls short of saying anything substantial about God, but analogical language actually does express something of the very nature of God. It is true that in an analogy, all the terms we predicate of God we know first from human experience; as St. Thomas says, "we can name God only from creatures."[10] However, because of the relationship between creatures and God—that is, God is the cause of creatures—what we say analogously about God can really express something substantial about Him.[11] In a proper analogy, we name God from what we know in us; but because God contains all the perfections of our nature, we can say that it first exists in Him. Thus, we find an intrinsic connection between God and creatures that allows us to say something about the essence of God:

These names are applied to God not as cause but also as essential. The words, "God is good or wise" signify not only that He is the cause of wisdom or goodness, but that these exist in Him in a more excellent way. Hence, in regard to what the name signifies, these names are applied primarily to God rather than to creatures because these perfections flow from God to creatures; but in regard to the imposition of the names, they are primarily applied by us to creatures that we know first. Hence, they have a mode of signification that belongs to creatures.[12]

Of course, the theologians mentioned above have a point because of the vast difference between God and creatures, the analogy has to admit elements of abstraction. Any word predicated of God will fall short of a full representation of God. As St. Thomas says:

Therefore the aforesaid names signify the divine substance, but in an imperfect manner, even as creatures represent it imperfectly. So when we say, God is good, the meaning is not, God is the cause of goodness, or, God is not evil; but the meaning is, Whatever good we attribute to creatures, pre-exists in God, and in a more excellent and higher way. Hence it does not follow that God is good because He causes goodness; but rather, on the contrary, He causes goodness in things because He is good; according to what Augustine says (De Doctr. Christ. i, 32), "Because He is good, we are."[13]

Since every analogy is imperfect, it is the task of theology to discern the essence of an analogy—what makes the intrinsic connection? What exactly does it tell us about God, and what part of the analogy cannot be directly applied?[14] This task becomes extremely important when applied to a scriptural analogy because scriptural analogies are revealed by God. As Benedict Ashley says:

> The fundamental terms of the Bible, of worship, and of theology are not mere metaphors but proper analogies by which we know the Creator through his works of creation and redemption. St. Paul says, "ever since the creation of the world, his [God's] invisible attributes of eternal power in divinity have been able to be understood and perceived in what he has made" (Rom 1:20; cf. Wis 13:1-9).[15]

For example, in Ephesians 3:14-15, a proper analogy is used to describe God as Father. St. Paul says, "For this reason I kneel before the Father, from whom every family in heaven and on earth is named." St. Thomas uses this as an example of an analogy in Scripture in his *Summa Theologiae*.[16] Here, we can see that St. Paul knows what a Father is from creatures, but he is pointing out that in reality, the term "Father" should be first applied to God (i.e., God is the real Father, the primary referent in the analogy. Human fathers, then, should contain something of the perfection of fatherhood found in Him.) Yet there is also an element of abstraction as Benedict Ashley explains: "The term 'Father' used of God in no way implies that he is male, but only that as our father gave us life and loves and cares for us, so does God."[17] The Father gives us life and cares for us in a way analogous to what a human father does, in a way that is similar but also different. Armed with this understanding of analogy, we now turn to the image of the bridegroom to see how it, too, is a scriptural analogy.

The Analogy of Ephesians 5:21-33

In Ephesians 5:21-33, St. Paul uses the understanding of Christ as the bridegroom of the Church as a scriptural analogy. St. Paul says, "Husbands, love your wives, even as Christ loved the church and handed himself over for her" (Eph 5:25). Thus, he shows that human married love is to reflect the covenantal love of Christ and His Church. Christ's self-giving love is held up as the archetype of marriage and the model to be followed. We know what marriage is, and what a bridegroom is, through our human experience; and we apply that knowledge to Christ and His Church. But St. Paul shows us that this is a scriptural analogy: Christ is the real bridegroom and His relationship with the Church is the real marriage. From this marriage, every bridegroom and every marriage take their name. The mystery of the marriage relationship of Christ and the Church is the deeper and more profound reality, the covenantal relationship, that sheds light on human marriage (as is done in the Old Testament, Mal 2:14-16). This can be seen clearly in Ephesians 5:32, which is the theological summit of the passage: "This is a great mystery, but I speak in reference to Christ and the church." St. Paul's use of the term "μυστήριον" (mystery) to describe the spousal relationship of Christ and the Church reveals the centrality of this reality for understanding the covenant and, as a result, all marriages. St. John Paul II explains this in his *Theology of the Body*: "In the overall context of Ephesians and further in the wider context of the words of Sacred Scripture, which reveal God's salvific plan 'from the beginning,' one can see that here the term "mystérion" signifies the mystery, first hidden in God's mind, and later revealed in man's history."[18]

Thus, the Holy Father says that the spousal image used in Ephesians 5 is a scriptural analogy based on the love that Christ has for His Church:

By quoting the words of Genesis 2:24 ["the two shall become one flesh"], the author emphasizes that the basis of this analogy should be sought in the line that unites, in God's salvific plan, marriage as the most ancient revelation (and "manifestation") of that plan in the created world with the definitive revelation and "manifestation," namely, the revelation that "Christ loved the Church and gave himself for her" (Eph 5:25), endowing his redemptive love with a spousal nature and meaning.[19]

This passage has the key characteristic of an analogy. Human marriage is being compared to the love of Christ for the Church, arguing that it must have the same intrinsic reality: the self-giving love of the bridegroom for the bride.[20] Just as St. Thomas described a proper analogy above, St. Paul is naming the relationship of Christ and the Church as a marriage that he knows first from human marriage, but it is the marriage of Christ to the Church, which is the primary analogue being proposed because "as regards what the name signifies, these names are applied primarily to God rather than to creatures."[21]

St. Thomas himself also interprets Ephesians 5:32-33 as a scriptural analogy. He says in his commentary on St. Paul's letter to the Ephesians that certain passages in Scripture "can be explained as referring to Christ and others; to Christ principally, and to others as they were types (figurae) of Christ."[22] St. Thomas believes that when St. Paul says, "This is a great mystery, but I speak in reference to Christ and the Church" (Eph 5:32), it has the key characteristic of an analogy. It really says something about Christ and secondarily, is applied also to humans: "It must first be interpreted in reference to Christ and afterwards concerning others."[23]

Now we are in a place to answer the questions with which we started this section: When Scripture uses the bridegroom image to speak about Christ in His relationship with the Church, what does that actually tell us? Does it tell us anything about Christ per se, in His essence? The answer is yes. Scripture reveals that the marriage between Christ and the Church is the archetypal marriage upon which all marriages are based. As Robert Pesarchick says:

> God's original intentions for the old Adam and Eve only are fully manifest in the relationship between the New Adam and Eve, Christ and his Body/Bride, the Church. It is within this relationship, witnessed to in the New Testament (e.g., Eph 5), that the relationship intended by God for man and woman, and their union in marriage becomes visible.[24]

This is why we can speak of human marriage as a sacrament that should make present the covenant of Christ with His Church.[25] As St. John Paul II says, "The Church professes that Marriage, as the Sacrament of the covenant between husband and wife, is a 'great mystery', because it expresses the spousal love of Christ for his Church."[26] Ephesians 5 reveals that the covenant, "the great mystery," is a nuptial reality; and, thus, there is a profound connection between the nuptiality found in creation and in God's redemptive plan. As de la Potterie says:

> The original plan of salvation formulated by God was that of a symbolic couple. With that image in front of himself, God created man and woman in order that

they would represent and prepare through their mutual relationship the archetypal and final couple of Christ and the Church."[27]

Ephesians 5 not only tells us something about the essence of the covenant but it also tells us something about Christ in himself—that is, Christ is the true bridegroom. Christ is the primary analogue who reveals the heart of spousal love in laying down His life for the Church.[28] What was foreshadowed in the Old Testament becomes reality in the person of Christ who lays down His life for the Church. As Grelot summarizes:

> Having occurred at the heart of history, as the act above all others in which earth and heaven, the human and the divine, time and eternity meet—for this is the meaning of Christ's death followed by his resurrection. . . . The divine archetype of the couple is therefore no longer that of the pagan mythologies, a mere mental personification, invented by men to account for the sacral nature of sex, of which they had an intuitive or instinctive knowledge and which they sought to explain to themselves. It is no longer, as in the Old Testament, a shadow which shares the imperfections of the actual human condition, or a simple promise. It is a fact, the central fact of history, in which a mysterious reality is both fulfilled and revealed, a reality which embraces in its fullness the relationship between man and God.[29]

We know that we cannot fully comprehend how Christ is the bridegroom because the spousal analogy does not allow us to fully enter into the mystery. As John Paul II says: "the mystery remains transcendent with respect to this analogy as with any other analogy with which we try to express it in human language. At the same time, however, this analogy offers the possibility of a certain cognitive 'penetration' into the very essence of the mystery."[30]

Who is the Bride?

It is interesting that although the Gospels clearly refer to Christ as the bridegroom, they speak only indirectly about the bride. The disciples are referred to as wedding guests[31] and as the virgins or bridesmaids ready to escort the groom,[32] but it is never specified that they are to be seen as the bride.

It is left completely open who the bride is: whether the bridegroom, in fact, has an individual bride, of whom the invited guests are friends or relations, or whether the nature of the bride is to be looked for as present, in a hidden manner, in the guests, the "children of the bridegroom," the ten virgins and, so, in those very persons to whom the Lord is speaking.[33]

Based on the Old Testament, where we saw that Israel (i.e., the people of God) was always the bride, in the New Testament, "the thought readily suggests itself that the new community of the covenant is the bride."[34] St. Paul and the book of Revelation make this connection explicit. We saw both in 1 Corinthians 2:11 and in Ephesians 5:21-33 how St. Paul speaks of the Church as the bride of Christ. The bride is presented not as an individual but as a corporate reality. In fact, the very name "Ἐκκλησία" (Ecclesia) implies this, since it signifies a group of people having been called together.[35] As St. John Paul II explains, "according to the Letter to the Ephesians, the bride is the Church, just as for the Prophets the bride was Israel. She is therefore a collective subject and not an individual person."[36] We also saw how the Book of Revelation speaks about the bride as the redeemed people. She is the saints who have clothed themselves in righteous deeds[37] and also the city which descends from heaven.[38] Thus, we can say that in the Scriptures the Church, the redeemed people, is the bride of Christ.

But is it possible, and perhaps even necessary, to find another, more concrete, reference to the bride in the Scriptures? Christ is a particular person who is also the universal savior, is it enough for the individual Christ to have a corporate bride? Hans Urs von Balthasar argues that the spousal self-gift that Christ makes must find in humanity a particular response, if it will be truly a marriage. Thus, there must be an individual bride who also represents all people:

> Since the man Jesus Christ is an individual human being, his relationship to woman will be individual too; the woman to whom he relates is a particular person. On the other hand, insofar as he is the incarnate Word of God, carrying out in his earthly existence the Father's commission to reconcile God's entire creation with God (2 Cor 5:19), there will necessarily be a social aspect to his "helpmate," since she represents mankind (which, in relation to God, is female).[39]

Balthasar sees the Scriptures presenting Mary as the particular bride of Christ. She is the one who will offer her "fiat" on behalf of all humanity. We know that marriage is not a one-sided action but requires mutual consent. According to St. Thomas Aquinas, this is why, at the Annunciation, the Angel Gabriel does not command Mary to say "Yes," but rather "proposes" to her. God wants that Mary give this bridal consent on behalf of all of humanity:

> It was reasonable that it should be announced to the Blessed Virgin that she was to conceive Christ . . . in order to show that there is a certain spiritual wedlock (*matrimonium*) between the Son of God and human nature. Wherefore in the Annunciation the Virgin's consent was besought in lieu of that of the entire human nature (*loco totius humanae naturae*).[40]

But Mary does more than give a bridal "Yes" at the Annunciation, where she also is most clearly mother. John's Gospel shows us the connection between Cana and Calvary, where the woman's request evokes the new wine of the wedding feast. Mary can, perhaps, be seen most clearly as the bride at Calvary, for there, at the foot of the Cross, she must repeat her fiat. Balthasar explains how Mary—and in her, the whole Church—has a role to play in the nuptial self-gift of redemption at the Cross:

> The Mother is here the prototype of this Church which Paul describes as immaculate: Ecclesia sancta et immaculata (holy and immaculate Church, Eph 5:27), whose consent to Christ's passion is infinitely sorrowful, but expressly required, because the solidarity that Christ wants to establish between himself and his Church is not satisfied by a faith granted post factum, but demands a simultaneous, instantaneous, consent, in order that his sacrifice may be truly total: inseparably that of the head and its members.[41]

What this bridal "Yes" means for Mary is that "she somehow embodies the Church as the cherished spouse for whom

Christ gives himself up on the Cross."[42] In her, the analogy of the bride becomes concrete. She "is the Mother of God, the one who in faith and love gave flesh and blood to God the Son, and she is the Church, Holy Church's personal embodiment as immaculate bride."[43]

This biblical word "woman" that Jesus uses to address Mary at Cana and Calvary leads us to connect Mary with the woman spoken of in Genesis 3:15 and Revelation 12. This is an idea firmly rooted in Patristic theology. The Fathers often spoke of Mary as the New Eve, the bride of the New Adam and the mother of all the children of God. John Paul II explains this patristic teaching:

> In the tradition of faith and of Christian reflection throughout the ages, the coupling Adam-Christ is often linked with that of Eve-Mary. If Mary is described also as the "new Eve," what are the meanings of this analogy? Certainly there are many. Particularly noteworthy is the meaning which sees Mary as the full revelation of all that is included in the biblical word "woman": a revelation commensurate with the mystery of the Redemption. Mary means, in a sense, a going beyond the limit spoken of in the Book of Genesis (3:16) and a return to that "beginning" in which one finds the "woman" as she was intended to be in creation, and therefore in the eternal mind of God: in the bosom of the Most Holy Trinity.[44]

Mary is the woman of redemption, the new Eve, whose relationship with the New Adam is manifold.

Von Balthasar points out that, in the relationship between the sexes in creation, the position of the woman in regard to the man is two-fold or dyadic: "she is bride and spouse to the man mother to the child."[45] This dyadic role of the woman is taken over into the mission of Mary. She is to be the virgin mother of the Incarnate Son, yet at the same time, the New Eve, the Bride and Helpmate to the New Adam, for she is the "epitome" of the Church. Her mission then is two-fold in nature.[46] As St. Aelred of Rievaulx points out, Mary, in some way, encompasses all femininity in relationship with Christ: "Let us come to his bride, his mother, his perfect handmaid, for the blessed Mary is all of this."[47]

In Balthasar's theology, he calls Mary a Realsymbol, because she makes present the Church in her person. As John Saward explains:

> In the Patristic eyes of Balthasar, the Lady who stands by the Cross is indistinguishably both Mary and the Church. When, like Vatican II, he says that Mary is the Church's "type" or "model", he means much more than that she is a poetic symbol of the Church, a Realsymbol, as the Germans say, a symbol which contains the very thing it symbolizes.[48]

Here, we are entering into the mysterious relationship between Mary and the Church, a relationship that Balthasar will call "perichoresis between Mary and the Church."[49] In one way, we can say Mary represents the Church; but in another way, we can say she is the Church. One cannot be understood without the other because she is the Church's "deepest origin and unsullied kernel: as that point in the center of the community where, by God's grace, that was truly achieved which as sinners we are all quite incapable of achieving."[50] Therefore, Mary as a historical person becomes the "concrete universal" of the Church.[51] Cardinal Ratzinger points out that this does not reduce the fact that Mary is a real person. Precisely the opposite, her concrete "Yes" is essential:

> Mariology can never simply be dissolved into
> an impersonal ecclesiology. It is a thorough
> misunderstanding of patristic typology to reduce Mary
> to a mere, hence, interchangeable, exemplification of
> theological structures. Rather, the type remains true to
> its meaning only when the non-interchangeable personal
> figure of Mary becomes transparent to the personal
> form of the Church herself. In theology, it is not the
> person that is reducible to the thing, but the thing to the
> person. . . . Only the Marian dimension secures the place
> of affectivity in faith and thus ensures a fully human
> correspondence to the reality of the incarnate Logos.[52]

There must be a fully human yes offered to the matrimonial covenant of Christ. Mary does this on behalf of the whole Church. For this reason, as St. Isaac of Stella said, "that which is understood of the virgin mother Church in a universal sense, is understood of the Virgin Mother Mary in a singular sense."[53]

This idea that Mary is the "form," "type," "sacrament," "mirror," "heart" of the Church is deeply rooted in patristic theology. As Henri de Lubac explains, for the Fathers of the Church, Mary and the Church are "one single mystery":

> Our Lady speaks and acts in the name of the Church at
> every moment of her existence—"She shows forth in
> herself the figure of the holy Church"[54]—not of course,
> in virtue of some decision which is an afterthought nor,
> obviously, because of an explicit intention on her part,
> but because she already carries the Church within her,

so to speak, and contains it, in its wholeness, in her own person. She is "the whole of the Church." [55]

Vatican II emphasized this patristic idea that Our Lady is the "type" and "exemplar" of the Church. The council fathers say that she is the new Eve:

> As St. Ambrose taught, the Mother of God is a type of the Church in the order of faith, charity and perfect union with Christ. For in the mystery of the Church, which is itself rightly called mother and virgin, the Blessed Virgin stands out in eminent and singular fashion as exemplar both of virgin and mother. By her belief and obedience, not knowing man but overshadowed by the Holy Spirit, as the new Eve she brought forth on earth the very Son of the Father, showing an undefiled faith, not in the word of the ancient serpent, but in that of God's messenger.[56]

Jesus is the perfect bridegroom who gives Himself completely in the archetypal marriage. The nature of Jesus' gift calls for perfect receptivity (i.e., the perfect bride). Through the Immaculate Conception, Mary is made capable of this perfect receptivity, this complete openness. Balthasar explains:

> for the Lord wills to see his Church standing before him, not a singular, palpable failure, but as a glorious bride worthy of him. Here the Marian principle in the Church necessarily comes into play. Mary is the subjectivity that, in its womanly and receptive manner, is enabled fully to correspond to the masculine subjectivity of Christ, through God's grace and the overshadowing of his Spirit. The Church flowing forth from Christ finds her personal

center in Mary as well as the full realization of her idea
as Church.⁵⁷

As the fathers of Vatican II say, in Mary, the perfection
that will be achieved in the whole Church is already present:
"But while in the most holy Virgin the Church has already
reached that perfection whereby she is without spot or wrinkle, the followers of Christ still strive to increase in holiness
by conquering sin (cf. Eph. 5:27)."⁵⁸

We are reminded of the eschatological nature of the
wedding feast that is central to the use of the marriage image
in the Old and New Testaments. The marriage of God with
humanity happens at the Cross, when Christ pours out His
life for the Church; but it will ultimately only be fulfilled in
heaven when the wedding feast of the Lamb will include
all the elect: the wedding has already happened but is not
yet fulfilled in the kingdom. It is through Mary that the
eschatological tension of the marriage feast is held together.
Mary, who cooperates in the marriage at the Cross, is the
sign of the heavenly Jerusalem where all those saved will be
fully espoused to Christ. What is predicted in Revelation, the
wedding feast of the lamb, is already fulfilled in Mary at the
Cross. Balthasar explains:

> In this, too, she points us, in anticipation, to the real place
> for which we strive, to the wholeness and savedness of
> our whole spiritual and material existence; because it is
> fitting that not only the bridegroom but also his bride, the
> heavenly Jerusalem, should really (and not only "ideally")
> partake of the ultimate salvation gained on the cross, and
> the eschatological marriage feast, of which the Book of
> Revelation speaks, should not be put off till some far

distant future but should now already in a mysterious present be beginning.[59]

Mary has a unique relationship with the Church as bride. On one level, she is the archetype of the bride, just as Christ is the archetype of the bridegroom. Her spousal "Yes" is what every member of the Church must seek to imitate. Mary is the bride in whom the wedding feast of the Lamb has already been realized in her spotless purity. However, even in the Scriptures, her role as a Realsymbol allows her never to be separated from the people she represents; she always has this relationship with the Church, which Balthasar calls perichoresis. Thus, saying Mary is the bride does not intend to remove the rest of the Church from being fully the bride but to say that Mary is what the rest of the Church is still becoming. "Everything said about the ecclesia in the Bible is true of her, and vice versa; the Church learns concretely what she is and is meant to be by looking at Mary."[60]

The Church as Body and Bride

The nuptial nature of the covenant has important ramifications for appreciating Christ's ongoing relationship with the Church. St. Paul primarily uses two images for the Church: the body of Christ and the bride of Christ. In terms of the mere number of references, one could argue that St. Paul sees the image of the Church as the Body of Christ as primary.[61] However, we saw in Ephesians 5 that these two images are related to each other; and, in fact, the nuptial image is primary because it is the foundation for calling the Church the Body of Christ. This nuptial understanding of the Church is, therefore, essential for a proper ecclesiology and, we will argue, for a proper understanding of the priesthood.

Recent ecclesiology, dating at least from the encyclical *Mystici Corporis* of Pope Pius XII in 1943, has seen a greater emphasis on the Church as the Body of Christ, but this was not the case throughout the history of the theology.[62] Although both images are present in *Lumen Gentium*, the image of the bride of Christ receives only a brief mention compared to the full treatment of the image of the Church as Christ's Body.[63] Understanding the Church as the Body of Christ has been an important development of twentieth century theology, yet, as St. John Paul II has pointed out, ecclesiology needs both images: "The Church is indeed the body in which Christ the head is present and active, but she is also the bride who proceeds like a new Eve from the open side of the redeemer on the cross."[64]

Based on the Scriptures, the image of the Church as the Body of Christ derives from the understanding of the Church as the Bride of Christ. As noted in Chapter One, the understanding of the Church as the Body of Christ is a New Testament development; in the Old Testament, the image of Israel as Yahweh's bride had no attached conception of being the body of Yahweh.[65] It is the letter to the Ephesians that makes the connection between these two images clear. Ephesians bases its claim that the Church is the body of Christ on the application of Genesis 2:24 to the marriage of Christ with His Church: "'For this reason a man shall leave [his] father and [his] mother and be joined to his wife, and the two shall become one flesh' [Gen 2:24]. This is a great mystery but I speak in reference to Christ and the church" (Eph 5:31-32). Sara Butler describes the relationship between the two images:

The head-body and bridegroom-bride analogies in Ephesians 5 are not simply placed side by side. The one is within the other. There is a tradition of seeing the entire symbolism as marital: the bridegroom and bride become "one body" through their mutual gift of self. Taken in this way, the comparison of the Church to Christ's body appears to derive from the nuptial relationship.[66]

Ephesians 5 demonstrates to us how the two images of body and bride must be held together. Christ and the Church are one body because they have become "one flesh" through the marriage covenant of the cross. As Cardinal Ratzinger explains:

> In Pauline terms, however, the claim that we are the "Body of Christ" makes sense only against the backdrop of the formula of Genesis 2:24: "The Two shall become one flesh" (cf. 1 Cor 6:17). The Church is the body, the flesh of Christ in the spiritual tension of love wherein the spousal mystery of Adam and Eve is consummated, hence, in the dynamism of a unity that does not abolish dialogical reciprocity.[67]

As Ratzinger is explaining, there is a theological complementarity to these two images of the Church; both of them emphasize different but important aspects of the relationship between Christ and the Church. The image of the Church as the Body of Christ emphasizes the unity of the Church with Christ, while the image of the bride of Christ emphasizes the distinction between Christ and the Church, while still maintaining the unity. As the *Catechism of the Catholic Church* says, "The unity of Christ and the Church, head and members of one Body, also implies the distinction of the two within a personal relationship. This aspect is often expressed by the image of bridegroom and bride."[68] This balance between emphasis on union and emphasis on distinction creates the unique relationship of Christ with the Church. It is a paradox that must be held in tension, as Ernest Best explains:

> But while the Church is set over against Christ as owing subjection to him it is also regarded as "one flesh" with him. Here is the paradox which we have continually found: distinction from and identity with. The Church is a person in her own right—a Bride, yet she is also part of a fuller and more comprehensive person; she is one person with Christ. . . . The relationship of the Church cannot be simply regarded as one of unity with Christ nor can it be regarded as one of independence from him. It is the second of these which is brought out most effectively by the nuptial metaphor, in so far as the Church is considered to be a separate person for whom Christ gives his life and whom he marries.[69]

Cardinal Ratzinger has pointed to a danger in recent theology of an overemphasis on the image of the body to the exclusion of the image of the bride. An overemphasis on the Church as the body of Christ implies an identity between Christ and His Church and fails to recognize the reason for the distinction. "The concept of the body of Christ needs clarification in order not to be misunderstood in today's context: it could easily be interpreted in the sense of a Christomonism, of an absorption of the church, and thus of the believing creature, into the uniqueness of Christology."[70] The image of the Church as Bride corrects this danger. The Church, because she is separate from Christ, is completely dependent on Him. She needs His power, which she does not find in herself, to sanctify her and make her holy. If the focus is too much on union between the Church and Christ (i.e., the body image exclusively) the Church ends up being Christ and not needing Him. Gisbert Greshake makes this very point:

> The Church is not merely the body of Christ, the fullness of him who fulfills all, but also the "bride of Christ," who in her infinite need and poverty receives everything from him; it is the people of God, which he gathers together, the building which he builds. These images express an essential and even the most fundamental aspects of the Church: the Church owes everything to the Lord: its origin is not the spontaneous coming together of those who wish to be the people of God; it does not adopt its fundamental structure and form of life in a kind of a spiritual enthusiasm; its journey and goal are not determined by human reflection or social contact. It is essentially the ekklesia, the community of those who are chosen, gathered together by Jesus Christ, by his word in work.[71]

The key is that Christ is always antecedent to His Church, and although the Church is drawn into a life-giving union with Him, such that she can be considered His body, on the other hand, the element of distinction is a constant reminder of the absolute dependence of the Church upon Christ. This is also why the priest must be seen to represent the bridegroom. Seeing the priest as representing the bridegroom helps the Church understand herself as bride. It reminds the Church of her constant dependence on Christ. The priest makes present not only the head of the body but the bridegroom, who through the sacraments is continually pouring out his life for the bride. The spousal relationship in the covenant is part of the Church's deepest nature: she is the bride of Christ as well as the body. Thus, this reality must also be reflected in her self-understanding; it must be represented sacramentally in the Church through the priesthood.

The Nature of Christ's Spousal Love

As has already been mentioned, nuptial theology was extremely popular for the Fathers of the Church. Patristic theology, because it was so rooted in Scripture, was deeply imbued with the idea of Christ as the bridegroom and the Church as the bride of Christ. This was one of the main lenses through which they saw the theology of redemption. An exploration of the main themes of the Church Fathers' nuptial theology will reveal to us a deeper understanding of Christ's spousal love, which we can then apply to our understanding of the priesthood.

Many Fathers speak about the Incarnation as the time when Christ espoused Himself to human nature in the nuptial chamber of Mary's womb. As St. Augustine wrote: "The bridal chamber of this bridegroom was the womb of the virgin, because in that virginal womb the two were joined, the bridegroom and the bride, the Word was the bridegroom and the flesh was the bride . . . the Church was joined to that flesh and the Totus Christus was made, head and body."[72]

However, Balthasar points out that for the Fathers, the spousal love expressed in the Incarnation cannot be separated from the Cross because for the Fathers "to speak of the incarnation is already to speak of the Cross."[73] Emile Schmitt makes this point when he comments on St. Augustine's teaching: "The union of the Word with flesh is, for the bishop of Hippo, the point of departure for the divine wedding, the fundamental principle of the whole doctrine of salvation. However, the potentialities of these espousals have to be prolonged and actualized in what will be the mystical wedding of Calvary."[74] One might say that the marriage begins in Mary's womb, but it is consummated on the Cross. For the Fathers, the Cross is the central moment when Christ gives Himself to His bride. One example that demonstrates this patristic belief is the constant comparison between the creation of Eve from the side of Adam and the birth of the Church from the side of Christ on the Cross. The Fathers almost universally saw the creation of the Church and her espousal happening in the solemn moment of Christ's Death.[75]

One of the early western Fathers, Tertullian, explains the connection: "If Adam was the figure of Christ, the sleeping of Adam was the figure of the death of Christ, who in death was falling asleep. Thus, coming from the wound of his side in a like manner is prefigured the Church, true mother of the living."[76] Some of the most beautiful passages describing this mystical marriage come from St. Augustine who frequently uses the image. In his commentary on Psalm 127, he compares the rib of Adam by which Eve was made to the blood and water from the side of Christ, the sacraments by which the Church are made:

> Therefore his wife is the Church, and we ourselves, his Church are his wife . . . While the man was sleeping, Eve was made, while Christ was dying, the Church was made. In the first from the side of the man a rib was taken, in the second when the side was pierced by a lance and from the wound the sacraments flowed out.[77]

The Fathers spoke about the Passion of Christ as the divine wedding of Christ with His Church. In the West, St. Ambrose, meditating on Psalm 118, says that the moment "when the king introduced [the bride] into the nuptial chamber, the time of the passion, the puncture of the side, the effusion of the blood, the anointing for burial and the mystery of the resurrection are indicated."[78] The eastern father St. Cyril of Alexandria says, "The day of the marriage he calls the day of the passion, in which he betroths the Church in his blood."[79] In a very clear reference, Quodvultdeus simply identifies the "wood" of the cross as the "bed" of the wedding chamber:

> The bridegroom goes up to the wood of our wedding chamber; the bridegroom goes up to the bed of our wedding chamber. Dying he sleeps, his side is opened and the virgin Church comes forth: just as Eve was made from the side of Adam sleeping, so also the Church is formed from the side of Christ hanging on the Cross.[80]

For the Church Fathers, there was no contradiction in considering the Cross both as the moment of the birth of the Church and the marriage of the Church with Christ. This can be easily understood in light of the connection between Christ and Adam, and Eve and the Church. Quodvultdeus gives us an example of the patristic teaching:

> O great mystery of this bridegroom and this bride! It cannot be worthily explained by human words. From the bridegroom the bride is born, and as she is born, at the same time she is married; and then the bride marries, when the bridegroom dies. And then he is joined to the bride when he is separated from mortals; when he is

exalted above the heavens, then she is made fruitful in all the earth. What is this? Who is this bridegroom both absent and present?[81]

The Fathers explain how Christ sacrifices Himself in love for His spouse on the Cross, noting the incredible nature of Christ's spousal love. As we see in Ephesians, Christ, in dying for His bride, goes far beyond what could have been imagined in the Old Testament. Sacrificial love draws the Word down from heaven to suffer and die for His bride, as is clearly expressed by St. Methodius of Olympus: "It was for this cause that the Word, leaving His Father in heaven, came down to be 'joined to His wife;' and slept in the trance of His passion."[82] St. John Chrysostom, musing on the sacrificial love of Christ, asks to what lengths Christ will go to obtain His bride; rhetorically, Chrysostom puts these words in the mouth of Christ: "Even if I have to be covered in spit . . . even if I have to receive blows, even if I have to go to the cross itself, I will not seek to avoid being crucified in order to obtain my bride."[83]

In this same movement of Christ's love for His bride, we also see the self-emptying character of Christ's spousal love; it is part of the divine kenosis. The Fathers describe Christ leaving His Father (and even His Mother) in order to be wed to His bride. They make a connection based upon the quote of Genesis 2:24 in Ephesians 5:31: "For this reason a man shall leave [his] father and [his] mother and be joined to his wife, and the two shall become one flesh." Through this, they link Ephesians with Philippians 2:6-8: "Though he was in the form of God, [he] did not regard equality with God as something to be grasped. Rather, he emptied himself, taking the form of a slave, coming in human likeness; and found human in appearance, he humbled himself, becoming obedient to death, even death on a cross." St. Augustine gives us a good example of this teaching in his commentary on the wedding feast of Cana.[84] St. Augustine is explaining what each of the six stone water jars symbolizes. About the first one, he says that through the light offered by St. Paul,[85] we can properly understand the wedding at Cana. For Augustine, the wedding at Cana is the prefiguration of the Christ-to-Church marriage that will happen on the Cross:

> What great mystery is this, "the two shall be one flesh?" While Scripture, in the Book of Genesis, was speaking of Adam and Eve, it came to these words, "Therefore shall a man leave his father and mother, and shall cleave to his wife; and the two shall be one flesh" (Eph 5:31-32). Now, if Christ cleaves to the Church, so that the two should be one flesh, in what manner did He leave His Father and His mother? He left His Father in this sense, that when He was in the form of God, He thought it not robbery to be equal with God, but emptied Himself, taking to Himself the form of a servant (Phil 2:6-7). In this sense He left His Father, not that He forsook or departed from His Father, but that He did not appear unto men in that form in which He was equal with the Father. But how did He leave His mother? By leaving the synagogue of the Jews, from which He was born in the flesh, and by cleaving to the Church which He has gathered out of all nations. Thus the first water-pot then held a prophecy of Christ. . . . Adam sleeps, that Eve may be formed; Christ dies, that the Church may be formed. When Adam sleeps, Eve is formed from his side; when Christ is dead, the

spear pierces His side that the mysteries from which the Church is formed may flow forth.[86]

This patristic insight reveals the self-emptying nature of Christ's spousal love. Christ leaves His Father in heaven to be joined to His bride because He did not deem equality with God "something to be grasped" (Phil 2:6). Thus, He empties Himself first through His Incarnation and secondly, through His Death on the Cross, making of Himself a total self-gift that gives birth to His bride, the Church.

This self-sacrificing, self-emptying love of Christ is what brings forth new life (i.e., Christ's spousal love is fruitful). The Fathers speak of different ways that Christ's spousal love is fruitful. For example, St. Methodius of Olympus demonstrates how through His Death on the Cross, Christ sows a seed of new life:

> [He] willingly suffered death for her, that He might present the Church to Himself glorious and blameless, having cleansed her by the laver, for the receiving of the spiritual and blessed seed, which is sown by Him, who with whispers implants it in the depths of the mind; and is conceived and formed by the Church, as by a woman, so as to give birth and nourishment to virtue.[87]

Christ's fruitful love coming from the Cross continues to give life in the Church through the sacraments. St. Leo the Great explains how this happens in Baptism:

> He is the one who having gone out by the Holy Spirit from the virgin mother gave fecundity through his breath to his same incorrupt Church, that through the baptismal birth of an immense number, a multitude of sons of God may be brought forth, about whom it is said: they

are not born from blood, nor from the will of men, nor from the will of flesh but from God (Jn 1:13).[88]

The fruitfulness of Christ's Death is most completely communicated in the Eucharist. The Fathers show how it is through the Eucharist that Christ and the Church are united in one flesh. In a very interesting passage, St. Clement of Alexandria makes clear how Christ nourishes His people through the union of the Church and Christ on the Cross. Clement, arguing against the Gnostics, has a long commentary on 1 Corinthians 3:2: "I fed you milk, not solid food," which he connects with 1 Peter 2:2: "like newborn infants, long for pure spiritual milk so that through it you may grow into salvation." Clement shows that Christ feeds His children through the Church, their mother, by giving them the spiritual milk of His Body and Blood in the Eucharist:

> What a wonderful mystery! There is only one Father of the universe, and only one Logos of the universe, and also only one Holy Spirit, identical in everything; there is also only one virgin who has become mother, as I love to call the Church. This mother alone does not have milk, because alone she did not become a wife; she is at the same time virgin and mother, as a virgin she is intact, as a mother she is full of love; she draws to herself her little children and feeds them with a sacred milk, the Logos of the infants.[89]

Clement makes clear that this spiritual milk with which Christ feeds the Christians through the Church is, in fact, the Eucharist: "He has said: 'Eat my flesh and drink my blood' (Jn 6:53). Here is the nourishment well made for you that the Lord gives generously: He offers his flesh and pours out his blood. Nothing is lacking to the little children in order that they might grow."[90]

For Clement, this milk that nourishes the children through the Church is the blood of Christ, a symbol of His Passion: "It is then the same thing—blood and milk—which is the symbol of the passion and the teaching of the Lord."[91] The Passion is what makes the Church fruitful, through which she receives the spiritual milk of the Eucharist. St. Methodius of Olympus makes this teaching even more explicit. He shows how the kenosis of Christ is continued in the Eucharist. Christ's spousal love nourishes us and unites us to Him even now in the Eucharist, which makes present the wedding feast of the Cross:

> For in this way, too, the command, "increase and multiply," is duly fulfilled, the Church increasing daily in greatness and beauty and multitude, by the union and communion of the Word who now still comes down to us and falls into a trance by the memorial of His passion; for otherwise the Church could not conceive believers, and give them new birth by the laver of regeneration, unless Christ, emptying Himself for their sake, that He might be contained by them, as I said, through the recapitulation of His passion, should die again, coming down from heaven, and being "joined to His wife," the Church, should provide for a certain power being taken from His own side, so that all who are built up in Him should grow up, even those who are born again by the laver, receiving of His bones and of His flesh, that is, of His holiness and of His glory.[92]

From this brief patristic study, we are able to see the central aspects of Christ's spousal love. First, His spousal love is self-sacrificing—that is, He gives Himself in the pursuit of His bride; to unite Her to Himself, He is willing to die on the Cross. Second, His love is kenotic; that is, to be joined to His bride, He empties Himself. He leaves His Father in heaven to become incarnate, and He even empties Himself further through His Death on the Cross. Third, His love is spiritually fruitful: His self-sacrificing and self-emptying love pours new life into His bride, the Church, through faith and the sacraments, especially the Eucharist.

Further Exploration of the Central Aspects of Christ's Spousal Love

This theology of the Fathers of the Church leads us to the central point of our study of nuptial theology that we must explore even further. To understand the call for the priest, we must explain fully the nuptial self-gift of Christ for the Church on the Cross. What is the depth of the meaning of St. Paul's expression, "Christ loved the Church and handed himself over for her" (Eph 5:25)? What is the depth of this nuptial redeeming love? The Fathers showed us that Christ's spousal love is self-sacrificing, kenotic, and fruitful; and further exploration will show us how we can apply Christ's spousal love to the priest.

First, Christ's spousal love is self-sacrificing. By the gift of Himself on the Cross, Christ expresses the depths of His love. Through His sacrifice, He pours out Himself for us completely, "to the end" (Jn 13:1). This gift of self for the Church is the fullest expression of love: "No one has greater love than this, to lay down one's life for one's friends" (Jn 15:13). The sacrifice that Christ makes is for the remission of sins[93]; this also shows the depth of Christ's love. As St. Paul explains: "Christ loved us and handed himself over for us as a sacrificial offering to God for a fragrant aroma" (Eph 5:2). This reveals the incredible love of God for us,[94] since God pays Himself the price of our deliverance. As Jean Galot says:

> It is true that God wanted the sacrifice of Jesus in order to give salvation to humanity. But if Christ has been immolated as a ransom for the liberation of men, this ransom has been furnished by God himself. God has paid the price of our deliverance: he has purchased us. In the same way, here, under the appearance of justice and an exchange of benefits, there is a love all the more vast which is revealed.[95]

"God proves his love for us in that while we were still sinners Christ died for us" (Rom 5:8). The sacrificial love of the Cross is the extreme end of self-renunciation. It is the fulfillment of the way of self-renunciation Jesus taught to His disciples:

> When he talks about discipleship, he speaks of the Cross as the fundamental form and synthesis of self-renunciation (Mk 8:34). It consists in "drinking the cup" that he must drink, and "being baptized" with the baptism with which he must be baptized (10:38). He himself longs for this ending (Lk 12:50), just as he longs for the supper where he will be able at last to distribute his immolated flesh and poured out blood (Lk 22:15).[96]

In this longing, Jesus lays down His life freely out of love, not out of coercion: "This is why the Father loves me, because I lay down my life in order to take it up again. No one takes it from me, but I lay it down on my own. I have power to lay it down, and power to take it up again. This command I have received from my Father" (Jn 10:17-18).

St. Thomas underlines this absolute freedom of Christ's self-gift by pointing out that there was no absolute necessity for Christ to deliver us through His Passion. God could have delivered us in another way, but this way shows more love: "and this came of more copious mercy than if He had forgiven sins without satisfaction."[97] Thus, to say Christ's spousal love is sacrificial is to say that it is offered for our forgiveness, in total renunciation of self, freely, out of love for His bride.

Second, Christ's spousal love is self-emptying (i.e., kenotic).[98] His self-emptying begins with His Incarnation, is fulfilled in His Death on the Cross, and continues in the Eucharist. The central text that explains the kenotic nature of Christ's Death is found in Philippians 2:6-8:

> Though he was in the form of God, [Christ] did not regard equality with God something to be grasped. Rather, he emptied himself, taking the form of a slave, coming in human likeness; and found human in appearance, he humbled himself, becoming obedient to death, even death on a cross.

As we have already seen, the Fathers of the Church theologically connected this kenosis with Christ's spousal love. The kenosis described in Philippians 2:6-8 shows us the extent of Christ's self-renunciation by emphasizing His divinity. He did not cling to "equality with God," a right based on His being "in the form of God." As Galot comments: "In the hymn there is even a deliberate insistence on this initial divine state because it indicates the extent of the self-emptying that accompanied his passage to the condition of a servant."[99] Also we see that coming after His bride means a self-emptying for Christ happening in two stages: first, He lowers Himself and takes the form of a slave,[100] and then He humbles Himself further by "becoming obedient to death, even death on a cross" (Phil 2:8). The first kenotic act is the Incarnation:

> It is remarkable that this very ancient hymn should conceive of the Incarnation as a "making into nothing," an "emptying." Even though certain exegetes would prefer to interpret this annihilation as applying only to the redemptive sacrifice, it is difficult to deny that Paul is referring to the very act of the Incarnation, inasmuch as the one who was in "in the form of God" "emptied himself, . . . being made in human likeness" and "taking the form of a servant."[101]

The kenosis of the Incarnation reaches its apex in the kenosis of the Cross. As Balthasar explains: "In this primary Kenosis the second is already contained: As man, not only does he tend to the same condition . . . as other human beings. He goes yet further, in obedience, by stooping lower still, down to the death of the Cross."[102]

St. Augustine makes this same connection clear when he explains the image of Jesus washing the feet of His disciples. For Augustine, the foot washing is a symbol of the kenosis of Christ's Incarnation and His Death:

> What is the wonder if he rises from dinner, and lays aside his clothes, who when he was in the form of God, emptied himself? And what is the wonder if he girds himself with a towel, he who taking the form of a slave was found in the likeness of a man (Phil 2:6-7)? What is the wonder, if he poured water into a basin from where

he would wash the feet of his disciples, who poured out his blood upon the earth to wash away the filth of sins?[103]

Jesus' whole life and mission can be seen in terms of this self-emptying and taking the form of a servant because Jesus' greatest act of self-emptying service for His bride is His Death on the Cross: "the Son of Man did not come to be served but to serve and to give his life as a ransom for many" (Mt 20:28; Mk 10:45). Joseph Ratzinger echoes Augustine's insight:

> In the washing of the disciples' feet is represented for us what Jesus does and what he is. He, who is Lord, comes down to us; he lays aside the garments of glory and becomes a slave, one who stands at the door and who does for us the slave's service of washing our feet. This is the meaning of his whole life and Passion: that he bends down to our dirty feet, to the dirt of humanity, and that in his greater love he washes us clean.[104]

Here, in Christ's kenosis, we can already see a connection to His obedience and poverty. Philippians 2:8 makes it clear that Christ's kenosis is expressed in obedience to the Father's will. It also shows that His self-emptying involves accepting poverty, both the poverty of our limited human nature, and the additional emptying of any material good, whether power or possessions, through His Death on the Cross. It is in Christ's clinging to nothing for Himself that He makes Himself completely free to be used as the instrument for our salvation.

Philippians 2 also makes clear that the self-emptying of Christ is connected with His glorification. Because Christ emptied Himself, "God greatly exalted him and bestowed on

him the name that is above every name" (Phil 2:9).[105] And it
is also through His self-emptying that we are raised up.[106] As
St. Gregory of Nazianzen said, "He who makes rich is made
poor; he takes on the poverty of my flesh, that I may gain
the riches of his divinity. He who is full is made empty; he is
emptied for a brief space of his glory that I may share in his
fullness."[107] We will see when we examine the life of the priest
that this same reality is at work. As St. Paul says, it is through
Christ's own sacrificial self-emptying that the Church is made
fruitful: "death is at work in us, but life in you" (2 Cor 4:12).

Christ's self-giving nuptial love is fruitful. We see this in
the life of the Church through the sacraments, especially in
the Eucharist. In the Eucharist, we receive Christ poured
out for us in love: "What more could Jesus have done for
us? Truly, in the Eucharist, he shows us a love which goes
'to the end' (cf. Jn 13:1)."[108] In an ordination homily, Pope
Emeritus Benedict XVI explains how the Eucharist is Christ
stripping Himself to be united with us: "We also learn what
celebrating the Eucharist properly means: it is an encounter
with the Lord, who strips himself of his divine glory for our
sake, allows himself be humiliated to the point of death on
the Cross and thus gives himself to each one of us."[109] We
can say that the Eucharist carries the kenosis that began at
the Incarnation to its furthest end, union with us. As St. John
Paul II explained:

> In the Eucharist the logic of the Incarnation reaches
> its extreme consequence. It is the culmination of that
> way towards man, which drove Jesus to strip himself
> of the privileges of divinity, to assume the condition
> of a servant and take his place beside each of us, as our

brother; to become in the end Food and Drink for our soul on its spiritual journey."[110]

Cardinal Ratzinger puts it even more succinctly: "He became flesh so that he might become bread."[111]

It is through the connection between the Eucharist and the Cross that we can see how Christ's spousal love is fruitful. Jesus explained that life comes from His Death: "Amen, amen, I say to you, unless a grain of wheat falls to the ground and dies, it remains just a grain; but if it dies, it produces much fruit" (Jn 12:24). This promise becomes concrete in the Eucharist: "By means of the Eucharist, he distributes his death, spilling it as life into the womb of his Church."[112] This is the nuptial nature of the Eucharist, the wedding feast of the Lamb, making Christ's spousal gift fruitful for all time.

The Eucharist is essentially nuptial for two reasons: First, because it makes present the sacrifice of the Cross. As the Second Vatican Council stated:

> At the Last Supper, on the night when He was betrayed, our Savior instituted the eucharistic sacrifice of His Body and Blood. He did this in order to perpetuate the sacrifice of the Cross throughout the centuries until He should come again, and so to entrust to His beloved spouse, the Church, a memorial of His death and resurrection: a sacrament of love, a sign of unity, a bond of charity, a paschal banquet in which Christ is eaten, the mind is filled with grace, and a pledge of future glory is given to us.[113]

Second, the Eucharist is "a foretaste of [the] heavenly liturgy"[114] "because it anticipates the wedding feast of the Lamb in the heavenly Jerusalem (cf. 1 Cor 11:20; Rev 19:9)."[115]

As St. John Paul II has pointed out, the spousal relationship is the relationship that is most fully characterized by
self-gift.[116] In a marriage relationship, husband and wife are
intended to give all of themselves to the other, and this is why
it most fully captures the scriptural covenant. Here, the two
become one. It is for this reason that the Eucharist is nuptial.
Here, Christ makes a gift of Himself to us and invites us into
this nuptial relationship. The Eucharist is the place where the
faithful ratify and renew their spousal covenant with Christ.
The Church becomes, through the Eucharist, both body and
bride because she becomes "one flesh" wither her bridegroom in communion. As St. John Paul II explained:

> The Eucharist is the Sacrament of our Redemption. It
> is the Sacrament of the Bridegroom and of the Bride.
> The Eucharist makes present and realizes anew in a
> sacramental manner the redemptive act of Christ, who
> "creates" the Church, his body. Christ is united with
> this "body" as the bridegroom with the bride. All this is
> contained in the Letter to the Ephesians. The perennial
> "unity of the two" that exists between man and woman
> from the very "beginning" is introduced into this "great
> mystery" of Christ and of the Church.[117]

For this reason, the Fathers of the Church frequently
explain the Eucharist in nuptial terms. Once again, St.
Augustine serves as a classic example; for him, every Mass is
a celebration of the marriage between Christ and the Church,
where the two become one flesh:

> Concerning the bride let us see what [Christ] says: for
> you, when you know the bridegroom and bride, it is not
> without reason that you come to the wedding. For every

celebration is a celebration of nuptials: the nuptials of
the Church are being celebrated. The king's son is about
to take a wife, and the son himself is a king: and those
who attend, they are the bride. This marriage is not like
the carnal ones where some attend the wedding, and
another marries; in the Church those who attend, if they
attend well, become the bride. For all the Church is the
bride of Christ, of which the beginning and the first-
fruits is the flesh of Christ: there the bride was joined
to the bridegroom in the flesh. Fittingly then, when he
entrusted his own flesh, he broke bread; and also fittingly
in the breaking of the bread the eyes of the disciples were
opened and they knew him."[118]

Thus, Holy Communion, in the language of the Fathers,
becomes an intimate, nuptial moment when Christ and the
soul become one flesh. Jean Danielou, S.J., makes this clear in
summarizing how the Fathers applied the Song of Songs to
the Liturgy:

> The Eucharistic communion in which the Body of
> Christ is placed on the lips of the baptized who has been
> purified from his sins, is truly the kiss given by Christ to
> the soul, the expression of the union of love which He
> has contracted with her. Here it is the marriage union
> which directly typifies the Eucharist.[119]

An example from St. John Chrysostom exemplifies this
theology of the nuptial union that the Fathers saw happening
in the Eucharist:

> For you I was spit upon, I was scourged. I emptied
> myself of glory, I left My Father and came to you,
> who hate me, and turn from me, and are loath to hear

my name. I pursued you; I ran after you, that I might overtake you. I united and joined you to myself, "eat me, drink me," I said. Above I hold you, and below I embrace you. Is it not enough for you that I have your first-fruits above? Does not this satisfy your affection? I descended below: I not only am mingled with you, I am entwined in you. I am masticated, broken into minute particles, that the interspersion, and commixture, and union may be more complete. Things united remain yet in their own limits, but I am interwoven with you. I would have no more any division between us. I will that we both be one.[120]

This theology of the Eucharist as a nuptial union is found throughout the Tradition right up to the present day. As Pope Emeritus Benedict XVI writes in his encyclical *Deus Caritas Est*, it is through the marriage union of the Eucharist that we are drawn into a union with God at a radically new level. He shows how the marriage image in the New Covenant, although fulfilled in a spiritual way, goes beyond a mere metaphor:

The Eucharist draws us into Jesus' act of self-oblation. More than just statically receiving the incarnate Logos, we enter into the very dynamic of his self-giving. The imagery of marriage between God and Israel is now realized in a way previously inconceivable: it had meant standing in God's presence, but now it becomes union with God through sharing in Jesus' self-gift, sharing in his body and blood. The sacramental "mysticism," grounded in God's condescension towards us, operates at a radically different level and lifts us to far greater heights than anything that any human mystical elevation could ever accomplish.[121]

This nuptial theology brings us deeper into understanding the mystery of the self-gift of Christ to the Church. These sacrificial, kenotic, and fruitful aspects of Christ's spousal love are the defining example of spousal love from the Scripture, implicitly contained in St. Paul's exhortation: "Husbands, love your wives, even as Christ loved the church and handed himself over for her" (Eph 5:25). As noted in the Introduction, St. John Paul II in his *Theology of the Body* has drawn out the richness of this meaning by explaining what he calls the "nuptial meaning" of the body. Written into the very creation of humanity as male and female is the idea that the human person was created with a capacity for expressing nuptial love: "that love in which the person becomes a gift and—by means of this gift—fulfills the meaning of his being and existence."[122] St. John Paul II quotes the Second Vatican Council speaking about the truth of human existence: "Man, who is the only creature on earth which God willed for itself, cannot fully find himself except through a sincere gift of self."[123] Thus, at the heart of human existence is this law that we find ourselves through a self-gift. This self-gift is seen most clearly in married love. In his book *Love and Responsibility*, John Paul II points out that what makes betrothed love distinct from all other loves is that it involves the "giving of one's own person to another."[124] In human experience, married love is the deepest expression of love because in this love, a person makes of himself or herself a gift:

> The essence of betrothed love is self-giving, the surrender of one's "I." This is something different from and more than attraction, desire or even good will. These are all ways by which one person goes out towards another, but

none of them can take him as far in his quest for the good of the other as does betrothed love. . . . Betrothed love is something different from and more than all the forms of love so far analyzed, both as it affects the individual subject, the person who loves, and as regards the interpersonal union which it creates. When betrothed love enters into this interpersonal relationship something more than friendship results: two people give themselves each to the other.[125]

The words at the center of the marriage Liturgy express this self-gift: "I, N., take you, N., to be my wife/husband. I promise to be true to you in good times and in bad, in sickness and in health. I will love you and honor you all the days of my life."[126] It is through this self-gift, expressed and confirmed in the conjugal act, that the couple becomes "one flesh." Here again, we see how the nuptial image becomes indispensable for theology, which seeks to understand the union between God and humanity, established through Christ's self-gift. Christ's Death is nuptial love because it is through Christ's death that He is given for us. St. John Paul II explains:

> The analogy of the love of spouses (or spousal love) seems to emphasize above all the aspect of God's gift of himself to man who is chosen "from ages" in Christ (literally, his gift of self to "Israel," to the "Church"); a gift that is in its essential character, or as a gift, total (or rather "radical") and irrevocable. This gift is certainly "radical" and therefore "total." One cannot speak here of totality in the metaphysical sense. As a creature, man is in fact not capable of "receiving" the gift of God in the transcendental fullness of his divinity. Such a "total

gift" (an uncreated gift) is shared only by God himself
in the "Trinitarian communion of persons." By contrast,
God's gift of himself to man, which is what the analogy
of spousal love speaks about, can only have the form
of participation in the divine nature (see 2 Pet 1:4) as
theology has made clear with precision. Nevertheless,
according to such a measure, the gift given by God
to man in Christ is a "total" or "radical" gift, which is
precisely what the analogy of spousal love indicates: it
is in some sense "all" that God "could" give of himself
to man, considering the limited faculties of man as a
creature. In this way the analogy of spousal love indicates
the "radical" character of grace: of the whole order of
created grace."[127]

What Scripture and theology show us is that this nuptial
self-gift finds its origin and fulfillment in the self-gift of
Christ on the Cross. Christ on the Cross is the perfection of
love, love that must be described as spousal, since it is a total
self-gift. Thus, we can say that Christ in His self-giving love
on the Cross is the source of every vocation in the Church.
As St. John Paul II said, "It is in the contemplation of the
Crucified Christ that all vocations find their inspiration."[128]

A traditional Orthodox icon can help to summarize this
chapter by demonstrating the sacrificial and kenotic nature of
Christ's spousal love. It is interesting to note that the image
that in the West is often called "Ecce Homo," in the East
is called "Ὁ νυμφίος." In the Orthodox Church, Christ the
Bridegroom is depicted as Christ in His Passion. The Orthodox Church of America explains the icon this way:

> The name comes from the central figure in the well-
> known parable of the ten virgins (Matthew 25:1-13).

The title bridegroom suggests the intimacy of love. It is not without significance that the kingdom of God is compared to a bridal feast and a bridal chamber. The Christ of the Passion is the divine Bridegroom of the Church. The imagery connotes the final union of the lover and the beloved. . . . "The Bridegroom" icon portrays Christ during His Passion, particularly during the period when our Lord was mocked and tortured by the soldiers who crowned Him with thorns, dressed Him in purple and placed a reed in His Hands, jeering Him as the "King of the Jews."[129]

The bridegroom icon is central to the services of Holy Week in the Orthodox Church. Beginning on Palm Sunday evening, the icon is brought out and processed throughout the church during the evening prayer service, which is called the "Office of the Bridegroom." The icon remains stationed in the center of the church until Holy Thursday.[130] Our own presentation of Christ's spousal love being sacrificial and self-emptying helps us understand why the Orthodox Church presents the Divine Bridegroom as the one who is ready to suffer His Passion. Christ's spousal love is His readiness to make of Himself a total self-gift for us. As one Orthodox priest expresses it:

In the Icon of the Bridegroom Christ does not look like a spouse prepared for a Wedding. Grooms usually are neatly dressed in the best suit of clothes. How could he possibly be the Bridegroom? He is wearing a crown of thorns. He holds a reed in his hands tied together, designed to mock him and his claim to be a king. There is blood dripping over his brow. He was just flogged at the whipping post and his back is bleeding. But such an Icon

portrays a mystery. He is the spouse who must suffer
birth pangs, because he is birthing the members of the
new humanity."[131]

Here, we come to understand more fully who is Christ,
the Bridegroom of His Church. The ancient icon of Christ
the Bridegroom reveals the true nature of His spousal
love for us. Here is the one who is completely given for
us, stripped of glory, and suffering His Passion. Here, we
shall find the explanation for His obedience, chastity, and
poverty, which are fulfilled in His Death on the Cross. Here,
also, we will find the true nature of the priesthood and the
explanation for the priestly life of self-gift in imitation of
the bridegroom.

Questions for Discussion, Reflection, and Prayer

1. We have seen that the spousal image as applied to our
    relationship with God is not just a metaphor but an
    analogy, and that Christ and the Church are the prime
    analogate by which all marriages are to be understood.
    What does it mean for the identity of the priest that
    Christ is the Bridegroom?

2. What do you find most striking, what moves you the
    most about how the Fathers of the Church explain
    redemption through the nuptial image? Which image
    would you like to pray with?

3. How can your relationship with Mary grow by seeing
    her as "his bride, his mother, his perfect handmaid"
    (St. Aelred of Rievaulx)?

4. What are practical ways that a priest's nuptial gift
    should become like Christ's: self-sacrificing, kenotic,
    and fruitful?

5. Calling to mind the truth of Christ's spousal love
    revealed on the Cross, while looking at the icon
    of Christ the Bridegroom, what do you hear the
    Bridegroom saying to you about how you are to live
    the priesthood?

NOTES

1. See Paul VI, *Lumen Gentium* (1964), sec. 6: "The inner nature of the Church is now made known to us in different images taken either from tending sheep or cultivating the land, from building or even from family life and betrothals."

2. Elizabeth Johnson, *She Who Is: The Mystery of God in Feminist Theological Discourse* (New York: Crossroad, 1992), 117. Johnson's book is important because she attempts to use "Classical Theology" (104-23), including Aquinas, to support her thesis that "the designation 'he' is subject to all the limitations found in any other positive naming of God, and in the end does not really tell us anything about the divine" (117). However, as Benedict Ashley, O.P., points out in his critique of Johnson, she does not take into account the "classical distinction, which is mentioned only in passing (Johnson, 114), between *metaphor* (improper analogy) and *proper analogy*" (Benedict Ashley, *Justice in the Church: Gender and Participation* [Washington, D.C.: Catholic University of America, 1996], 197). Johnson seems to place all images of God in the same category. For her, when Jesus says, "I am the gate" (Jn 10:9), there is no different from when he says, "I am the truth" (Jn 14:6). But as we shall see, the first is a metaphor and the second is a proper analogy (See Ashley, *Justice in the Church*, 197).

3. George Peter Klubertanz, "Analogy," in *New Catholic Encyclopedia*, 2nd ed., vol. 1, ed. Berard L. Marthaler, O.F.M.Conv., et al. (Detroit: Thomson Gale, 2003), 373.

4. John Paul II, *Fides et Ratio: Encyclical Letter on the Relation between Faith and Reason*, in *Acta Apostolicae Sedis* (AAS) 91 (1999): sec. 84. Balthasar makes it clear that all theological knowledge about God rests on this teaching of analogy, that without it we can have no direct knowledge of God; see Balthasar, *Theodrama: Theological Dramatic Theory*, vol. II: *The Dramatis Personae: Man in God*, trans. Graham Harrison (San Francisco: Ignatius Press, 1992), 118 ff.

5. Fourth Lateran Ecumenical Council, *De Errore Abbatis Ioachim*, II: DS 806.

6. *Fides et ratio*, sec. 83. Specifically, the Holy Father warns that in the field of "hermeneutics and the analysis of language," there is a danger that "some scholars working in these fields tend to stop short at the question of how reality is understood and expressed, without going further to see whether reason can discover its essence" (Ibid., sec. 84).

7. Thomas Aquinas, *Summa Theologica* (ST) I, q.13, a.2.

8. Benedict Ashley explains this distinction well using technical philosophical language: "When a term is used to mean one thing only it is *univocal*. When used in several senses it is *equivocal*. When these diverse senses are nevertheless related, it is *analogical*. When the relation between

them is based on the similarity that is extrinsic to their essences it is *improper analogy* (metaphorical); when it is based on an intrinsic, essential likeness it is *proper* or *proportional analogy*; and when proper analogy results from giving the name of an effect to its cause or vice versa it is *attributed analogy*" (Ashley, *Justice in the Church*, 105: note 82).

9.   Ashley, *Justice in the Church*, 105-06.

10.   ST I, q.13, a.5, corpus.

11.   As Thomas explains: "Thus whatever is said of God and creatures, is said according to the relation of a creature to God as its principle and cause, wherein all perfections of things pre-exist excellently. Now this mode of community of idea is a mean between pure equivocation and simple univocation. [Perhaps "mode of community" of idea is better translated "mode of participation" or "joint use of an idea." The original Latin says: "Et iste modus communitatis medius est inter puram aequivocationem et simplicem univocationem"]. For in analogies the idea is not, as it is in univocals, one and the same, yet it is not totally diverse as in equivocals; but a term which is thus used in a multiple sense signifies various proportions to some one thing" (Ibid.).

12.   ST I, q.13, a.6, corpus.

13.   ST I, q.13, a.2, corpus.

14.   Ashley, *Justice in the Church*, 197.

15.   Ibid., 106.

16.   ST I, q.13, a.6.

17.   Ashley, *Justice in the Church*, 107.

18.   John Paul II, *Man and Woman He Created Them: A Theology of the Body* (Boston: Pauline Books and Media, 2006), 488, emphasis in original.

19.   Ibid., 487, emphasis in original.

20.   Thus, St. John Paul II can say: "the whole text of Ephesians 5:21-33 is permeated by the same analogy: that is, the reciprocal relationship between spouses, husband and wife, should be understood by Christians *according to the image of the relationship between Christ and the Church*" (John Paul II, *Man and Woman He Created Them*, 475, emphasis in original).

21.   ST I, q.13, a.6, corpus.

22.   Thomas Aquinas, *Commentary on Saint Paul's Epistle to the Ephesians*, trans. Matthew L. Lamb, O.C.S.O. (Albany: Magi Books, 1966), 226.

23.   Ibid.

24.   Robert Pesarchick, *The Trinitarian Foundation of Human Sexuality as Revealed by Christ According to Hans Urs von Balthasar: The Revelatory Significance of the Male Christ and the Male Ministerial Priesthood, Tesi Gregoriana Serie Teologia*, vol. 63 (Roma: Gregorian University, 2000), 187.

25.   See *Catechism of the Catholic Church*, sec. 1617.

26.   *Letter to Families*, AAS 86 [1994], sec. 19.

27.   La Potterie, *Mary*, xxvi. See ST III, 1, ad 5, where St. Thomas explains that the creation of woman described in Genesis 2:23 is, in fact, a

foreshadowing of the Incarnation of Christ and His relationship with the Church as an effect is related to a cause. As John Paul II says in commenting on Ephesians 5:21-33, "In this Letter the author expresses the truth about the Church as the bride of Christ, and also indicates how this truth is *rooted in the biblical reality of the creation of the human being as male and female*" (*Mulieris Dignitatem*, sec. 23, emphasis in original).

28. Just as in other analogical knowledge of God that we saw above, there are parts of the analogy that do not apply from humans to God. Here, too, when we speak about Christ as the true Bridegroom and His relationship with the Church, the true marriage, we can see from our own understanding of marriage some aspects that have to be purified before "marriage" can be applied to Christ. The clearest example of this is the equality of dignity between a man and woman versus the vast difference between the human Church/bride and Christ. As Balthasar comments, "Between Adam and Eve, the dignity of the person is equal, even if we retain the legend that the woman was formed out of the side of the man. Concerning the parity between Christ and the new Eve—who may be Mary or the Church—, Mary is only the servant, even though full of grace, the Church is only the receptacle of the fullness of Christ, and the vase which receives the one who is in himself the source of this plenitude" (*Au cœur du Mystère Rédempteur* [Paris: Socéval Éditions, 1980], 85). Or as John Paul II says about Ephesians 5, "Reading this rich and complex passage, which *taken as a whole is a great analogy*, we must *distinguish* that element which expresses the human reality of interpersonal relations from that which expresses in symbolic language the 'great mystery' which is divine" (*Mulieris Dignitatem*, sec. 23, emphasis in original). Part of this distinction has to do with subjection in marriage as noted above: "However, whereas in the relationship between Christ and the Church the subjection is only on the part of the Church, in the relationship between husband and wife the 'subjection' is not one-sided but mutual" (*Mulieris Dignitatem*, sec. 24).

29. Pierre Grelot, *Man and Wife in Scripture* (New York: Herder and Herder, 1964), 102.

30. John Paul II, *Man and Woman He Created Them*, 500, emphasis in original.

31. See Mark 2:19; Matthew 9:15; Luke 5:34.

32. See Matthew 25:1-13.

33. Hans Urs von Balthasar, *Explorations in Theology*, Vol. 2: *Spouse of the Word*, trans. A.V. Littledale (San Francisco: Ignatius Press, 1991),151.

34. Ethelbert Stauffer, "γαμεώ γάμος." in *Theological Dictionary of the New Testament*, s.v. edited by Gerhard Kittel (Grand Rapids, MI: Eerdmans, 1968), 655.

35. As Luis Alonso-Schökel points out in *Símbolos matrimoniales en la Biblia* (Navarre: Editorial Verbo Divino, 1997): "The feminine person

is the Church, the name says that it consists in a group which has been
gathered together. Ἐκκλησία is assembly, congregation, reunion, as results
from a call or convocation. The congregation is a response to a call" (91).

36.   *Mulieris Dignitatem*, sec. 25, emphasis in original.

37.   See Revelation 19:7-8.

38.   See Revelation 21:2.

39.   Balthasar, *Theodrama: Theological Dramatic Theory*, vol. III: *Dramatis
Personae: Persons in Christ*, trans. Graham Harrison (San Francisco: Ignatius
Press, 1992), 288. This argument is central to Balthasar's understanding of
the nuptial nature of salvation. He argues that Mary acts as bride, saying
"Yes" to the spousal marriage at the Annunciation and at the Cross. She
does this both on behalf of the Church and as a member of the Church.
He explains it briefly in his article "The Marian Principle" (*Communio* 15
[Spring 1988]:122-130), and much more in depth in his book *The Office of
Peter and the Structure of the Church* (trans. Andrée Emery [San Francisco:
Ignatius Press, 1986], especially 183-222) and *Theodrama*, Vol. III, chap. 3,
especially 306-317.

40.   ST III, q.30, a.1, corpus. As Pope Leo XIII expressed: "When, for
man's redemption and adornment, the eternal Son of God willed to take
man's nature, and by this very fact was about to enter into a kind of mystical marriage with the whole human race, He did not complete this act
before the accession of the most free consent of His designated Mother,
who in a certain way acted in the person of the human race" (*Octobri
Mensi*, in *AAS* 24 [1892], 195).

41.   Balthasar, *Au Cœur du Mystère Rédempteur*, 87.

42.   John Saward, *The Mysteries of March: Hans Urs von Balthasar on
the Incarnation and Easter* (Washington, DC: Catholic University Press,
1990), 76.

43.   Ibid., 80, emphasis in original.

44.   *Mulieris Dignitatum*, sec. 11.

45.   *Theodrama: Theological Dramatic Theory*, vol. III, 290.

46.   Pesarchick, 198-199.

47.   *Sermo 20, In Nativitate beatae Mariae* (*Patrologiae Cursus Completus,
Series Latina* [PL]: 195: 322).

48.   Saward, *Mysteries of March*, 75.

49.   Balthasar, *The Office of Peter and the Structure of the Church*, trans.
Andrée Emery (San Francisco: Ignatius Press, 1986), 200.

50.   Balthasar, "The Marian Principle," *Communio* 15 (Spring 1988):127.

51.   Balthasar, *Office of Peter*, 198.

52.   "Thoughts on the Place of Marian Doctrine and Piety in Faith
and Theology as a Whole," printed in Hans Urs von Balthasar and Joseph
Cardinal Ratzinger, *Mary: the Church at the Source* (San Francisco: Ignatius
Press, 2005), 27.

53. *Sermone 51 in Assumptione Beatae Virginis Mariae*, 8 (St. Thomas Aquinas, *Summa Contra Gentiles* [SC], 339, 204).

54. St. Ambrose, *In Luc.*, bk. ii., no.7 (PL 15, 1555a); St. Augustine, *De Symbolo ad Cat.*, ch. I (PL 40, 661).

55. De Lubac, *The Splendour of the Church* (New York: Sheed and Ward, 1956), 242-243. For a full explanation on this patristic teaching see chap. 9: The Church and Our Lady.

56. Paul VI, *Lumen Gentium* (1964), sec. 63.

57. Balthasar, *Spouse of the Word*, 161.

58. *Lumen Gentium*, sec. 65.

59. Balthasar, "Marian Principle," 130. "En Marie, l'Épouse a déjà atteint son plein salut; toute entière celle-ci l'atteindra un jour pour fêter les noces eschatologiques de l'Agneau, telles que nous les décrit l'Apocalypse."

60. Ratzinger, "Hail Full of Grace," in Hans Urs von Balthasar and Joseph Cardinal Ratzinger, *Mary: The Church at the Source* (San Francisco: Ignatius Press, 2005), 66.

61. St. Paul refers to the Church as the Body of Christ in many passages (Romans 12:4-5; 1 Corinthians 10:17, 12:12-27; Ephesians 1:22-23; Ephesians 3:6; Ephesians 4:4-16; Colossians 1:18-24); however, he only makes direct reference to the Church as the bride of Christ in the two passages investigated above (2 Corinthians 11:2; Ephesians 5:31-37).

62. See Balthasar, *Spouse of the Word*, 154.

63. See *Lumen Gentium*, sec. 6, 7.

64. *Pastores Dabo Vobis*, sec. 22.

65. Balthasar, *Spouse of the Word*, 149: "This had to be made explicit, since one might well think of a 'bride' who was not, at the same time, 'body,' as was the case with the Old Testament Israel of Zion."

66. Sara Butler, M.S.B.T., "Priest as Sacrament of Christ the Bridegroom," *Worship* 66 (1992): 510.

67. Joseph Ratzinger and Hans Urs von Balthasar, *Mary: The Church at the Source*, trans. Adrian Walker (San Francisco: Ignatius Press, 2005), 26. Ratzinger goes on to point out why Mary must be bride, see p. 27 ff.

68. *Catechism of the Catholic Church*, 796.

69. Ernest Best, *One Body in Christ: a Study in the Relationship of the Church to Christ in the Epistles of the Apostle Paul* (London: SPCK, 1955), 183.

70. Ratzinger, *Mary: The Church at The Source*, 26.

71. *The Meaning of Christian Priesthood*, trans. Peadar MacSeumais, S.J. (Westminster, MD: Christian Classics, 1989), 26-27.

72. Augustine, *In Epistolam Ioannis ad Parthos* 1, 2 (*Sources Chrétiennes* 75, 117). For a summary of this teaching in the Fathers, see Tromp, *Corpus Christi quod est Ecclesia*, pt. I, chap. 1, 32 ff; and John Saward, *Cradle of Redeeming Love* (San Francisco: Ignatius Press, 2002), 164-68.

73.   Hans Urs von Balthasar, *The Glory of the Lord: A Theological Aesthetics*, Vol. VII: *Theology: The New Covenant*, trans. Brian McNeil, C.R.V. (San Francisco: Ignatius Press, 1989), 212; see also *Mysterium Paschale: The Mystery of Easter*, trans. Aidan Nichols, O.P. (Edinburgh: T & T Clark, 1990), 20-23.

74.   Emile Schmitt, *Le mariage chrétien dans l'Oeuvre de Saint Augustin. Une théologie baptismale de la vie conjugale* (Paris: Etudes Augustiniennes, 1983), 243.

75.   Emile Schmitt points out just how common this idea is among the Fathers: "The image of Eve taken from the side of her sleeping bridegroom, among the Fathers, is often put parallel, with the Church being born from the pierced side of Christ on the Cross. This comparison goes back to the oldest Christian antiquity" (Ibid., 243).

76.   Tertullian, *De Anima*, CSEL What is CSEL? 20, 372.

77.   Augustine, *Enarrationes in Psalmos*, 127, 11 (CCSL 40, 1875). Or similarly in his commentary on Psalm 126: "When the Lord was sleeping on the cross, his side was pierced by a lance, and the sacraments flowed out, by which the Church was made. For the Church, the bride of the Lord, was made from his side, in the same way that Eve was made from the side; but just as the one was not made except from the side of the sleeping one, so also the other was not made except from the side of the dying one" (Augustine, *Enarrationes in Psalmos*, Ps. 126,7 [*Corpus Christianorum Series Latina* {CCSL} 40, 1862]).

78.   Ambrose, *Expositio in Ps. 118*, 1, 16 (*Corpus Scriptorum Ecclesisticorum Latinorum* [CSEL] 62, 16).

79.   Cyril of Alexandria, *In Cantica Canticorum Commentarii Reliquiae, Patrologiae Cursus Completus, Series Graeca* (PG) 69, 1288). St. Cyril is commenting on the Song of Songs 3:10-11: "Daughters of Jerusalem, go out and look upon King Solomon In the crown with which his mother has crowned him on the day of his marriage, on the day of the joy of his heart."

80.   Quodvultdeus, *De Symbolo* I, 6 (CCSL 60, 320). The ideas expressed in this sermon on the creed are so thoroughly Augustinian that until modern times, it was attributed to St. Augustine, and only recently (c. 1975) was it discovered to be that of the Bishop of Carthage, one of Augustine's disciples; see CCSL 60, introduction.

81.   Quodvultdeus, *De Symbolo* I, 6 (CCSL 60, 320).

82.   St. Methodius of Olympus, *Symposium*, Discourse 3, c. 8 (*Source Chrètiennes*, 95, 10).

83.   Chrysostom, Third Catechesis (Sources Chrétiennes 366, 214).

84.   See John 2:1-11.

85.   See Ephesians 5:31.

86.   Augustine, *In Joannis Evangelium Tractatus*, 9,10, in CCSL 36, 96-97. Many other times, Augustine makes the same connection: See *Sermo.* 95, 4

(PL 38, 582); *Sermo.* 91, 6 (PL 38, 576); *En. in ps.*, 44, 12 (CCSL 38, 502); *De sancta virginitate* 2, 2 (CSEL 41, 236) and 6,6 (CSEL 41, 240); *Contra Faustum* 12, 8 (CSEL 25.1, 337).

87. Methodius, *Symposium*, Discourse 3, c. 8 (*Sources Chrétiennes* 95, 106): English translation: *Ante-Nicene Fathers*, vol. 6, 319).

88. Leo the Great, *Sermon* 50, 6 (*Sources Chrétiennes* 74 bis, 158).

89. Clement of Alexandria, *Pedagogos*, 1, 6 (*Sources Chrétiennes* 70, 187).

90. Ibid. (*Sources Chrétiennes* 70, 189).

91. Ibid.

92. Methodius, *Symposium*, Discourse 3, c. 8 (*Sources Chrétiennes* 95, 106-108). English translation: *Ante-Nicene Fathers*, vol. 6, 319-320). See also Gregory of Nyssa. *In Sanctum Pascha et de Triduano Festo Resurrectionis Christi*, 1 (PG 46, col. 604).

93. See Matthew 26:28.

94. See John 3:16.

95. Jean Galot, *La Rédemption mystère d'alliance* (Paris: Desclée de Brouwer, 1965), 107.

96. Balthasar, *Mysterium Paschale*, 18.

97. ST III, 46, a. 1, ad. 3.

98. "κενόω: to empty, divesture of position or prestige … ἑαυτὸν ἐκένωσεν emptied himself, divested himself of his prestige or privileges Phil 2:7" (*A Greek-English Lexicon of the New Testament and Other Early Christian Literature*, fourth edition, 1979 [BDAG], s.v. "κενόω").

99. Galot, *Who Is Christ? A Theology of the Incarnation*, trans. M. Angeline Bouchard (Chicago: Franciscan Herald Press, 1981), 78.

100. See Philippians 2:7.

101. Galot, *Who Is Christ?*, 183-184.

102. Balthasar, *Mysterium Paschale*, 24.

103. Augustine, *In Ioh. Evang. Tractatus* 55, 7 (CCSL 36, 466).

104. Joseph Ratzinger, *God Is Near Us*, trans. Henry Taylor (San Francisco: Ignatius Press, 2003), 30.

105. The "inferential conjunction" διό, meaning "therefore, for this reason," makes this causal connection clear (BDAG, s.v.).

106. See Romans 6:4; Ephesians 2:6; Colossians 2:12.

107. Gregory of Nazienzen, *Oratio* 45, 9 *In Sanctum Pascha* (PG 36, 636), English Translation, *Liturgy of the Hours*, Vol I, 162).

108. John Paul II, *Ecclesia de Eucharistia* (2003), sec. 11.

109. Benedict XVI, "Ordination Mass, St. Peter's Basilica: Sunday, 7 May 2006," in *L'Osservatore Romano*, English Edition (10 May 2006): 3.

110. John Paul II, "Angelus Address, July 19, 1981," in *Bread of Life* (Athlone, Ireland: St. Paul Publications, 1982), 155.

111. Ratzinger, *God Is Near Us*, 102.

112. Balthasar, *Theodrama*, Vol. IV, 359.

113. Paul VI, *Sacrosanctum Concilium* (1963), sec. 47.

114.   Ibid., sec. 8.

115.   *Catechism of the Catholic Church*, sec. 1329.

116.   John Paul II, *Man and Woman He Created Them*, 186.

117.   *Mulieris Dignitatem*, sec. 26, emphasis in original.

118.   Augustine, *In Epistolam Ioannis ad Parthos*, 2,2 (*Sources Chrétiennes* 75, 154). See also his commentary on the wedding feast at Cana: *In Ioh. Evang.*, 8,4 (CCSL 36, 83-84).

119.   Jean Daniélou, *The Bible and the Liturgy* (Notre Dame, IN: University of Notre Dame Press, 1956), 205.

120.   Chrysostom, *Homilies on Timothy*, *Homily*, 16 (PG 62, 586); English Translation: St. John Chrysostom, *Homilies on Timothy*, in *Nicene and Post-Nicene Fathers of the Christian Church*, First Series, ed. Philip Schaff, vol. 13 (Grand Rapids: Eerdmans Publishing, 1979), 463-464.

121.   Benedict XVI, *Deus Caritas Est* (2005), sec. 13.

122.   John Paul II, *Man and Woman He Created Them*, 186.

123.   Paul VI, *Gaudium et Spes* (1965), sec. 24.

124.   Karol Wojtyla, *Love and Responsibility* (San Francisco: Ignatius Press, 1993), 96.

125.   Ibid.

126.   *The Rite of Marriage* (New York: Catholic Book Publishing, 1970), n 25.

127.   John Paul II, *Man and Woman He Created Them*, 501, emphasis in original.

128.   John Paul II, *Vita consecrata* (1996), sec. 23.

129.   "The Services of the Bridegroom: Sunday Evening Through Tuesday Evening," by The Greek Orthodox Church of America, available from http://lent.goarch.org/bridegroom_services/learn/, accessed 18 August 2013.

130.   Georges Gharib, *Le icone di Cristo: Storia e culto* (Roma: Città Nuova, 1993), 258.

131.   Rev. Archimandrite Fr. Eusebius A. Stephanou, Th.D., "Look! The Bridegroom is Coming," available from http://www.stsymeon.org/archive/bridegroom.htm, accessed 18 August 2013.

CHAPTER 3

CHRIST'S SPOUSAL LOVE AND THE EVANGELICAL COUNSELS

Most people today do not understand the importance of the evangelical counsels of poverty, chastity, and obedience. Those outside the Church often see them as outdated modes of life; and even within the Church, they are often seen only as revered penances for religious life. It is not uncommon today for people to question if these qualities should at least be "optional" for the priesthood. Are the evangelical counsels actually necessary for holiness? Why are they essential, and how do these counsels apply to the life of the priest?

As with everything in the priesthood, to understand the meaning of the evangelical counsels one must go back to Christ Himself. We must discover why and how Christ lived the evangelical counsels to understand their importance in the Tradition and their relationship to the priesthood. If one argues that the evangelical counsels are optional, one must ask, "Were they optional for Christ?" If one understands Christ's spousal love, one can see that the evangelical counsels were the most perfect manifestation of this love. Far from being optional, they are a means of total self-gift.

Were the Evangelical Counsels Optional for Christ?

Was it required that Jesus be poor, chaste, and obedient? Could He have lived another way? This is not a ridiculous question because asking it helps us see the relationship between the counsels and Christ's own life and mission. As soon as we begin to ask the question, we see that the counsels are not accidental to Christ's life. As Gianfranco Ghirlanda says:

> The life of virginity, poverty and obedience was not for Christ something accidental or simply functional according to the mission which he had to fulfill; rather it was the visible and revelatory, earthly expression of his unique and unrepeatable relationship with the Father in the Spirit, through which in some way we can say that Jesus could not be other than virgin, poor and obedient.[1]

The evangelical counsels are intimately tied to Christ's relationship and mission of total openness and availability to the Father. They are the expression of His self-gift.

It is true that it was not absolutely necessary for Christ to live the evangelical counsels. There are two reasons why this statement is true. First, the counsels by their very nature, require a free response. Obedience, celibacy, and poverty would lose their value if they were the result of compulsion and not free choice. Second, it is impossible to demonstrate absolute necessity with regard to almost anything in Christ's life and mission because of God's sovereign freedom. At one point in his writing, St. Thomas Aquinas asks about the necessity of the Incarnation. He asks whether the Incarnation was "necessary for the restoration of the human race?"[2] St. Thomas points out that God was not absolutely required to save us, nor was He required to save us by the means of the Incarnation. He could have found other means for salvation.[3] This being said, however, God chose the most fitting means. The word that St. Thomas uses to describe this fittingness is: "conveniens." Conveniens is usually translated in English as "fitting to something, appropriate to, meet, fit, suitable, or congruens."[4] It means that these two things "come together" in their very nature; they are "co-natural."[5] But it is important to note that for St. Thomas, conveniens or "fitting" does not at all mean "optional."

In fact, when St. Thomas asks whether it was necessary for the restoration of the human race that the Word of God should become incarnate, he answers, "Yes, it was necessary!" He then qualifies just what kind of necessity he is talking about. St. Thomas says a thing can be necessary in two different ways. First, there is what we call absolute necessity, which he defines as "when the end cannot be without it." He gives an example: "as food is necessary for the preservation of human life."[6] The Incarnation was not absolutely necessary; God could have saved mankind another way. But St. Thomas admits of another type of necessity: "when the end is attained better and more conveniently, as a horse is necessary for a journey."[7] Thus, it is not absolutely necessary, but for Thomas, here, the word conveniens implies a kind of necessity—that is, it is, in a certain way, required for a better, more expedient, more fitting attainment of the end.

The distinction becomes even clearer when St. Thomas speaks about the necessity of the Passion of Christ. St. Thomas rules out absolute necessity, noting that Christ's Passion was voluntary: "It was not necessary for Christ to suffer from necessity of compulsion, either on God's part, who ruled that Christ should suffer, or on Christ's own part, who suffered voluntarily."[8] This voluntary nature of Christ's suffering is important, since Christ's freedom to embrace His Passion is what reveals His spousal love. Yet, St. Thomas says there is a kind of necessity to Christ's Passion. Christ embraced His Passion freely because it was required in light of the desired end: "But if the extrinsic cause inducing necessity is a desired end, then a necessity arises in view of that end; without it, in other words, the objective either cannot be attained at all or cannot be otherwise so well attained."[9] Again, the word "conveniens" is used here to speak about attaining the end in a better, more fitting way, which St. Thomas calls a kind of necessity. He will say clearly that Christ suffered voluntarily, not because it was absolutely necessary, nor from any kind of compulsion, but from the necessity of the end proposed.[10]

Some authors call this type of necessity "hypothetical necessity."[11] Given the end in mind, this means is necessary to achieve it in the most fitting way. St. Thomas would say the means is conveniens. This is the type of necessity that the evangelical counsels had in Christ's life. If the desired end, the plan of God, requires that Christ be the Bridegroom of the Church who makes His life a total self-gift on the Cross, it is hypothetically necessary (conveniens) that He live His life and make His offering in obedience, chastity, and poverty. Thus, the counsels are "co-natural" with Christ's mission because they respond to a need contained in the inner nature of Christ's spousal self-gift for the Church. And if these counsels are co-natural to Christ's mission, it is possible to show how they are co-natural to the life and mission of the priest.

Christ's Mission and the Evangelical Counsels

Jesus speaks of His mission as something required of Him. His first recorded words to His parents at age twelve reveal this necessity: "Why were you looking for me? Did you not know that I must be in my Father's house?" (Lk 2:49). The "must" of Jesus' mission shows up in all His predictions of His Passion: "He began to teach them that the Son of Man must suffer greatly and be rejected by the elders, the chief priests, and the scribes, and be killed, and rise after three days" (Mk 8:31).[12] It is seen in the way He speaks about His hour.[13] It even shows up when He speaks about His Passion after His Resurrection: "Was it not necessary that the Messiah should suffer these things and enter into his glory?" (Lk 24:26). Given who He is, given what He must do, He must make His life a gift for us. For Him, it is necessary: "There is a baptism with which I must be baptized, and how great is my anguish until it is accomplished!" (Lk 12:50).[14]

This necessity in the life and mission of Jesus reveals the essential unity in Christ between His mission and His person. One could say in as much as every person is created by God, every person has a mission, since every person's existence is directly willed by God. To have a mission is to be called by one who sends to carry out a specific task; it is a calling to be a certain kind of person. However, Jesus is different from any other human person. With every human person, there is a gap between the mission and the person, between who the person is and who the person is called to be by God. But this is not the case with Jesus, for He so completely embodies His mission that there is no distinction between His mission and His person. As Hans Urs von Balthasar points out, Jesus is "'sent' in such an absolute sense that his mission coincides with his person, so that both together constitute God's exhaustive self-communication."[15] This explains Jesus' determination about His actions and reveals the unity of person and mission in Him:

> Who must he be, to behave and act in this way? If we stay with this question, we shall begin to ascend the path that leads from Christ's overt function to his covert being (which the former presupposes); but, in doing so, we shall be faced with a problem: while in the case of the prophets, their being (or person) and function are—at least relatively—distinguishable, here we are presented with Someone who never was, and never could have been, anyone other than the One Sent.[16]

This is the uniqueness of the person of Jesus. He is the eternally begotten Son who is the Incarnate Word of the Father; and, therefore, He could not but fulfill His mission in obedience to the Father. As Jean Galot explains:

> Jesus himself indicates the link which exists between his person and his mission. The one who is sent is the Son who lives in the Father. In receiving his life from the Father, he receives also his mission from him. By this fact his obedience is linked to his quality as Son; it is the expression of his filial relation and belongs to his filial love.[17]

Here, we already see the interior necessity of Jesus' obedience, given who He is and what He must do. Jesus will be so completely given to His mission that His entire life will be poured out as a sacrifice. This is, in fact, the unique mark of the New Covenant priesthood: Jesus' mission is to be both priest and victim.[18] However, this offering does not only happen on the Cross but begins with the kenosis of the Incarnation and is expressed in His life of poverty and celibacy. As we will see, all three of the counsels are required to make Jesus' self-gift total. Thus, Jesus' whole life is a sacrificial offering in obedience to the will of the Father. "The effective power of this sacrifice arises from the resolution of the Son who, from the first moment of the Incarnation, puts himself totally at the disposal of the plan of salvation, in an existential act of pure instrumentality."[19] It is this unity that marks Jesus, the unity between His person and His mission, the unity of being both priest and victim. This unity makes His self-offering as our bridegroom a total self-gift. Because of who He is, it could be no other way.

Based on this unity of the person and mission in Christ, we can demonstrate two reasons why the evangelical counsels are co-natural with Christ's mission. First, Jesus lived the counsels as a means of unconditional adhesion to His Father. He had to be obedient, celibate, and poor in order to allow Himself to be completely given for His mission from the Father. His mission required this freedom from anything that would prevent His total self-gift in poverty and chastity. He places everything completely at the Father's disposal. As Balthasar explains:

> Jesus' existence in and for his mission is an unconditional existence in poverty, chastity and obedience, insofar as these three modes of life guarantee exclusive freedom for mission. . . . Together they effect his perfect readiness to undertake the task, a task proposed by the Father in the Spirit and taken up in total freedom by the Son.[20]

Second, Jesus' mission required that He Himself be both the priest and the victim offered. Here obedience, chastity, and poverty become part of the internal sacrificial offering Christ makes to the Father on our behalf. Ghirlanda elaborates:

> Jesus has loved to the end (Jn 13:1), he has gone into the very depths, in the sense that in his death he reached the most complete radicalization of his virginity, precisely by the totality and the exclusivity of his love for the Father and for all men; of his poverty, by the way in which he despoiled himself of every human support and experienced the feeling of being abandoned by God; of his obedience, by having fulfilled everything according to the design of the Father, overcoming every temptation of realizing his own autonomy.[21]

This reveals the explicitly spousal nature of the evangelical counsels. As we have seen, Christ's spousal gift is a total self-gift through which He empties Himself in sacrificial love to give birth to His bride, the Church. His gift becomes a total only through obedience, celibacy, and poverty. This means that the Bride of Christ, "the Church of the New Covenant is herself a product of the total gift of self, or of the life of the counsels."[22]

Theology of the Evangelical Counsels

Fundamentally, the evangelical counsels draw their meaning from the life of Jesus "as the approximation of his loving gift of himself to the Father and to men."[23] St. John Paul II points out in his post synodal apostolic exhortation on consecrated life that all the counsels were lived by Jesus and they are embodied in His self-offering to the Father:

Jesus is the exemplar of obedience, who came down from heaven not to do his own will but the will of the One who sent him (cf. Jn 6:38; Heb 10:5, 7). He places his way of living and acting in the hands of the Father (cf. Lk 2:49). In filial obedience, he assumes the condition of a servant: he "emptied himself, taking the form of a servant . . . and became obedient unto death, even death on a cross" (Phil 2:7-8). In this attitude of submissiveness to the Father, Christ lives his life as a virgin, even while affirming and defending the dignity and sanctity of married life. He thus reveals the sublime excellence and mysterious spiritual fruitfulness of virginity. His full acceptance of the Father's plan is also seen in his detachment from earthly goods: "though he was rich, yet for your sake he became poor, so that by his poverty you might become rich" (2 Cor 8:9). The depth of his poverty is revealed in the perfect offering of all that is his to the Father.[24]

Christ lived in unconditional availability and surrender to the will of the Father. The evangelical counsels were the means for this union with the Father; and in this way, they become a central expression of His filial response to the Father. The counsels are not only external ways for Christ to live, but part of His interior life; they express His disposition of complete openness before His Father. Christ is obedient, celibate, and poor because He must be completely given to the Father. The counsels are revelatory of His whole way of life:

> One thing is certain, it would be reductive to consider the virginity, poverty and obedience of Jesus as simple facts. These three dimensions of his life express the unity and

totality of his being Son completely turned towards the Father in the substantial love of the Spirit. . . . These are founded on the filial life of the incarnate Word, who in the Spirit is totally given to the Father, in an act of chaste and exclusive love which becomes a complete stripping away of everything and obedience unto the end, unto death on a Cross (Phil 2:5-8).[25]

The second reason that Jesus lives the counsels is that through the counsels, Jesus becomes a victim for our redemption.[26] Christ was victim for our salvation, throughout His life, not just on the Cross. Christ's poverty,[27] celibacy,[28] and complete obedience to the Father[29] are the forms of visible mortification that exemplify His living of the Cross daily. This threefold self-gift of His daily life is the visible prefiguration of His total sacrifice on the Cross. This is why John Paul II says that on the Cross, we behold poverty, chastity, and obedience in their perfection as the means of Christ's redemptive love: "There his virginal love for the Father and for all mankind will attain its highest expression. His poverty will reach complete self-emptying, his obedience the giving of his life."[30] Heidi Böhler's important work on the Evangelical Counsels after Vatican II emphasizes this central point:

Who is more chaste than him, when upon the cross, for our love, he breaks himself free from every affective bond of body and soul accepting even to be abandoned by the Father? Who is more poor than him who has lost everything in order to bring us back to the Father? Finally who is more obedient than him who desired not else than to fulfill in himself the will of the Father even unto death on the cross?[31]

The evangelical counsels form part of Christ's redemptive gift because they are fitting with the nature of the way
we are redeemed. They were required for the self-gift of His
mission, and they formed His daily self-sacrifice, which was
fulfilled on the Cross.

The evangelical counsels are also at the heart of response
to Christ's self-gift. We see this perfect response of the disciple to Christ's call in Mary. In her "yes," we also find the
heart of the counsels, a self-gift without reservation:

> What counts is the open fiat to the entire will of the
> Lord: unconditional, unlimited, not anticipated by human
> plans. No "Up to this point, and no further!", but:
> "Behold the handmaid of the Lord, let your word alone
> be done unto me. I am the matter, you are the form."[32]

One sees in Mary's fiat an essential aspect of the evangelical counsels: their unity. Even as we will speak about the
individual nature of the counsels and their relationship to
the total self-gift, in fact, they are one self-gift. It is this total
"yes" that Mary gave, the total "yes" that Jesus gave; that
must always be the heart that unifies obedience, chastity, and
poverty.[33] This total surrender will always be the norm of
the counsels, the central movement that makes them one. It
is a yes that wants to give everything to the beloved in order
to become totally dispossessed of one's self. Here, we can
see again the connection between the evangelical counsels
and nuptial love. For, in marriage, we also see this desire to
give oneself completely: "This attitude has only one analogy: the indivisibility and indissolubility of the yes given
in marriage."[34]

The Primacy of the Evangelical Counsels

What we begin to see as we study poverty, chastity, and obedience is that these three counsels are not only set above all other counsels of Jesus, but also in some way include them all.[35] First, we see the preeminence of the evangelical counsels in their universality; they are the way for someone to offer everything one has to God. "Together they so completely exhaust the possibilities of what can be given that they are in no way subordinate to any of Jesus' other counsels."[36] This is the main reason St. Thomas Aquinas argued that the *tria principalia vota* were to be singled out among all the counsels of Jesus. According to St. Thomas, "all the particular counsels may be reduced to these three general and perfect counsels."[37] St. Thomas uses an image from the Old Testament sacrificial system, and he says that through poverty, chastity, and obedience, one makes of one's whole life a "holocaust,"—that is, a sacrifice that is totally consumed. He defines a holocaust as "offering to God all that one has."[38] As St. Thomas explains:

> Now man has a threefold good, according to the Philosopher (Ethic. i. 8). First, the good of external things, which he wholly offers to God by the vow of voluntary poverty: secondly, the good of his own body, and this good he offers to God especially by the vow of continence, whereby he renounces the greatest bodily pleasures: the third is the good of the soul, which man wholly offers to God by the vow of obedience, whereby he offers to God his own will by which he makes use of all the powers and habits of the soul.[39]

In other words, what else is there to give to God? The one who embraces the counsels gives all.

In this way, the three evangelical counsels have often been seen as the antidote to what the Tradition calls the "threefold lust" in our fallen human nature.[40] St. John Paul II explains:

It tends therefore to conquer the threefold lust. "The lust of the flesh, the lust of the eyes and the pride of life" are hidden within man as the inheritance of original sin. . . . Against the background of the phrases taken from the first letter of St. John, it is not difficult to see the fundamental importance of the three evangelical counsels in the whole economy of Redemption. Evangelical chastity helps us to transform in our interior life everything that has its sources in the lust of the flesh; evangelical poverty, everything that finds its source in the lust of the eyes; and evangelical obedience enables us to transform in a radical way that which in the human heart arises from the pride of life.[41]

The counsels include all the radicalism of the Gospel because they represent the call to give up everything and counteract the main ways we are tempted to be drawn away from God.

The Unity of the Evangelical Counsels

It is because of this universality that the evangelical counsels are meant to be seen as a unity. Living the counsels is not giving God three separate gifts (control over one's possessions, one's body, and one's will); rather, as we saw in Mary, the counsels are one total donation of self that is concretized in three areas of human existence:

What counts for the Bible is man's total gift of self to God, the total "Yes, Father" (Mt 11:26), "thy will!" (Lk 22:42; Mk 6:10), "handmaid of the Lord!" (Lk 1:38). This is faith and love. Insofar as God's call demands it this is the love that is subsequently articulated into the three areas of poverty, obedience, and virginity. There exists only one vowing of oneself, one vow (with three areas) that makes no exceptions but is available in such a way that God can dispose over everything.[42]

This unity of the counsels makes a very important point. The individual value of poverty or chastity or obedience only makes sense in light of the whole. Individually, they are only one aspect of a total offering. If one separates one of the counsels from the others, the offering is not total. It is still a sacrifice to live chastity; but if I do not also give my possessions and my will, I am not living the total self-gift that Christ lived. In this sense, as Gianfranco Ghirlanda explains, one cannot be chaste if one is not also poor and obedient:

> Precisely because they express one attitude, the "major" evangelical counsels are considered in their unity. With the profession of the evangelical counsels the person is inserted more deeply in the mystery of the life of Christ, which is a manifestation of the same intra-Trinitarian life. Given the oneness of Trinitarian love and the love of Christ, the three counsels are three aspects of one reality. One is not able to be chaste without being poor and obedient, one is not able to be poor if one is not chaste and obedient, one is not able to be obedient if one is not chaste and poor. True love, in fact, is nakedness and humility."[43]

Christ placed everything in His life at the disposal of the Father. He made of His life a total self-gift for His bride. Seeing this unity of the counsels is important for the life of the

priest. If celibacy is proposed for the priest in imitation of
the attitude of Christ, then it cannot be separated from obedience and poverty, which form an essential part of that same
attitude of Christ, the desire to make a total self-gift.

The Order of the Counsels

There is within the counsels a kind of hierarchy, as one
sees, for example, within the unity of the three theological
virtues of faith, hope, and charity.[44] Virginity and poverty are
the entrance to the life of the counsels while obedience is its
core. Balthasar theorizes that poverty is traditionally listed
first because it is necessary to "leave all things" before one
can embrace the other two counsels:

> With a certain comprehensiveness and urgency, *poverty*
> is always placed first. The demand that one sell one's
> possessions and give the proceeds in alms is so striking
> and so impossible to dismiss with subtleties that it is
> presented as the most visible manifestation of "leaving
> all things." It would be folly to try to clear a path to
> evangelical obedience without passing through this gate.[45]

If poverty is the gate to enter into the counsels, perhaps
virginity is its most distinguishing characteristic. The absolute
demand of perpetual chastity marks those who embrace the
counsels as the most radical response of following Christ
throughout the history of the Church.[46] Celibacy, in this
way, is considered "the most natural thing in the state of the
counsels" because it allows a person to fix "one's attention
on the Lord, as one chooses to be like him a 'eunuch for
the kingdom of Heaven' (Mt 19:12), in attitude of humility
that forbids any self-regard."[47] It makes sense in this context
because it expresses the heart of the one who is totally given.

St. Thomas affirms with the entire Tradition that obedience has primacy among the three evangelical counsels. This is because obedience is the most essential and decisive in the gift of self. This vow binds one more than the other two because it binds at the deepest level—one's very person.[48] In order to fully give oneself, one has to give what is most intimate, one's own will: "In the vow of obedience, man offers to God something greater than the rest: his will, the value of which surpasses that of his body, which he offers to God through the vow of continence, and that of external goods, which he offers to God through the vow of poverty."[49] Obedience is so central that it contains the other two vows; without obedience, the other vows would not be embraced with the same value. Jacques Servais explains this insight:

> In fact, virginity and poverty are not lived in spirit and in truth except insofar as they are embraced in a spirit of obedience, which is not only the external form of the counsels, but also their interior form. Without obedience, the former would end up turning into the opposite of that to which it is ordered; it would merely serve to enclose the person into a guarded personal sphere, rather than opening him up even unto his innermost affective core. Without obedience, poverty would risk devolving into a rigid habit, diametrically opposed to that to which it is supposed to bear witness: unrestricted availability in relation to the superabundant riches that God reserves to those who love him above all things. Obedience dispossesses the disciple of these two "virtues," and by the same token it confers on the two other counsels their positive evangelical significance of the radical surrendering of one's entire will to the Lord: " . . . when you become old, you will extend your hands and another

will gird you and will lead you to where you do not wish to go" (Jn 21:18).[50]

For the one seeking to respond fully to the call of Christ, obedience is the real goal. It is ultimately through obedience that one is able to make a complete gift of self. Poverty and chastity provide the necessary freedom for the person to give oneself completely in obedience. Obedience guides one's life because the person has "given up everything" in order to follow Christ (Mk 10:28). Thus, the one who is completely given seeks to be completely obedient, with a boundless openness to the divine plan. Clearly, this is far from being slavery, as we shall see when we look at Christ's obedience; rather, it leads to a true freedom, "to that outer and inner freedom that enables the apostle to follow the Master wherever he goes."[51]

Redemption and the Evangelical Counsels

Hans Urs von Balthasar points out the essential connection between the salvation Christ wins for us and the evangelical counsels. He argues that since the Fall, we have been tempted to sin in the threefold "lust" mentioned above (1 Jn 2:16). Christ enters into our humanity and lives the poverty, chastity, and obedience to redeem the effects of the Fall in us. Thus, Christ's evangelical life opens up the way to heaven:

> Christ emptied himself so that he might experience the full reality of earthly life as it had been lived since man was driven from the Garden of Eden. . . . In the Incarnation, Jesus' descent took the form of poverty, virginity, and obedience, and it was these forms that enabled him to live here below as he has lived above. He bore witness that what is impossible for man is possible for God, but likewise that what God makes possible

thereby becomes possible for man. . . . Man could live on earth as though the laws of paradise were still in effect.[52]

Christ's living of the evangelical counsels heals these three areas of sin in us and restores humanity to a life in relationship with God—that is, the way human beings would have lived in Eden and the way they will live in heaven. It is very clear that all of us will live the evangelical counsels in heaven. The Lord clearly states there will be no marriage in heaven,[53] and there will certainly be no possessions and no self-will. However, Balthasar makes a strong argument for the evangelical counsels based on the mode of life both in the state of original justice and in heaven.[54] He demonstrates, with the help of the Fathers of the Church, that both in the Garden of Eden and in heaven, life is lived according to the evangelical counsels. It was Original Sin that brought about disobedience, un-chastity, and covetousness, which he lists as three inseparable consequences of the Fall.[55] The life of the evangelical counsels is an attempt to live the perfect love of the state of original justice that existed before the Fall. But the counsels not only mark the life of the original state, they also mark the life of heaven. In heaven, where love will reach its perfection, the human person must return to the unity of the threefold gift of self. "Man will not be admitted to the kingdom of heaven until he has learned in the anteroom of heaven to renounce every will of his own, every desire, all personal autonomy that would oppose itself to the will of God as an independent authority."[56] Thus, the evangelical counsels are meant to be embraced by every Christian in some way, as all will embrace them fully in heaven.[57] Even those in marriage must learn not to be ruled by the threefold

lust and live a kind of chastity, poverty, and obedience proper
to their state.

Celibates who are called to the full embrace of the evangelical counsels on earth witness to the heavenly way of life
here and now. They are a reminder to all Christians that they
must remember they are living for heaven, and they must
learn to let Jesus be Lord of their possessions, their bodies,
and their hearts and minds. Thus, as we will see in the next
chapter, by living the evangelical counsels, the Lord opened
up a new state of life—a state of life to which only some are
called and which is possible only by His grace, the state of
sharing in the Lord's own way of life, living His obedience,
chastity, and poverty:

> The new state created by the Lord and possible only on
> the basis of his own way of life . . . [is] a synthesis of
> earthly and paradisial life. It means taking one's stand
> by the Cross, which is the gateway to paradise, or taking
> one's stand in the paradise that has been restored to
> mankind in the form of the Cross. It is fullness despite
> renunciation, happiness despite suffering.[58]

Living the counsels is living the Lord's own way of
life; it is living the beauty and sacrifice of the Cross. It is
paradoxical, a sign of contradiction in our world today; but
it is redemptive, life-giving, and points to a life beyond this
one. It is nuptial love, a love which we saw was sacrificial,
self-emptying, and fruitful. Christ redeems us through the
Cross, and His daily life of poverty, chastity, and obedience
is His daily living of the Cross. In this, he repairs all that is
wrong in humanity by going against the threefold lust in total,
self-emptying love. He also invites others to share in His

redemptive way of life by embracing these same evangelical counsels. This is the foundation of the evangelical state of life from which both the priesthood and the religious life come. As we will see, both are real ways of entering the nuptial relationship of Christ with His Church.[59]

Questions for Discussion, Reflection, and Prayer

1. What has been your attitude toward the evangelical counsels, and how is Christ inviting you to see them differently?

2. Meditating on Christ's total openness to the Father and how His life is completely given, how can you allow your life to be more open to God and more free to be given? Are there areas of your life which you have not surrendered completely to Christ?

3. How does the essential unity of the evangelical counsels affect your living of them? Is it possible that you find celibacy difficult because you have not fully embraced poverty or obedience?

4. Since obedience is the most importance of the counsels, how is Christ calling you to be obedient today? How will this obedience lead you to deeper union with Christ?

NOTES

1.   Gianfranco Ghirlanda, S.J., "Formazione del prete al carisma della paternità," 12. Ghirlanda cites St. John Paul II who, as we will see, supports this teaching. See *Vita Consecrata* (1996), sec. 16, 21, 22, 23, 24.

2.   Thomas Aquinas, *Summa Theologica* (ST) III, 1, a. 2.

3.   See ST III, 1, a. 2; ST III, 46, a. 1.

4.   S.v., "conveniens," in Charlton Lewis and Charles Short (Lewis and Short), *A Latin Dictionary* (Oxford: Clarendon Press, 1958), see definition B.

5.   This definition is my own, based on Thomas' use of the word *conveniens* in the *Summa Theologiae;* see ST, I-II, 108, a. 4; ST, III, 40, a. 2; ST, III, 46, a. 3, ad 3.

6.   ST III, 1, a. 2, corpus.

7.   Ibid. The Blackfriars version translates the phrase into English this way: "it is required for a better and more expeditious attainment of the goal" (*St. Thomas Aquinas Summa Theologiae: The Incarnate Word (3a. 1-6)*, vol. 48, trans. R. J. Hennessey, O.P. [New York: McGraw-Hill Book Co., 1976], 11).

8.   ST III, 46, a. 1.

9.   Ibid. English translation in text is from Gilbey version, vol. 54, 5.

10.   Ibid. The Angelic Doctor lists three ends that required, by way of *conveniens*, that Christ suffer: first, on our part, in order to deliver us (Jn 3:16); second, on Christ's part, in order to merit the glory of being exalted (Lk 24:26); and third, on God's part, whose determination regarding Christ's passion was foretold in the Scriptures (Lk 24: 44, 46) (ibid.).

11.   This is the term that Jacques Servais, S.J., uses when commenting on St. Thomas's understanding of the Passion of Christ: "Hypothetical necessity concerns the 'convenient' means for arriving at the pursued end, not only by relationship to us, but by relationship to Christ himself and to God" (Servais, Jacques, S.J. "La doctrine thomiste de la Rédemption," postface in Hans Urs von Balthasar, *Au cœur du mystère rédempteur* [France, Magny-les-Hameaux: Socéval Éditions, 2005], 148). Garrigou Lagrange calls it "necessitate finis," necessity of the end: "It was necessary for Christ to suffer by necessity of the end" (Garrigou-Lagrange, *De Christo Salvatore*, 401).

12.   See also Matthew 16:21, 17:22; Mark 9:12; Luke 9:22, 8:31-34.

13.   See John 2:4; 12:23; 13:1; 16:21, 25, 32; 17:1.

14.   See John 10:11-18; 12:32; Mark 10:38.

15.   Balthasar, *Theodrama: Theological Dramatic Theory,* vol. III trans. Graham Harrison (San Francisco: Ignatius Press, 1992), 150.

16.   Ibid., 149, emphasis in original. This corresponds with the comments of Cardinal Ratzinger who shows Jesus' existence is in being the

one sent. Commenting on John 7:16, Ratzinger says, "his teaching is not his own because even he is not his own. Rather in his entire existence as Son he is from the Father and to the Father. But for the same reason, because he has nothing that is his own, all that belongs to the Father is his: 'The Father and I are one' (10:30). Returning his entire existence and action to the Father, he did not seek his own will (3:30). . . . Here the mystery of the divine Trinity, which is the exemplar of our existence as well, shines forth in its splendor" (Cardinal Ratzinger: "The Formation of Priests in the Circumstances of the Present Day," *Communio*, 17.4 [1990]: 620).

17.   Jean Galot, S.J., *Vivre avec le Christ: La vie consacrée selon l'Évangile* (Louvain: Sintal, 1986), 170.

18.   See Hebrews 9:11-12; 10:4-9.

19.   Jacques Servais, S.J., "The Evangelical Counsels and the Total Gift of Self," in *Communio* 31 (Fall 2004): 369.

20.   Balthasar, *Theodrama*, Vol. III, 182, emphasis in original.

21.   Ghirlanda, *Il diritto nella Chiesa: mistero di communione* (Milan: San Paolo, 1993), 180.

22.   Hans Urs von Balthasar, *The Laity and the Life of the Counsels*, trans. Brian McNeil, C.R.V. with D.C. Schindler (San Francisco: Ignatius Press, 2003), 241, emphasis in original.

23.   Hans Urs von Balthasar, *The Christian State of Life*, trans. Sister Mary Frances McCarthy (San Francisco: Ignatius Press, 1983), 14. The Second Vatican Council declared that the evangelical counsels draw their "origin from the doctrine and example of the divine Master." The Council fathers explain that evangelical counsels flow from "Christ, who chaste and poor (cf. Matt. 8:20; Luke 9:58) redeemed and sanctified men through obedience even to the death of the Cross (cf. Phil. 2:8)" (*Perfectae Caritatis* [PC] 1)

24.   *Vita Consecrata*, sec. 22.

25.   Ghirlanda, "Formazione del prete al carisma della paternità," 12.

26.   Balthasar points out how the Scriptures often speak of redemption in terms of the counsels: "Christ's *total self gift*, through which I am redeemed and have become a child of God is delineated precisely through the sphere of the 'evangelical counsels': 'For you know the grace of our Lord Jesus Christ, that though he was rich, yet for your sake he became poor, so that by his poverty you might become rich' (2 Cor 8:9). And 'though he was in the form of God, he did not count equality with God a thing to be grasped, but emptied himself, taking the form of a servant, being born in the likeness of men. And being found in human form he humbled himself and became obedient unto death, even death on a cross' (Phil 2:6-8; cf. Heb 5:8-9). And in order to make his human nature the pure instrument of the redemption of all, letting himself be exhibited as last of all, like a man sentenced to death . . . the refuse of

the world, the offscouring of all things' (1 Cor 4:9, 13), and to become, thanks to this total and exhaustive exploitation, the Eucharistic flesh and blood that is distributed ad infinitum, he remained virginal" (Balthasar, *Laity and the Life of the Counsels*, 238). He goes so far as to say: "Christ's life in poverty, obedience, and virginity is not only the expression of divine love for us, but it is the effective, indeed the only effective, means of our redemption" (Ibid.).

27.   See Matthew 8:20.

28.   See Matthew 19:10-12.

29.   See Luke 22:41-42, Matthew 26:42, Mark 14:36.

30.   *Vita Consecrata*, sec. 23.

31.   Heidi Böhler, *I consigli evangelici in prospettiva trinitaria: Sintesi dottrinale* (Milano: San Paolo, 1993), 17.

32.   Balthasar, *Laity and the Life of the Counsels*, 188.

33.   "The Marian *availability* is so indivisible and comprehensive that it is pointless and impossible to distinguish within it the elements of virginity, of poverty, and of obedience. They are integrated in the fundamental act to the point of mutual compenetration. . . . Mary might, for example, have said: 'God can have everything but my body,' on the grounds that the she was already promised to the man named Joseph; but she makes no such reservation" (Ibid., 24, emphasis in original).

34.   Ibid., 188.

35.   *Lumen Gentium* (sec. 42) lists the evangelical counsels as distinct from the other counsels proposed by our Lord. For an explanation of their role in the documents of Vatican II, see Jean Beyer, S.J., "Life Consecrated by the Evangelical Counsels: Conciliar Teaching and Later Developments," in *Vatican II Assessment and Perspectives: Twenty-five Years After (1962-1987)*, vol. 3, ed. René Latourelle, S.J. (New York: Paulist Press, 1989), 64-89, esp. 68.

36.   Balthasar, *Christian State of Life*, 14.

37.   ST I-II, 104, a.4, corpus.

38.   ST III, 186, a. 7, corpus.

39.   Ibid. In SCG 3, 130, 2, St. Thomas makes a similar observation in that the vows offer every aspect of a human life to God: "first, to one's own person, what he should do, or where he should spend his time; second to the person of those connected with him, chiefly his wife and children, and third, to the acquisition of external things, which a man needs of the maintenance of life."

40.   See John 2:16.

41.   John Paul II, *Redemptionis Donum* (1984), sec. 9. St. Thomas speaks about the same threefold lust in ST I-II, 108, a. 4, corpus, and about three kinds of attachments corresponding to the three vows in ST II-II, 196, a. 7, corpus. See also *Catechism of the Catholic Church*, sec. 377.

42.   Balthasar, *Laity and the Life of the Counsels*, 243.

43.   Gianfranco, Ghirlanda, S.J., "La Vita Consacrata," in *Commento Teologico al Catechismo della Chiesa Cattolica,* ed. by Rino Fisichella (Casale Monferrato: Edizioni Piemme, 1993), 272.

44.   See 1 Corinthians 13:13.

45.   Balthasar, *Christian State of Life,* 154, emphasis in original.

46.   For this reason, St. John Paul II called chastity the first of the counsels (*Vita Consecrata,* sec. 14).

47.   Servais, "Evangelical Counsels," 363.

48.   See ST II-II, 183, a.1, corpus.

49.   St. Thomas, ST II-II, 186, a. 8, corpus.

50.   Servais, "Evangelical Counsels," 364. St. Thomas points out that without obedience the other two would not have the same value: "That which is done out of obedience is more acceptable to God than that which is done of one's own will" (ST II-II, 186, a. 8, corpus).

51.   Balthasar, *Christian State of Life,* 155.

52.   Christian State of Life, 160.

53.   See Matthew 22:30.

54.   See *Christian State of Life,* chap. 2, "From the Original State to Final State," 67-119.

55.   *Christian State of Life,* 120 f. At the very least, we can say that in the state of original justice, Adam and Eve could have lived the perfection of chastity even as they were married, by having intercourse without any "deformity of excessive concupiscence" (ST I, 98, a. 2, corpus). But the Fathers of the Church went a step further. Balthasar gives extensive references to show that the Fathers were, in fact, almost unanimous that in Eden, there "could be no *corruption* in man's virginity," and yet they were "also convinced that man would have 'increased and multiplied' even in his paradisal state" (*Christian State of Life,* 95). Even St. Thomas, who readily admits that there could have been intercourse in the state of original justice, also argues with the help of St. Augustine (*De Civitate Dei* 14, 26 [CCSL 48, 449]) that this intercourse would not have destroyed virginal integrity (ST I, 98, a. 2 ad. 4). Balthasar points out the Fathers defended virginity in the original state based on the conviction that in the original state, there was somehow a "synthesis between the married state and the state of virginity" (*Christian State of Life,* 95). So the Fathers offer many different explanations, some of which would seem problematic to us today, all for the purpose of defending what was for them a central truth: "*their unanimous conviction of the unity that must have once existed* [in original justice] *in the states of life* [i.e. marriage and the consecrated state] *that today are so diverse*" (Ibid., 96, emphasis in original). See Balthasar's many references to the Fathers including St. Augustine, St. Gregory of Nyssa, St. John Chrysostom, St. John of Damascus, St. Jerome, in *Christian State of Life,* 95-103.

56. *Christian State of Life*, 124. Ghirlanda makes the point that, at least in death, every Christian must become poor, chaste, and obedient when speaking about baptismal consecration: "In death the Christian realizes fully the spirit of the beatitudes according to which he should have conducted his whole life, to consecrate himself to the Father in response worthy of the consecration he received; and it is in death that the spirit of the beatitudes comes to be lived by every Christian in a real poverty, obedience and total and exclusive love of the Father. It is through this realization of the spirit of the beatitudes according to the evangelical counsels, at least in the moment of death, that every Christian is lead to the perfection of Charity, in Christ, and becomes a Eucharistic offering to the Father" (*Diritto nella Chiesa*, 89-90).

57. Matthew 22:30: "At the resurrection they neither marry nor are given in marriage, but are like the angels in heaven."

58. *Christian State of Life*, 161.

59. The priest and the religious enter into the relationship differently as we will see in chapter 7. The priest stands in the person of Christ, representing the bridegroom through his office. The religious (whether male or female) stands in the person of the Church within Mary's total "Yes," offering herself completely on behalf of all.

CHAPTER 4

THE EVANGELICAL COUNSELS AS LIVED BY CHRIST

The Scriptures and the Church Fathers showed us how Christ's gift of Himself on the Cross was a nuptial self-gift. On the Cross, we behold obedience, poverty, and chastity in their fullest expression, a life poured out in love for His bride. But as we have seen, Christ did not live this nuptial love only on the Cross, rather He lived it concretely through His daily life of obedience, chastity, and poverty. Each of the evangelical counsels, as lived by Christ, is in some way nuptial. In order to see the nuptial nature of the counsels, we will reflect on them in detail. This kind of reflection can become a rich source of meditation to inspire those who seek to imitate Christ's own way of life.

The Obedience of Christ

Obedience is the principle of all Jesus' actions. It is the deepest expression of who he is in relation with the Father. He refers consistently to His union with the Father in His mission: "a son cannot do anything on his own, but only what he sees his father doing; for what he does, his son will do also. For the Father loves his Son and shows him everything that he himself does, and he will show him greater works than these" (Jn 5:19-20).[1] Christ's life of obedience finds its greatest expression in His Passion. We get a glimpse into the cost of His obedience in Gethsemane where we see Jesus' agony before His Passion. He goes forward in obedience, submitting to the mission given Him by the Father. "Not my will but yours be done" (Lk 22:42) is the deepest expression of the heart of Christ.

Christ's obedience is the source of our salvation. This is how St. Paul presents the whole drama of salvation. It is Christ's obedience, the true heart of His self-gift, that undoes original sin: "For just as through the disobedience of one person the many were made sinners, so through the obedience of one the many will be made righteous" (Rom 5:19).[2] Christ is the new Adam. Unlike the old Adam, He gives Himself for us in obedience to the Father, and through this brings forth "the abundance of grace and of the gift of justification" (Rom 5:17) for His bride.

Obedience is the heart of Christ's priesthood. When the book of Hebrews explains how Christ is our High Priest, it makes clear that this happens through His obedience. The author puts on the lips of Christ the words of Psalm 40:

> For this reason, when he came into the world, he said: "Sacrifice and offering you did not desire, but a body you prepared for me; holocausts and sin offerings you took no delight in. Then I said, 'As is written of me in the scroll, Behold, I come to do your will, O God.'" (Heb 10:5-7)

Thus, the Incarnation is the means for Christ to make an obediential sacrifice. This sacrifice is fulfilled on the Cross. In fact, we have to say that the true heart of Christ's priestly sacrifice on the Cross was obedience, a sacrifice made in Christ's heart. As Jean Galot says: "There was there an oblation of the body, and in this sense a sacrifice which was not less physically real than those which were being offered in Jewish worship. But the oblation attained its objective in virtue of the obedience of the son to the will of the Father."[3] It is obedience that makes Christ's offering a sacrifice in the true sense of the term. As St. Thomas explains, "Christ offered Himself up for us in the Passion: and this most voluntary enduring of the Passion was most acceptable to God, as coming from charity. Therefore it is manifest that Christ's Passion was a true sacrifice."[4] It is His suffering through love and obedience that made Christ's sacrificial offering truly salvific: "By suffering out of love and obedience, Christ gave more to God than was required to compensate for the offense of the whole human race."[5]

In understanding the salvific nature of Christ's sacrifice in obedience, we can understand why there is no contradiction between the obedience of Christ and His freedom. For the sacrifice of the Cross to be salvific, it must be both free and obedient. Christ explains that He freely lays down His life in obedience: "No one takes it from me, but I lay it down on my own. I have power to lay it down, and power to take it up again" (Jn 10:18).[6] In Christ, therefore, there is all the freedom of the Son of God, and all the freedom of man, freedom He sacrificially places completely at the disposal of the Father in His mission. As Balthasar says, "He is so divinely free that he can bind himself to the obedience of a slave."[7]

There is another aspect of Christ's kenosis to be seen in His obedience. In obedience, He empties His will so completely that at every moment, He does only the will of the Father. "A son cannot do anything on his own, but only what he sees his father doing" (Jn 5:19). Jesus empties His will to allow Himself to be an instrument of love for the salvation of His bride. This self-dispossession of the will is what Balthasar calls "expropriation." This self-emptying existence is the way Jesus lives:

> At the beginning of all his work there is found obedience: the readiness to let himself be disposed of by the Father according to his total will. This is a letting go, an indifference that never chooses this as opposed to that. Already the way from the bosom of the eternal Father to the womb of the temporal Mother is a path of obedience, the most difficult and consequential of ways, but one which is trod on mission from the Father: "See, I come to do your will" (Heb 10:7).[8]

It is because Jesus allows Himself to be expropriated that He becomes a transparent image of the Father. Jesus speaks about this transparency in obedience when He says, "The Father and I are one" (Jn 10:30) or "Whoever has seen me has seen the Father" (Jn 14:9). Jesus has allowed Himself to be given so completely to the Father in obedience that in Jesus, person and mission are completely one. This is the complete expropriation in obedience, which the priest must also imitate by virtue of his mission to be another Christ.

This surrender of Jesus in obedience should not be seen as a passive action but an active self-giving. Christ is both priest and victim, offerer and offering. As the Book of Hebrews makes clear, it is this offering of Himself that makes Jesus' priesthood unique from the sacrifices of the Old

Testament.[9] Thus, Christ has an active part in His own sacrifice. St. Thomas speaks about a mutual handing over: "The Father handed over the Christ, and the Christ handed himself over out of love."[10] Through Christ's daily obedience, He lives in a state of being given. We can say Christ's whole life is explained in the words of institution: "my body, given up for you," "my blood, poured out for you." As Balthasar says, Jesus is paradosis, the one given:

> These [words] are the Eucharist and the verbalizing of Jesus' life in the sphere of the early Church. Both are the work of the paradosis: which is understood not as the act of God who gives up the Son, nor as the act of the Church which hands on further what has been handed on to her, but as Jesus' handing over of himself (1 Pet 2:23; Heb 9:14), so that by the power of this handing over, he may become what he should be.[11]

Understanding the suffering of Jesus in obedience leads us to enter more deeply into the mystery of the relationship between the Father and the Son. The Letter to the Hebrews says that Christ "learned obedience from what he suffered" (Heb 5:8). Through His Incarnation, Christ was made capable of suffering; and, thus, He was brought in some way to a new experience of obedience.[12] The essence of this mystery is revealed in Christ's "not my will" prayer in the garden, where we get a glimpse of the sacrifice he makes in obedience. Galot describes this mystery: "The prayer of Gethsemane revealed how suffering entered into the relations of intimacy so affectionate of the Son with the Father and brought Jesus to an obedience which in some way condensed his whole sacrifice."[13]

Here, we see how obedience makes the gift of Jesus a total self-gift and, thus, a nuptial self-gift. Obedience is central to nuptial love because it opens a person to another completely, uniting that person with the other, allowing one to make a total self-gift, placing one totally at the disposal of the other. As Balthasar explains with regard to Jesus:

> The obedience made manifest in this action of love (Jesus' surrender unto death) had always lain hidden in the nature of love. The person who loves renounces, in ever greater measure, every autonomous determination or ordering of his own deeds and omissions, his own thoughts and feelings, so that everything he has may be left more freely and more completely at the disposal of the beloved.[14]

A total self-gift to another must first and foremost include the gift of one's will, either by submission to the other or on behalf of the other. Thus, the Church, the bride of Christ, is united to her bridegroom through obedience.[15] Christ's obedience that united Him completely with His Father also united Him completely with His bride. This is because Christ's obedience is rooted in His love, His love for the Father and His love for the Church; and, thus, it unites Him with both.

From this union of wills with God through obedience comes the fruitfulness of the divine marriage. Obedience is always central to fruitfulness. Bishop Fulton Sheen pointed out the connection between kenosis and pleroma, between "emptying" and "filling," which is seen in Philippians 2. It was because Jesus emptied Himself that "Because of this, God greatly exalted him and bestowed on him the name that is above every name" (Phil 2:9): "Because He emptied

Himself, He was exalted. Because there was Calvary, there was the sending of the Holy Spirit. Because His physical Body was broken, His Mystical Body grows in age and grace and wisdom before God and men."[16] In this, we see the fruitfulness of the obedience of Christ. By his kenotic obedience, He was raised up and He raised us up. His death in obedience bears fruit. "Unless a grain of wheat falls to the ground and dies, it remains just a grain of wheat; but if it dies, it produces much fruit" (Jn 12:24).

The Celibacy of Christ

The celibacy of Jesus is an established fact.[17] Jesus Himself spoke about the meaning of celibacy in Matthew 19:10-12. In this context, He begins speaking about the indissolubility of marriage,[18] and in response to this Jesus' disciples exclaim, "If that is the case of a man with his wife, it is better not to marry" (Mt 19:10).[19] Interestingly, Jesus takes advantage of their negative statement and uses the opportunity to propose a new vision for a radically new way of life.

> Not all can accept [this] word, but only those to whom that is granted. Some are incapable of marriage because they were born so; some, because they were made so by others; some, because they have renounced marriage for the sake of the kingdom of heaven. Whoever can accept this ought to accept it. (Mt 19:11-12)

It must be noted that in the Jewish cultural milieu of Jesus, His praise of "eunuchry" was shocking. There were eunuchs in the time of Jesus, but they were, for the most part, considered outcasts.[20] Marriage was considered by the Jews as a religious obligation and the lack of children, as at best, a

great tragedy and at worst, a curse from God. St. John Paul
II describes the Jewish mindset at the time of Jesus: "Marriage was not only the common state of life but, through the
promise made to Abraham, it had acquired a consecrated
significance. Marriage, as a source of fruitfulness and descen-
dants, was 'a religiously privileged state: and privileged by
revelation itself.'"[21]

Yet, despite the shame attached to being a eunuch, Jesus
shows the complete newness of His teaching by proposing
freely chosen eunuchry as an ideal: "In using this image, he
wants to underline very vividly the audacity of this option:
the voluntary renouncement of marriage and most especially
of procreation comes from a decision which is not afraid to
expose itself to contempt and misunderstanding."[22] Because
Jesus uses a word that normally refers to a physical condition,
the strength of the choice He proposes is emphasized. The
word shows that it is intended to be seen as a choice for a
permanent state of life, an irrevocable gift.[23]

Some scholars propose that the word "eunuch" was
actually borrowed by Jesus from others who had used it as
an attack upon Him and His disciples. Since Jewish tradition
regarded a celibate as somebody less than a man, His scoffers
had likely used this pejorative term to chide Jesus and those
among His disciples who were celibate about their renunciation of marriage.[24] The word, thus, emphasizes the profound
nature of the sacrifice that someone makes "for the sake of
the kingdom of heaven." Jesus is making a radical statement:
"By making a pitiful condition a state fit to be admired, he
would bring out the distance between his own kingdom and
the Jewish mind. Far from glossing over the break between
the two, he stressed it. The logion is one of the strongest

passages in the gospels."[25] This is also why Jesus emphasizes that this teaching is not intended for all, "only those to whom that is granted" (Mt 19:11).

Why would someone make this incredible sacrifice? Jesus says it is done "for the sake of the kingdom of heaven" (Mt 19:12). It is worth noting that this is a theological and spiritual motivation, not just a practical one. It is a reason of the heart. Galot explains: "The 'kingdom of heaven' is not, after all, an exterior kingdom; it implants itself in man, and here it tends to take the entire person to the point of making the person renounce marriage and family."[26] Those to whom Jesus gives this call to live for the sake of the kingdom find their whole lives consumed by this love. The phrase "kingdom of heaven" is synonymous in the Scripture with "kingdom of God." Celibacy is proposed by Jesus as a way of totally dedicating oneself to God and His kingdom.

Of course, Jesus is, in fact, describing His own life and the motivation for His own celibacy:

In the concrete example of Jesus' celibate life, it is easy to find out to whom the third category of eunuchs refers. When the disciples heard that saying, they could only think of Jesus himself and possibly also of John the Baptist. It is clear that Jesus here speaks of his own case and explains it. He does not advocate self-mutilation; he sets up his own example.[27]

It is also important to point out that Jesus is proposing a positive ideal but not a negative one. Jesus is proposing a way of giving oneself; his "eunuchry" is not sterile but instead, reveals a different kind of fecundity. Living totally dedicated to the kingdom is living so that all may come to enter this kingdom. It is living totally open to God and others, totally given for the sake of the kingdom.

Matthew 19:10-12 is not the only place in the Scripture where we find reference to giving up marriage for the sake of the kingdom. In response to Peter's statement, "We have given up our possessions and followed you" (Lk 18:28), Jesus promises a reward to His closest disciples for having left marriage to follow Him: "Amen, I say to you, there is no one who has given up house or wife or brothers or parents or children for the sake of the kingdom of God who will not receive [back] an overabundant return in this present age and eternal life in the age to come" (18:29-30). Although this passage is applicable in some ways to all, it refers explicitly to a special group of Christ's disciples.[28] Jean Galot has made a special study of the phrase "follow me" as it is used by Christ in the Gospels. He points out that Christ gives this invitation only to those whom He has invited into a special relationship with Himself, sharing His own way of life:

> Many indications show that the invitation "follow-me" was really pronounced by Jesus. It is attested to by the four evangelists, each time in a context where it is appropriate in order to express the essential importance of the call (Mt 8:22; 9:9; 19:2; Mk 2:14, 20:21; Lk 9:59; 18:22; Jn 1:43; 21:19). It corresponds to a Semitic expression which is perhaps more literally rendered "come behind me."[29]

Notice that in this passage, Peter defines the community of Apostles who have responded to this call: "We have given up everything and followed you" (Mt 19:27).[30] This passage seems to refer to a special group of people who have received the call to "follow me." Here the *sequela Christi* for Christ's closest disciples is shown to include the necessity of giving up marriage.[31] As the context of Peter's question shows, Christ is speaking only to a select group of apostles (those who have "left everything"), since the command to embrace celibacy obviously could not be valid for all. In the parallel passages, Matthew 19:27-29 and Mark 10:29-30, there are two important differences from Luke. Neither of the passages mentions "wife" but both mention "children." Yet, one can see that giving up children must also include giving up a wife. Thus, Mark and Matthew's versions are focusing on the important cultural aspect of giving up offspring, which is the natural result of giving up marriage.[32] Notably, all the passages mention the reward (which Matthew calls "a hundred times more " [Mt 19:29]) for having "given up everything" (Mt 19:27). This reveals the spiritual fruitfulness not only of the celibacy of the Apostles but also of their poverty and obedience.

We can also explain theologically the fittingness (conveniens nature) of Jesus' celibacy. It is important to note that the celibacy of Jesus was not absolutely necessary. Jesus was fully human; he was like us in everything but sin, and there is no reason to suppose that marriage for Him was a physical impossibility. It is this free choice that makes Jesus' celibacy significant. He chose it as part of His total self-gift in fulfilling the plan of the Father to be our priest and bridegroom.[33] However, we can say that Jesus' celibacy was required in the same way the Passion of Christ was required: it was necessary, given His mission. Jesus was totally dedicated to the mission given to Him by His Father, and it is in this light that His celibacy makes sense. "The virginity of Jesus is above all communion of charity with the Father and therefore an adequate and

necessary existential repercussion of the salvific mission."[34]
He chose it because it was co-natural with who he was—that
is, His person and His mission.

In the exploration of Jesus' celibacy, an interesting question comes up: In what way is it possible to say Jesus lived the
virtue of chastity? St. Thomas defines chastity as the virtue
that allows us to control our concupiscence according to right
reason.[35] However, Jesus did not experience the temptations
of the flesh which result from the concupiscence of our
fallen nature.[36] Yet, St. Thomas admits another "metaphorical" understanding of the virtue of chastity:

> If the human mind delight in the spiritual union with
> that to which it behooves it to be united, namely God,
> and refrains from delighting in union with other things
> against the requirements of the order established by
> God, this may be called a spiritual chastity, according to 2
> Corinthians 11: 2: "I have espoused you to one husband,
> that I may present you as a chaste virgin to Christ."[37]

This kind of chastity might be called a chastity of the
heart: an undivided clinging to God with the affections of
the heart. Surely, this kind of chastity could be practiced by
one in any state of life but is more easily practiced in a life of
celibacy.[38] This is why St. Thomas says that virginity is a virtue
where one keeps oneself free from all venereal pleasure in
order to "have leisure for Divine things,"[39] that is, freedom to
be with God in love. Virginity, in this way, goes beyond chastity of the body, since chastity of the body would require one
to abstain only from unlawful venereal pleasure. This virginity
includes a virginity of the heart, to be more "anxious about
the things of the Lord" (1 Cor 7:33).[40]

From this, we can say that in a certain way, Jesus lived chastity because Jesus clings to the Father with an undivided heart. Jesus exemplifies the greater freedom of celibacy in His total surrender to His mission. He is so totally dedicated that it consumes every aspect of His life. Christ's sexuality, too, forms part of this total offering to the Father. He must have an undivided heart, a heart that is unattached to any other commitment than the will of his Father, a heart free for union: "His celibacy is first of all an expression of total love which united him to the Father; it forms a part of the homage of the total person of the incarnate Son to the Father from whom he has come and towards whom he goes."[41]

Jesus' total dedication to the Father means loving the Father's will and, therefore, loving those to whom the Father has given Christ. In this way, there is no separation between Jesus' love of the Father and His love of us. In fact, Jesus' celibacy allows Him to be open to us in a new and deeper way. This love of the Father allows Christ to be universally given to everyone. As Galot says, "He was able to manifest in his human conduct total openness to the heart of the Father, the divine love that, in its universality, has no preference for anyone and is directed equally towards all."[42]

However, it must be added that Jesus is not just given for humanity as a whole but is given for each person as an individual. His love reaches out to every person, and He dies in the place of, not just humanity as a whole, but each person.[43] This is the chaste love of Jesus' celibacy, not given in any particular human relationship but allowing Christ to be completely given to each person:

The true chastity of Jesus, the secret of his liberty
. . . is basically his way of approaching any human being
whatsoever, his way of giving himself to that person
entirely, of giving that person all his experience, all his
riches, all his attention, and of calling that person to a
total response. Incapable of demanding less than the
entire heart, incapable of exerting the least pressure, he
gives to each being exactly himself.[44]

In a certain way, every person becomes the spouse of
Jesus Christ; Jesus gives each one His full attention. This
dispels the myth that celibacy makes a person distant from
others. Jesus' celibacy did not separate Him from the people
He came to save but allowed Him to be more completely
united to them:

By means of celibacy, the Son of God could belong more
completely to all men. If he did not enter into the way
of marriage and if he had refused to found a family, it is
because he wanted, through his life and through his heart,
a more universal openness. A particular family would have
taken him in part from all the other families and all the
other men.[45]

In the life of Jesus, we see that celibate love is not at all
distant or cold but rather, rich in tenderness and emotion.
Celibacy fully lived by Jesus did not wither His heart but, in
fact, expanded it toward all. Thus, we see Jesus' tenderness
toward children,[46] towards women,[47] and towards his own disciples.[48] The chaste love of Jesus is not at all distant but open
to the heart of each individual.

What we see is that through His chastity, Jesus redeems
sexuality and reveals the true meaning of sexual love. As

noted above, the "sensual lust" (1 Jn 2:16) is one of the primary results of original sin that Christ came to repair. Yet, some would argue that to redeem sexuality, it would have been better for Jesus to have exercised it, in order to be a real man. "They are afraid that, without sexual life, Christ would not be truly a man, since desire is necessarily in the constitution of the psyche. But this is sophistry, which substitutes wounded nature for nature tout court."[49] Jesus redeems sexuality by revealing its inner truth; through chastity lived in charity, He reveals the meaning of sexuality and shows it is meant to be a way of self-giving. This chaste love of Jesus fulfills the essence of nuptial love as much as, if not more than, human marriage. John Paul II defines nuptial love as "that love in which the human person becomes a gift and—through this gift—fulfills the very meaning of his being and existence."[50] Jesus, through His chastity, made His life a gift of self-sacrificing and self-emptying love. He sacrificed sexual activity not because sex was something evil but because it was required by His mission.[51] In making this sacrifice, He actually fulfilled the self-giving nature of His sexuality by consecrating it to His Father on behalf of His bride:

> This sacrifice was neither a destruction nor a mutilation, but truly a consecration of the sexuality of Jesus. Far from being a renunciation by the Man-God of human sexuality, the celibacy of Jesus constituted its salvific offering up for the world. Already made sacred by reason of the Incarnation, the human sexuality of Jesus— which, in Him, was never exclusively natural or profane, much less profaned—was further consecrated by a free and continual offering, issuing from the human love of His heart.[52]

In this way, we can even argue that Jesus' celibacy was part of His priestly sacrifice for our salvation. In offering His sexuality through celibacy, He was offering an intimate part of Himself. Daily, He offered His life through the mission given by His Father, allowing every area of His life to be completely consumed, a consummation that was ultimately fulfilled in His Death on the Cross. As Antonio Sicari said, "Virginity was for him a daily offering of his entire being to the world as incarnated love for every creature of the Father."[53]

Another reason that marriage would have been incompatible for Jesus' mission is that He came to found a spiritual family, not a physical one. He came to give the gift of supernatural life, establishing the spiritual family of the Church. This is why Christ speaks about this spiritual family of His when someone points out that His natural family has come looking for Him. He explains that His family is not founded by physical generation, rather "whoever does the will of God is my brother and sister and mother" (Mk 3:35). Jesus' family will not be physical but rather, founded on union with Him through obedience to the word of God in faith. Jesus Himself founds His spiritual family in celibacy by His own obedience, even unto Death on the Cross:

> Jesus creates a new reality. He proclaims and at the same time realizes a new familial relationship not born from carnal union, but from the need to fulfill the will of God. . . . It is this bond which Christ, the virgin, establishes with his incarnation and with his obedience even unto death on a cross (cf. Phil 2:8) to the will of the Father.[54]

Given this mission, we can see how a particular marriage would have been an obstacle:

> Had he chosen to marry, he would have ushered into his life a particular love which would have concealed and hampered his universal love. His predilection for one woman would have put a distance between himself and all other women. In this connection, the episode of the woman who raised her voice in a crowd to proclaim the blessedness of Jesus' mother is significant. Jesus declared that this blessedness is accessible to all (Lk 11:27-28).[55]

Another way to speak about this reason for celibacy is to say that Jesus chose not to be the bridegroom of an individual bride in order to be the bridegroom of the Church. Clement of Alexandria opposed the rigorists of his time who taught that Jesus did not marry because marriage was evil by arguing that "he had his own spouse, the Church."[56] Jesus has His marriage; He is the bridegroom exclusively wed to His Church, as we saw in chapter 1. This is why He refuses a particular marriage; He has a marriage of superior value:

> In the light of this quality of bridegroom, one can understand the importance of the celibacy of Jesus. This is the refusal of a particular marriage, but not the refusal of every marriage: as Bridegroom, Christ realizes the supreme matrimony, that which unites God and man. . . . For Jesus, to be celibate signifies to be married to all humanity and to create a more superior love which must nourish and sustain the love of all marriages.[57]

This is clear also in the Eucharistic self-giving of Jesus. The Eucharist is Christ giving Himself totally to us as in a marriage. His gift of Himself as our bridegroom in the

Eucharist reveals the incongruity of another physical marriage for Jesus. As James Cardinal Stafford says, "The affirmation of either symbolism, whether of the Eucharist or of matrimony, is exclusive and irrevocable."[58] Marriage is an exclusive relationship because it is an exhaustive one. It is not possible for someone to give themselves totally to two people; you cannot have two total self-gifts. If Christ's self-giving to His bride in the Eucharist is exhaustive, then it must also be exclusive. As Balthasar says, "Our Lord's Eucharistic giving of his whole Body would be unthinkable if, even in the most devout spirit of the Old Testament, he had been married."[59] In this way, we can say that it would have been adultery for Christ to have participated in a physical marriage.

Jesus' celibacy is co-natural with His person and His mission. It is a sacrificial and kenotic expression of His spousal love; and as a result, it is spiritually fruitful. Jesus' begetting shows the positive power of His sacrificial, spousal love. He was a real bridegroom and a real father, but He was not passing on natural life, rather He was sharing with us the supernatural life of grace. This why the Fathers saw so clearly the nuptial significance of His Cross. Through His celibacy, lived also in obedience and poverty, Jesus also established a new state of life for some of His followers. This state of life was completely new to the Jewish milieu of His time. He founded it upon His own virginal life and inviting some of His followers to share the spiritual fruitfulness of His own way of life. This state of life only makes sense in light of Jesus teaching that "whoever loses his life for my sake will find it" (Mt 10:39), where the grain of wheat has to die before "it produces much fruit" (Jn 12:24). It is a state of life where one is called to embrace a fruitfulness that comes from consecrated celibacy—that is, they "who have renounced marriage for the sake of the kingdom" (Mt 19:12). John Paul II explains this new state of life founded on Christ:

> The detachment from the tradition of the Old Covenant, in which marriage and procreative fruitfulness "in the body" were a religiously privileged condition, must have been brought about above all on the basis of the example of Christ himself. Only little by little did it consciously take root that for "the kingdom of heaven" a special significance attaches to man's spiritual and supernatural fruitfulness—which comes from the Holy Spirit (the Spirit of God), and which, in a specific sense and in determined cases, is served precisely by continence— and that this is precisely continence "for the kingdom of heaven."[60]

The celibate priest is called to live in this state of life and carries on Christ's spiritual paternity when he acts *in persona Christi* in the sacraments, especially the Eucharist. Being a eunuch for the sake of the kingdom is not at all a kind of sterility. Rather, as we will see in the upcoming chapters, it is entering into the virginal, life-giving relationship that Jesus has with His Church.

We can say in conclusion that Jesus' celibacy is a revelation of His life and mission as bridegroom. Jesus' celibacy makes Him the model and source of chaste love because it enables Him to unite Himself completely with His Father and with us, and allows Him to fulfill His role as the Bridegroom of the Church. It is part of His spousal self-gift, demonstrating further the sacrificial, kenotic, and fruitful nature of that self-gift. Thus, celibacy becomes necessary for Jesus by virtue of the end proposed. The end is that He might make His life a total self-gift for His bride:

> In this sense, it is by celibacy that the mystery of the Incarnation was able to attain its objective fully, the diffusion of divine love into humanity through the human love of Jesus. Detached from family obligations, the savior was able to offer his heart more freely to all, and to live closer to those to whom he was directing his mission.[61]

Again, we see the bridegroom image is essential to understand who Jesus is and how He lives His life in self-gift: "With this nuptial name [bridegroom] Jesus reveals the foundation of his being, which is not the dry solitude of a cold and distant, human-divine perfection, but the great joy of nuptial love offered without limits."[62]

The Poverty of Christ

Christ lived poverty both materially and spiritually. His life on earth was one with the materially poor, and He lived this poverty also in His spirit. Both of these aspects of His poverty are nuptial in that they form part of the total self-gift He makes for His bride. As we will see, Christ proposes the poverty that He lived as a way of life for His closest followers, part of the state of life of those He called when he said, "Follow me."

When meditating on the Incarnation, St. Thomas Aquinas asks the question "whether Christ should have led a life of poverty in this world."[63] Was it right that the God Man, the King of Kings and Lord of Lords, be poor? He gives four reasons that poverty was fitting for Christ.

First, St. Thomas argues that material poverty fits with Christ's mission to preach the Gospel. Here, we see how poverty frees Christ from worldly concerns so that He may be completely given to His mission: "In order that the preachers of God's word may be able to give all their time to preaching, they must be wholly free from care of worldly matters: which is impossible for those who are possessed of wealth."[64] St. Thomas is speaking about the dangers of what he calls solicitudes, things that take up the energy of our mind and heart and keep us from being focused on God and free to serve God. He sees the simple truth that the more things we have, the more we have to be solicitous for them; and this can be an obstacle for one who should be totally dedicated to God. [65]

Second, St. Thomas connects Christ's poverty to His sacrificial Death. Just as with the other evangelical counsels, poverty is one of the ways that Christ daily lives His mission, which is fulfilled on the Cross. Thomas says: "Just as He took upon Himself the death of the body in order to bestow spiritual life on us, so did He bear bodily poverty, in order to enrich us spiritually according to 2 Cor. 8:9: He became poor for our sakes that through His poverty we might become rich."[66] Here, St. Thomas cites an important Scripture passage from St. Paul about Christ's poverty. And when we look at St. Thomas' commentary on 2 Corinthians 8:9, we find that according to St. Thomas, Jesus' poverty enriches us in two ways, by example and by means of a sacrament:

> Certainly by means of an example, because if Christ loved poverty, then also we, by his example, should love it. Also loving poverty in temporal things, we are made

rich in spiritual things, see James 2:5, 'Did not God choose the poor in the world, to be rich in faith, etc…'

Moreover by means of a sacrament, because everything which Christ chose or suffered, was on our behalf. Thus, according to this principle, since he suffered death, we have been liberated from eternal death and have been restored to life; so also, according to this principle, since he suffered want in temporal things, we have been liberated from want in spiritual things, and we have been made rich in spiritual things., see 1 Cor 1:5, "You have been made rich in all knowledge in him, etc . . . . "[67]

For St. Thomas, Christ's poverty is a sacrament because it is a sign that gives grace. Thus, it is nuptial, because it is a means by which He gives Himself so that we receive life. St. Thomas repeatedly affirms the principle that all Jesus' actions are a cause of grace for us, not only His Death and Resurrection: "For his humanity was the instrument of his divinity. And so his actions brought salvation to us through the power of the divinity. They caused grace in us both by meriting it and by some kind of efficient causality."[68] Thus, Christ's poverty gives us grace, supernatural life.

In the third place, St. Thomas says poverty was fitting to Christ so that His mission provided Him with no personal gain. If He had had wealth, he might have appeared to be preaching for selfish reasons, and not for the salvation of the world.[69]

Lastly, St. Thomas shows us that Christ's poverty reveals His dependence upon divine power; thus, it was spiritual poverty and not only physical:

Christ desired to be poor, and of humble estate, in his earthly life so that the transformation of the world might be shown to come from the power of God and not from any human power: "the more lowly He seemed by reason of His poverty, the greater might the power of His Godhead be shown to be."[70]

Here, Thomas demonstrates the connection between material poverty and humility: "In one who, like Christ, is poor willingly, poverty itself is a sign of very great humility."[71] For St. Thomas, poverty of spirit is humility. Thus, there is a connection between material poverty and humility; when one chooses material poverty, as Christ did, it is a sign of humility.[72] Thus, poverty in Christ, both in fact and in spirit, provides these four things: freedom for His mission, a means of self-gift, freedom from personal gain, and humility that demonstrates the power of God.

The Scriptures consistently attest to the material poverty of Jesus life. He was born in poverty,[73] lived his mission in poverty,[74] and died stripped of every possession as the poorest of the poor.[75] Although he was the Son of God, he never lived among the privileged class, but lived rather as a poor servant.[76] During his ministry he lived in a state of material dependence, not even having a place of his own to lay his head.[77] Jesus' poverty, like His celibacy, points to His way of being, His person, and His mission. His poverty is relational; it allows Him to live in total dependence upon the Father:

He does not possess what the animals possess, a place to rest that belongs to him. It is his permanent situation; he has no fixed home. . . . In this is affirmed the profound root of the poverty of Jesus: the relations of the incarnate Son with the Father. The renunciation of earthly goods expresses a filial belonging to the Father: there is no earthly treasure for him who has the Father as his unique treasure, and there is no earthly home for the one who is only able to live in the home of the Father.[78]

Jesus lives materially poor because He is united with His Father and is given completely to His mission.[79]

Jesus not only lives in material poverty Himself but He also invites those who would be His closest followers to embrace material poverty with Him. Galot explains that "when Jesus invites someone to follow him, he demands of him that he share his mode of life: it is a sharing in common of his self-abnegation."[80] The Scriptures clearly show that one of the aspects marking the *sequela Christi* is that these disciples are asked to give up everything to follow Him. One sees this in the call of each of the Apostles, since almost every time an apostle is called, the Gospel writers mention what they left behind.[81] Also, when Jesus is describing what will be given to those who have "given up everything and followed" Him (the description of those in the *sequela Christi*, Mt 19:27 and parallels), He emphasizes that besides leaving family, they have left their possessions and livelihoods (e.g., "houses" and "lands" [Mt 19:29 and parallels]). And when He sends out His disciples to preach, He specifically tells them to take nothing for their journey: "neither walking stick, nor sack, nor food" — not even an extra tunic (Lk 9:3 and parallels).[82] Those whose lives are taken completely for the Kingdom must be poor.

The starkest example of how the call "follow me" is a call to embrace poverty is found in the story of "the rich young man." In this story, recorded in all three synoptic Gospels,[83] a man who "had many possessions" asks Jesus, "Good Teacher, what must I do to inherit eternal life?" (Mk 10:22, 17). Jesus responds to this question on two levels.[84] First, He tells the young man what could be expected of all Christians: to follow the commandments. Second, seeing the young man's deeper desire, He gives him an invitation to join His disciples in the *sequela Christi*. The uniqueness of this second call is seen clearly in the text. The young man responds to Jesus' first answer: "Teacher, all of these I have observed since my youth" (Mk 10:20), which evokes a further invitation from the Lord. This second invitation is especially clear in Mark's Gospel where the evangelist describes Jesus' gaze upon the rich young man: "Jesus, looking at him, loved him and said to him, 'You are lacking in one thing. Go, sell what you have, and give to [the] poor and you will have treasure in heaven; then come, follow me.'" (Mk 10:21).[85] As Jean Galot points out, this request is totally different than the first one and marks a new invitation:

> In the second part, the request is completely different; it enunciates demands unknown in the Old Covenant, it is understood as well beyond the commandments which were recalled. God has never demanded in Judaism that one sell all that he possesses and that he give it to the poor. Moreover, this stripping only justifies itself by a call particular to the gospel: "Come, follow me."[86]

The refusal of the rich young man is the only recorded time in the Scriptures when someone walks away from the invitation, "Follow me." It is important to note, though, that the invitation given is a positive one, "Come, follow me"; the renunciation of riches is the requirement that makes the total following of Jesus possible:

> What the rich man lacks, more precisely, is the following of Jesus. The abandoning of goods is only mentioned, according to the text, in view of this fundamental step. . . . In inviting him to follow, Jesus wants to open to the rich man access to a new way, which must transform his entire existence. The condition of this is the renunciation of all goods. Poverty is demanded, but as an aspect of a mode of life which consists in accompanying the Master."[87]

This special invitation draws attention to the fact that all of Christ's apostles and His closest disciples were poor. Poverty seems to be a pre-requisite for following Christ in total dedication to His mission.[88] Certainly, Jesus invites all to the spirit of poverty in His Beatitudes,[89] but to some, He proposes a new and more radical command. In fact, this command of actually leaving behind one's possessions must be considered as revolutionary as His call to celibacy for the sake of the kingdom. The Old Testament contains no command to sell all for the sake of following God.[90] And yet, Jesus sees it as essential for His closest disciples. Again, poverty is relational; those who share in Christ's mission must also share His life. They, too, must live His fundamental readiness to be completely given.[91]

Like all aspects of the nuptial self-gift, material poverty is also spiritually fruitful, even for the disciples:

> Jesus said, "Truly I tell you, there is no one who has left house or brothers or sisters or mother or father or children or fields, for my sake and for the sake of the

good news, who will not receive a hundredfold now in this age—houses, brothers and sisters, mothers and children, and fields with persecutions—and in the age to come eternal life." (Mk 10:29-30)

Jesus lives poverty of spirit through His humility. Despite His power and authority seen in the things He does, the way He preaches, and how He identifies Himself with the Father, Jesus presents Himself as the poor one who is gentle and humble of heart.[92] He does not come demonstrating His power as a master but rather, declares He is the humble servant: "Rather, let the greatest among you be as the youngest, and the leader as the servant. For who is greater: the one seated at table or the one who serves? Is it not the one seated at table? I am among you as the one who serves" (Lk 22:26-27).[93]

Jesus' greatest act of humility is seen in His kenosis, emptying Himself to accept the poverty of our human condition. As St. Gregory of Nyssa commented, "Is there any greater poverty for God, than the form of a slave? Is there greater humility than for the King of the universe to share voluntarily in the poverty of our nature?"[94] This poverty of spirit is reflected not just in the act of the Incarnation, but also in the entire way that Jesus lives His earthly life. Jesus' spiritual poverty is expressed in His total dependence on the Father's will. This shows how His poverty is really rooted in His obedience. Not claiming anything for Himself, even His own will, He makes a total gift of Himself. As Jean Beyer explains:

> He is poor because it is himself: filial in the gift of the Father and in his total, eternal abandonment to him. This poverty will show itself in the fact that he does not

> consider anything as belonging to himself. He is himself
> in so far as he gives himself totally. In order to manifest
> this gift, he will be the Son of one sole love in full
> dependence.
>
> Christ is poor, born poor in order to belong completely
> to the Father to teach us to abandon everything in order
> to be completely God's.
>
> Christ is poor, he who from being wealthy, became poor
> incarnating himself, offering himself, renouncing himself,
> he who is the life.[95]

This passage allows us to see more clearly how poverty is
essential for Jesus' mission. For Jesus, poverty of spirit flows
from the unity of His mission and person. Since He is poor,
He is completely free to be given, holding nothing back; He
is even free to be abandoned to God. Poverty and obedience
come together in this complete availability to the Father. It
is the combination of both His material poverty and His
poverty of spirit that allows Him to make a total self-gift. In
pursuit of His mission, He has renounced any place to lay
His head: He will not lay down His head until He lays it on
the Cross.

In Jesus' Passion and Death, in His extreme kenosis, His
poverty reaches its deepest expression, since in His Death,
He takes on in some way the poverty of our sin.[96] Jesus
takes on our poverty to the point of experiencing in some
mysterious way our abandonment from God.[97] Edward Schillebeeckx, O.P., describes this mystery of Christ's total kenosis
in poverty:

In his earthly life Jesus, as Messiah or representative of sinful mankind, did truly go forth from the Father. So truly, in fact, that he can pray with us, "Out of the depths I cried to thee, Lord"—not in a local but in a qualitative sense: "Out of the depths of the miserable state of fallen mankind, I call upon you, my God." This cry echoes above all from the Cross. It is the outburst of a man who, even though knowing himself personally bound to the Father in love from the depths of his human heart, was nevertheless living in utter truth, though to the very end, the experience of the estrangement from God belonging to our sinfulness, identifying himself with everything there ever was or will be of sin-spawned alienation from God in this world.[98]

The poverty of Christ goes far beyond His material stripping; the poverty of the Cross goes all the way to taking on our suffering, even in its worst form, suffering our experience of separation from God, as a result of sin.

Jesus also calls His followers to poverty of spirit in humility.[99] Living Gospel poverty for the disciples means more than just giving up material possessions; Gospel poverty goes further. Being poor means taking the last place[100] and becoming like a child.[101] It means following Jesus who is "meek and humble of heart" (Mt 11:29). As St. Paul exhorts the early Christians, they must learn to imitate the humility of Jesus in His kenosis:

> Do nothing out of selfishness or out of vainglory; rather, humbly regard others as more important than yourselves, each looking out not for his own interests, but [also] everyone for those of others. Have among yourselves the same attitude that is also yours in Christ Jesus, Who,

though he was in the form of God, did not regard
equality with God something to be grasped. (Phil 2:3-6)

As we saw above in St. Thomas, there is a relationship
between material poverty and humility. The abandonment
of material goods is meant to lead to a life of humility.[102]
Material poverty helps to create the conditions for spiritual
poverty to thrive because it makes the disciple dependent
upon God. As Raniero Cantalamessa says, "real poverty is the
privileged road to spiritual poverty."[103] Material poverty and
spiritual poverty are connected in that they both make the
disciple dependent:

> The Sermon on the Mount and the Sermon on the Plain
> emphasize the essential poverty of human existence,
> its dependence on God (Mt 6:25 ff.): God cares for
> tomorrow, and if man cares about God, then his
> tomorrow is also taken care of. The rebuke to Martha
> makes this very clear (Lk 10:41). The lack of care goes
> so far that one must not only avoid amassing possessions
> which God will anyhow require tomorrow of us "fools"
> (Lk 12:20), and must avoid gathering on earth rusting
> treasures that hold fast the heart in what passes away (Mt
> 6:19 ff.); one must willingly let oneself be robbed, without
> striking back (Mt 5:39-42; 1Cor 6:7), without anxiety,
> because we are kept safe in God (Lk 12.6), and we will
> lack nothing when we are sent out by Christ.[104]

This state of total dependence upon God is an invitation
to share Christ's own way of life, as He was the first one to
count nothing as His own and lay everything at the feet of
His Father, making His life a total gift. As Heidi Böhler says,
"The poverty of Christ also consisted in considering nothing

as his own, but everything given to the Father. Conscious of this, do not retain anything for yourself, but make your life a gift of love to the Father."[105]

Having investigated the poverty of Christ, we can also say that it is nuptial because it fulfills three characteristics of Christ's spousal love: it is sacrificial, kenotic, and fruitful. Both in His material poverty and His poverty of spirit, Jesus lives a sacrificial and kenotic existence. The sacrifice and kenosis of His poverty is fulfilled in the total self-gift of the Cross. However, His poverty can be called fruitful not only because it is a visible element of the Cross, which is the primary cause of grace for us; but, as we saw in St. Thomas, by the power of the Incarnation, the whole of Christ's existence causes grace for us: "Since he suffered want in temporal things, we have been liberated from want in spiritual things, and we have been made rich in spiritual things."[106] In this way, Christ's material poverty and His poverty of spirit were central to His mission of becoming a total self-gift for us; and through Jesus' poverty of spirit and poverty of material things, we have become rich because we have received His life poured out for us.

Conclusions from Christ's Living of the Evangelical Counsels

The unity of Christ's person and mission demanded that He live His life in obedience, celibacy, and poverty. His mission as our bridegroom required a total-self gift. Obedience, celibacy, and poverty were the inner form that made His gift complete. They were the daily means by which He poured out His life for us through sacrificial, self-emptying, and fruitful love. Not only do they make Christ completely free to give all, but they also form part of His sacrificial self-offering by which He gives His life so that we may have life.[107]

The counsels, thus, form the perfect response of Christ to His mission; and as we saw in Mary, they form the perfect response of the disciple to Christ.

From this perspective, one might argue that all Christians are called to live the evangelical counsels. There is a way in which this is true. Since the counsels, by their nature, include all there is to be given, they represent the heart of the availability that every Christian ought to have before God. All followers of Jesus are called to be obedient to God, to chasten their sexual drives, and to surrender their possessions to His will as they attempt with all their heart to be led by Him. Yet, as we have already seen in the Scriptures, there is a more radical following of Christ to which only some are called ("Not all can accept [this] word, but only those to whom that is granted" Mt 19:11). It is in the very nature of this radical call that Christ could not invite everyone to the explicit demands of obedience, celibacy, and poverty.[108] Some are invited to an undeniably "special" call, and this is a life of closer conformation to the spousal self-gift of Christ on the Cross:

> For all the baptized, in conformity with the diverse conditions of life, there is a real demand of poverty, but not up to the freedom from every earthly good; of chastity, but not up to the renouncement of marriage; of obedience, but not up to depriving oneself of one's own will before those who have the place of God. In the consecrated life the precepts and the evangelical values valid for all are lived, in the most profound insertion of the mystery of the cross of the Lord and his resurrection, as a closer and more radical following of Jesus, to represent in the Church, in a permanent and visible

mode, the form of life that Jesus embraced and proposed to his disciples.[109]

Our study has been, however, to investigate a specifically priestly call to the evangelical counsels. This will be clearly demonstrated in the next chapters which show how the priest's configuration to Christ the Bridegroom calls him to live the counsels. Before concluding this chapter on how Christ lives the evangelical counsels, however, it is important to see briefly how the counsels are connected specifically to Christ's priesthood and to Christ's pastoral care for His flock. These connections will be relevant to the priest who stands *in persona Christi*, as priest, head and shepherd, and bridegroom.

We have seen that the Cross is the wedding between Christ and the Church. Since it is also on the Cross that Christ is our priest and victim, this means that Christ is both priest and bridegroom at the same moment. He is both offering Himself to the Father on our behalf as our priest and offering Himself to us to share His life with us as our bridegroom.[110] We already saw this theme of the bridegroom consummating the marriage through sacrifice in chapter 1. It is this same sacrificial consummation of the marriage that "sanctifies" the people of God that St. Paul described in Ephesians 5:25-26: "Christ loved the Church and handed himself over for her to sanctify her." The word "sanctify," (ἁγιάζω) which St. Paul uses in this passage, could also be translated "consecrate" and has strong priestly connotations.[111] It is used to describe Christ's atoning sacrifice (Heb 2:11) —that is, His priestly offering for the sanctification of the world.[112] This is the point made in the *Directory on the Ministry and Life of Priests*: "The letter to the Ephesians closely relates the priestly oblation of Christ (cf. 5:25) with the sanctification of the Church (cf. 5:26) loved with a spousal love."[113] This same connection can be made in the Book of Revelation where the bridegroom is also the lamb "slain" (Rev 5:6) in order to sanctify the bride.[114] As St. John Paul II said, Christ is priest and bridegroom at the same moment:

> That gift of self to the Father through obedience to the point of death (see Phil. 2:8) is at the same time, according to Ephesians, an act of "giving himself for the Church." In this expression, redeeming love transforms itself, I would say, into spousal love: by giving himself for the Church, with the same redeeming act, Christ united himself once and for all with her as the Bridegroom to the Bride, as the husband with the wife, giving himself through all that is included once and for all in his "giving himself" for the Church. IN this way, the mystery of the redemption of the body conceals within itself some sense of the mystery "of the marriage of the Lamb" (see Rev. 19:7).[115]

This is also why the Tradition of the Church brings these images—priest and bridegroom—together in the celebration of the Eucharist, which both makes present the sacrifice of the Cross and foreshadows the wedding feast of the Lamb. This connection between redeeming love and spousal love means that Christ's priesthood cannot be separated from His role as bridegroom. They are two aspects of His one sacrifice.

It also follows from this unity that Christ's priesthood cannot be separated from His obedience, celibacy, and poverty. Just as we showed that obedience, celibacy, and poverty were necessary for Christ's mission as bridegroom, they are also necessary for His mission as priest. As we mentioned above, Christ is both priest and victim. Through obedience, celibacy, and poverty, He places Himself completely at the disposal of the Father so that He can be given as a victim. As we saw in the section on obedience, an essential part of Christ's priesthood is His internal self-offering.[116] Robert Pesarchick explains that "this total self-abandonment on the part of Christ constitutes one essential aspect of his priesthood. His self-offering . . . is the expression of his entire 'priestly' Being. His kenotic self-gift is then one with his mission/person."[117] But as Balthasar points out, this internal self-offering of Christ finds its "form" in the evangelical counsels:

> When the Son stands before the Father in readiness to give himself and to renounce what is his . . . ; when, in poverty, chastity and obedience, he thus abandons to the Father the disposal of what is his, he becomes potentially a victim to be sacrificed, and the Father can turn this potentiality into actuality whenever he chooses.[118]

Thus, obedience, celibacy, and poverty are at the very heart of Christ's priestly and spousal self-offering. They are the "inner modalities of the Son's perfect love" by which he offers himself for our sake as our priest and bridegroom:

> What is truly fruitful and redemptive in his (as in every) sacrifice is the frame of mind that depends on the inner disposition of love. To the extent, then, that poverty, chastity and obedience are the inner modalities of the Son's perfect love, which becomes, through them, a sacrificial offering, these modalities cannot fail to signify the establishment of his priesthood."[119]

Christ's priestly, spousal self-gift is made precisely by His internal offering in total obedience, celibacy, and poverty.

This is because he is both priest and victim, and the counsels form the mode of his internal offering. The ministerial priest, who acts in the sacraments *in persona Christi*, by the very nature of his priesthood, must also seek through the evangelical counsels to be both priest and victim. As Dermot Power explains: "It is the obedient love of the Son towards the Father that is the mode of his priestly office, and it is only within the Form of this redemptive love that the continuation of the office of priesthood in the Church can be correctly perceived and understood."[120]

The evangelical counsels bring together Christ's spousal love and His shepherd's heart. Christ is the Good Shepherd who lays down His life for His sheep.[121] This shepherd's heart is what John Paul II calls "pastoral charity," which forms the very heart of his doctrine of priesthood in *Pastores Dabo Vobis*. However, for John Paul II, pastoral charity must also be understood as the spousal love of Christ.[122] The good shepherd who lays down his life for the sheep is also the bridegroom who gives his life for his bride.[123] And according to John Paul II, Christ's pastoral charity is also seen in Christ's living of the counsels, which then become necessary for the priest as part of the means of his own pastoral charity.[124] If the priest is configured to Christ the Bridegroom through ordination, then he is called to take on the spousal love of Christ—that is, pastoral charity—by living in imitation of Christ's self-emptying love. This means in order to be a "living image of Christ the bridegroom of the Church," he must imitate Christ's own sacrificial, kenotic, spousal self-gift in obedience, chastity, and poverty.

Questions for Discussion, Reflection, and Prayer

1. What inspires me most about how Christ lived the evangelical counsels?

2. What do I find most challenging about Christ's living of the evangelical counsels?

3. The obedience of Christ is obedience unto death.[125] What are the ways that Christ has asked or is asking me to embrace death through obedience? How can I do that in love?

4. Christ witnesses to a celibacy that is fruitful. How do I experience the fruitfulness of celibacy in my priesthood?

5. What does Christ want me to learn from His own living of poverty? How is He calling me to embrace poverty with Him?

6. In what ways is the spiritual poverty of humility difficult for me? How does poverty of spirit allow me to receive "the kingdom of heaven" (Mt 5:3)?

7. As I meditate on Christ's living of the evangelical counsels, where do I feel drawn to deeper union with His way of life?

NOTES

1.   See also John 4:34, 5:30, 6:38, 8:28-29, 9:4, 12:49, 14:10.

2.   As St. Thomas notes (ST III, 1, a. 2, ad 2), it is precisely Christ's unique offering in obedience as God and man that is able to save us, since only the satisfaction of one who is God and man could have the infinite effect required to undo the disobedience of all the sons of Adam. Servais comments: "the burden of this obedience, in contrast to the disobedience of the one who made the many sinful (cf. Rom 5:19), remains a demand that far surpasses anything that his human nature could bear" (Jacques Servais, S.J., "The Evangelical Counsels and the Total Gift of Self," in *Communio* 31 (Fall 2004): 372).

3.   Jean Galot, S.J., *Vivre avec le Christ: La vie consacrée selon l'Évangile* (Louvain: Sintal, 1986), 164. See also ST III, 48, a. 3, ad. 2.

4.   ST III 48, a. 3, corpus; he is citing Augustine's *De civitate Dei*, 10, 6 (*Corpus Christianorum Series Latina* [CCSL] 47, 278).

5.   ST III 48, a. 2, corpus.

6.   St. Thomas points out that even though it was not possible for Christ to choose against the Father's plan, this does not limit Christ's true freedom. The possibility of choice is not essential to the freedom that consists in self-determination. As Margerie explains, "With perfect knowledge of the purpose fixed by the Father, i.e., the salvation of mankind, and with complete and inner acceptance of this purpose, Christ decided to die, not under any violent pressure from the Father, but through a spontaneous and human impulse of his 'voluntas ut ratio, se determinans et causans' without option or choice" (336: note 28). See also ST III, 47, a. 2, ad. 2: "Although obedience implies necessity with regard to the thing commanded nevertheless it implies free-will with regard to the precept. And, indeed, such was Christ's obedience, for, although His Passion and death, considered in themselves were repugnant to his natural will, yet Christ resolved to fulfill God's will with respect to the same according to Ps 39 (40): *That I should do thy will: O my God, I have desired it.* Hence He said (Matt 26:42): *If this chalice may not pass away, but I must drink it, Thy will be done.*"

7.   Hans Urs von Balthasar, *Mysterium Paschale: The Mystery of Easter*, trans. Aidan Nichols, O.P. (Edinburgh: T & T Clark, 1990), 28.

8.   Hans Urs von Balthasar, *The Threefold Garland*, trans. Erasmo Leiva-Merikakis (San Francisco: Ignatius Press, 1982) 30.

9.   See Hebrews 10:8-10.

10.   ST III, 47, a. 3, ad. 3.

11.   Hans Urs von Balthasar, *The Glory of the Lord: A Theological Aesthetics*, vol VII trans. Erasmo Leiva-Merikakis (San Francisco: Ignatius Press, 1982; reprint, 1989), 148.

12. Antonio Sicari explains this "learning": "The word who becomes incarnate reveals himself as the obedient word. Beginning with the Incarnation, there will also be for Him a continual human apprenticeship until this obedience leads him to the total powerlessness of death upon the Cross (cf. Phil 2) in which his activity will be a supreme passivity joined to an abandonment (Mk 15:14) tried and accepted (Lk 13:17). 'Thus, Son though he was, he learned, by his sufferings, obedience' (Heb 5:8)" (Antonio Sicari, "Inspiration and Genesis of the Evangelical 'Counsels'" *Communio* 9.1 [Spring 1982]: 51-66).

13. Galot, *Vivre avec le Christ*, 165.

14. Hans Urs von Balthasar, *The Christian State of Life*, trans. Sister Mary Frances McCarthy (San Francisco: Ignatius Press, 1983), 37.

15. This is why obedience plays a central role in Ephesians 5:22-23: "Wives should be subordinate to their husbands as to the Lord. For the husband is head of his wife just as Christ is head of the church, he himself the savior of the body." Thus, as the Church is united with Christ through obedience, so wives should be united with their husbands. Of course, we remember John Paul II's commentary on Ephesians 5 cited in chapter 1: "Whereas in the relationship between Christ and the Church the subjection is only on the part of the Church, in the relationship between husband and wife the 'subjection' is not one-sided but mutual" (*Mulieris Dignitatem*, sec. 24).

16. Fulton J. Sheen, *The Priest is Not His Own* (New York: McGraw-Hill, 1963), 20.

17. There have been some attempts to present arguments that Jesus was married: See William E. Phipps, *The Sexuality of Jesus: Theological and Literary Perspectives* (New York: Harper and Row, 1973). Phipps states that at the time of Jesus, the Jewish and cultural milieu would have made marriage essential. Secondly, he argues that the Scripture is silent about the married state of Jesus (an argument we challenge below when talking about Matthew 19:10-12); therefore, we must presume Jesus was married. However, this argument from silence fails to take into account all the facts. As Angelo Amato, S.D.B., points out in *Gesù il Signore. Saggio de cristologia*, Corso di teologia sistematica, 4 (Bologna: Edizioni Dehoniane, 1999): "This hypothesis concerning the theological necessity of marriage during the time period of Jesus is historically denied by the existence of a celibacy in a few groups of Essenes." (Amato, 499). In addition, Amato says: "The Gospels speak often of the family of Jesus (cf. Mc 3,31; 6,3; Jn 6:42; 7:3). However a wife and any possible children are always excluded from these lists (cf. Acts 1:14)" (Ibid.). Today, most Scripture scholars argue that the celibacy of Jesus is an undeniable fact: see Marco Adinaolfi, "Il celibato di Gesù," in *Bibbia e Oriente* 13 (1971): 145-158; Thaddée Matura, O.F.M., "Le célibat dans le Nouveau Testament d'après l'exégèse récente," in *Nouvelle Revue Théologique* 97 (1975): 481-500, 593-604. Galot,

who has done extensive study on the issue, calls the celibacy of Jesus an "indisputable fact" (Jean Galot, S.J., *Theology of the Priesthood* [San Francisco: Ignatius Press, 2014], 230; see also *Vivre avec le Christ*, 35). Pius XII in his encyclical *Sacra Virginitas* states that Christ was a lifelong virgin: "The Teacher of divine things was a virgin from the beginning of his life to his death" (AAS 46 [1954], n. 167).

18. See Matthew 19:1-9.

19. Although the disciples began the conversation with this exclamation about marriage, one cannot see in Jesus' words any degradation of the married state—in fact, just the opposite: celibacy has value because marriage is such a highly valued state (see Galot, *Theology of the Priesthood*, 235). The two states being treated together in this one passage reveals also their unity (see *Catechism of the Catholic Church*, sec. 1618-1620).

20. "The eunuch, born thus or made so, was an outcast, denied by Jewish law the right to bring offerings to the Temple (cf. Lev 21:17-20), and excluded from the assembly of Yahweh (cf. Deut 23:2), because it seemed improper that a person deprived of the power of transmitting life would associate with the God of life" (Thomas McGovern, *Priestly Celibacy Today* [Downer's Grove, IL: Midwest Theological Forum, 1997], 78-79).

21. Address, 17 March 1982, no. 3, emphasis in original. We already noted that there were other examples of celibacy in the time of Jesus, most notably, John the Baptist and the Essenes; but these were considered to be rare and extreme.

22. Galot, *Vivre avec le Christ*, 74-75.

23. "This is not simply about abstaining from certain carnal acts, as in the rules for sexual purity, but it puts some one voluntarily in a state which excludes the married life." (Ibid, see also Galot, *Vivre avec le Christ*, 78). Galot points out that not even Jesus' audience thought He was speaking about self-mutilation (Jean Galot. "La motivation évangélique du célibat." *Gregorianum* 53.4 (1972): 743).

24. See Béda Rigaux, O.F.M., "Le Célibat et le radicalisme évangelique," *Nouvelle Revue Theologique* 94 (1972): 159; Léopold Sabourin, "The Positive Values of Consecrated Celibacy," *The Way Supplement* 10 (1970): 52; Galot, *Theology of the Priesthood*, 235; McGovern, *Priestly Celibacy Today*, 79.

25. Galot, *Theology of the Priesthood*, 235.

26. Galot, "La motivation évangélique du célibat," 745.

27. Lucien Legrand, M.E.P., *The Biblical Doctrine of Virginity* (London: Geoffrey Chapman, 1963) 40.

28. John Paul II (*Redemptionis Donum*, in *Acta Apostolicae Sedis* [AAS] 76 [1984]: n. 3) uses the call to the rich young man (Mark 10:17-22; Matthew 19:16-22; Luke 18:18-23) as a prime example of the invitation to follow Christ by means of the evangelical counsels. See also Paul VI, *Perfectae Caritatis* (PC) (1965), sec. 5.

29.   Galot, *Vivre avec le Christ,* 17-18.

30.   See also Mark 10:28 and Luke 18:28.

31.   It would be difficult to explain Jesus' encouraging His disciples to abandon their current wives and children, especially in light of His teaching on the indissolubility of marriage. We will handle the question of whether or not we can know if the apostles were married in chapter 7.

32.   For this reason, Galot argues that the Lucan passage is more original to Jesus Himself because it contains a more complete list (Galot, *Vivre avec le Christ,* 52). Galot will also argue ("La motivation évangélique du célibat," 752) that the texts where Jesus says His disciples must love Him more than their families (Lk 14:26, Mt 10:37) are examples of the call to leaving everything to follow Christ. Thus, he defends the idea that these passages are not addressed to all would-be followers of Jesus, rather to His intimate disciples who experience the call "follow me." We will evaluate this idea in chapter 7 when we consider the origin of the priesthood in the apostolic call.

33.   Galot also points out this should say something about the connection between priesthood and celibacy, since "in its most perfect realization, the priesthood entails the renunciation of marriage" (Galot, *Theology of the Priesthood,* 230).

34.   Amato, 502.

35.   ST II-II, 151, a. 1, corpus.

36.   "He never experienced and he could not experience any temptation of the flesh (this double affirmation is theologically certain, for the first part see canon 12 of the Second Council of Constantinople, DS, 224)" (Gabriel Jacquemet, "Célibat," in *Catholicisme: hier, aujourd'hui, demain* Vol. 2, 763-769 Dirigée par G. Jacquemet [Paris: Letouzey et Ané, 1947], 765). St. Thomas makes it clear that for Christ, there was no painful mortification of His flesh since He had no concupiscence. Christ practiced temperance and not continence (ST III, 7, a. 2, ad. 3).

37.   ST II-II, 151, a. 2., corpus.

38.   See 1 Corinthians 7:32-35

39.   ST II-II, 152, a. 3, corpus.

40.   Being "anxious about the affairs of the Lord" is not to be seen as simply activity for the Lord; but, according to St. Thomas's definition of virginity, includes freedom from things of the world also for the life of contemplation. The life of virginity provides more freedom to be concerned about the one necessary thing (see Luke 10:42-43). When St. Augustine quotes St. Paul speaking about presenting the Church to Christ as a "chaste virgin" (2 Corinthians 11:2), he speaks about what he calls *"virginitas fidei"* or *"virginitas cordi."* He holds up Mary as the example of this virginity of the heart (*Sermo.* 72/A, 8 [*Sancti Augustini Sermones Post Maurinos Reperti* in *Miscellanea Agostiniana: Testi e Studi,* vol. 1 (Roma: Tipographia Poliglotta Vaticana, 1930), 163]; see also *Sermo.* 341, 4 [PL

39, 1495], *En. in ps.*, 147, 10 [CCSL 40, 2146], *En. in ps.* 75, 16 [CCSL 39, 1048]).

41.   Galot, *Vivre avec le Christ*, 37.

42.   Galot, "Celibato sacerdotale," 366.

43.   As St. Paul emphasizes: "insofar as I now live in the flesh, I live by faith in the Son of God who has loved *me* and given himself up for *me*." (Gal 2:20, emphasis added). The *Catechism* also makes this clear: "Jesus knew and loved us each and all during his life, his agony, and his Passion and gave himself up for each one of us" (CCC, sec. 478).

44.   Jacques Guillet, S.J., "La chasteté de Jésus Christ," in *Christus* 17 (1970), 173.

45.   Galot, "Celibato sacerdotale," 366.

46.   See Mark 10:13-14.

47.   See Luke 7:37-38.

48.   See John 13:25.

49.   Xavier Tilliette, S.J., "The Chastity of Jesus." *Communio* 24 (Spring 1997): 53.

50.   John Paul II, *Man and Woman He Created Them: A Theology of the Body* (Boston: Pauline Books and Media, 2006),185-186, emphasis in original; see also *Gaudium et Spes*, sec. 24.

51.   As Pope Paul VI said, "Wholly in accord with this mission, Christ remained throughout His whole life in the state of celibacy, which signified His total dedication to the service of God and men" (*Sacerdotalis Caelibatus*, in AAS 59 [1967]: n. 21).

52.   Bertrand de Margerie, *Christ for the World* (Cincinnati, OH: Franciscan Press, 1974), 321.

53.   Sicari, 58.

54.   Amato, 501.

55.   Galot, *Theology of the Priesthood*, 230. Betrand de Margerie adds, "It was not fitting that the Son of the Virgin should physically beget a limited number of children, destined in their turn to continue His line; on the contrary, it was for Him to communicate spiritually, without any possible admixture, a participation in His divinely filial life to *all* mankind, including His own ancestors" (319).

56.   Clement of Alexandria, *Strom. III*, chap. 6, par. 49, 3 in *Clemente de Alejandría, Stromata II-III: Conocimiento religioso y continencia auténtica* in *Fuentes Patrísticas*, Vol. 10, ed. Marcelo Merino Rodríguez (Madrid: Editorial Cuidad Nueva, 1998), 387.

57.   Galot, "Celibato sacerdotale," 372. For this reason, one cannot see Jesus' refusal of a human marriage as somehow degrading marriage; in fact, by accepting this supernatural marriage, He reveals the true meaning of human married love: "If Jesus entered the way of celibacy, it is by no means by a lack of appreciation for marriage. Far from underrating the

matrimonial union, he wants to confer upon it a superior value, and bring to it his own spousal love" (Galot, *Vivre avec le Christ*, 40).

58.   James Stafford, "The Eucharistic Foundation of Sacerdotal Celibacy," *Origins* 23 (1993): 215.

59.   Hans Urs von Balthasar, *Our Task: A Report and a Plan*, trans. John Saward (San Francisco: Ignatius Press, 1994), 160.

60.   John Paul II, *Man and Woman He Created Them*, 422, emphasis in original.

61.   Galot, *Vivre avec le Christ*, 38. This is also why Gabriel Jacquemet called Jesus' celibacy essential: "In fact we must quickly insist that it is inconceivable that he could ever have held the idea of making a woman the center of his life. Besides, his consecrated being was not free for these bonds." (765).

62.   Amato, 503.

63.   ST III, 40, a. 3.

64.   Ibid.

65.   St. Thomas is clear that attaining to the perfection of charity requires "that a man wholly withdraw his affections from worldly things" (ST II-II, 186, a. 3, corpus). Jan G. J. van den Eijnden, O.F.M., in his study, *Poverty on the Way to God: Thomas Aquinas on Evangelical Poverty* (Louvain: Peeters, 1994), points out that St. Thomas mentions this aspect every time he speaks about poverty. Aquinas emphasizes that property and wealth are "said to confuse the mind and to cause many solicitudes, because they encourage greed and man has to take care of property which causes solicitudes he would not have were he not to have property" (Eijnden, 101). For St. Thomas's explanation of this teaching, see ST II-II, 188, a. 7, corpus.

66.   Ibid.

67.   *Super Epistolam ad Corinthios lectura*, in *Super epistolas S. Pauli Lectura*, ed. Raffaele Cai (Roma: Marietti, 1953), c. 8, lect. 2.

68.   ST III, 8, 1, ad. 1, emphasis in original, Blackfriars Translation, Vol. 49, trans. Liam Walsh, gen. eds. Thomas Gilby, O.P., and T. C. O'Brien, O.P. (New York: McGraw-Hill Book Co., 1973).

69.   ST III, 40, a. 3.

70.   Ibid. Thomas quotes a homily from the Council of Ephesus by St. Theodotus of Ancyra who says "He chose all that was poor and despicable, all that was of small account and hidden from the majority, that we might recognize His Godhead to have transformed the terrestrial sphere. For this reason did he choose a poor maid for His Mother, a poorer birthplace; for this reason did He live in want. Learn this from the manger" (quoted in ST III, 40, a. 4, corpus).

71.   ST III, 40, a. 3, ad. 3. See also ST III, 35, a. 7, ad 1, where St. Thomas emphasizes the importance of the witness of Christ's poverty as humility, citing St. Paul who said, "God chose the foolish of the world

to shame the wise, and God chose the weak of the world to shame the strong" (1 Cor 1:27).

72.   As St. Thomas says in his commentary on the beatitudes: "Thus, first blessed are the poor, that is the humble, who are the ones that who deem themselves poor; indeed those are truly humble, who deem themselves as poor, not only in exterior things, but also in interior things" (*Lectura Super Matthaeum*, in *Sancti Thomae Aquinatis opera omnia*, ed. Roberto Busa, S.J. [Stuttgart: Frommann-Holzboog, 1979], c. 5, lect. 2).

73.   See Luke 2:7

74.   See Matthew 8:20.

75.   See Matthew 27:35. Both Jean Galot and Luke Buckles quote a famous passage by St. Catherine of Siena meditating on this reality: " . . . he taught you not only with words but by his example as well, from his birth right up to the end of his life. For you he took poverty as his bride, though he was wealth itself by his union with the divine nature, for he is one thing with me and I with him, eternal wealth" (St. Catherine of Siena, *The Dialogue*, trans. Suzanne Noffke, O.P. [Mahwah, NJ: Paulist Press, 1980], 320).

76.   See Mark 10:43-45.

77.   See Matthew 8:20 and Luke 9:58.

78.   Galot, *Vivre avec le Christ*, 148-49.

79.   "The material poverty which characterized the human life of Jesus was a visible expression of the constant interior attitude of self-abnegation with regard to seeking anything apart from the perfect fulfillment of the Father's will in his life." Luke Douglas Buckles, O.P., *The Descent of Divine Love and Mercy: A Study of the Kenosis of Christ in Relation to the Eucharist and the Priesthood in the Writings of St. Catherine of Siena*, S.T.D. diss. Roma: Pontificia Universitas a S. Thoma Aq., 1985, 66.

80.   Galot, *Vivre avec le Christ*, 148.

81.   See, for example, Matthew 4:18-22: "As he was walking by the Sea of Galilee, he saw two brothers, Simon who is called Peter, and his brother Andrew, casting a net into the sea; they were fishermen. He said to them, "Come after me, and I will make you fishers of men." At once they left their nets and followed him. He walked along from there and saw two other brothers, James, the son of Zebedee, and his brother John. They were in a boat, with their father Zebedee, mending their nets. He called them, and immediately they left their boat and their father and followed him." (See also Mark 1:17-20). Luke 5:10-11: "Jesus said to Simon, 'Do not be afraid; from now on you will be catching men.' When they brought their boats to the shore, they left everything and followed him." Luke 5:27-28: "After this he went out and saw a tax collector named Levi sitting at the customs post. He said to him, 'Follow me.' And leaving everything behind, he got up and followed him."

82.   Although all the Gospels mention the importance of poverty for Christ's disciples, Luke's Gospel gives it special prominence: "Luke weaves together from the very beginning this general directive about the attitude of poverty with the particular instruction to those who 'follow' to *sell all* (12:33 f.). For these, perfect poverty is one with perfect obedience: at the call of Christ, they must leave everything (Lk 5:11, 28), must 'renounce all that they have' (14:33), 'sell all that they have and distribute to the poor (18:22), without taking farewells, without burying a father (9:59 ff.)" (Balthasar, *Glory of the Lord*, Vol. VII, 132).

83.   See Mark 10:17-22; Matthew 19:16-22; Luke 18:18-23.

84.   Jean Galot (*Vivre avec le Christ*, 113 ff.) defends strongly his insistence upon the two levels of Jesus' invitation to the young man found in the passage, levels that correspond to the two states of life we see in the Scriptures. He notes that some modern commentators have challenged this traditional exegesis, a position which he finds untenable. They argue that the second invitation to "follow me" is simply a continuation of the first and therefore "selling all" is a command directed to all Christians; see Paul Lamarche, "Les fondements scripturaires de la vie religieuse" in *Vie Consacrée* 41:6 (novembre-décembre, 1969), 321-27, esp. 323; John Burchill, O.P., "Biblical Basis of Religious Life," in *Review for Religious* 36 (1977): 900-917, esp. 903. Our explanation of the passage will demonstrate with Galot what John Paul II affirms: "Christ's words: 'If you wish to be perfect, go, sell what you have, and give to the poor, . . .' clearly bring us into the sphere of the evangelical counsel of poverty, which belongs to the very essence of the religious vocation and profession" (*Redemptionis Donum*, sec. 4), and, therefore, the words mark a special call not given to all.

85.   Ceslas Spicq, O.P., in his work *Agapè dans le Nouveau Testament. Analyse des textes*, vol. I ([Paris: Gabalda, 1958], 82), points out that this is the only place in the Synoptic Gospels where the verb *agape* is predicated of Jesus. Matthew describes the this special invitation with the words: "If you wish to be perfect, go, sell your possessions, and give the money to the poor, and you will have treasure in heaven; then come, follow me" (Mt 19:21), hence the traditional description of those who are invited to selling all in order to follow Christ more intimately as the "state of perfection."

86.   Galot, *Vivre avec le Christ*, 115-116.

87.   Ibid., 118.

88.   See Gisbert Greshake, *The Meaning of Christian Priesthood*, trans. Peadar MacSeumais, S.J. (Westminster, MD: Christian Classics, 1989), 139-140. As Basil Cole, O.P., and Paul Conner, O.P., explain: "Not a single rich person was given Christ's power, the authority of apostleship in his Kingdom, and the rich young man was told to give his wealth to the poor and to adopt the apostles' lifestyle if he would become perfect" (149).

89.   See Matthew 5:3 and Luke 6:20.

90.   "The instructions he sends out to his disciples are almost incomprehensibly extreme (Mt 19:9). There was no place in the Old Testament for such a voluntary poverty taken literally" (Hans Urs von Balthasar, "The Poverty of Christ," *Communio* 13.3 [Fall 1986]: 197). See also Burchill, "Biblical Basis for Religious Life," 913.

91.   As Balthasar explains, "This unconditional leaving of all things is the presupposition of the necessary readiness for all things on the part of the disciple ('Master, I will follow you wherever you go,' Mt 8:19): not only the general readiness 'with loins girt' for the approaching kingdom of God (Lk 12:35ff), but already in the present the readiness to let oneself be sent out by Jesus 'like sheep among wolves' (Mt 10:16) in the service of the coming kingdom 'without pay' and without means of support (10:8-10), and indeed unprepared spiritually, because the Spirit will inspire what is needed (10:19f.)" (*Glory of the Lord*, Vol. VII, 133). Balthasar notes that though Jesus does not ask anything of His disciples that He has not already embraced, "These unheard-of requirements, seemingly inhuman, can be based upon only one presupposition—that Jesus himself is the one who is *absolutely poor*. How could he make such demands, unless he had first accomplished this archetypically, representatively and inclusively?" (Ibid., emphasis in original).

92.   See Matthew 11:29.

93.   See Luke 20:26-28; Mark 10:42-45.

94.   *De Beatitudinibus*, 1, in *Gregorii Nysseni: De Oratione Dominica, De Beatitudinibus*, ed. Johannes F. Callahan (New York: Brill, 1992), 84. This poverty of spirit in Jesus demonstrated in His accepting of human limitations in the Incarnation has often been the mediation of spiritual theologians. As, for example, Reginald Garrigou-Lagrange, O.P., wrote, "He wished to be rendered like His brethren in all things, sin excepted; even more, He wished to be born among the poor. He was cold and hungry, like a man of humble condition. He was tired and worn out, as we are and more than we are" (*The Three Ages of the Interior Life*, vol. 2, trans. Sr. Timothea Doyle, O.P. [St. Louis: Herder Book Co., 1951], 128-29).

95.   Beyer, "Valori essenziali," 45-46.

96.   See 2 Corinthians 5:21; Galatians 3:13; Romans 8:3; 1 Peter 2:2.

97.   See Mark 15:34.

98.   Edward Schillebeeckx, *Christ the Sacrament of the Encounter with God* (Kansas City: Sheed & Ward, 1963), 27, emphasis in original. Schillebeeckx tries to explain here what theologians have often struggled to explain, the final kenosis of the Cross. Christ, in order to redeem us, had to experience in some way the poverty of sin, which is separation from God. Christ's own cry of dereliction from the Cross testifies to this (Matthew 15:34). John Paul II has said in a catechetical address on the "cry of dereliction" from the Cross that "if sin is separation from God, Jesus

had to experience, in the crisis of his union with the Father, a suffering proportionate to that separation" (General Audience: 30 November, in *L'Osservatore Romano* 49 [5 December 1988]: 15). Or, as the Holy Father said in *Salvifici Doloris*: "Together with this horrible weight, *encompassing the 'entire' evil of the* turning *away from God* which is contained in sin, Christ, through the divine depth of his filial union with the Father, perceives in a humanly inexpressible way *this suffering which is the separation,* the rejection *by the Father,* the estrangement from God" (*Salvifici doloris,* in AAS 76 [1984]: n. 18, emphasis in original). Yet, also here, it is important to remember what St. Thomas argues, that even though Christ suffered in His "whole soul," because of who He was, He could not be completely separated from the Father. Therefore, St. Thomas stated that Christ still enjoyed the Beatific Vision in his "higher reason" (ST III, 46, a. 7 and 8). Again, St. John Paul II explains why: "If Jesus feels abandoned by the Father, he knows however that it is not really so. He himself said: 'I and the Father are one' (Jn 10:30). . . . Dominant in his mind Jesus has the clear vision of God and the certainty of his union with the Father. But in the sphere bordering on the senses, and therefore more subject to the impressions, emotions and influences of the internal and external experiences of pain, Jesus' human soul is reduced to a wasteland, and he no longer feels the 'presence' of the Father, but he undergoes the tragic experience of the most complete desolation" (General Audience: 30 November, 1).

99.   See Matthew 5:3.

100.   See Luke 14:10.

101.   See Matthew 18:3-5.

102.   ST III, 40, a. 3, ad. 3.

103.   Raniero Cantalamessa, O.F.M. Cap., *Poverty* (New York: Alba House, 1997), 94.

104.   Balthasar, *Glory of the Lord,* Vol. VII, 132, emphasis in original. Balthasar illustrates that this state of total abandonment is especially the call of those who share Christ's way of life in the *sequela Christi*: "This state becomes the place where one as a poor man may, indeed must, entrust oneself, without care for the next day, to the care of the Father (Mt 6:25-34)" ("The Poverty of Christ," 197).

105.   Heidi Böhler, *I consigli evangelici in prospettiva trinitaria: Sintesi dottrinale* (Milano: San Paolo, 1993), 20.

106.   *Super Epistolam ad Corinthios lectura,* c. 8, lect. 2.

107.   John 12:24.

108.   All are called to the fundamental recognition that their whole life ultimately belongs to God. As St. Paul says, "None of us lives for oneself, and no one dies for oneself. For if we live, we live for the Lord, and if we die, we die for the Lord; so then, whether we live or die, we are the Lord's" (Rom 14:7-8). Yet, it is clear that in this obedience, Christ calls some to a more radical self-emptying in the *sequela Christi* through a more

explicit embrace of the life of the counsels. Not all are called to this intimate following as we see in the example of the Gerasene demoniac who, when Jesus was leaving the Decapolis, "pleaded to remain with him." Yet Jesus did not invite him to the *sequela*: "But he would not permit him but told him instead, 'Go home to your family and announce to them all that the Lord in his pity has done for you'" (Mk 5:18-19). As Balthasar points out, this does not mean that those who are not called to the *sequela Christi* are not called to the perfection of love: "True love is radically and fundamentally disposed to renounce everything. . . . It is ready to follow any path. . . . It is ready to follow the way of the commandments as the way of the counsels. Such a love is perfect even when the ultimate gift is not required of it. . . . They accept it as a sacrifice not to have been called upon to sacrifice all they were willing to sacrifice" (*Christian State of Life*, 55).

109.　Gianfranco Ghirlanda, S.J., *Il diritto nella Chiesa: mistero di communione* (Milan: San Paolo, 1993), 181; see *Vita Consecrata*, 18; 22; 23; 31; 32. Here Ghirlanda is speaking about the consecrated life; yet, as we will demonstrate in chapter 7, these same values are applicable to the priest.

110.　See McGovern, who says: "Christ's supreme priestly act is then a spousal one, as St. Paul explains when he encourages husbands and wives to love each other 'as Christ loved the Church and gave himself up for her' (Eph 5:25). This is why 'Christ stands 'before' the Church, and 'nourishes and cherishes her' (Eph 5:29), giving his life for her' (PDV 22)" (*Priestly Identity*, 113).

111.　Erlangen Otto Procksch, "ἁγιάζω," in *Theological Dictionary of the New Testament*, ed. Gerhard Kittel (Grand Rapids: Eerdmans, 1968), 111. Procksch says, "In the LXX ἁγιάζειν is usually rendering the root (Hebrew: "Kadosh"), so that we are everywhere concerned with a cultic state" (Ibid.).

112.　See Hebrews 10 which uses the word ἁγιάζω three times when describing Christ as the priest who sanctifies us through His Death on the Cross.

113.　*Directory*, 81.

114.　Revelation 21:9.

115.　*Man and Woman He Created Them*, 478, emphasis in original.

116.　See p. 151 above. As Balthasar says, "In its essence, Christ's high priesthood is characterized by his self-sacrifice (Heb 9:12-14), hence, by an inward priesthood" ("Thoughts on the Priesthood of Women," *Communio* 23 [Winter 1996]: 703).

117.　Robert Pesarchick, *The Trinitarian Foundation of Human Sexuality as Revealed by Christ According to Hans Urs von Balthasar: The Revelatory Significance of the Male Christ and the Male Ministerial Priesthood*, in Tesi Gregoriana Serie Teologia, vol. 63 (Roma: Gregorian University, 2000), 253.

118.　Balthasar, *Christian State of Life*, 252.

119.   Ibid., emphasis in original.

120.   *A Spiritual Theology of the Priesthood: The Mystery of Christ and the Mission of the Priest* (Washington, DC: Catholic University of America Press, 1998), 2.

121.   See John 10:11.

122.   As Cole and Conner comment: "Pastoral charity, the pope continues, is itself best understood as the spousal love of Christ, the bridegroom, for his bride, the Church (see PDV 22)." (Basil Cole, O.P., and Paul Conner, O.P., *Christian Totality: Theology of the Consecrated Life*, revised edition [Mumbai, India: St. Paul's, 1997], 321).

123.   See Ephesians 5:25.

124.   *Pastores Daho Vobis*, sec. 30.

125.   See Philippians 2.

CHAPTER 5: THE PRIEST AS A LIVING IMAGE OF CHRIST

Through the priest's consecration at ordination, he is configured in a special way to Christ for the purpose of his mission. This sacramental configuration, which makes the priest a representative of Christ, also makes him a representative of Christ the Bridegroom.[1] The Sacrament of Holy Orders makes the priest a representative of Christ through sacramental character. This character, which configures the priest to Christ, makes the priest a living instrument. It consecrates him objectively, making him a participant in the consecration and mission of Christ, and it calls forth from him a subjective response to this consecration. This subjective response is expressed by pastoral charity, which makes the priest a living image of Christ the Good Shepherd and Bridegroom. The sacramental grace of Holy Orders, which complements the sacramental character and normally is received with it in ordination, allows the priest to become more and more subjectively, in his person, what he is objectively by virtue of his ordination. Responding to this grace through the self-offering of pastoral charity, he becomes a "living and transparent image of Christ the priest."[2]

The Priest as a Representative of Christ

The purpose of the Sacrament of Holy Orders is to continue Christ's presence in the Church. More specifically, it is demanded by the very nature of the Church's divine constitution through the sacraments that the ministerial priesthood, exercised in various degrees, makes present Christ, the head and shepherd of His Church. Of course, it is true that all Christians are representatives of Christ, and they participate in the priesthood of Christ by virtue of their baptism. By virtue of this baptismal consecration, they are called to make Christ present in the world as priest, prophet, and king and to learn to make their own lives a sacrificial offering united with Christ's offering on the Cross.[3] Yet this representation of Christ in the baptized is distinct from the representation of the ministerial priest in the sacrament. Through the Sacrament of Holy Orders, men are given a special participation in Christ's priesthood to make His saving power present by acting *in persona Christi capitis*. Vatican II made clear that this ministerial priesthood differs in essence and not only in degree from the common priesthood of the faithful because the ministerial priesthood has the specific duty of making Christ present in the sacraments and in the Church.[4] As the 1971 Synod of Bishops clearly explained:

> The priestly ministry of the New Testament, which continues Christ's function as mediator . . . alone perpetuates the essential work of the Apostles: by effectively proclaiming the Gospel, by gathering together and leading the community, by remitting sins, and especially by celebrating the Eucharist it makes Christ, the head of the community, present in the exercise

of his work of redeeming mankind and glorifying God perfectly."[5]

As the bishops make clear, Christ bestowed upon His Apostles His three-fold ministry of shepherding, teaching, and sanctifying which they, in turn, handed on to their successors.[6] This ministry requires them to represent Him. The representational nature of the priesthood can already be observed in the New Testament where we see that Christ makes His Apostles participate in His own mission and ministry. Jesus, who represented the Father in such a way that He made Him present,[7] sends His own Apostles out with the mission and power to represent Him and to make Him present. As Jesus says when He sends out His disciples, "Whoever listens to you listens to me. Whoever rejects you rejects me. And whoever rejects me rejects the one who sent me" (Lk 10:16). Or as He says when He rises from the dead in John's Gospel: "As the Father has sent me, so I send you" (Jn 20:21).[8] This representational role of the ministerial priesthood is essential for the Church's mission. The healing power and salvific authority of Christ must remain present to His Church through the hierarchy as a permanent and living foundation of the Church.[9] This apostolic mission protects the absolute priority of Christ in the Church. As Gisbert Greshake writes:

> Christ communicates himself, his word and the gifts of his Spirit to us "sacramentally" that is, in signs which he uses and to which he gives power, signs which point to his person and "represent" him, produce his effective presence. Among these mediating signs apostolic office is primary and essential. In it the permanent priority of

Christ to the people of God is continued and becomes the permanent foundation of the Church.[10]

New covenant priestly ministry is a participation in and continuation of the mission of Christ in the Church. Priests, through the Sacrament of Holy Orders, participate with their bishops in the kingly, prophetic, and priestly role passed on through the Apostles and their successors.[11] As St. John Paul II said, "The priest finds the full truth of his identity in being a derivation, a specific participation in and continuation of Christ himself, the one high priest of the new and eternal covenant."[12] It is the priest's role to represent Christ—that is, to make Christ visible in the Church. This understanding of the priest as a representative of Christ derives from a central Church teaching about the priesthood: the priest acts *in persona Christi.*

The phrase *"in persona Christi"* has its roots in the Scriptures. The Greek word *apostolein*, which refers to the sending, is rooted in a Hebrew idea of *shaliach*, which means missionary or one sent. This idea has the connotation of an ambassador or representative; as Walter Kasper says:

> The idea of representation is found in another form in the New Testament, namely, in the shaliach (missionary) formulae that are inseparably linked to the concept of apostle. In Jewish Law, the one sent has the same status as the one who sends him. This is why Jesus can say: "He who hears you hears me, and he who rejects you rejects me, and he who rejects me rejects him who sent me" (Lk 10:16).[13]

A similar idea can be seen in the way St. Paul speaks about himself. Scholars cite 2 Corinthians 5:20 where St. Paul says, "So we are ambassadors for Christ, as if God were appealing through us. We implore you on behalf of Christ, be reconciled to God" Here, St. Paul says that he is exhorting the Corinthians because "Christ . . . has given us the ministry of reconciliation . . . entrusting to us the message of reconciliation" (2 Cor 5:18-19). Aimé-Georges Martimort argues that this is an early version of the concept in persona Christi where the apostle is understood as a representative of Christ: "The voice of the apostle expresses God's own voice, or rather God speaks the word of reconciliation through the apostle's mouth."[14]

The Fathers of the Church further develop this sacramental understanding of the priest or bishop acting in Christ's person. The earliest and most explicit reference is found in St. Cyprian's phrase "vice Christi"—that is, in place of, in one's stead. Cyprian writes a letter explaining why wine must be used in the celebration of the Eucharist, even though the time of persecution made the use of wine potentially dangerous. Despite the danger, the priest must do exactly what Christ does in the Eucharist, since he acts in His stead. St. Cyprian says:

> If our Lord and God, Christ Jesus, is Himself the high priest of God the Father, and offered Himself as a sacrifice to the Father, and commanded this to be done for a memorial of Himself, certainly that priest truly performs his office in the place of Christ (vice Christi) who imitates what Christ did, and then offers in the Church to God the Father a real and complete

sacrifice, when he begins to offer as he sees Christ Himself offered."[15]

The theological meaning is clear. It is by virtue of being *in persona Christi* that the priest offers the same sacrifice of Christ offering it to God in the Church.

St. Augustine strongly affirms the direct action of Christ Himself through the person of the minister when he is debating with the Donatists. They are arguing that an unholy priest cannot validly perform the sacraments, but Augustine makes the point that regardless of the holiness of the priest, he is acting in Christ's person and, so, Christ Himself is acting: "When Judas baptized, Christ baptized. Therefore if a drunkard baptized, the one who was baptized by a murderer, the one who was baptized by an adulterer, if the baptism was of Christ, Christ baptized."[16] We have to say that in the patristic period, the idea of *in persona Christi* is implicit in the teaching of many Fathers who consistently speak about the bishop as an icon or image of Christ or the Father.[17]

St. Thomas Aquinas develops this patristic idea and makes the formula a classic one. He shows how "Christ is the fountain-head (fons) of the entire priesthood," and for St. Thomas the fact that the priest acts "in persona Christi" marks the distinctive aspect of the New Covenant priesthood: "for the priest of the Old Law was a figure of Him; while the priest of the New Law works in His person (*in persona ipsius operatur*)."[18] For St. Thomas, this teaching is required by the very nature of the sacraments as effective signs of grace—that is, signs that cause what they signify. Sacraments are truly effective means of grace only because Christ with His power acts through them: "Christ himself perfects all the sacraments: it is He who baptizes; it is He who forgives sins; it is He, the true priest, who offered Himself on the altar of the cross, and by whose power His body is daily consecrated on the altar."[19] The sacraments are not just objects we receive; they are, in fact, actions of God through His ministers. These actions require that the priest act as an instrument because it is through the instrumentality of the priest that the matter and form are united into the life-giving action. This is why the priest's intention is required for the validity of the sacrament, and through intending this action, he exercises a true instrumental power.[20] Of course this instrumental power would be nothing if Christ Himself were not the chief cause of the sacraments.[21]

This can be seen most clearly in the Eucharist where the sacrifice of Christ on the Cross is re-presented. No one but Christ would be capable of re-presenting this offering, but Christ is not physically present. Therefore, it is required that a human being do this, acting in Jesus' power, in His person:

> Such is the dignity of this sacrament that it is performed only as in the person of Christ. Whoever performs any act in another's stead (*in persona alterius*), must do so by the power bestowed by such a one. But as the power of receiving this sacrament is conceded by Christ to the baptized person, so likewise the power of consecrating this sacrament on Christ's behalf is bestowed upon the priest at his ordination.[22]

Thus, in the Sacrament of the Eucharist, we see the truest expression, the heart of the meaning of *in persona Christi* for St. Thomas. The Eucharist emphasizes the priestly role even more than the other sacraments do because "the form of this sacrament is pronounced as if Christ were speaking in person, so that it is given to be understood that the minister does nothing in perfecting this sacrament, except to pronounce the words of Christ."[23] In the words of consecration, it is as if the priest himself becomes transparent to Christ. As Bernard Marliangeas comments in his important study, "This representative effaces himself in some way before the one whom he represents, so that it is no longer he but the one 'represented' who speaks and acts in person. Now this is verified par excellence in the case of the words of consecration."[24]

Although, for St. Thomas, the priest's actions *in persona Christi* are most properly in the Eucharist, there are some rare but significant exceptions where St. Thomas also speaks about some juridical actions of a prelate done in the person of Christ.[25] This follows for Thomas because the bishop leads in the person of Christ the head: "Christ is the Head of the Church by His own power and authority; while others are called heads, as taking Christ's place (*inquantum vicem gerunt Christi*)."[26] From this, we will see the roots of a natural expansion that will only become clear at Vatican II. As Martimort says, priests "act in the Lord's name, they carry out his role, they take his place and that not only when they exercise the sacramental ministry proper, but also in the whole of their ecclesial activity."[27]

The Second Vatican Council emphasizes that the priest acts *in persona Christi* in numerous places.[28] What is noteworthy about the Council's treatment of the phrase is the expanded use it is given. The Council fathers affirm the Thomistic insight that the priest acts *in persona Christi* in the Eucharist,[29] but they add that the bishop and the priest act *in persona Christi* also when they are governing and teaching.[30] *Lumen*

Gentium, section 21, affirms that bishops "take on the functions of Christ the teacher, shepherd and pontiff and act in his person." The Council fathers use the phrase again, in section 28 of the same document, when explaining that although presbyters do not share the fullness of the priesthood of Christ, they still participate in the priesthood of Christ. From an analysis of the *Acta Synodalia*, Sara Butler points out that "Lumen gentium, art. 28, reflects the Council's deliberate intention to affirm that presbyteral priesthood derives from Christ, that the priest participates in his function as Mediator and acts in his person, especially—but not exclusively—in the Eucharistic liturgy."[31]

The expansion in the use *of in persona Christi* becomes even clearer in *Presbyterorum Ordinis* when the Council fathers use the phrase *in persona Christi capitis*. It seems the addition of the term *capitis* was desired for two reasons. First, it would clarify the distinction between the priesthood of the laity and the ministerial priesthood. Representation *in persona Christi* could in some way be applied to all Christians, but *in persona Christi capitis* is specifically limited to the ministerial priesthood. Walter Cardinal Kasper explains, "as such, it is a *repraesentatio* of the ministry that Jesus Christ, its Head, performs for the Church, keeping it alive, nourishing it, purifying, sanctifying, leading, guiding, governing, unifying it, and keeping it together. The official ministry is not only *repraesentatio* Christi in some general sense; it is *repraesentatio Christi capitis Ecclesiae*."[32] In the second place, the expansion was desired so as not to limit the understanding of the priest's or bishop's acting *in persona Christi* only to the Eucharist or the sacraments. As Lorenzo Loppa details, the debates that gave birth to section 2 of *Presbyterorum Ordinis* emphasized that "there is an action of Christ the head in his body to build it up, to guide it, and to sanctify it, and the priests, together with the bishops, are the living sacraments and living instruments by means of which Christ continues to exercise his mission and his authority as head."[33] The text of *Presbyterorum Ordinis* makes this expansion of the meaning of the phrase clear:

> As it is joined to the episcopal order, the priesthood shares in the authority with which Christ himself constitutes, sanctifies and rules his body. . . . Priests are sealed with a special mark by the anointing of the Holy Spirit, and thus are patterned to the priesthood of Christ, so that they may be able to act in the person of Christ, the head of the body.[34]

Those who act *in persona Christi capitis* share in the work of shepherding the Church; they exercise the ministry of ruling, teaching, and sanctifying for the sake of the others. This representation of Christ *in persona Christi capitis* is not separate from the priest's role at the Eucharist, but rather is derived from it. As the whole life of the Church centers around the Eucharist—"the other sacraments and indeed all ecclesiastical ministries and works of the apostolate are bound up with the Eucharist and are directed towards it"[35]—so also the sanctifying, teaching, and shepherding roles of the bishop and priest find their source and summit in the Eucharist. Thus, it is because they represent Christ at the moment when the Church is most herself in the Eucharist that bishops and priests act *in persona Christi capitis*, as shepherds, teachers, and sanctifiers in the entire life of the Church. Thus, the priest's representation of Christ in the Church and on behalf of the Church is unique because of his unique role in the Eucharist.

As Martimort explains, "The priest of Jesus Christ cannot be defined uniquely from his liturgical duties, of which the consecration of the Eucharist is the principal . . . yet he cannot be understood without this. He is the one that is able to bring evangelization to its culmination: Baptism and Eucharist."[36]

It should be noted that this participation in the priesthood of Christ such that the priest acts *in persona Christi capitis* is for the sake of the Church. As *Lumen Gentium*, section 10, makes clear, the two participations in the priesthood of Christ are "ordered one to another," and, thus, the ministerial priest is essentially linked to the Church. Therefore, the priest cannot be understood in isolation, nor can the priesthood be defined only in relationship to Christ—even if this relationship is "the absolute key."[37] The priest must also be understood in his relationship to the Church. Cardinal Ratzinger argued that this was a "new" emphasis of Vatican II. In discussing the document *Presbyterorum Ordinis*, he says, "what we may see as being new, by contrast with Trent, is the marked insistence on interrelations in the Church and on the communal journey of the whole Church, in the context of which this classic vision is set."[38]

This relationship of the priesthood to Christ and the Church can be seen in the priest's dual representation. The priest not only acts *in persona Christi*, but also *in persona Ecclesiae*. As *Lumen Gentium* explains, the priest also offers the Eucharist in the name of the Church: "The ministerial priest, by the sacred power he enjoys, teaches and rules the priestly people; acting in the person of Christ, he makes present the eucharistic sacrifice, and offers it to God in the name of all the people."[39] Of course, this representation of the priest is founded on Christ's priestly mediation. Christ not only represented the Father to His people, but also represented the people to the Father. Both mediations are contained in His life and Death, and the priest also fulfills both mediations in his life and ministry. However, there is an important connection between these two ways the priest is a representative: it is precisely because the ministerial priest is conformed through ordination to the priesthood of Christ that he also can act and speak to God *in persona Ecclesiae*. Benedict Ashley, O.P., explains how these two aspects of the priest's representation go together:

> The two aspects of the priestly ministry are complementary and inseparable, as they must be in a mediator. Yet the principal reality symbolized by the priest as mediator is not in the Church he leads in prayer to God, but Christ the Mediator without whose grace no prayer and no sacrament is efficacious. The Bishop in ordaining acts not simply as an agent of the Church, but as an instrument of Christ who alone can incorporate the candidate through the sacramental character into the priestly college. Thus it is not primarily because he represents the people that an ordained priest represents Christ when he leads the people in prayer, but because through ordination he represents Christ that he is empowered to lead them.[40]

The Sacramental Character of Holy Orders

The priest is able to carry out this sacramental and ecclesial role *in persona Christi capitis* because he is configured to Christ through ordination in which his soul is marked with a sacramental character. As *Presbyterorum Ordinis* says, "Through that sacrament priests by the anointing of the Holy Spirit are signed with a special character and so are configured to Christ the priest in such a way that they are able to act in the person of Christ the head."[41] This indelible spiritual mark cannot be repeated or temporarily conferred.[42] Vatican II, when speaking about the character imprinted in the Sacrament of Baptism,[43] cites St. Thomas where he says that the character is an instrumental spiritual power:

> The sacraments of the New Law produce a character, in so far as by them we are deputed to the worship of God according to the rite of the Christian religion. . . . Now the worship of God consists either in receiving Divine gifts, or in bestowing them on others. And for both these purposes some power is needed; for to bestow something on others, active power is necessary; and in order to receive, we need a passive power. Consequently, a character signifies a certain spiritual power ordained unto things pertaining to the Divine worship.
>
> But it must be observed that this spiritual power is instrumental: as we have stated above (q. 62, a. 4) of the virtue which is in the sacraments. For to have a sacramental character belongs to God's ministers: and a minister is a kind of instrument.[44]

The character can be understood as an instrumental power that enables the person to do what would otherwise be impossible to him or her. This is because through sacramental character, the Christian is given a participation in the priesthood of Christ.[45] Specifically referring to the character of Holy Orders, we can say that it is through the sacramental character that "the priest is given a *deputatio* and receives a spiritual power in order to do God's work *in persona Christi et*

Ecclesiae."[46] Jean-Hervé Nicolas summarizes well the Thomistic understanding adopted by the Church:

> The character is a power which authorizes the Christian to receive or to effect sacramental actions. The sacrament is an action of the minister, and its efficaciousness depends, not only on the institution of Christ who has made in it an efficacious sign of sanctification, but also on the sacramental power that the one who confers them possesses or does not possess.[47]

Although the roots of the teaching on character can be found in the Scriptures and from the early church Fathers,[48] St. Augustine is the first to assert that ordination imprints a permanent character on the soul. In his debate with the Donatists, he uses sacramental character to affirm the earlier tradition that ordination cannot be repeated.[49] His doctrine is rooted in the idea that sacramental character is a kind of personal belonging to Christ, a configuration to him that cannot be undone. Central to Augustine's debate with the Donatists was the idea that the effectiveness of the sacraments does not depend on the holiness of the minister. Rather, because of the character, God can even work through an unholy priest or bishop.[50] This essential teaching on character guarantees the effectiveness of the sacraments and, therefore, the very life of the Church, by guaranteeing the link between the priest and Christ. As Nicolas illustrates, the sacramental action "depends before all else on this sacramental designation [the character], which assures the Church and each of its members that when the one who has received it ritually performs the sacramental action, it is Christ the priest who performs it through him."[51] Here, we see how the ontological aspect of the priestly ministry is, in fact, a great gift because it promises the faithful and the priest that, no matter how weak the minister, God's power continues to work. As Cardinal Kasper says:

> For many priests who feel unequal to the high claims that their ministry imposes on them—and for what priest would this not be the case?—precisely this "ontological" understanding is a help and a consolation, because they can say to themselves that the salvation of their communities and of the people committed to them does not ultimately depend on their own accomplishments and their own success. This is a consolation, as well, for many communities.[52]

The sacramental character also shows us another link between the priest and the community. The purpose of the character is not for a kind of status in the Church, but most clearly for the sake of the mission with which the priest is entrusted. This is a mission the whole Church needs:

> Without this working of the Spirit of Christ in the members, purely through the objective, sacramental and official mode of action, nothing in the body of Christ is built up and established. The whole objective and official element is simply the substructure and means to bring forth the subjective form of Christ in each Christian.[53]

That being said, it is important to remember that the priest is not an inert instrument or an inanimate sign. As St. John Paul II said, "indeed, the priest is chosen by Christ not as an 'object' but as a 'person.' In other words, he is not inert and passive, but rather is a 'living instrument,'"[54]

The character is what empowers the priest to be an instrument who acts *in persona Christi capitis* and *in persona Ecclesiae*; however, because he is marked with this character and given this sacred power, the priest becomes a sign or a sacrament of Christ in the Church. The priest needs to remember that because of this, his whole life is meant to be a living sign. The priest accomplishes objectively holy actions when he celebrates the sacraments; but, since he is a person, a living instrument, his subjective actions may or may not be holy. His subjective holiness depends on the conformation of his life to the one whose actions he performs. The dignity of his holy actions calls forth from the priest holiness. As St. Thomas says, this "most august ministry of serving Christ Himself in the sacrament of the altar . . . requires a greater inward holiness."[55] This is what St. Paul means when he calls himself a steward "of the mysteries of God" and points out that "it is of course required of stewards that they be found trustworthy" (1 Cor 4:1-2).

Since the priest is a living instrument, his ministry does depend in some measure on his personal holiness, even though his sins do not invalidate the sacraments. First of all, his holiness affects the disposition of the people who receive the sacraments. Although the sacraments are always effective by their valid celebration *ex opere operato*, the grace received in the sacraments is conditioned by the disposition of the recipients,[56] and the holiness of the priest can play an important role in helping the recipients to be properly disposed. If the priest witnesses the power of the sacraments through his own holiness, it will help the people to understand more how they should approach the sacraments. St. John Paul II explains:

There can be no doubt that the exercise of the priestly ministry, especially in the celebration of the sacraments, receives its saving effects from the action of Christ himself who becomes present in the sacraments. But so as to emphasize the gratuitous nature of salvation which makes a person both "saved" and a "savior"—always and only in Christ—God's plan has ordained that the efficacy of the exercise of the ministry is also conditioned by a greater or lesser human receptivity and participation. In particular, the greater or lesser degree of the holiness of the minister has a real effect on the proclamation of the word, the celebration of the sacraments and the leadership of the community in charity.[57]

Also, the effectiveness of many of the priest's non-sacramental duties is not guaranteed *ex opere operato* (e.g., his preaching, teaching, guiding, counseling, visiting, and other actions in his ministry). The degree to which these actions bring God's grace often depends upon the priest's personal conformity with Christ. Vatican II emphasized this point:

> Holiness does much for priests in carrying on a fruitful ministry. Although divine grace could use unworthy ministers to effect the work of salvation, yet for the most part God chooses, to show forth his wonders, those who are more open to the power and direction of the Holy Spirit, and who can by reason of their close union with Christ and their holiness of life say with St. Paul: "And yet I am alive; or rather, not I; it is Christ that lives in me" (Gal 2:20).[58]

Given this truth that the sacramental character makes the priest a living instrument of Christ, and the call to holiness which flows from this, the character cannot be considered only as a capacity to engage in certain sacramental activities. The character is not something only external or functional, rather the Tradition speaks about the sacramental character as a configuration of the priest's very being. As Thomas McGovern says, "it is primarily a relationship to God by which Christ takes possession of the being of the priest to imprint his own reflection on him."[59] In his book *La Nature du Caractère Sacramentel,* Jean Galot argues that the character is understood as a mark that is a reflection of God. He traces the original meaning of the Greek word "character" back to this idea of a likeness, an image, or a figure impressed upon the soul. He points out that St. Thomas and other medieval theologians reference the only place the word is used in the Bible, in Hebrews 1:3: "He is the reflection of God's glory and the exact imprint (χαρακτὴρ) of God's very being."[60] Character here expresses the resemblance or likeness of the Son to the Father. Galot comments, "Thus the first and the most far-reaching foundation of the sacramental character resides in the very person of the Son, 'character' of the substance of the Father; Christ transmits His resemblance to us [priests], makes of us His image as He Himself is the image of the Father."[61] The character marks the priest in his inner being and makes the priest belong to Christ in a new way. Here, you see how priesthood must be more than just performing certain functions; it involves the whole life of the priest. Through ordination, he is grasped by Christ, configured to Him, and called to become a man of God, Christ's own unique representative. As Jean Galot comments:

If the priest is to be capable of doing God's work, he must belong to God with his whole self. It is not in vain that he is called not merely God's messenger, but the man of God. Grasped by God in his whole being, he can radiate and communicate God by everything he is.[62]

Through ordination, the priest's whole life is taken for a priestly purpose. This flows from the permanent nature of the character; he is always a priest, even when doing ordinary things. And the character, therefore, makes it incongruent if his life is not in accordance with his nature. As St. John Paul II said, "in him everything, even what is secular, must become priestly as in Jesus, who was always a priest, and always acted as a priest, in all the expressions of his life."[63] The priestly character with which the man is marked in his being calls forth from him a life in conformity with the love of Christ. For the priest, this means a life of pastoral charity.

The Consecration and Mission of the Priest

When Vatican II speaks about the priest's interior conformation worked by the Sacrament of Holy Orders through the character, it calls it a "consecration." One could argue that the central theme of Vatican II's document on the priesthood is the "consecration and mission" of the priest.[64] St. John Paul II picked up this theme and made it central to his post synodal apostolic exhortation *Pastores Dabo Vobis*. When we come to understand the consecration and mission of the priest, we will see the priest's call to become a living image of Jesus Christ.

The consecration and the mission of the priest is another way to explain some aspects of the priesthood we have already seen. It is through the priestly consecration that the priest is signed with sacramental character and configured to Christ so that he can act in His person and with His power. As St. John Paul II explains:

> Indeed, the priest, by virtue of the consecration which he receives in the sacrament of orders, is sent forth by the Father through the mediatorship of Jesus Christ, to whom he is configured in a special way as head and shepherd of his people, in order to live and work by the power of the Holy Spirit in service of the Church and for the salvation of the world.[65]

All Christians are consecrated through the Sacrament of Baptism and participate in Christ's mission, but priests receive a special consecration for their unique work. The consecration and mission of the priest is a unique participation in Christ's priestly consecration and mission. Vatican II describes the priest's participation in Christ's consecration and mission this way:

> Christ, whom the Father sanctified or consecrated and sent into the world (Jn 10:36), "gave himself for us to redeem us from all iniquity and to purify for himself a people of his own who are zealous for good deeds" (Tit 2:14), and in this way through his passion entered into his glory (Lk 24:26). In a similar way, priests, who are consecrated by the anointing of the Holy Spirit and sent by Christ, mortify the works of the flesh in themselves and dedicate themselves completely to the service of people, and so are able, in the holiness with which they have been enriched in Christ, to make progress towards the perfect man (Eph 4:13).[66]

Three things are explained here: first, Christ's own priestly consecration and mission; second, the priest's participation in that consecration and mission; and, third, the demands this makes on the priest's life. To understand fully the meaning of the priest's consecration and mission, we must explain these three dimensions.

Christ's consecration and mission has two dimensions: an objective one and a subjective one. Objectively, Christ is sanctified, sent by the Father; and, subjectively, he responds by consecrating Himself to His mission through the gift of His life. The objective consecration and sending can be seen in the Incarnation when Christ's humanity is sanctified by God through its union with the divinity.[67] Gianfranco Ghirlanda explains this consecration:

> The humanity of Christ, in virtue of the hypostatic union, is the creaturely reality that is supremely and primarily consecrated by God, in that, completely saved from the corruption of sin and death, it fully enters into the divine sphere. The initiative is by the Father, who, in the fullness of the gift of the Spirit, totally consecrates the humanity of the Son (Mt 3:16-17; Lk 4:18-19), such that Christ manifests his being Son also in His humanity. In this divine consecration the humanity of Christ is consecrated to the worship of the Father, to bring to the Father the world that he had lost.[68]

This objective consecration for the sake of mission calls forth from Christ a subjective response. Jesus speaks about the subjective aspect of this consecration in John 17:15-19. Here, we see that Christ consecrates Himself for the sake of the world to fulfill His salvific mission: "And I consecrate myself for them, so that they also may be consecrated in truth" (Jn 17:19). The sanctification or consecration of Jesus in this passage refers to His mission to make Himself the priest and the victim of our redemptive sacrifice. Andre Feuillet, P.S.S., in his study of this high priestly prayer, points out:

> the verb 'sanctify' (*hagiazein*) does not mean moral sanctification or a setting apart for a mission, but a setting apart for sacrifice. The proper translation, therefore, is, "For their sake I consecrate myself," and it is another allusion to Isaiah 53:10 where the Servant offers himself as an expiatory victim.[69]

Ghirlanda explains how this describes Christ's subjective response, His act of true and perfect worship for the Father, His response to the Father's objective consecration:

> To this act of the Father, the Son responds in a personal way, consecrating himself to the Father for the redemption of the world. With this *personal consecration* Christ freely accepts the consecration-mission of the Father, so that all of humanity and all the creation can be consecrated to the Father in him (Jn 17:15-19). Christ expresses the totality of the consecration to the Father in the oblation of the cross. The sacrifice of the cross has the maximum power of consecration, because it is the exercise of the supreme, unique, and eternal priesthood, of which Christ is the priest, altar and victim. In this is expressed as an act of personal offering the supreme testimony of the absolute transcendence of God, eternal praise and glory, the full and perfect worship which are due to him.[70]

Christ's subjective consecration is not seen exclusively in His Death on the Cross. As we saw in chapter 4, He also consecrates Himself daily through His life of self-gift to the Father.[71] In fact, as St. John Paul II says, this response to the Father, this subjective consecration of Christ, happens through His daily living of the evangelical counsels:

> Jesus is the One whom "God anointed . . . with the Holy Spirit and with power" (Acts 10:38), the One "whom the Father consecrated and sent into the world" (Jn 10:36). Accepting his consecration by the Father, the Son in turn consecrates himself to the Father for the sake of humanity (cf. Jn 17:19). His life of virginity, obedience and poverty expresses his complete filial acceptance of the Father's plan (cf. Jn 10:30; 14:11). His perfect offering confers an aspect of consecration upon all the events of his earthly existence.[72]

This life of self-offering through the counsels is intimately connected to Christ's consecration and mission. Through offering Himself in poverty, chastity, and obedience, He daily lives His mission as priest and victim for the salvation of the world.

It is also important to see that because of who Christ is, the objective and subjective dimensions of Christ's consecration and mission are perfectly united. As we saw in chapter 4, there is no distinction between His person and His mission. Christ's subjective response to the Father is the perfect fulfillment of His objective consecration and mission. It is toward this union of objective and subjective consecration and mission that Vatican II calls the priest to strive.[73]

Understanding the consecration and mission of Christ, we can now comprehend the consecration and mission of the priest. As we have already seen, ordination is an objective consecration. This consecration, which makes the priest participate in Christ's mission, requires from him a subjective consecration through giving himself to the mission, just as was required for Christ. God has taken possession of him in this consecration; and, thus, it requires of him the surrender of self-dispossession, letting himself be given for mission. As Gisbert Greshake says:

> Consequently, the decree *Prebyterorum ordinis* (12) rightly connected ordination (*consecration*—a word also used in the early Church to denote baptism) with the Johannine concept of "sanctification" (cf. Jn 10:36). To be consecrated and to be sanctified mean to be dispossessed of oneself and to be handed over to God, for life of service and for special mission.[74]

Many authors see this consecration of the priest foreshadowed in Christ's consecration of the Apostles in His high priestly prayer: "Consecrate them in the truth. Your word is truth. As you sent me into the world, so I sent them into the world. And I consecrate myself for them, so that they also may be consecrated in truth." (Jn 17:17-19).[75] The sanctification in this passage is connected with the sending of the Apostles; Raymond Brown points out that it is consecration for mission:

> The consecration of the disciples is directed toward their mission. This is in harmony with the Old Testament understanding of consecration; for example, Moses, who himself has been consecrated by God, is told in Exodus

28:41 to consecrate others so that they may serve God as priests. The disciples are to be consecrated so that they may serve as apostles, that is, as ones sent."[76]

Feuillet goes a step further than some authors and argues that this passage, in fact, refers to the consecration of the Apostles as priests:

> John 17:17-19 is dominated by the idea of complete assimilation to Jesus. Jesus himself had been consecrated a priest by the Father with a view to being sent into the world (10:36); now he asks the Father to bestow a similar consecration on the apostles whom he is sending into the world; that is, to consecrate them as priests."[77]

In one way, Jesus' priestly consecration is unique in that He becomes both the priest and the victim who is offered for our sins; no other priest is victim in the same way as Christ. However, the Apostles receive some share in Christ's priestly consecration as they are sent into the world. Since their priesthood derives from Christ's, it should have some similarity to His. As Feuillet says, "The prayer of John 17 shows Christ giving his apostles a share in his own twofold consecration as priest and victim."[78] Therefore, the exercise of the Apostles' priesthood will also involve a subjective consecration through self-sacrifice, as Christ's priesthood did. Jean Galot elucidates this point:

> Consecration, too, establishes a special bond between priests and the redeeming mystery of Christ. Because Jesus brings his own consecration to fruition through sacrifice, those on whom he bestows his pastoral power are called upon to realize in themselves the definition

of the good shepherd who gives his life for his sheep. Priests cannot limit their sacrificial offering to the ritual performance of the Eucharist. They are called upon to commit themselves completely by making the total gift of their own selves which the Eucharist implies for their own personal lives."[79]

Ordained priests can have no other model than Christ's own priesthood. Thus, in this priestly consecration is found the basis of the priest's special call to holiness of life, as *Presbyterorum Ordinis* makes clear: "Priests are bound by a special reason to acquire this perfection. They are consecrated to God in a new way in their ordination and are made the living instruments of Christ the eternal priest."[80] They will find their holiness by their interior conformation to Christ, seeking subjectively to consecrate themselves to what they are objectively: "In order to realize their mission, [priests] need to nourish in themselves a life which is a pure reflection of their identity, and to live a union of love with Jesus Christ Eternal High Priest, Head and Master, Spouse and Pastor of his Church."[81]

The Priest as a Living Image of Christ through Pastoral Charity

Seeing the meaning of the priest's consecration and its intimate connection to his mission to represent Christ, we can now understand why St. John Paul II asserts that the priest must seek to become a living image of Christ. Becoming a living image is the subjective consecration of the priest, conforming himself to the life and attitudes of the one he represents:

The priest, who is called to be a "living image" of Jesus Christ, head and shepherd of the Church, should seek to reflect in himself, as far as possible, the human perfection which shines forth in the incarnate Son of God and which is reflected with particular liveliness in his attitudes toward others as we see narrated in the Gospels.[82]

What is this attitude that Christ exemplifies toward others, which the priest must embody? Here, we arrive at the true heart of St. John Paul II's understanding of the priesthood, his favorite way of describing Christ's self-gift as priest and victim. It is found in the attitude of Christ's priestly heart which, following the fathers of Vatican II, St. John Paul II calls "pastoral charity."[83] We recognize his description of pastoral charity from our understanding of Christ's spousal self-gift described in chapter 4. The pastoral charity of Christ is exemplified in the self-sacrificing and kenotic total self-gift of the Cross:

> Jesus' service attains its fullest expression in his death on the cross, that is, in his total gift of self in humility and love. "He emptied himself, taking the form of a servant, being born in the likeness of men. And being found in human form, he humbled himself and became obedient unto death, even death on a cross" (Phil 2:7-8). The authority of Jesus Christ as head coincides then with his service, with his gift, with his total, humble and loving dedication on behalf of the Church. All this he did in perfect obedience to the Father; he is the one true Suffering Servant of God, both priest and victim."[84]

Pastoral charity is the mode of Christ's priesthood. It is a sacrificial service, a love that is self-giving; it is Christ's laying down his own life for the sake of the beloved. Pastoral charity is Christ's subjective response to His objective consecration.

This sacrificial, kenotic, gift of self in Christ's priesthood must be imitated in the life of the ordained priest.[85]

St. John Paul II uses two images to explain further this subjective consecration of Christ in pastoral charity: the good shepherd and the bridegroom. First, Christ is the Good Shepherd who lays down His life for His sheep[86]:

> His whole life is a continual manifestation of his
> "pastoral charity," or rather, a daily enactment of it.
> He feels compassion for the crowds because they were
> harassed and helpless, like sheep without a shepherd
> (cf. Mt 9:35-36). He goes in search of the straying and
> scattered sheep (cf. Mt 18:12-14) and joyfully celebrates
> their return. He gathers and protects them. He knows
> them and calls each one by name (cf. Jn 10:3). He leads
> them to green pastures and still waters (cf. Ps 22-23) and
> spreads a table for them, nourishing them with his own
> life. The good shepherd offers this life through his own
> death and resurrection.[87]

In addition, St. John Paul II argues, a fuller understanding of pastoral charity can be gained by seeing Christ as the bridegroom of the Church:

> Christ's gift of himself to his Church, the fruit of his
> love, is described in terms of that unique gift of self
> made by the bridegroom to the bride, as the sacred texts
> often suggest. Jesus is the true bridegroom who offers to
> the Church the wine of salvation (cf. Jn 2:11). He who
> is "the head of the Church, his body, and is himself its
> savior" (Eph 5:23) "loved the Church and gave himself
> up for her, that he might sanctify her, having cleansed
> her by the washing of water with the word, that he might

present the Church to himself in splendor, without spot or wrinkle or any such thing, that she might be holy and without blemish" (Eph 5:25-27). The Church is indeed the body in which Christ the head is present and active, but she is also the bride who proceeds like a new Eve from the open side of the redeemer on the cross.[88]

Both of these images help us to understand the priest's subjective consecration. First, the priest is called to be a "living image" of the Good Shepherd: "By virtue of their consecration, priests are configured to Jesus the good shepherd and are called to imitate and live out his own pastoral charity."[89] Secondly, the priest is also called to be a living image of Christ the Bridegroom of the Church: "Hence Christ stands 'before' the Church and 'nourishes and cherishes her' (Eph 5:29), giving his life for her. The priest is called to be the living image of Jesus Christ, the spouse of the Church."[90]

This is St. John Paul II's unique insight into pastoral charity; it is not only the love of the Good Shepherd who lays down His life for His sheep, but also the love of the Bridegroom who pours out His life for His bride. St. John Paul II sees that "in virtue of his configuration to Christ, the head and shepherd, the priest stands in this spousal relationship with regard to the community."[91] The spousal character of the priest's self-gift on behalf of the Church is discovered in pastoral charity. It is through self-sacrificing love that the priest re-presents the love of the Good Shepherd and Bridegroom. As St. John Paul II says:

> In his spiritual life, therefore, he is called to live out Christ's spousal love toward the Church, his bride. Therefore, the priest's life ought to radiate this spousal

character, which demands that he be a witness to
Christ's spousal love and thus be capable of loving
people with a heart which is new, generous and pure—
with genuine self-detachment, with full, constant and
faithful dedication and at the same time with a kind of
"divine jealousy" (cf. 2 Cor 11:2) and even with a kind
of maternal tenderness, capable of bearing "the pangs
of birth" until "Christ be formed" in the faithful (cf.
Gal 4:19).[92]

Another way that the Tradition speaks about this subjective consecration of the priest is by telling the priest that he
must imitate the mysteries he celebrates.[93] The Eucharist,
which makes present the marriage of the Cross, is the place
where the priest's objective consecration and subjective
consecration should come together. At Mass, he most clearly
represents Christ; and it is from the Eucharistic celebration
that the priest finds the inspiration and grace for his subjective self-gift. As Vatican II says: "This pastoral charity flows
mainly from the Eucharistic sacrifice, which is thus the
center and root of the whole priestly life. The priestly soul
strives thereby to apply to itself the action which takes place
on the altar of sacrifice."[94] St. John Paul II comments on
this passage:

> Indeed, the Eucharist re–presents, makes once again
> present, the sacrifice of the cross, the full gift of Christ to
> the Church, the gift of his body given and his blood shed,
> as the supreme witness of the fact that he is head and
> shepherd, servant and spouse of the Church. Precisely
> because of this, the priest's pastoral charity not only flows
> from the Eucharist but finds in the celebration of the

Eucharist its highest realization—just as it is from the Eucharist that he receives the grace and obligation to give his whole life a "sacrificial" dimension.[95]

The Sacramental Grace of Holy Orders

Understanding more precisely how the priest becomes an image of Christ through ordination is connected to the two effects of the Sacrament of Holy Orders: character and grace. When the fathers of Vatican II speak about the consecration and mission of the sacrament, they are referring to both the character and the grace of the Sacrament of Holy Orders. We have already seen that character is an objective configuration that gives the priest a share in Christ's priesthood, allowing the priest to act in Jesus' person. The grace of the sacrament, strictly related to the character, allows the priest to respond subjectively to his consecration by living his mission, making him a living image of Christ.

The main purpose of the sacraments is to bring people to share in the life of grace. Sacraments are "efficacious signs of grace."[96] St. Thomas points out that sacraments have both a principal effect and a secondary effect.[97] The principal effect is grace, and the secondary effect, in the three Sacraments of Baptism, Confirmation, and Holy Orders, is character. Of course, all the sacraments bestow sanctifying grace, giving people a share in the life of God,[98] but sacraments also bestow grace proper to each sacrament called "sacramental grace." Sacramental grace is given for attaining the ends of that particular sacrament.[99] With regard to the Sacrament of Holy Orders, the grace is given in order for the priest to live in a manner worthy of his consecration. Vatican II spoke about this grace of orders:

Since, therefore, every priest in his own fashion acts in place of Christ himself, he is enriched by a special grace, so that, as he serves the flock committed to him and the entire People of God, he may the better grow in the grace of him whose tasks he performs.[100]

There is an important relationship between the character and the grace in the Sacrament of Holy Orders. They are, of course, always intended to come together.[101] However, if the grace is gone, the character "remains forever in the Christian as a positive disposition for grace, a promise and guarantee of divine protection, and as a vocation to divine worship and to the service of the Church."[102] Such is the link between character and grace that if the grace is lost, the character almost "calls" for the grace to return. Antonio Miralles explains this relationship between the character and grace in the Sacrament of Holy Orders:

> Sacramental grace and character are strictly linked. Grace presupposes the character, because it is, precisely, the thing necessary for the worthy and fruitful accomplishment of the ministry to which the character enables the minister in the corresponding level of orders; and, equally, the character impressed by virtue of the anointing of the Holy Spirit assures the sanctifying action of the Spirit, unless the subject interposes there the obstacle of sin, in which case the sign of the character constitutes a permanent call to conversion.[103]

The grace is given to the priest to enable him to make a subjective response to his objective consecration and mission. Nicolas describes this grace:

The grace of the sacrament of orders gives rise to this burning desire in the soul of the priest, which every day is manifested by prayer for the salvation of souls, and ordinarily by action in the service of Christ the Savior and of the men whom he wants to save. This action is multiform. It has its beginning, its font in the priestly grace which makes the priest participate in the redeeming charity of Jesus Christ.[104]

This "redeeming charity of Jesus Christ" is, of course, pastoral charity. As St. John Paul II says, "The sacrament of holy orders confers upon the priest sacramental grace which gives him a share not only in Jesus' saving 'power' and 'ministry' but also in his pastoral 'love.'"[105] Configured to Christ by the sacramental character, the priest is also given sacramental grace which helps the priest to be subjectively conformed to the mode of Christ's priesthood. This grace makes him capable of loving with Christ's own pastoral charity. This is why some authors speak about a "double conformity to Christ the priest" in the sacrament: a conformity of character and grace:

> [There are] two types of conformity to Christ the priest: the first according to which the priest receives in sacred ordination a certain number of powers . . . properly of Christ the Head; the second according to which the priest receives (normally) in sacred ordination a specific help which makes him more apt to put in practice this power for the good of the Church.[106]

It is by this complex of grace and character that the priest is able to become conformed to Christ. This is why it is possible to say the priest should be a living image of Christ. A priest who is not seeking by the grace of the sacrament through his subjective self-gift to become a living image of Christ is not fully living his objective consecration.

The Distinction between Office and Person in the Priest

An important distinction must be made because of the representational nature of the priesthood. The priest is a representative of Christ and should be a living image of Christ. But even at the moments when he most clearly represents Christ—i.e., when speaking *in persona Christi* in the Eucharist—there is always a distinction between the subjective person and the objective office he represents. The priest is consecrated to represent someone who he is not, who is radically different from him. He becomes a kind of sacramental sign of Christ and makes Christ present in the Church, but he is not Christ. Balthasar explains that this is the very nature of representation:

> Representation . . . says at the same time something positive: the representative has received from the one he represents full powers to make something of his superiority or dignity present, without being able to claim for himself—and here we have the negative element—this superiority or dignity.[107]

The office of the priest, through the character, provides an objective link with Christ, guaranteed sacramentally by the power of the Holy Spirit, which makes him capable of acting *in persona Christi*. Yet in exercising this office, in doing these sacred actions, he must realize that he is doing something completely beyond him. It is not by his power that he realizes his most important activities. The office provides a power, an authority, and a certitude that are not his. Cardinal Ratzinger explains how this distinction of office and person reveals a profound paradox in apostolic ministry:

> This "nothing" which the apostles share with Jesus expresses at one and the same time the power and weakness of the apostolic ministry. Of themselves, on their own resources, they can do nothing that apostles ought to do. How on their own could they say, "Your sins are forgiven"? How could they say, "This is my Body"? How could they impose hands and say, "Receive the Holy Spirit"? Not one of these things which make up apostolic activity happens by virtue of their proper authority. But in this expropriation of their own resources is their communion with Jesus, who is wholly from the Father: with him all things, without him nothing.[108]

This distinction between person and office reveals the priority of grace in the ministry and life of the priest and the Church, and ought to make the priest conscious of his profound unworthiness to carry out this ministry. His own holiness will never be equal to the task he is given. As Pesarchick explains:

> Only in Christ does this unity of Person and representational Office/Mission occur. In the realm of the Church, the official mission of ministerially representing the Son Incarnate is bestowed on sinners whose lives never adequately correspond to the profound mission they receive.[109]

This knowledge of the gap between himself and Christ, between his person and his office ought to foster humility on the part of the priest. Because the priest acts *in persona Christi,* he cannot take credit for his works. Even when exercising the munera of teaching or shepherding, he does these things in the name and the person of Christ. He should always exercise his authority as a service to Christ and not himself. As Gisbert Greshake says, "Because it is the priest's office that points to Christ, it is inadmissible that he should put himself in place of Christ."[110] The sin of clericalism in the tradition of the Church is a result of the priest appropriating his office to his own person. The "clericalist" priest forgets whom he is serving and forgets the strong words of Jesus to His Apostles:

> He said to them, "The kings of the Gentiles lord it over them and those in authority over them are addressed as 'Benefactors'; but among you it shall not be so. Rather, let the greatest among you be as the youngest, and the leader as the servant. For who is greater: the one seated at table or the one who serves? Is it not the one seated at table? I am among you as the one who serves. (Lk 22:25-27)

The humble priest does not confuse his office with his person; he is seeking to become a pure reflection of his office. As he seeks to become a living image of Christ, he becomes more and more aware of the distinction between himself and Christ. As Balthasar says:

> The more the servant, sent out and commissioned, represents the Lord—not only externally by a function to be discharged but also internally by his life and person—the more profoundly does he see himself in contradistinction to the Lord. As long as he is really the Lord's servant, nothing can be further from his mind than to equate himself, in any point whatever, with the Lord.[111]

The priest who is seeking to live like Christ will not fall into the danger of using his office to draw others to himself or for his own advantage. Many Fathers and saints could be named who have written strong words about those who use office for the promotion of their own personal advantage. Let it suffice for us to cite once again the teaching of St. Augustine.

St. Augustine saw clearly this representational nature of Church office. He pointed out in many places that a bishop is called a shepherd only because he is a member of the Good Shepherd and represents Him.[112] It would, therefore, be a betrayal of the authority of the bishop to use his office for selfish advantage, to draws others to himself. Augustine says that a minister who is not like the Good Shepherd laying down His life for His sheep[113] is a mercenary or a hireling: "Shepherds do not watch over themselves, but the sheep. This is the principal reason why these [bad] shepherds are accused, because they watch over themselves and not the sheep."[114] Augustine adds that these shepherds "who watch over themselves and not the sheep, seek from the people the comfort of having their needs supplied and the favor of honor and praise."[115] For Augustine, the good bishop must be like the good shepherd who suffers for his sheep. For when Jesus said to Peter "watch over my sheep," he meant "to suffer on behalf of my sheep. A good bishop should be of this kind; if he will not be of this kind, he will not be a bishop."[116] Of course, Augustine, the anti-Donatist, is not questioning the validity of the sacraments of such a bishop, but simply pointing out, as he does elsewhere: "For someone to be a true priest, he needs not only a Sacrament, but also to be clothed with righteousness."[117]

The real goal of the priest is not to draw people to himself but to Christ. To do this, the priest in some way must seek to disappear so that Christ can appear more clearly in and through the priest. To explain this transparency, Cardinal Ratzinger cites an image from St. Augustine, who explains what it means for John the Baptist to call himself the "voice" while Jesus is the "word":[118]

> The relation of "voice" (vox) to "word" (verbum) helps to make clear the mutual relationship between Christ and the priest. . . . Ultimately, the task of the priest is quite simply to be a voice for the word: "He must increase, but I must decrease"—the voice has no other purpose than to pass on the word; it then once more effaces itself.[119]

What is required is John the Baptist's attitude of humility, the surrender of one's own glory to glorify Christ completely. "He must increase, I must decrease."

This humility follows from the truth of the priest's office. Because of this distinction between the office of the priest and his person, the priest will always live in a tension. He is always striving to live fully his office, to consecrate himself subjectively through self-gift. And yet, he will always fail to some degree because he will never be able to live the office perfectly. It is in this failure that there is an important opportunity for the priest. This failure can lead to discouragement; or it can lead to self-emptying humility. It can, and often does, lead to giving up on the high call to priestly holiness; or it can, and often does, lead to deeper confidence in the one who works through the priest despite his weakness. When lived rightly, this tension in the priestly life leads to a deeper experience of what St. Paul came to know: "My grace is sufficient for you, for power is made perfect in weakness" (2 Cor 12:9). This is the essential role that humility plays in the life of the priest. As Balthasar says:

> In his effort to be worthy of his office and, in the process, increasingly to sacrifice and submerge his subjectivity, the priest can expect as his only reward the consciousness, not that he has become equal to the office, but that the office has been able to succeed in him despite his inadequacies. In the ethos of the priest, the contrast between office and person is dominant to the end—a static dualism that no existential effort can overcome or weaken. His gift of self has primarily the form of humility.[120]

In learning to live in this tension, we find in the Scriptures a great example for the priest in the life of St. Peter. St. Peter is a great example precisely because his failure is so often recorded in the Scriptures. Balthasar theorizes that one of the reasons that the Gospels recount in detail Peter's failure, even as they recount his investiture with the most important office of the Apostles, is to reveal this tension between office and person that must always exist in the priestly office.[121] As Balthasar explains:

> In his failure, in his subsequent sorrow at being the kind of man he was, he was installed in his unique office as shepherd of the Lord's flock (Jn 21: 15-17). Only because he was first among his brethren in the priestly office does the New Testament offer such a minute description of Peter's character and fate; for it was not until they had been jolted out of their pleasant self-complacency by their manifold failures and their shameful abandonment

of the Lord in his Passion that the other apostles also learned to perceive the difference between person and office, to distinguish between the significance of their office, of which the Lord was the only true measure, and the insignificance of their persons, and so to become worthy ministers in the Lord's service."[122]

Balthasar refers to the important scene of the commissioning of Peter after the Resurrection, when Peter is asked three times by the Lord, "Do you love me?" According to Balthasar, the Lord is asking Peter for "an 'advance installment' of subjective love toward himself (cf. Jn 21:15)."[123] This means that Peter must seek subjectively to conform his life to his office. "He must bend all his powers toward harmonizing his life with the ethos of his office."[124] The threefold questioning cannot but remind Peter of his threefold denial. Here also is the vivid reminder for the priest. He knows that many times, he has failed to live his calling. Yet, he is also still called; the Lord still asks, "Do you love me? . . . Feed my sheep"(Jn 21:17). He must allow his experience of failure to empty him of himself, to expropriate him, so that he can be taken for Christ's Mission. So he can be led to total self-gift. As Christ said to Peter when He entrusted him with pastoral authority, "you will stretch out your hands, and someone else will dress you and lead you where you do not want to go" (Jn 21:18).

Is this not what the Tradition of the Church means when it says that the priest is *alter Christus*, another Christ. Through his consecration, effected by the sacramental character, the priest is called to make a total self-gift of his life, just as St. Peter did or St. Paul did. He is called to do this, very aware of the distinction between his office and his person. If he responds rightly to his weakness, he will realize that it is not an obstacle but the means of growing in humility. This humility allows him to see that the power of Christ is made perfect in his weakness.[125] Through this humility, and his continually seeking to subjectively conform his heart to Christ, through pastoral charity, he becomes a living image of Christ.

Questions for Discussion, Reflection, and Prayer

1. How do you experience being conformed to Christ through your ministry?

2. How do you see Christ is using you as His representative, and what is that like for you?

3. How does your daily celebration of the Eucharist affect your relationship with Christ and His people?

4. Where do you find pastoral charity most challenging, and how can you grow there?

5. Can you experience in your failure to live your priestly life adequately Jesus looking at you and asking you, "Do you love me?" What is your response?

NOTES

1.   This chapter is not intended to be a complete treatise on the Sacrament of Holy Orders, but rather a more limited study on the priest as a sacramental representative of Christ—that is, a living image, which, when properly understood, is one of the unique aspects of his role in the Church. Among other important emphases, Vatican II and subsequent magisterial teaching have emphasized the priest as a representative of Christ, a living instrument that carries on Christ's work in the Church and in the world. This unique role of the priest has not been unchallenged by theologians in the forty years since Vatican II. An excellent summary of these challenges and an important response is found in Toups, ch. 2, "Post-Conciliar Confusion," 97-132.

2.   John Paul II, *Pastores Dabo Vobis* (1992), sec. 12.

3.   See Paul VI, *Lumen Gentium* (1964), sec. 11-13, 1 Peter 2:9; Revelation 1:5, 5:10, 20:6.

4.   As *Lumen Gentium* says: "Though they differ from one another in essence and not only in degree (*essentia et non gradu tantum*), the common priesthood of the faithful and the ministerial or hierarchical priesthood are nonetheless interrelated: each of them in its own special way is a participation in the one priesthood of Christ. The ministerial priest, by the sacred power he enjoys, teaches and rules the priestly people; acting in the person of Christ, he makes present the eucharistic sacrifice, and offers it to God in the name of all the people"(*Lumen Gentium*, sec. 10; see *Apostolicam Actuositatem*, sec. 2). Sara Butler, M.S.B.T., points out, from her study of the *Acta Synodalia* of Vatican II, that the council fathers, when speaking about the essential difference referenced in *Lumen Gentium* 10, "located the distinctive feature in the priest's role as Christ's representative" ("Priestly Identity: 'Sacrament' of Christ the Head." *Worship* 70 [1996]: 295). The *Directory* says, "The specificity of the ministerial priesthood, however, is defined not on the basis of its supposed 'superiority' over the common priesthood, but rather by the service it is called to carry out for all the faithful so they may adhere to the mediation and Lordship of Christ rendered visible by the exercise of the ministerial priesthood." (6).

5.   *Ultimis Temporibus*, Synod of Bishops, 30 November 1971, in *Vatican II, Volume 2: More Post Conciliar Documents*, ed. Austin Flanner, O.P. (Collegville, Minn.: Liturgical Press, 1982), 679. See also *Lumen Gentium*, sec. 24, 27, 28; *Catechism of the Catholic Church*, sec. 1581; *Directory for the Life and Ministry of Priests*, 6.

6.   See *Lumen Gentium*, sec. 21, 26-28.

7.   See John 14:7-9.

8. Raymond Brown explains that "in the Jewish notion of apostolate the one sent (*shalûah, shaliah*) represents the one who sends, carrying not only the sender's authority but even his presence to others" (*Priest and Bishop: Biblical Reflections* [New York: Paulist Press, 1970], 28). Walter Kasper adds, "The idea of representation is found in another form in the New Testament, namely, in the *shaliach* (missionary) formulae that are inseparably linked to the concept of apostle. In Jewish Law, the one sent has the same status as the one who sends him. This is why Jesus can say: 'He who hears you hears me, and he who rejects you rejects me, and he who rejects me rejects him who sent me' (Lk 10:16)" (*Leadership in the Church: How Traditional Roles Can Serve the Christian Community*, trans. Brian McNeil [New York: Crossroad Publishing Co., 2003], 54).

9. Robert Pesarchick, *The Trinitarian Foundation of Human Sexuality as Revealed by Christ According to Hans Urs von Balthasar: The Revelatory Significance of the Male Christ and the Male Ministerial Priesthood*, Tesi Gregoriana Serie Teologia, vol. 63 (Roma: Gregorian University, 2000). Pesarchick says, "It is the official (sacramental), hierarchical ministry (sanctifying, teaching and governing) of the institutional Church that makes present the 'authority' of Christ to the entire Church, and thus makes discipleship itself possible" (236). Pesarchick draws this argument from Balthasar who says that true discipleship, at times, requires the submission to the absolute authority of Christ Himself, exercised through the Church. This biblical understanding of the absolute authority of God cannot simply be limited in Christianity to a personal encounter with God and the soul (Balthasar, *The Office of Peter and the Structure of the Church*, trans. Andrée Emery [San Francisco: Ignatius Press, 1986], 61). Peter and his successors have been given the power to bind and to loose, and thus through this "in the person of Peter—as the head of the Twelve, in whom their real authority receives its final cogency—real biblical authority is to be addressed to the faithful of all times, including those living today" (Ibid., 63).

10. Gisbert Greshake, *The Meaning of Christian Priesthood*, trans. Peadar MacSeumais, S.J. (Westminster, MD: Christian Classics, 1989), 48, emphasis in original.

11. *Presbyterorum Ordinis*, sec. 2; *Lumen Gentium*, sec. 20 and 28. The Council fathers in *Lumen gentium*, using the image from the *Sacramentarium Veronense*, chose to speak of the bishop as the fullness of the priesthood (LG 21), while also maintaining that priests, although "dependent on the bishops in the exercise of their power, nevertheless are united with the bishops in sacerdotal dignity" (LG 28).

12. *Pastores Dabo Vobis*, sec. 12.

13. Walter Kasper, *Leadership in the Church: How Traditional Roles can serve the Christian Community*, trans. Brian McNeil (New York: Crossroad Publishing Co., 2003), 54.

14. "The Value of the Theological Formula *in persona Christi*" in *From "Inter Insigniores" to "Ordinatio Sacerdotalis,"* ed. *Congregation for the Doctrine of the Faith* (Washington: USCC Publishing, 1998), 110).

15. St. Cyprian, *Epistula* 63, 14 (CCSL 3c, 410).

16. *In Ioh. Evang.*, 5, 18 [CCSL 36, 51]; see also *In Ioh. Evang.*, 6, 7 [CCSL 36, 57]; *Sermo.*, 293a, 15 (François Dolbeau, "Nouveaux sermons de saint Augustine pour la conversion des païens et des donatistes [VI]," in *Revue des Études Augustiniennes*, 39 [1993]: 393).

17. Yves Congar summarizes how this truth is both scriptural and patristic: "This idea [*in persona Christi*] has antecedents of a very firm kind in the biblical notion of the *shaliah*, the messenger commissioned by an authority that he makes present by representing, and also in the idea so well known in the early centuries of Christianity that the bishop (the priest) was the image of the Father or the image of Christ in the midst of the Christian community and over and against the people" (*I Believe in the Holy Spirit III: The River of the Water of Life flows in the East and in the West*, trans. David Smith [New York: The Seabury Press, 1983], 234-35).

18. ST III, 22, a. 4, corpus.

19. Thomas Aquinas, *Summa Contra Gentiles* 4, 76, n. 7.

20. As St. Thomas says, "When a thing is indifferent to many uses, it must be determined to one, if that one has to be effected. Now those things which are done in the sacraments, can be done with various intent; for instance, washing with water, which is done in baptism, may be ordained to bodily cleanliness, to the health of the body, to amusement, and many other similar things. Consequently, it needs to be determined to one purpose, i.e., the sacramental effect, by the intention of him who washes. And this intention is expressed by the words which are pronounced in the sacraments" (ST III, 64, a. 8, corpus).

21. "For instrumental power lies in several instruments through which the chief agent acts" (ST III, 82, a. 1, ad. 1).

22. ST III, 82, a. 1, corpus. See also ST III, 83, a. 1, ad. 3. St. John Paul II explains this point clearly: "The priest offers the Holy Sacrifice *in persona Christi*; this means more than offering 'in the name of' so or 'in the place of' Christ. *In persona* means specific sacramental identification with the eternal High Priest who is the Author and principal Subject of this sacrifice of his, a Sacrifice in which, in truth, nobody can take his place. Only he – only Christ – was able and is always able to be the true and effective 'expiation for our sins and ... for the sins of the whole world' (1 Jn 2:2; cf. 4:10)" (*Dominicae cenae*, in AAS 72 [1980]: n. 8).

23. ST III, 78, a. 1, corpus. Pope Pius XII in his encyclical *Mediator Dei* (69) quotes St. John Chrysostom who says the priest "lends his tongue, and gives his hand" to Christ (ΟΜΙΛΙΑΙ ΕΙΣ ΤΟΝ ΑΓΙΟΝ ΙΩΑΝΝΗΝ, 86:4 [*Corona Patrum Salesiana, Series Graeca*, 13, 460]).

24.   Bernard D. Marliangeas, *Clés pour un théologie du ministère: "in persona Christi, in persona Ecclesiae,"* in *Théologie Historique*, vol. 51 (Paris: Beauchesne, 1978), 97.

25.   See ST IIa IIae, 88, a. 12, corpus; ST III, 82, a. 1, ad. 4.

26.   ST III, 8, a. 6, corpus.

27.   Martimort, *"in persona Christi,"* 110.

28.   *Sacrosanctum Concilium*, sec. 7, 33; *Lumen Gentium*, sec. 10, 21, 28; *Presbyterorum Ordinis*, sec. 2, 13; similar formulas in *Presbyterorum Ordinis* sec. 6 and 12.

29.   *Sacrosanctum Concilium*, sec. 20, 33; *Lumen Gentium*, sec. 10, 28; *Presbyterorum Ordinis*, sec. 13.

30.   The thesis of Lorenzo Loppa ("In persona Christi"-"Nomine Ecclesiae": Linee per una teologia del ministero nel concilio ecumenico Vatican II e nel magistero post-conciliare [1962-1985], in Corona Lateranensis, 34 [Roma: Pontificia Università Lateranense, 1985], 182-83) makes clear this intentional expansion of the use of the phrase. As Walter Kasper explains it: "Just as Jesus Christ is the primary celebrant of the sacraments, so he is also the primary and the real teacher and shepherd in the Church" (Leadership in the Church, 53).

31.   "Priestly Identity," 298.

32.   Kasper, *Leadership in the Church*, 58.

33.   Loppa, 63.

34.   *Presbyterorum Ordinis*, sec. 2. Sections 6 and 12 also reflect this expanded use of the phrase including the whole mission of the priest as part of his role *in persona Christi*, not just his role at the Eucharist.

35.   Ibid., sec. 5.

36.   "La testimonianza della liturgia," in *Il prete per gli uomini d'oggi*, opera collettiva diretta da Gino Concetti, con la collaborazione di J.L. Acebal, O. Barlea (Roma: A.V.E., 1975), 219.

37.   *Pastores Dabo Vobis*, sec. 12.

38.   *Pilgrim Fellowship of Faith: The Church as Communion*, ed. Stephan Otto Horn and Vinzenz Pfnür, trans. Henry Taylor (San Francisco: Ignatius Press, 2005), 157.

39.   *Lumen Gentium*, sec. 10.

40.   *Justice in the Church*, 87. Pope Pius XII emphasized strongly this doctrinal point: "We deem it necessary to recall that the priest acts for the people only because he represents Jesus Christ, who is Head of all His members and offers Himself in their stead" (*Mediator Dei*, sec. 84). The question becomes important today in the debate surrounding the ordination of women since it is argued that a priestly representation *in persona Ecclesiae* could just as easily, or better, be done by a woman. For this reason, the Sacred Congregation of the Doctrine of the Faith also clarified this point: "It is true that the priest represents the Church, which is the Body of Christ. But if he does so, it is precisely because he first

represents Christ himself, who is the Head and Shepherd of the Church" (*Inter insigniores*, 15 October 1976, in AAS 69 [1977]: n. 5). In spite of this doctrinal clarification, several authors still argue the point (e.g., David Coffey, "Priestly Representation and Women's Ordination," in *Priesthood: The Hard Questions*, ed. Gerald Gleeson [Newton, Australia: E.J. Dwyer, 1993], 80 ff.; Susan Wood, "Priestly Identity: Sacrament of the Ecclesial Community," *Worship* 69 [March 1995]: 109-127) and they are aptly responded to by the following authors: Ashley, *Justice in the Church*, Appendix I, 169-188; Butler, "Priestly Identity," 291; Lawrence J. Welch, "Priestly Identity Reconsidered: A Reply to Susan Wood," *Worship* 70 (1996), 314.

41.   *Presbyterorum Ordinis*, sec. 2. For a full explanation of the development of the Church's teaching on sacramental character showing its importance for today, see Toups, 31-96.

42.   *Catechism of the Catholic Church*, sec. 1585. As St. Thomas makes clear in his treatment of character "Christ's Priesthood is eternal. . . . Consequently, every sanctification wrought by His Priesthood, is perpetual, enduring as long as the thing sanctified endures. . . . Since, therefore, the subject of a character is the soul as to its intellective part, where faith resides, as stated above; it is clear that, the intellect being perpetual and incorruptible, a character cannot be blotted out from the soul" (ST III, 63, a. 5, corpus).

43.   See *Lumen Gentium*, sec. 11.

44.   ST III, 63, a. 2, corpus. Jean Galot says of St. Thomas' understanding of character that it "won such prestige as to be adopted as if no other theory were in sight" (*Theology of the Priesthood*, 197).

45.   ST III, 63, a. 3, corpus.

46.   Toups, 55.

47.   Jean-Hervé Nicolas, O.P., *Synthèse Dogmatique: de la Trinité à la Trinité*, Éditions Universitaires Fribourg Suisse (Paris: Beauchesne, 1985), 752.

48.   St. Paul speaks about a spiritual seal in baptism (2 Corinthians 1:22; Ephesians 1:13; 4:30) and the Fathers pick up this idea of σφραγίς with which the soul is marked by the Holy Spirit, see Galot, *Theology of the Priesthood*, 198-199; Toups, 33-54.

49.   *Contra epistulam Parmeniani*, II, 13, 30 (CSEL 51,82); *De Baptismo*, I, 1, 2 (CSEL 51, 146); *See* Jean Galot, S.J., *La nature du caractère sacramentel* (Paris: Desclée de Brouwer, 1958): 36-41; Toups, 49-51.

50.   "At the time the Church decided in favor of Augustine that the holiness of the ministry is not founded in the personal holiness of the minister—thus not in whether or not he carries out his praxis in a holy manner—but in the gift of grace and the commission that is given him by Jesus Christ in the Holy Spirit, which precedes his own activity, i.e., that is due him because of his 'being'" (Walter Kasper, "Ministry in the Church: Taking Issue with Edward Schillebeeckx," *Communio* 10 [Summer 1983]: 189).

51. Nicolas, *Synthèse dogmatique*, 1088.

52. Kasper, "Ministry in the Church," 189.

53. Balthasar, *Spouse of the Word*, 126, emphasis in original. Of course, this truth flows from the teaching of St. Thomas himself who saw the priestly character as a gift given for the sake of bestowing divine gifts on others (ST III, 63, a. 2, corpus).

54. *Pastores Dabo Vobis*, sec. 25. See St. Thomas, *In IV Sent.*, d. 18, q. 1, a. 3, sol.

55. ST II-II, 184, a. 8, corpus; see also a. 6, corpus. Vatican II used the same logic in *Presbyterorum Ordinis*, sec. 13: "Priests as ministers of the sacred mysteries, especially in the sacrifice of the Mass, act in a special way in the person of Christ who gave himself as a victim to sanctify men. And this is why they are invited to imitate what they handle, so that as they celebrate the mystery of the Lord's death they may take care to mortify their members from vices and concupiscences." Nor is this idea foreign even to simple saints: "'this is my body; this is my blood.' How clean your heart must be to utter those words, and to give Jesus to someone else! How clean your hands must be when you raise them in absolution, and wash sinners with the Blood of Jesus" (Mother Teresa of Calcutta, "Mary, Mother of All Priests," in *Be Holy: God's Call to Priests Today*, proceedings from Worldwide Retreat for Priests, Vatican City, October 5-9, 1984, ed. Tom Forrest, C.Ss.R. [South Bend, Ind.: Greenlawn Press, 1987], 73).

56. Apart from infant baptism, which must be considered a separate case (see ST III, 69, a. 8, corpus), the grace of the sacraments is received in proportion to the disposition of the recipients: "if they are to produce their proper effect, it is absolutely necessary that our hearts be properly disposed to receive them" (Pius XII, *Mediator Dei*, sec. 31). See also *Catechism of the Catholic Church*, sec. 112.

57. *Pastores Dabo Vobis*, sec. 25. In addition, the examples of priest saints, like St. John Marie Vianney or St. Pio of Pietrelcina, show well how the devout disposition of the priest can have the effect of disposing the people to receive the sacraments more devoutly. As Pope Paul VI said of Padre Pio, "Look what fame he had, what a worldwide following gathered around him! But why? Perhaps because he was a philosopher? Because he was wise? Because he had resources at his disposal? Because he said Mass humbly, heard confessions from dawn to dusk and was—it is not easy to say it—one who bore the wounds of our Lord. He was a man of prayer and suffering" ("Padre Pio da Pietrelcina," available from: http://www.vatican.va/news_services/liturgy/saints/ns_lit_doc_20020616_padre-pio_en.html; accessed 11 Nov. 2013).

58. *Presbyterorum Ordinis*, sec. 12.

59. McGovern, *Priestly Identity*, 73.

60. See St. Thomas, ST III 63, a. 1, ad. 3.

61. Galot, "The Priesthood and Celibacy," 942

62.   Galot, *Theology of the Priesthood*, 202. As Dulles says, character "grasps the whole being of the person ordained, so that he becomes a man of God, not simply a delegate of the community" (*Priestly Office*, 12).

63.   "Called by God to Act in His Name," homily at the ordination of priests, 2 July 1980, in *L'Osservatore Romano*, English Edition 28 (14 July 1980): 18.

64.   Blessed Alvaro del Portillo, who worked as a secretary to the doctrinal committee that produced *Presbyterorum Ordinis*, points out in his commentary: "All three chapters are imbued by the one basic idea already developed in *Lumen gentium* in connection with the episcopacy—the close link that exists between consecration and mission. *Presbyterorum ordinis* aims at showing the intimate connection between these two aspects" (*On Priesthood* [Chicago: Scepter Press, 1974], 31). See *Lumen Gentium*, sec. 28, *Presbyterorum Ordinis*, sec. 5 and 12.

65.   *Pastores Dabo Vobis*, sec. 12.

66.   *Presbyterorum Ordinis*, sec. 12.

67.   See John 10:36.

68.   Ghirlanda, *Diritto nella Chiesa*, 87-88, original emphasis.

69.   Andre Feuillet, P.S.S., *The Priesthood of Christ and His Ministers*, trans. Matthew J. O'Connell (Garden City, New York: Double Day, 1975), 206.

70.   Ghirlanda, *Diritto nella Chiesa*, 88, original emphasis.

71.   Edward Malatesta, S.J., said, "Throughout his life on earth, Jesus sanctifies himself *in the truth* by living his sonship and by revealing this sonship to others. . . . To speak of Jesus' sanctification of himself is to stress the personal and active aspect of his holiness, to highlight in particular his obedience towards and perfect communion with the saving will of the Father (Jn 5:19; 8:28-29)" ("Consecration and Mission," *The Way Supplement* 13 (1971), 10).

72.   *Vita Consecrata* 22.

73.   See *Presbyterorum Ordinis*, sec. 12.

74.   Greshake, 55; see also 28.

75.   Feuillet, in *The Priesthood of Christ and His Ministers*, argues that the consecration spoken about in these verses refers specifically to consecration of the Apostles, not the general consecration of all the baptized by Christ's death: "This consecration is not given to all the disciples of Jesus without distinction but only to the apostles" (212). He bases this on a detailed study of the similarities between this high priestly prayer of Jesus and the Yom Kippur liturgy (49-68). Feuillet says that, "the narrowing of perspective in the present passage is readily explained once we accept the priestly interpretation of the prayer in John 17 as a whole and the transposition of the liturgy of the Day of Atonement which the chapter represents. Jesus' intention in the verses under consideration is to show his redemptive suffering to be the wellspring of the priesthood of the apostles, just as elsewhere in the fourth gospel the same suffering is clearly

shown to us as being the source of the sacraments of baptism and the Eucharist" (147).

76.   Brown, *John*, vol. 29a, 765.

77.   Feuillet, *Priesthood of Christ and His Ministers*, 213. Although not all scholars accept this position, The International Theological Commission, adopts Feuillet's position as its own in its document entitled "The Priestly Ministry" (in *International Theological Commission Texts and Documents 1969-1985*, 38).

78.   *Priesthood of Christ and His Ministers*, 15.

79.   Galot, *Theology of the Priesthood*, 124.

80.   *Presbyterorum Ordinis*, sec. 12. See also *Pastores Dabo Vobis*, sec. 20. This does not mean that priests are called to greater holiness than all Christians. Vatican II (*Lumen Gentium*, sec. 39) made it clear that all Christians are called to the summit of holiness regardless of their state in life. But as Greshake (117) says, the priest has his own special motivation for holiness, seeking to live his life in accord with his unique consecration and mission. This will also provide some specific demands upon his spiritual life.

81.   Cardinal Jose Sanchez, "Introduction," *Directory on the Ministry and Life of Priests*, 1994 edition.

82.   *Pastores Dabo Vobis*, sec. 43.

83.   See *Presbyterorum Ordinis*, sec. 14; see *Lumen Gentium*, sec. 41.

84.   *Pastores Dabo Vobis*, sec. 21.

85.   Jean Tillard explains the same reality: "The Spirit wants the minister to be united as intensely as possible with what lay at the heart of the *teliosis* (consecration) of the priesthood of Jesus: his gift of all of himself of those who belonged to him" ("Ordained 'Ministry' and the 'Priesthood' of Christ," 239).

86.   See John 10:11, 14, 16

87.   *Pastores Dabo Vobis*, sec. 22.

88.   Ibid.

89.   Ibid.

90.   Ibid.

91.   Ibid.

92.   Ibid.

93.   As the ordination rite says at the moment the newly ordained receives the chalice and the paten: "Receive the oblation of the holy people, to be offered to God. Understand what you do, imitate what you celebrate, and conform your life the mystery of the Lord's cross" (*Rites of Ordination of a Bishop, of Priests, and of Deacons*, second typical edition (Washington, DC: USCCB, 2003), n. 163).

94.   *Presbyterorum Ordinis*, sec. 14

95.   *Pastores Dabo Vobis*, sec. 23.

96.   *Catechism of the Catholic Church*, sec. 1131.

97.   ST III 62, Preface.

98.   *Catechism of the Catholic Church*, sec. 1129; ST III, 62, a. 1 and 2.

99.   As the *Catechism* says, "'Sacramental Grace' is the grace of the Holy Spirit, given by Christ and proper to each sacrament" (*Catechism of the Catholic Church*, sec. 1129).

100.   *Presbyterorum Ordinis*, sec. 12. St. Thomas explains that God gives sacramental grace for the priest to live in accord with his office: "Now, this belongs to divine liberality: that, if the power for some operation is conferred on one, there can be conferred also those things without which this operation cannot suitably be exercised. But the administration of the sacraments to which the spiritual power is ordered is not suitably done unless one be helped to it by divine grace. Accordingly, grace is bestowed in this sacrament as it is in other sacraments" (SCG 4, 74, n. 5).

101.   When grace is lost through sin, the character remains along with the power to effect the sacraments (ST III, 63, a.5, corpus). Still, normally, both are intended to be present together in the priest (ST III, 63, a, 4, ad. 1).

102.   *Catechism of the Catholic Church*, sec. 1121.

103.   "Sacramenti del servizio," 401.

104.   "La grâce du sacrement de l'ordre suscite en l'âme du prêtre cette sollicitude ardente, qui se traduit toujours par la prière pour le salut des hommes, et dans le cas ordinaire par l'action au service du Christ Sauveur et des hommes qu'il veut sauver. Cette action est multiforme. Elle a son principe, sa source dans la grâce sacerdotale qui fait participer le prêtre à la charité rédemptrice de Jésus-Christ" (Nicolas, *Synthèse Dogmatique*, 1129).

105.   *Pastores Dabo Vobis*, sec. 70. See also *Pastores Dabo Vobis*, sec. 72: "If he is to live daily according to the graces he has received, the priest must be ever more open to accepting the pastoral charity of Jesus Christ granted him by Christ's Spirit in the sacrament he has received."

106.   Daniel Ols, O.P. "La dimensione cristologica del sacerdozio ordinato" *Sacrum Ministerium* 5 (1999), 35-36. See also Nicolas, *Synthèse Dogmatique*, 1130.

107.   Balthasar, "How Weighty Is the Argument," 102-03. Balthasar points out the danger that comes with the nature of representation, which we will explore: "This duality makes the concept of representation, and therefore also of apostolic office, so vulnerable and also so liable to misuse" (ibid.).

108.   Ratzinger, "Formation of Priests," 620.

109.   Pesarchick, 238.

110.   Greshake, 64.

111.   Balthasar, *Spouse of the Word*, 108.

112.   *In Ioh. Evang.*, 46, 7. See also *Sermo.* 46, 13 (CCSL 41, 539); *Sermo.* 46, 30 (CCSL 41, 556); Sermon 138, 5 (PL 38, 765).

113.   See John 10:11-13.

114. *Sermo.* 46, 2 (CCSL 41, 529).

115. *Sermo.* 46, 6 (CCSL 41, 533).

116. *Sermo.* 340/a, 3, 4 (PLS 2, 640).

117. *Contra Litteras Petiliani*, 2, 30, 69 (CSEL 52, 58).

118. See Augustine, *Sermo.* 288, 4 (PL 38, 1306); 289, 3 (PL 38, 1309); 293a, 5-16 (Dolbeau, 387-395); 293c, 1 (PLS 2, 497).

119. Ratzinger, *Pilgrim Fellowship of Faith*, 164.

120. Balthasar, *Christian State of Life*, 269, emphasis in original.

121. Balthasar shows what Peter teaches us about Church office in many places, but two important examples are found in *Office of Peter*, 149 ff. and *Christian State of Life*, 262 ff.

122. Balthasar, *Christian State of Life*, 262.

123. Hans Urs von Balthasar, *Theodrama. Theological Dramatic Theory.* vol. III: *Dramatis Personae: Persons in Christ*, trans. Graham Harrison. (San Francisco: Ignatius Press, 1992), 357.

124. Ibid.

125. See 2 Corinthians 12:9.

CHAPTER 6

THE NUPTIAL IMAGE AND THE
SACRAMENT OF HOLY ORDERS

Throughout the Catholic Tradition, theologians and
Fathers of the Church have seen that ordained ministry has
a role in the nuptial relationship that Christ has with His
Church, and they have used the nuptial image to understand
the Sacrament of Holy Orders.[1] In seeking to understand
how the spousal relationship has been applied to the Sacrament of Holy Orders, we find it has been primarily used
to explain three aspects of priestly life and ministry. First,
the image is used as an explanation for clerical celibacy or
continence; second, as an explanation for the self-gift of the
bishop or the priest on behalf of his people; and third, as an
explanation of the spiritual fruitfulness of ordained ministry.[2]
As we explore each of these areas, we will see that the nuptial
image is applied to the Sacrament of Holy Orders in diverse
ways, for we are dealing with a symbolic language which has
not followed a strict uniformity.

The Nuptial Image and Clerical Celibacy or Continence

Throughout the history of the Church, the nuptial image has been used as an explanation for the reason that a bishop or a priest lives celibately or in a continent relationship with his wife after ordination. There is debate about how early the tradition of clerical continence and celibacy became widespread;[3] nevertheless, the use of the nuptial image to defend these practices can be traced to the early Church Fathers, and some would even argue it is found in the writings of St. Paul.

The only explicit reference in the Scriptures to the married state of bishops, presbyters, or deacons is found in the Pastoral Epistles; it is the Pauline formula: *unius uxoris vir.* The phrase that might be literally translated "a man of one woman" or "husband of one wife" is found in 1 Tim 3:2, 1 Tim 3:12, and Titus 1:6. Ignace de la Potterie, S.J., points out that the formula in these passages is "especially important from the strictly biblical point of view . . . they are the only passages in the New Testament where an identical norm is laid down for the three groups of ordained ministers, and only for them."[4] There is much debate among scholars about how to interpret this passage.[5] What is interesting is that in the tradition of the Church, the phrase was always cited as a biblical argument that celibacy or continence was of apostolic origin. It seems to have been presumed by many Fathers and popes that the Pastoral Epistles make a condition of ordination that a man be a husband of one wife (*unius uxoris vir*), since this could be considered one indication of his ability to live continently once he is ordained. Alfons Cardinal

Stickler demonstrates the traditional interpretation of this Pauline phrase:

> The official interpretation of a well-known passage of Scripture, made by Popes and also adopted by councils, implies that those who feel the need to remarry demonstrate by that fact that they are not able to live the continence required for sacred ministers and therefore cannot be ordained. Thus, this passage from Scripture, far from being a support for marriage and its use by clerics, is in fact a proof for continence, something that was already demanded by the apostles.[6]

Most modern readers find this traditional interpretation goes against the natural sense of the phrase.[7] However, Ignace de la Potterie, S.J., has argued this is because we fail to see the connections between the phrase "husband of one wife" and the spousal covenant of Christ. De la Potterie believes the phrase is a covenantal formula that refers to the fact that the ordained man symbolizes Christ's relationship with the Church—that is, he must be like Christ who is the husband of one wife, the Church.

De la Potterie first points out the unique nature of the phrase "husband of one wife," which is used only for bishops, presbyters, or deacons and its immediate counterpart "wife of one husband" (*unius viri uxor*), which is used to describe the woman seeking to be enrolled as a widow.[8] This fact alone, says de la Potterie, "invites us to think that the quality seen in our expression surpasses in some way the level of common morality, and should have a special nuance, related to the exercise of the ministry in the Church."[9] It is this unique nature of the phrase that will cause de la Potterie to look for a deeper understanding: "one first needs to realize the fact that the stereotypical formula used by the Apostle is in reality a covenantal formula."[10] When looked at in this light, he argues that we should see a connection:

> One can only with difficulty get out of one's mind the impression that this turn of phrase is a direct echo of the formula of 2 Corinthians 11:2, where Paul describes the Church of Corinth as a chaste virgin who has been betrothed to Christ, and who should be presented to him as to a "single husband."[11]

The connection is not hard to trace. In 2 Corinthians 11:2, as we saw in chapter 1, St. Paul describes the Church of Corinth as a woman whom he has betrothed to one husband. When one looks closely at this passage, one finds a striking parallel between the vocabulary in 2 Corinthians 11:2 and 1 Timothy 5:9. In 2 Corinthians 11:2, we see St. Paul telling the Corinthian community that it has been betrothed to one husband (*uni viro*), and in 1 Timothy 5:9, where St. Paul tells the widow she must be the wife of one husband (*unius viri*):[12]

> 2 Cor 11:2: "I feel a divine jealousy for you, for I promised you in marriage to one husband (*uni viro*), to present you as a chaste virgin to Christ.

> 1 Tim 5:9: "she has been married only once (*unius viri uxor*).[13]

As de la Potterie says, "The same formula *unus vir* is used of the relations whether of the Church with Christ, or of the widow who has only had one husband and discharges a ministry in the community."[14] The ramifications for this connection are far reaching:

> If the author of the Pastoral Epistles alludes to this image
> [2 Cor 11:2], when he says to the widow who is at the
> service of the Church that she should be the "wife of
> one husband," and when he says in a parallel way, each
> married minister of the community that he should be the
> "husband of one wife," it is that he wanted, for each of
> these persons, to place a relation between their ecclesial
> ministry and the mystery of Christ and the Church.[15]

By connecting "husband of one wife" with 2 Corinthians 11:2, de la Potterie sees the minister of the Church entering into this nuptial relationship of Christ with His Church. To be "husband of one wife" is to enter into the covenantal relationship of Christ with the Church. This is precisely what we see St. Paul doing in 2 Corinthians 11:2. He takes upon himself God's own jealous love for His Bride: "The jealousy of which Paul speaks is a sharing in God's jealousy over his people. It is the zeal devouring the Apostle in order that his Christians may remain faithful to the covenant made with Christ, who is their true and only bridegroom."[16] Paul places himself in the nuptial relationship between Christ and the Church. Representing the bridegroom, he becomes, so to speak, a man of one wife. We have seen just how deep are the roots of the nuptial image for understanding the covenant in the Scriptures. Based on this, de la Potterie posits that the Pastoral Epistles apply this covenantal relationship to those who dedicate themselves completely to Church ministry:

Unius uxoris vir was a covenantal formula: it introduced
the married minister into the marriage relationship
between Christ and the Church. . . . already in New
Testament times it actually does propose the model
for the ministerial priesthood of a marital relationship
between Christ the bridegroom and the Church his bride,
on the basis of the mystical view of marriage which St
Paul frequently mentions in his letters (cf. II Cor. 11:2;
Eph. 5:22-32).[17]

From this understanding, de la Potterie will propose two
possible interpretations of this passage. First, that "husband
of one wife" means that the minister images Christ's spousal
relationship with the Church in his own spousal relationship with his wife. If a man admitted to ministry in the early
Church was married, he had to be a "husband of one wife."
That is, he must have imaged in his own married life the
fidelity of Christ for His Church. And yet, as we have seen,
Ephesians five proposes this model for every man in the
Church: every man must love his wife as Christ loved the
Church. Therefore, "husband of one wife," which is a unique
qualification only applied to those in ministry, would seem
to imply some form of sexual control over and beyond what
is required of others. De la Potterie, in line with most of the
Tradition, will argue that this formula refers to the practice
of continence for the married minister, especially since it is
connected to Christ's spousal love for the Church, which, as
we have seen, was always virginal.[18] A second possible interpretation of "husband of one wife" is that the formula refers
to the relationship of the married man with the Church.
The minister must be the husband of one wife—that is, he

must either be celibate or continent because his one wife is the Church.

This second argument becomes stronger when one tries to understand the formula for widows, "married only once" (1 Tm 5:9), which must be related since it is so similar. This formula seems to refer to the widow's undivided love for Christ. For the widow, this formula cannot be seen as a negative prohibition against polygamy, since a woman having more than one husband at a time is almost unheard of, and the woman is currently a widow. Nor does it make sense that it is a negative prohibition against marrying a second time since just five verses later (1 Tm 5:14) the author specifically counsels, "I would like younger widows to marry." St. Paul would be forever banning these younger widows from entering the order of widows should their second husbands die. St. Paul tells Timothy, "But exclude younger widows, for when their sensuality estranges them from Christ, they want to marry and will incur condemnation for breaking their first pledge." (1 Tm 5:11-12). What is this "first pledge" of which St. Paul speaks? It must be a pledge to be the "wife of one husband," to have undivided love for Christ in chastity. Since this life of chastity is difficult for younger widows, they should not be enrolled. Thus, the formula for widows makes the most sense when it is interpreted as referring to their undivided love for Christ. Given the relationship between this formula and the one for men, a similar meaning is likely intended for the bishop, presbyter, or deacon. This formula, unius uxoris vir, is a positive command about chaste love for the Church or at the very least, chaste love for his wife as a symbol of Christ's love for the Church.

Some have argued that this interpretation of de la Potterie is too allegorical or "mystical," and that it does not have real connections to the text.[19] However, others have argued it is a very Pauline interpretation. As E. Tauzin wrote at the beginning of the twentieth century: "I believe that Saint Paul would have an intention rather mystical at times, let us say religious, and moral. The persons consecrated to God should represent Christ who himself is the only Bridegroom of the one Bride, the Church "to present you to Christ as a chaste virgin" (2 Cor 11:2)."[20] De la Potterie also argues that this "mystical" idea of marriage is authentic Pauline theology. He recalls the properly exegetical observations of his article:

> 1) The formula is employed only for those who exercise ministry in the Church; 2) it is found always at the top of the list, and has in this regard an archetypal value; 3) this formula is absolutely unique in its genre; 4) it is, however, surprisingly similar to that which St. Paul uses to speak about Christ and the Church, a theme particularly dear to the Apostle (cf. Eph. 5:22-32).[21]

What is, perhaps, most interesting, though, is that when one studies the history of how the nuptial image was applied to the ordained minister, de la Potterie's exegesis is in accord with most of the Tradition; only in the last two hundred years did the exegesis begin to change.[22] For example, Cornelius Lapide, the great synthesizer of patristic exegesis in the post-tridentine period, comments that St. Paul says that the bishop must be "husband of one wife," "not only because of the appearance of incontinence, about which I have already said, being married twice is excluded, but also for the sake of the mystical signification. For the Bishop should represent Christ, who had only one spouse, and she was a virgin, namely the Church."[23] As we will see, this exegesis is much more in accord with the way the Fathers employed the nuptial image for a minister of the Church to explain celibacy or continence.

For the Fathers, since Christ is the Bridegroom of the Church, they can also see the bishop and the priest as a bridegroom, since he is a representative of Christ. Although there are earlier examples of the use of the image,[24] one of the first important witnesses from the East is found in St. Ephrem. The deacon Ephrem is writing to a bishop named Abraham, explaining the meaning of the bishop's celibacy:

> Thou who answerest to the name of Abraham, in that Thou art made father of many; but because to Thee none is spouse, as Sarah was to Abraham,-lo! Thy flock is Thy spouse; bring up her sons in Thy truth; spiritual children may they be to Thee, and the sons be sons of promise, that they may become heirs in Eden.[25]

The image moves between the people as a collective spouse and individual children as Ephrem encourages the bishop to "jealous" love like St. Paul:

> O virgin-youth that art become bridegroom, move to a little jealousy thy mind, towards her who is the wife of thy youth: cut off the attachments which she had, in her girlhood with many others . . . Be jealous O husbandman against the tares, which have sprung up and entangled themselves among the wheat.[26]

However, even in calling the bishop the spouse of the Church, Ephrem never loses sight of who the true spouse is. He tells the bishop: "rebuke her and call together her affections, that she may know what she is and whose she is. In thee may she desire yea love, Christ the Bridegroom of truth."[27] What we see is that Ephrem places the bishop within the nuptial relationship of Christ to the Church. He is not afraid to call the bishop the bridegroom of the Church, and yet he is not the true bridegroom. As Robert Murray comments about Ephrem:

> When he comes to apply nuptial imagery to the Apostles and bishops . . . he makes them share in Christ's own position as Spouse, though in a subordinate and representative way. . . . Of the bishops . . . Ephrem does not hesitate to say that they are wedded to their churches. . . . However, the bishop is not wedded to the Church in his own right. He may be more than a mere go-between, but he is still acting for the "true bridegroom," and therefore he lives in chastity.[28]

St. Jerome defends the idea that "man of one wife" refers to the continence of the bishop in his relationship with his wife. He explains that if the bishop does not live continently after his ordination, he becomes an adulterer: "You surely admit that he who goes on siring children during his episcopate cannot be a bishop. For if people find out about it, he will not be considered a husband but condemned as being adulterous."[29] Jerome sees the bishop as an adulterer even though he has relations with his own wife. This is because the ordination has made the Church his bride.[30]

When St. Augustine asks why it is possible to ordain as a minister of the Church only a man who has had one wife, he also answers by comparing the bishop to Christ the Bridegroom:

> As the many wives of the ancient Fathers symbolized our future churches of all nations, subject to the one man, Christ, so the guide of the faithful, our bishop, who is the husband of one wife, signifies the union of all nations, subject to the one man, Christ.[31]

Here, the bishop can have had only one wife before he is ordained because the bishop represents Christ in His relationship with the Church.[32] However, as we will explain later, Augustine never goes as far as others in actually calling the bishop or the priest the bridegroom of the Church.

St. Leo the Great also makes reference to the phrase "husband of one wife." He, too, sees the priest representing symbolically Christ the Bridegroom who gives Himself entirely to His Bride:

> For already at that time the spiritual marriage of Christ and the Church was being prefigured in the priests: because as the man is head of the woman, the bride of the Word learns to know no other bridegroom than Christ, who rightly chooses only one bride; he has only loved one bride and no other besides her is added to his company.[33]

Leo is explicit that a married man who is ordained a priest begins to live continently with his wife. Since he now must represent Christ's virginal love for His Church in his own marriage, "the carnal union should become a spiritual one."[34]

St. Peter Damian uses an explicit reference to the patristic image of the Cross as the marriage bed to explain the phrase "husband of one wife." Christ was the husband of one wife because He gave Himself totally for His Bride, and the same sacrificial love is to be modeled by the priest in His chastity:

> Christ who . . . clearly offered the lamb of his own body to God on the altar of the cross for the salvation of the world, is the husband of one bride, namely of the entire, holy Church . . . thus in the same way it is taught that the priest is a man of one wife, as he bears the image of this most high bridegroom.[35]

St. Thomas's explanation also points to "husband of one wife" as symbolic of Christ's relationship with the Church. When he explains why St. Paul says the bishop must be "husband of one wife," he says it is not only a proof for continence, but also has a symbolic meaning. The minister must be husband of one wife "not merely to avoid incontinence, but to represent the sacrament, since the Church's bridegroom is Christ, and the Church is one: *Una est columba mea* (Song of Songs 6:9)."[36] Here, St. Thomas is making a subtle but important point: the one who distributes the sacraments becomes himself a sacramental sign, in this case, a sign of the bridegroom who has only one bride. Thus, commenting elsewhere on "husband of one wife," Thomas will say that the recipient of Holy Orders should not have had more than one wife before ordination, that is, he has not re-married if his wife dies because he must signify more perfectly the relationship of Christ with His Church.

> Through the sacrament of orders someone is made a minister of the sacraments; and he who must minister sacraments to others, ought to incur no defect in the

sacraments. However there is a defect in a sacrament, when the signification of the sacrament is not found untainted. Moreover the sacrament of marriage signifies the union of Christ to the Church, which is of one to one; and therefore it is for the perfect signification of the sacrament that the man should be only one man and the woman only one woman. . . . Many wives successively is many secundum quid; and therefore does not remove the signification completely, nor does it empty the sacrament as far as its essence, but as far as its perfection, which is required in those who are dispensers of the sacraments.[37]

Thus, having more than one wife successively does not destroy the essence of the Sacrament of Marriage, which can still be a symbol of the relationship of Christ to His Church, as in the case when the first wife dies. But for a man having had more than one wife to be ordained would make the symbol less perfect, and since he is to be a dispenser of the sacraments, he should be held to a higher standard. The symbolic meaning of his life is more important, since he will signify Christ the Bridegroom.[38]

These examples serve to show that the Tradition, when speaking about the married state of bishops and priests, often sees the minister as a sign of Christ the Bridegroom; and some go so far as to place him within the spousal relationship of Christ with the community as a sacramental representative.

The Nuptial Image Used to Explain the Self-Gift of the Bishop to His Diocese

One of the important uses of the nuptial image in the Tradition has been to describe the relationship between the bishop and his diocese. In many cases, the image was used to prevent the transfer of a bishop from one diocese to another. The reason given was that a bishop should be completely dedicated to his flock, laying down his life for them as a husband for his wife. He is no more able to give up his flock and seek another than a husband is able to give up his wife. Thus, for a bishop to leave his diocese for another was considered adultery. One of the earliest and clearest examples comes from St. Athanasius, who cites 1 Corinthians 7:27: "Are you bound to a wife? Do not seek a separation." St. Athanasius applies St. Paul's words about marriage directly to the bishop and his diocese:

> Are you bound to a wife, do not seek to be free. If this is said about a wife, how much more can it be said about the Church, and about the bishop himself, for anyone having been bound should not seek another, lest he be considered an adulterer according to the Bible.[39]

St. John Chrysostom uses the bridal image in reference to his own relationship with the Church of Constantinople in two impassioned homilies, one that he gave right before his first exile in 403 AD and the second, the day after his return. Before the exile, he assures his people that, even though he will be away from them, nothing can really separate the husband from his wife:

> For my life is prolonged only for your sake; but I implore your charity, that you may have a calm spirit. For no one will be able to break us apart. For those whom Christ has joined, man will not separate. Because if it is said about a husband and wife: For this reason a man shall leave his father and mother, and cling to his wife, and they will be two in one flesh (Gen 2:24): and if in this way the union

of marriages among men is not able to be separated, then much more the Church is not able to be broken from her pastor.[40]

One gets a sense of the deep communion and trust Chrysostom envisions between the bishop and his people implied by this image. They have learned to depend upon his preaching, shepherding, and sanctifying as a bride depends upon her husband. Upon his return from exile, he acclaims them for their fidelity to him, comparing the fidelity to that of a bride for her husband. He begins his homily meditating on how God protected the chastity of Sarah from the Egyptians,[41] and he likens this to his bride the Church which, in his absence, repulsed the heretics as barbarian seducers. Chrysostom cries out against them: "You have not injured in any way my bride, but she has remained showing forth her beauty."[42] This clearly resembles the depth of pastoral charity(i.e., spousal love) that we saw in St. Paul,[43] which makes a priest or a bishop rightfully saddened when his people, his bride, abandon the faith he preaches. In our own age, many bishops and priests know this pain.

The image of the bishop espoused to his people persists with different levels of influence throughout the Tradition right up to the present day.[44] In fact, it was brought up by some of the Fathers at the Second Vatican Council in the discussions about mandatory retirement for bishops. Bishop Paolo Marella, President of the commission *De episcopis et de dioeceseon regimine*, in justifying the retirement and transfer of bishops, said such moves must be balanced with "that ancient and venerable opinion of the mystical marriage between the bishop and his bride the local church." And yet,

Bishop Marella says that although stability is a value in the episcopal office, a bishop is not "in every way unmovable until his death," because the "supreme law is the good of souls" counts even for bishops.[45] Thus, although the image continues to play a role, it is not an absolute prohibition, nor has it been considered as such during much of the Church's history.[46] Instead, Antonio Miralles has proposed that the permanent nature of the nuptial relationship is what links the bishop to the universal Church, not the local church. He argues that the bishop is an image of the universal mission of Christ,[47] and his relationship with a particular diocese is a concrete, even if a temporary, expression of this permanent nuptial relationship: "The role of the bishop in a spousal relationship versus the particular Church is none other than the particular projection of his indelible spousal relationship versus the universal Church."[48] A similar argument could be made about him being a bridegroom of the universal Church (as St. John Paul II did in *Pastores Dabo Vobis*). Since the priest, too, makes Christ present to the local community, although to a lesser degree than the bishop, he also makes present the Bridegroom to his local community by virtue of the priest's spousal relationship with the universal Church.

The spousal relationship of the bishop with the Church is expressed in the Liturgy of Ordination for the bishop. In the current ordination rite, when the bishop receives his episcopal ring, the ordaining prelate says: "Receive this ring, the seal of fidelity: adorned with undefiled faith, preserve unblemished the bride of God, the holy Church."[49] Although the use of a ring by the bishop goes back further, the nuptial significa-tion of the ring enters the Liturgy in the tenth century.[50] The prayers that accompany the giving of the ring throughout the

development of the Liturgy express different understandings of the bishop's spousal relationship with the Church.
Some address the nuptial mystery of Christ and the Church
by speaking of the bishop being entrusted as a "guardian"
with the duty to preserve or to protect the spouse of Christ.
For example, one of the Gallican liturgies says, "with this
ring of faith we commend to you this bride of Christ the
Church that you may preserve it holy and immaculate in his
sight in every good thing."[51] However, in the same Liturgy,
the prayer that follows implies more directly that the bishop
himself becomes the bridegroom and encourages him to the
self-donating love of Christ: "In the name of the Lord Jesus
Christ receive this ring, that just as he espoused the Church
to himself in his own blood and made it fruitful with spiritual
offspring so you are able from the same bride to bring forth
children of adoption also through saving instruction."[52]

The explanations of theologians and Fathers of the
Church on the ring of the bishop follow the same distinction between the bishop as guardian of the bride and the
bishop as bridegroom. Hugh of St. Victor explains the ring
this way: "The ring signifies a mystery of faith, in which the
bride of Christ the Church is married, whose guardians and
teachers are the bishops and the prelates, as a sign of which
they wear the ring testifying to this duty."[53] On the other
hand, St. Bernard of Clairvaux relates a scene in his *Life of St.
Malachy* where the bishop is choosing a successor for another
deceased bishop.[54] He speaks about a vision of a ring on the
hand of the man that will make him a bridegroom: "Do not
be afraid . . . For you have been seen worthy by the Lord,
because the gold ring, by which you are going to be espoused,
I have already seen on your finger."[55] At times, the bishop is

called the bridegroom of the diocese; at other times, he is the bridegroom's guardian. Yet in all the uses of the image, the bishop has a role in the nuptial relationship, and he is encouraged to give himself completely to the service and protection of the bride.

The Nuptial Image Used to Explain the Spiritual Fruitfulness of the Sacrament of Holy Orders

Many of the Fathers express the idea that the priest or the bishop raises up offspring with the bride through his preaching and celebration of the sacraments. St. Pacian of Barcelona cites St. Paul's First Letter to the Corinthians (4:15: "I became your father in Christ Jesus through the gospel") and applies this to the priests:

> Thus Christ begets in the Church through his priests, as also the apostle says: For in Christ I fathered you (1 Cor 4:15). And thus the seed of Christ, that is the Spirit of God, brings forth the new man having been formed in the womb of the mother and received by the hands of the priests in the birth at the font.[56]

It is noteworthy that the priest plays a role in the generation but is not the bridegroom. Pacian sees the generation coming from Christ through the means of the priest by the power of the Holy Spirit in the Church. St. John Chrysostom also speaks about the priest as begetting children through performing the Sacrament of Baptism: "For our fathers begot us 'of blood and the will of the flesh'; but they [priests] are responsible for our birth from God, that blessed second birth, our true emancipation, the adoption according to grace."[57] Eusebius of Caesarea sees spiritual fruitfulness as connected to the celibacy or continence of the bishop and the priest. Their preaching and teaching are their way to propagate offspring:

> Especially in the present time, a life separated from a wife is necessary by [teachers and preachers] that they may be more free for higher pursuits, just as it is desired by those who are concerned with bringing forth divine and spiritual offspring; they have undertaken the education and holy discipline not of only one or two children but of an innumerable multitude.[58]

In the first chapter, we looked at a scriptural image that becomes very important for understanding the patristic vision of the nuptial nature of the Sacrament of Holy Orders. As we noted, the Fathers see John the Baptist as the friend of the bridegroom who refers to the levirate law when he says that he is not worthy to untie the strap of Jesus' sandal.[59] But the Fathers take this image a step further when they see Jesus as the deceased brother and place the Apostles and their successors in the position of the levir who takes up the bride. Many of the Fathers link John 1:27 with 1 Corinthians 4:15 where St. Paul says, "for I became your father in Christ Jesus through the gospel." They see this as the fulfillment of the levirate law; the Apostle takes the bride and raises up children for his deceased brother, Christ.

Some of the best examples of this exegesis come from St. Augustine who seemed to prefer it as a nuptial image for apostolic ministry. In his letter *Contra Faustum*, Augustine uses this image as an example of how the Old Testament is fulfilled spiritually in the New Testament:

Without understanding Faustus objected to the commandments of the Old Testament as adultery, that one brother was commanded to take the wife of another brother in order that he should raise up progeny not for himself but for his brother and that the law would call them by the name from whence they were born [i.e., the deceased brother]. What else is prefigured in this, except that every preacher of the gospel should thus labor in the Church, as to raise up seed for his deceased brother, that is for Christ, who died for us, and that those who will have been raised up should be called by his name? Moreover, the apostle fulfills this not as it was previously signified in the flesh, but spiritually, in complete truth, he reminds them that Christ has begotten them; he is angry with them and reproving them he corrects those wanting to belong to Paul: Was Paul, he says, crucified for you? Or were you baptized in the name of Paul? It is as if he would say: "I have begotten you for my deceased brother, you are called Christians, not Paulinians."[60]

In another passage, St. Augustine points out that the Apostles were called "brothers" by the Lord, so this means they have to fulfill the levir's duty:

The Church is the bride of the deceased, which Christ has entrusted to these first faithful ones, he who through death and resurrection ascended to the Father. That she might bring forth children, the Church has been joined to the apostles and the leaders of the Church. For in the Gospel he calls "brothers" the apostles, who, working in the Church, should raise up offspring, not for themselves, but for their deceased brother. Indeed this is the reason that those who are born of the Gospel having the Apostles as fathers are called by the name of Christian.[61]

The image helps Augustine to balance his understanding of the nuptiality of Holy Orders: Yes, the apostle has a nuptial role; he is joined to the Church and raises up children. However, he does this not for himself, but for Christ, since Christ is the true bridegroom. St. Caesarius of Arles uses the image much as Augustine does, emphasizing that Jesus refers to the Apostles as His brothers who will take up His bride in His absence:

> We see that this figure is fulfilled in the apostles: since the brother is deceased, that is Christ has died, who had said: go and tell my brothers, they took up his wife, which is the Church. This is what the apostle Paul says: in Christ Jesus I fathered you through the Gospel. And still those born of the Church through the teaching of the apostles are not called Petrinians or Paulinians, but they are called Christians; in order that the figure might be completed, which was anticipated in the law concerning the wife of the deceased brother.[62]

St. Gregory the Great applies the levirate law to the scene where Jesus asks St. Peter "Do you love me?" (Jn 21:16). He sees Jesus asking Peter to take up the levir's role, shepherding as a kind of bridegroom in his place. For Gregory, this is a foreshadowing of all those charged to be shepherds, all of whom have a responsibility to take the levir's role and raise up children for Christ the Bridegroom. Gregory says:

> This he said to Peter: Simon do you love me? Who, when he responded that he loved him, immediately

heard: If you love me, feed my sheep (Jn 21:15-17). If
being a shepherd is a testimony of love, then anyone
having strong abilities to shepherd, and yet refuses to
shepherd the flock of God, this one is shown to have
no love for the supreme Shepherd. . . . This Moses said,
that a surviving brother should receive the wife of his
brother who died without children, and he should bear
a son in the name of his brother; if he should refuse to
accept her, the wife should spit in his face, and a relative
should take off the sandal from one of his feet. . . .
Obviously, he is the brother of the deceased, who after
his resurrection appearing in glory said: Go, and tell
my brothers (Mt 28:10). The brother died as if without
children, because he still had not filled up the number of
his elect.[63]

Perhaps Gregory was even thinking of his own reasons
for leaving the monastery to take on pastoral duty, called to
father children in Christ's place, he could not say no.

Other examples of this application of the levirate law
throughout the centuries could be cited,[64] but these examples
help to show us one of the ways the Fathers spoke about the
fruitfulness of apostolic ministry. The bishop or the priest
accepts being in the spousal relationship of Christ and the
Church to raise up children for Him. The advantage of how
the Fathers use the levirate image is that it reveals the nuptial
nature of the Sacrament of Holy Orders, without confusing
who is the real bridegroom.

Bridegroom or Amicus Sponsi

We have already seen a distinction when talking about the
spousal image; some Fathers do not call the bishop or the

priest the bridegroom. Seeking to protect Christ's unique role, some reserve to Him the title "bridegroom" and use the term *amicus sponsi* (friend of the bridegroom) for the minister. The title *amicus sponsi* is taken from St. John the Baptist. It is often applied to the Apostles and their successors in ministry as a way to explain their role in the nuptial relationship. The minister is not the bridegroom, even though he has a role in the spousal relationship; he is really the friend of the bridegroom who rejoices at the bridegroom's voice. A good example of this application to the priest or bishop is found in St. John Chrysostom. We have seen that at times, he refers to himself as the bridegroom of the Church, but in his commentary on John's Gospel, he holds up the example of John the Baptist. John is not the bridegroom but a friend of the bridegroom. His job is temporary, and he rejoices when it is finished. Then John is able to "hand over the bride because he is servant and minister."[65] This is an example for the bishop or the priest who must never forget his job is to prepare the bride for the real bridegroom, the one for whom he is a friend and servant. Chrysostom shows us that it is difficult to oppose too directly the distinct uses of the bridegroom image. Precisely because of the relationship of representation, the image is fluid, and we find the Tradition uses it in different ways at different times.

St. Gregory the Great also speaks about the priest or bishop as friend of the bridegroom. He uses this image to warn against being a priest or a bishop who seeks too much to please the people. When the priest or bishop seeks first the love of the flock and not of Christ, he is actually drawing the bride to himself and not to Christ:

For he is an enemy of the savior, the man who, through the good works he does, desires to be loved by the Church in the place of [Christ]. For a servant, through whom the bridegroom transmits his gifts, is guilty of adultery in his intentions, if he seeks pleasure in the eyes of the bride.[66]

This is a very real danger for every minister who begins to live for himself and not as a servant to Christ's mission. As we saw earlier, he fails to recognize correctly the distinction between the person and the office of the minister. He begins to appropriate his office to himself and in this way, takes the place of the true bridegroom and becomes an adulterer. The friend of the bridegroom transmits the gifts but always remembers he is not the source of them. He does not seek the benefits of the office for himself.

St. Augustine never applies the title "bridegroom" directly to the person of the bishop or the priest; he always prefers the title "friend of the bridegroom." He does this precisely because it helps to retain the distinction between office and person. He believes that it protects the humility of the minister by keeping him in right relationship with Christ. In his commentary on John's Gospel, St. Augustine applies the title "friend of the bridegroom" to the ministers of the Church. The Bishop of Hippo connects the example of St. John the Baptist to the apostolic ministry of St. Paul. First, he points out the humility of John who does not rejoice as if he is the bridegroom but rejoices that the true bridegroom comes:

Let us see what he says: He who has the bride, is the bridegroom, she is not my bride. And do you not rejoice in the marriage? Even more I rejoice, he says: For the

friend of the bridegroom who stands and listens to
him, he rejoices with joy at the voice of the bridegroom
(Jn 3:29). He did not say, I rejoice at my voice, he said
I rejoice at the voice of the bridegroom. I am the one
doing the listening, he is the one speaking: for I am the
one needing to be enlightened, he is the light; I am like
the ear: he is the Word. Therefore the friend of the
bridegroom stands and listens to him.[67]

Augustine then correlates this humility of the friend of
the bridegroom with St. Paul's jealous love for the bride.[68] He
points out that Paul embodies the jealousy of Christ. Paul is
not upset because the people have stopped loving him but
because they have stopped loving Christ!

So, also, the Apostle is a friend of the bridegroom; and
he is jealous, not for himself, but for the bridegroom.
Listen to the voice of the one who is jealous: with the
jealousy of God I am jealous for you, he said; not with
mine, not for myself, but with the jealousy of God. From
where? how? You are jealous for whom? Or of whom are
you jealous? For I have espoused you to one husband, to
present you as a chaste virgin to Christ (2 Cor 11:2). Why
therefore do you fear? Why are you jealous? I fear, he
said, lest just as the serpent seduced Eve by his subtlety,
so also your minds may be corrupted from the chastity
which is in Christ (2 Cor 11:3).[69]

For the Bishop of Hippo, this distinction becomes
important when he is embroiled in the Donatist crisis.[70] In
using the title "friend of the bridegroom," he emphasizes that
the priest should not be confused with the true bridegroom;
and it is from the true bridegroom that the real baptism

comes. For this reason, Augustine chooses the example of St. John the Baptist as the true friend of the bridegroom because, as Michael Sherwin, O.P., says, "John proclaims that Christ is the one who baptizes with the Holy Spirit. John reveals that it is Christ and Christ alone who administers this baptism."[71] The minister administers the baptism of Jesus, not of himself; therefore, he does not confuse himself with the bridegroom. Only the true bridegroom has the ability to give life to the bride. The bishop or the priest realizes that the life he gives does not come from himself—he does not confuse his office and his person—like John, he is the friend of the bridegroom and not the true bridegroom.

In fact, Augustine will go so far in his accusation of the Donatists as to say they push themselves into Christ's place, like adulterers. Augustine says they claim to do what only the real bridegroom can do:

> Why are you taking the place of Christ? He baptizes in the Holy Spirit. Therefore, he justifies. You, what are you saying? I baptize in the Holy Spirit, I justify. Certainly you are not saying, I am the Christ? Certainly you are not one of those about whom it was said: Many will come in my name saying, I am the Christ? (Mt 24:5) . . . Therefore don't continue to say, I justify, I sanctify; lest you be convicted of saying, I am the Christ. Say rather what the friend of the bridegroom said, not like you who wants to push yourself forward instead of the bridegroom: Neither the one who plants is anything, nor the one who waters, but it is God who gives the growth (1 Cor 3:7).[72]

For St. Augustine, John the Baptist and Paul become models for a true minister. Here, we see an important

Augustinian theme that was emphasized in the previous chapter: a sign of a true minister is his humility; he leads the people to Christ. He does not take credit for what ultimately belongs to Christ. He listens for the bridegroom and rejoices at the bridegroom's voice (Jn 3:29). He sees himself as the voice that passes away, as a servant of the Word. He must decrease so that Christ may increase. For Augustine, all who will minister in the name of Christ are called to be this kind of friend of the bridegroom. They have been entrusted to guard and prepare the bride, not for themselves but for Christ:

> He spent forty days with them: as he was about to ascend into heaven he again commended the Church to them. About to depart, the bridegroom commended his bride to his friends: not so that she would love any particular one of them; but that she may love him as the bridegroom, them as friends of the bridegroom, no one of them as if he were the bridegroom. For this the friends of the bridegroom are zealous, that they do not permit her to be seduced by flirtatious love. They hate it when they are loved this way.[73]

Then, Augustine gives an example from St. Paul of how St. Paul hated being put in the place of Christ, as if he were an adulterer taking the place of the bridegroom and not a friend of the bridegroom:

> Notice the jealousy of this friend of the bridegroom: when he sees the bride is in some way going to commit fornication with the friends of the bridegroom, he says: . . . each one of you says: certainly I belong to Paul, truly I belong to Apollos; I on the other hand

to Peter, and I to Christ. Is Christ divided? Was Paul crucified for you, and were you baptized in the name of Paul? (1 Cor 1:11-13). What a Friend! He repels the love of another's bride from himself. He does not want to be loved by the bride, that he may be able to reign with the bridegroom.[74]

The friend of the bridegroom prefers the love of Christ to the love of the bride. This distinction helps us to understand more clearly the role of the minister in the spousal relationship of Christ with the Church. The minister's primary relationship is not with the bride; his first love should be for Christ. He does love the bride but only in and for Christ. Of course, he wants to be loved by the bride and to love the bride, but he does not want to be loved in the place of Christ; and he wants to love only in and for Christ:

> Accordingly, my brothers, let no one deceive you, no one seduce you: love the peace of Christ, who was crucified for you, although he was God. Paul says: Neither the one who plants is anything, nor the one who waters, but it is God who gives the growth (1 Cor 3:7). And does any one of us say he is anything? If we say that we are something, and we do not give glory to him, then we are adulterers; we want to be loved and not the bridegroom. You, love Christ, and us in him, in whom also you are loved by us. Let the members love one another, but let them all live under the head.[75]

In this overview of the Tradition, we have seen that there are many times in the Tradition when the bishop and the priest are referred to as a bridegroom of the Church. Yet, some Fathers, especially St. Augustine, point out this should be done in a way that does not forget who the real bridegroom is. Their preference for the term "friend of the bridegroom" emphasizes again the virtue of humility. The priest or bishop must remember his life-giving power is not his own and that the authority he exercises is not for his own benefit. If he leads the bride to himself, he has usurped the true bridegroom and become an adulterer. The friend of the bridegroom always thinks first of the real bridegroom, even as he serves the bride.

Is there a contradiction in the applications of the title "bridegroom" to the ordained minister and the title "friend of the bridegroom"? Laurent Touze demonstrates clearly that either image can lead to an extreme, and yet we need both to understand fully the nuptial nature of the sacrament.[76] Those who insist too strictly on the minister's being a bridegroom risk the error of clericalism. Those who say we cannot call the bishop or the priest the bridegroom risk negating the real sacramental representation of the minister. We have entered into the complex reality of representation, which we spoke about in the previous chapter. This is the tension between office and person in which the priest lives. In his office, he represents the bridegroom; but he cannot seek the benefits of the office for himself. Rather, he is always seeking subjectively to allow everything within him to lead people to Christ: Christ must increase, and the priest must decrease. As we will see, the priest must seek in his life to continually live rightly in this tension, and the evangelical counsels will aid him in this goal.

Can the Bridegroom Image Be Applied to the Priest as Well as the Bishop?

In the Tradition, the nuptial image is more often applied to the bishop than to the priest. Many Fathers—St. John Chrysostom, St. Pacian of Barcelona, St. Leo the Great, and other theologians—do apply the image to the priest,—yet, the image is more often and more strictly applied to the bishop.[77] This is seen especially in the argument for limiting the transference of the bishop and in the giving of the ring during the ordination rite. It is much more common to see the bishop's total self-gift of his ministry in terms of the nuptial image.[78] Yet, as we have already shown, St. John Paul II uses the image to bring out a deeper understanding of the nature of the priesthood. St. Thomas Aquinas can show us how the application of the bridegroom image to the priest is justified.

St. Thomas was careful in his application of the nuptial image to the Sacrament of Holy Orders. Although he does apply the title bridegroom in some way to the bishop and also the priest, he does so analogously. He makes it clear that the real bridegroom of the Church is Christ; however, to the degree that he represents Christ, the bishop or the priest can be properly called the bridegroom of the Church. The bishop is referred to as the bridegroom of the Church in the Supplement to the *Summa Theologiae* of St. Thomas.[79] Here, a distinction is made in the way a priest and bishop represent Christ. The bishop is called the bridegroom of the Church because he represents Christ with a greater perfection: "A bishop represents [Christ] in that He instituted other ministers and founded the Church . . . For this reason also a bishop is especially called the bridegroom of the Church even as Christ is."[80] This text was taken almost exactly from St. Thomas's understanding of the episcopacy as it was outlined in his commentary on the *Sentences*.[81] Also in the *Sentences*, St. Thomas speaks about the symbol of the bishop's ring—again, it is because he has full power to dispense the sacraments and represent the Church juridically as a public person that the bishop receives the ring that marks him as a bridegroom: "Only the bishop is properly called a prelate of the Church: and therefore only he receives the ring as if a bridegroom of the Church; and only he has full power in the dispensation of the sacraments, and jurisdiction in the public tribunal as a public person."[82] It is the representation of Christ who continues to found the Church through the sacraments and the representation of Christ as juridical head of the Church that makes the bishop able to be called the bridegroom. Thus, it is a question of analogy. The real bridegroom is Christ, and the bishop is called a bridegroom because in these central aspects, he represents Christ.

In another passage, St. Thomas makes it even clearer that there is only one true bridegroom; but he also says that the ministers of the sacraments, including priests, who generate spiritual children for Christ, can be called the bridegrooms of the Church. Addressing whether parish priests are bridegrooms of the churches committed to their care, he says:

> The bridegroom of the Church, properly speaking, is Christ: about whom it is said: he who has the bride is the bridegroom (Jn 3:29), for he begets children with the Church in his own name. Others, who are called bridegrooms, are ministers of the bridegroom, cooperating in a more exterior way in the begetting of

spiritual children, whom nevertheless they do not beget for themselves, but for Christ. Indeed, ministers are called bridegrooms of the Church in as much as they occupy the place of the true bridegroom.[83]

St. Thomas goes on to say that priests, as well as bishops and the pope, can, by analogy, be called bridegrooms in their representation of Christ: "The Pope, who occupies the place of Christ in the whole church, is called the bridegroom of the universal Church, the bishop of his diocese, and the presbyter of his parish."[84] Thus, for St. Thomas, the application of the bridegroom image has to do strictly with the representative role of the minister. And the greater the degree of representation of Christ in that role, the more aptly he is called bridegroom.

The State of Perfection and the Nuptial Nature of Holy Orders

One more aspect of St. Thomas's theology of the episcopacy can help us come to a deeper understanding of the bridegroom image. Admittedly, St. Thomas himself did not use the nuptial image to describe this aspect of the episcopacy, although his commentators did. The question has to do with the relationship of the bishop to the state of perfection.[85] St. Thomas argues that bishops and religious are in the state of perfection because they are bound "to things pertaining to perfection . . . with a certain solemnity."[86] Religious bind themselves through the counsels to "refrain from worldly affairs," and bishops "bind themselves to things pertaining to perfection when they take up the pastoral duty, to which it belongs that a shepherd lays down his life for his sheep" (Jn 10:15).[87] St. Thomas adds that "the perfection of the episcopal state consists in this, that for love of

God a man binds himself to work for the salvation of his neighbor."[88] The common denominator for the state of perfection is binding oneself to make of one's life a total self-gift. The religious does this through counsels, which, as noted in Chapter Three, allow him to make his life a "holocaust . . . offering to God all that one has."[89] The bishop does it through the gift of self in pastoral care to the Church, which, according to St. Thomas, must also be a total self-gift, even to the point of laying down his life.

When he speaks about the total self-gift of the bishop, St. Thomas does not mention the nuptial image, yet some of his commentators easily make the connection. Sebastian of St. Joachim and Ildefonsus of the Angels, both from the school of Salamanca, integrate the state of perfection of the bishop and the nuptial nature of the episcopacy when questioning the licitness of transferring a bishop:

> Bishops by the force of office are in the state of perfection; but the state of perfection by its nature demands perpetual permanence: Therefore bishops by the force and dignity of the office are held to remain perpetually in exercising Episcopal care with respect to the Church, with which they have contracted a spiritual marriage.[90]

To support this, they explicitly cite the *Summa Theologiae* II-II questions 184 and 185. Here, we can see an important insight. St. Thomas's commentators see a connection between the nuptial relationship of bishops with the Church and those who profess the counsels. Both, as part of the state of perfection, are called to make their lives a total self-gift. If the evangelical counsels are the means of Christ's total self-gift, then one can argue that they should in some way be common to this state of perfection. If the bishop and the priest are called to make their lives a total self-gift, in imitation of Christ's nuptial self-gift, this can be argued to include in some way the evangelical counsels.

Interestingly, St. Thomas does not include the priest in the state of perfection with the bishops and the religious. According to the Angelic Doctor, priests cannot be in the state of perfection because the "parish priest or archdeacon does not pledge his whole life to the cure of souls, as a bishop does."[91] In other words, priests are not bound "under the obligation of a perpetual vow to retain the cure of souls; but they can surrender it . . . by entering religion, even without their bishop's permission."[92] Therefore, priests are not in the state of perfection because they do not have the same kind of unbreakable covenant with their parishes as a bishop has with his diocese. Their care of souls does not require in the same way a total self-gift for their flock. St. Thomas says that although their charge requires from them a sacrifice, the sacrifice is not a holocaust: "The comparison of their religious state with their [priests'] office is like the comparisons of the universal with the particular, and of a holocaust with a sacrifice, which is less than a holocaust."[93]

Yet, it is precisely this understanding of the nuptial nature of the episcopacy as a total self-gift, a holocaust, that can allow us to see the development in St. John Paul II's use of the nuptial image for the life of the priest. In the modern era, the bishop's spousal covenant is more clearly seen with the whole Church than with his individual diocese. As noted, this opens the door to seeing the priest also in such a permanent spousal relationship—indeed, a relationship that requires a total self-gift, a holocaust. This is precisely the way that St. John Paul II applies the nuptial image to the priest. When describing the pastoral charity that is the heart of the priesthood, he not only cites John 10:15 as the example of the good shepherd laying down his life for his sheep as St. Thomas does, but he also cites Ephesians 5:25-27. The Holy Father writes, "Christ's gift of himself to his Church, the fruit of his love, is described in terms of that unique gift of self made by the bridegroom to the bride, as the sacred texts often suggest."[94] St. John Paul II declares that the nuptial image is appropriate for describing the life and mission of the priest because, by his sacramental configuration to the bridegroom, he, too, is called to lay down his whole life for his bride—that is, to make a holocaust, not just a sacrifice. By this logic, one could make an argument that St. John Paul II's understanding of the priesthood places the priest with the bishops and the religious in what is traditionally called the "state of perfection."[95] This application of the spousal image to the priest, and its connection to the total self-gift, will allow us in our concluding chapter to explain the importance of the evangelical counsels in the priest's life.

The Priest as Bridegroom: An Ecclesiological Value

There are two primary images for the Church in the Scriptures: the Church as the Body of Christ and the Church as the Bride of Christ. Both images are essential for the Church's self-understanding because they emphasize different aspects of the Church's relationship with Christ. The body image, which emphasizes the unity between the Church and Christ, is necessarily complemented by the spousal image, which is primary in St. Paul, and which emphasizes the

distinction between Christ and the Church without destroy-
ing the unity. As we noted, some have argued that in our
present day, there is a risk of a misunderstanding of the
Church based upon an overemphasis of the body image. An
overemphasis on the body image implies an identity between
Christ and the Church that fails to recognize the need for
the distinction. This can cause the Church to lose her sense
of total dependence on Christ; she ends up being Christ and
not needing Him. It is the spousal image that reminds us
that Christ is always antecedent to His Church and that the
Church is continually dependent upon Christ for her new life.

This misunderstanding of ecclesiology has led to an
error about the nature of the priesthood proposed by some
scholars in the post-Vatican II period. As a reaction to many
factors, including the shortage of priests, the problem of
clericalism, and issues of democratic ideologies, these scholars promoted the idea that there is no ontological distinction
between the priesthood of the ordained and that of the
faithful.[96] They argue that the priesthood should be seen as
primarily a service to the community carried out by a delegated leader, and they downplay the emphasis on the cultic
role of the priest. The idea is that the community gives the
authority to a delegated leader who performs necessary functions within the Church—that is, presiding at the Eucharist
and the other sacraments, as well as preaching and teaching.[97]
In this view, the priest represents the head; but he has no
power which does not emanate from the body of which he is
a member. Gisbert Greshake explains this approach:

> This approach to a theological explanation not only sets
> the ministry completely inside the community of baptized

and confirmed Christians, but derives ministry entirely from the community. . . . It makes it clear that the people of God is the greater entity, because it includes both clergy and laity.[98]

Ultimately, these scholars reject the idea that Christ left His Church an apostolic ministry that serves as a representation of Christ continuing His life-giving presence.[99] Gisbert Greshake, in his critique of this view, puts the question poignantly:

> Has the ordained official a merely official responsibility for what is fundamentally the responsibility of the Church as a whole, or does ordination mean that some effect is produced by Christ on the ordained person (for the benefit of the Church, of course), an effect which the Church as a whole cannot confer and which is transmitted by Christ to the Church and through the ordained person?[100]

The Congregation for the Doctrine of the Faith answered the questions raised by these theologians by simply pointing out that the community does not have the power to give what it does not have: "no community has the power to confer apostolic ministry, which is essentially bestowed by the Lord himself."[101]

One might ask why it is important to emphasize that the priest is distinct from the Church, even though he is a member of it. This is because the priest must be seen to represent Christ who, although he is united to His body, is, in fact, distinct from it. As we noted in chapter 2, this distinction between Christ and the Church is essential for the Church's self-understanding. As Walter Kasper points out, the Church's official ministry reminds her that her life does not come from herself:

> Behind this specific task of the official ministry lies the conviction that individual Christians do not simply "possess" their own charisms; nor does the Church, as Christ's body, owe its life to itself or to its own power. The Christian existence and the life of the Church are possible only thanks to Jesus Christ, the Head of the Church. He did not found and equip the Church once and for all, so that it could now get on with things on its own; in all that they do, both the Church and every individual Christian owe their life completely to the Lord who is present in his body. Their life comes not "from below," but "from above," since "Christ is the Head, from whom the whole body, joined and knit together by every joint with which it is supplied when each part is working properly, makes bodily growth and upbuilds itself in love" (Eph 4:16).[102]

Here, it can be seen that the understanding of the Church as the Bride of Christ is a helpful complement to the understanding of the Church as the Body of Christ. The image of the Church as bride emphasizes more clearly the distinction between Christ and the Church while still maintaining the essential unity. Lawrence Welch explains this:

> What is needed is a symbol that clearly expresses not only the difference between Christ and his Church but their free union as well. A symbol capable of doing this is the symbol of Christ as bridegroom and Church as bride. Put simply, the relation of Christ the head to his body should be understood covenantally and nuptially as union of one

flesh. The relationship between Christ and his body is a marital kind of union where each subject exists in a union that is freely chosen but does not dissolve or collapse the subject into one another. It makes evident the difference between Christ the head and his body and bride while maintaining their unity.[103]

One can see how important it is to recognize the priest as representing the bridegroom of the Church. The priest as bridegroom, although certainly a member of the body and united to the body, is also distinct within it. Because of the priest's sacramental consecration, he represents Christ who stands in the forefront of His bride. It is through this representation of the priest, standing in the forefront, that the Church understands her life comes not from herself but from Christ:

> Through the ministerial priesthood the Church becomes aware in faith that her being comes not from herself but from the grace of Christ in the Holy Spirit. The apostles and their successors, inasmuch as they exercise an authority which comes to them from Christ, the head and shepherd, are placed—with their ministry—in the forefront of the Church as a visible continuation and sacramental sign of Christ in his own position before the Church and the world, as the enduring and ever new source of salvation, he "who is head of the Church, his body, and is himself its savior" (Eph 5:23).[104]

We see how necessary it is to understand that included in the priestly representation of Christ the Head is the priest's representation of Christ the Bridegroom who "stands 'before' the Church and 'nourishes and cherishes her' (Eph

5:29), giving his life for her."[105] Commenting on this passage
from *Pastores Dabo Vobis*, Antonio Miralles says, "One can
clearly say that being 'in front of the Church,' [is] characteristic of the participation of the priest in the spousal nature of
Christ."[106] The *Directory on the Ministry and Life of Priests* states
it clearly:

> Christ, the permanent and ever new origin of salvation,
> is the germinal mystery springing forth from which
> is the mystery of the Church, his Body and his Bride,
> called by her Spouse to be a sign and instrument of
> redemption. . . . Through the mystery of Christ, the
> priest, exercising his multifaceted ministry, is inserted into
> mystery of the Church, which "becomes aware in faith
> that her being comes not from herself, but from the grace
> of Christ in the Holy Spirit" (PDV 16). In this sense,
> while the priest is in the Church, he is also placed in the
> forefront of it (ibid.).[107]

The priest becomes a living sign of the bridegroom, a
sign that shows the bridegroom is distinct but not distant
from the Church. Distinction is not an obstacle to union, as
the marriage image shows us. Distinction is the means of
union; the union of two requires difference and does not
erase the distinctions. The priest, who as we have seen is set
apart by his consecration to the Bridegroom, is also a sign for
the Church of Christ's union with her. The Church needs this
living sign as a reminder of who Christ is for her. Gustave
Martelet, S.J., explains this need well:

> The fact remains, however, that the ministerial priesthood
> exercises, by virtue of the Spirit, a function that can
> easily be distinguished in the economy of salvation.

While Christ, with the gift of himself, guarantees the
Church a union that abolishes all spiritual distance, which
would leave the Church with her hunger unsatisfied, it
is necessary for the Bride herself, however, to possess
within herself the sign that reminds her efficaciously
of the incomparable personality of the Bridegroom.
Since union always presupposes the real difference of
persons, theirs will be all the deeper and more successful:
all confusion excluded, no distance, however, will be
established, but only the distinction which guarantees
union will be signified. In this sense the ministerial
priesthood, beyond all merit of the subjects invested with
it only to serve the whole Church, helps the Church not
only to forget the conditions of her union, but even more
to rejoice always in the originality of a Bridegroom whose
marvelous singularity is incessantly recalled to her by the
consecrated ministry.[108]

The need to see the priest as both head and bridegroom
can also be illustrated in the two aspects of priestly representation that we noted in the last chapter: *in persona Christi* and *in
persona ecclesiae*. One cannot make a strict correlation between
these representations and our two ecclesiological images,
but it can be observed that when the priest prays to God *in
persona ecclesiae*, he acts more like the head who is united to the
whole body; whereas when the priest speaks *in persona Christi*,
he stands in the forefront of the community and makes present the life-giving nuptial self-gift of Christ, as an image of
the bridegroom. As John Saward says:

> The difference between the two kinds of priestly
> representation can be expressed as follows: Representing
> the Church, the priest faces the Bridegroom as a living

part of the Bride, whereas representing Christ, he stands facing the Bride, not for his own glory, but in her service, as the living and transparent image of her Spouse.[109]

The Church needs the living sign of the Bridegroom for her own proper self-understanding. By representing the Bridegroom to the bride, the priest becomes a living sign of the dependence of the Church on the life-giving power of Christ her groom. One more excellent quote from Gustave Martelet brings home this important point:

> The Church, in fact, needs to know always that the riches which she so miraculously has for herself and for the life of the world, are nothing but the property of her Christ, and Christ himself. Hence the necessity for her to possess, in her living reality as a society unique in the world, the irrefutable sign that everything she possesses, everything she enjoys, she receives incessantly from Christ and from him alone. Now, since Christ, having become invisible for her, can no longer appear personally to affirm his irreplaceable presence and action, there will be in the Church a visible and efficacious reminder of her absolute and vital dependency on her irreplaceable Bridegroom. The ministerial priesthood is the sign.[110]

The Priest as Bridegroom at the Eucharist

In chapter 2, we saw the nuptial nature of the Eucharist. We have also seen how it is in the celebration of the Eucharist that the priest acts most clearly *in persona Christi*. At Mass, he most clearly represents Christ, and he represents Christ at the very moment when Christ sacramentally reveals himself to us as our Bridegroom: this moment of self-giving which the words of institution express, "this is my body given for you . . . my blood . . . poured out for you." If the priest at this moment represents Christ the Priest, then he also represents Christ the Bridegroom, for the two are essentially connected. Yves Congar, O.P., makes this argument in defense of why the priest must be male, since he must be a sign of the bridegroom:

> From Genesis to the Apocalypse the relationship between God and his people, Christ and the Church, is presented as a covenantal relationship, and even a spousal relationship. We do not give as a reason [for male priesthood] a representation of Christ by the authority of the minister, conceived of as power . . . but a signification, a representation at the level of the sign, of this relationship, in the encounter of the minister with the community, especially in the celebration of the Eucharist, which is the sacrament of the covenant. It seems to us that at this level of signification, a feminine minister would not have the same value.[111]

At the level of sign, the priest must represent the bridegroom. This same argument is made by St. John Paul II in his encyclical *Mulieris Dignitatem*:

> Since Christ, in instituting the Eucharist, linked it in such an explicit way to the priestly service of the Apostles, it is legitimate to conclude that he thereby wished to express the relationship between man and woman, between what is "feminine" and what is "masculine." It is a relationship willed by God both in the mystery of creation and in the mystery of Redemption. It is the Eucharist above all that expresses the redemptive act of Christ the

Bridegroom towards the Church the Bride. This is clear and unambiguous when the sacramental ministry of the Eucharist, in which the priest acts "in persona Christi," is performed by a man.[112]

One could say from this that, when he celebrates the Eucharist, the priest stands *in persona Christ sponsi Ecclesiae.*

Of course, in saying that the priest stands *in persona Christi Sponsi Ecclesiae,* we must remember what we have explained about the representational nature of the priesthood. The priest stands in the person of the Bridegroom and makes present the nuptial covenant through his ministry as a living instrument, but he is still only an instrument. The purpose of the Eucharist is to unite the Church to Christ the Bridegroom, not to the priest himself. As Sara Butler explains:

> The organic relationship is not between the priest-bridegroom and the Church-bride; it is between Christ the bridegroom and the Church-bride. Christ is the one who associates the ministerial priest and the rest of the assembly into an organic unity. The complete dependence of the Church's worship on Christ is visibly symbolized by the presence of the ministerial priest, the sacramental sign of Christ the bridegroom."[113]

This follows from the sacramental nature of the Church. The priest is a sacrament of Christ in the Liturgy. He discloses the presence of the Bridegroom as His living image, thus putting the people in touch with the Bridegroom and not himself. In this way, the priest becomes a means for the bride to encounter the Bridegroom. As Dermot Power says:

Priestly mediation does not eclipse the divine involvement but is the foundation of the possibility of the full encounter of love between Christ and his Church. In the Catholic tradition the priesthood is willed by Christ himself and is an intrinsic dimension to the disclosure in liturgy and in life of how much he "is love."[114]

Thus, the priest is called be in life what he is at the Eucharist: a living image of the Bridegroom—that is, to make present the love of the Bridegroom through his life.

Conclusion: In Persona Christi Sponsi Ecclesiae

Having studied the nuptial nature of the Sacrament of Holy Orders, we are now able to explain precisely how the priest can be seen *in persona Christi Sponsi Ecclesiae*. We saw in the first part of this chapter how the Tradition applied the nuptial image to the Sacrament of Holy Orders in various and fluid ways, sometimes applying the image directly to the bishop or priest and other times, speaking about them as the friend of the Bridegroom. One of the most popular and, perhaps, most helpful uses of the image we saw is the application of the levirate law to the minister. This image of the levirate law is, perhaps, the most helpful because it gives the minister a very clear place in the nuptial relationship of Christ with His Church. The term "friend of the bridegroom" laudably emphasizes the humility necessary for the priestly office, but taken strictly, does not express enough the sacramental representation of Holy Orders. Theologically, we have to say there is a key difference between John the Baptist and the Apostles. John was the friend of the Bridegroom, who gave his own baptism, but the Apostles are more than just friends of the Bridegroom; they are also representatives of the Bridegroom.

As His representatives, they are given an intimate share in His own power to impart His divine life through the sacraments. The levirate image allows that the minister has a proper role within the spousal relationship of Christ with the Church. In the absence of the brother, Christ, the minister sacramentally makes the bridegroom present. Yet, the levirate law also emphasizes that the minister is not the Bridegroom. He raises up children for his brother, who is, in fact, the source of his fecundity, and not for himself. The image also shows that the minister's first relationship is with Christ, and it is out of love for his brother that he gives himself on behalf of the bride. This image allows us to see the priest within the spousal relationship of Christ to the Church while still protecting the representational nature of his ministry, since the Church has only one true bridegroom.

We also observed how seeing the priest *in persona Christ Sponsi Ecclesiae* strengthens the Church's self-understanding and the perception of the priesthood by emphasizing the unity-in-difference between the priest and the community. And we saw how the priest is a representative of the Bridegroom at the Eucharist. Flowing from this is St. John Paul II's intuition that the priest must make present Christ's spousal love in his whole life. Based on this, it seems there is good reason for the proposal of Bishop Brom that "a deeper understanding and appreciation" of priestly identity and ministry could be gained if the priest were seen to act not only *"in persona Christi, capitis Ecclesiae,"* but also *"sponsi Ecclesiae."* [115]

Pastores Dabo Vobis does not use the phrase *in persona Christi Sponsi Ecclesiae*. It comes close to it when St. John Paul II says that the Sacrament of Holy Orders "configures them [priests] to Christ the head and shepherd, the servant and spouse of the Church."[116] And then, more precisely, he writes, "in virtue of [the priest's] configuration to Christ, the head and shepherd, the priest stands in this spousal relationship with regard to the community."[117] The *Directory on the Ministry and Life of Priests* picks up this theme and expands it. The document says that priesthood has a "participation in the spousal nature of Christ,"[118] and it adds, "The Sacrament of Holy Orders makes the priest partake not only in the mystery of Christ the Priest, Head and Shepherd but in some way also in the mystery of Christ, 'Servant and Spouse of the Church.'"[119] Noting that the spousal dimension of the episcopate can be seen in the giving of the ring, the *Directory* argues that this spousal dimension can also be applied to priests as collaborators of the bishops.[120]

Based upon this magisterial teaching, we propose that it is possible to see the priest *in persona Christi sponsi Ecclesiae*. In combining our explanation in chapters 5 and 6 of this book, this configuration to the Bridegroom can be seen as rooted in the sacramental character of the Sacrament of Holy Orders. We noted in the section on the sacramental character that it provides a link to the community because the character is given for the sake of the community. The character places the priest in relationship with the community, precisely because it guarantees the life-giving power of the sacraments for the community. Thus, the character makes the priest capable of fulfilling his spousal role, giving life in the name of Christ. Secondly, the character calls forth from the priest a sacrificial life for the sake of the Church; and here, too, we see a kind of configuration to the Bridegroom who lays down His life for the Church. Of course, it is the grace of the sacrament, with the character, which makes the priest able to become a living image of the Bridegroom, to whom he is configured.

Cannot one argue that all Christians are called to be living images of the Bridegroom by virtue of their baptismal consecration to the priesthood of Christ? It is true that Christ is both priest and bridegroom at the same time; and, therefore, whoever participates in the priesthood of Christ could also be said to participate in His nuptial self-gift.[121] Yet, as we saw in the previous chapter, the specific difference between the priesthood of the baptized and that of the ordained has to do with representation. Only the priest stands *in persona Christi capitis* because it is his job to make the Head sacramentally present to the Church, His body. In this way, we can argue also that only the priest stands *in persona Christi sponsi Ecclesiae* because it is his job to stand in front of the Church revealing the spousal love of the Bridegroom to the bride.[122] The laity, through their priesthood, are called to imitate Christ; the priest, through his ordination, is called to represent Him. As Touze explains:

> The precise meaning of the *repraesentatio Christi capitis* which distinguishes radically the imitation of Christ by all the baptized from the efficacious representation proper to the order of the minister: this representation ought to make shine forth in him the particular gift of which he is the instrument. It is also this which differentiates essentially the priestly, ministerial nuptiality from the non-ministerial: surely, all the baptized imitate the Bridegroom (a sacrifice for the fecundity of the community and nuptial love which belongs to the common priesthood), but the visible translation of the nuptial effects of character of order belong only to the priest.[123]

It is because of this distinction that we could expect to see a more radical imitation of Christ's own way of life asked of the ministerial priest than what is asked of the priesthood of all the baptized; his life must more clearly represent Christ's life.

Sacramental representation is the key to understanding the priest as bridegroom. It makes clear that through the Sacrament of Holy Orders, he does stand in a spousal relationship with the community. The representation that comes from the sacramental character creates the relationship, rooted in his ontology, between the priest and the community. This representation is better understood when the relationship is also seen in its nuptial dimension, thus, *in persona Christi capitis includes sponsi Ecclesiae*. It is not that the formula of Vatican II, *in persona Christi capitis*, should be changed or did not go far enough. Rather, based on the Tradition, ecclesiology, and the Eucharist, the formula should also be seen to include the nuptial relationship of the priest to the Church. Thus, it is also accurate to say the priest is *in persona Christi capitis et Sponsi Ecclesiae*.

The strength of seeing the priest *in persona Christi Sponsi Ecclesiae* is that it emphasizes the essentially relational nature of the priesthood. As we noted in the introduction of this work, St. John Paul II explains in *Pastores Dabo Vobis* that priestly identity is "fundamentally 'relational.'"[124] There are two fundamental relations for the priest: with Christ and with the Church. The primary point of reference for priestly identity is Christ Himself: "The priest finds the full truth of his identity in being a derivation, a specific participation in and continuation of Christ himself, the one high priest of the new and eternal covenant. The priest is the living and

transparent image of Christ the priest."[125] The second point
of reference is Christ's relationship to the Church: "Reference
to the Church is therefore necessary, even if it is not primary,
in defining the identity of the priest. As a mystery, the Church
is essentially related to Jesus Christ. She is his fullness, his
body, his spouse."[126] St. John Paul II explains how these two
relations work together:

> The priest's fundamental relationship is to Jesus Christ,
> head and shepherd. Indeed, the priest participates in
> a specific and authoritative way in the "consecration/
> anointing" and in the "mission" of Christ (cf. Lk 4:18-
> 19). But intimately linked to this relationship is the
> priest's relationship with the Church. It is not a question
> of "relations" which are merely juxtaposed, but rather
> of ones which are interiorly united in a kind of mutual
> immanence. The priest's relation to the Church is
> inscribed in the very relation which the priest has to
> Christ, such that the "sacramental representation" to
> Christ serves as the basis and inspiration for the relation
> of the priest to the Church.[127]

The image of the priest *in persona Christi Sponsi Ecclesiae*
expresses both of these relationships in a unique way. It helps
to locate the priest properly within the Church by expressing
his sacramental relationship both with Christ and with the
Church. The image is also helpful because it helps to inspire
practically one of the central aspects of the priesthood: the
priestly call to imitate in his own life the self-gift of Christ
in pastoral charity. Francis Stafford explains how the nuptial
image captures this central theme of *Pastores Dabo Vobis*:

The priestly spirituality which John Paul II has elaborated [in *Pastores dabo vobis*] is nuptial simply. . . . This spirituality is that manner of life in which each priest lives the full implication of his ordination by making to be his own Christ's self-sacrifice for his bridal Church: He is to exist in the person of Christ; his own nuptiality has no other expression than this.[128]

The priest's self-gift is expressed in nuptial terms. He is called to give his life on behalf of Christ's bride. The bride of Christ is the immediate object of the priest's self-gift. He gives himself in order to serve the people of God. As St. John Paul II said, "Church and souls become his first interest, and with this concrete spirituality he becomes capable of loving the universal Church and that part of it entrusted to him with the deep love of a husband for his wife."[129] Yet, the priest in doing this never treats the Church as his own bride. He is not seeking union primarily with the bride, but with Christ. The love of Christ's bride is the means of his self-gift, but the reason is love for Christ. Again, St. John Paul II explains:

> The gift of self to the Church concerns her insofar as she is the body and the bride of Jesus Christ. In this way the primary point of reference of the priest's charity is Jesus Christ himself. Only in loving and serving Christ the head and spouse will charity become a source, criterion, measure and impetus for the priest's love and service to the Church, the body and spouse of Christ.[130]

St. John Paul II then offers two scriptural examples of this kind of pastoral charity in action. Both Paul and Peter show us how the gift of the priest is concretely for the people, but it is for the sake of Jesus:

> The apostle Paul had a clear and sure understanding of this point. Writing to the Christians of the church in Corinth, he refers to "ourselves as your servants for Jesus' sake" (2 Cor 4:5). Above all, this was the explicit and programmatic teaching of Jesus when he entrusted to Peter the ministry of shepherding the flock only after his threefold affirmation of love, indeed only after he had expressed a preferential love: "He said to him the third time, 'Simon, son of John, do you love me?' Peter . . . said to him, 'Lord, you know everything; you know that I love you.' Jesus said to him, 'Feed my sheep'" (Jn. 21:17).[131]

Jesus' question to Peter, "do you love me?" shows the central requirement for pastoral leadership in the Church: union with Christ. The ministry is the means of the priest's self-gift, the means of his growing in a deeper union and identification with Christ Himself. The more he gives himself on behalf of the bride, the closer he comes to the Bridegroom, and the more he becomes the Bridegroom's living image. Thus, we return to the warning of St. Augustine, who criticized those who loved the bride in an exclusive way, drawing the bride to themselves, rather than showing properly disinterested love for the sake of Christ. As Sherwin explains:

> The bishop, like every other Christian, is called to love others in a way that leads them and him to Christ. Yet, the office of bishop places those who hold it in a unique relationship with Christ and imposes upon them unique demands. . . . A man of means has gone on a journey and has entrusted his friend with the care of his household

and bride. The friend is expected to be a faithful friend and not love the bride in a way that leads her away from her husband.[132]

The closer the priest is united to the Bridegroom, the more he will be able to give himself freely to the bride. He draws the strength necessary for his self-gift from the depth of his relationship with Christ. As McGovern summarizes for us:

> The priest, then, loves and gives himself to the Church as the Body and Bride of Christ. However, he will only be able to do this in so far as the person of Jesus Christ is the central reference and love of his life. It is from this primary relationship that he will be able to draw the necessary spiritual energy and apostolic zeal to exercise those virtues which are implicit in the spousal love for the Church which his vocation demands."[133]

Seeing that the priest stands *in persona Christ Sponsi Ecclesiae* allows us now to draw our conclusions in the final two chapters. We will see the call of the priesthood to embrace a life of total self-gift through the evangelical counsels. This call is unique because it flows from the priest's specific sacramental representation of Christ, his call to be a living image of the Bridegroom.

Questions for Discussion, Reflection, and Prayer

1. Which of the nuptial images used by the Fathers spoke to your experience of the priesthood, and how did it speak to you?

2. What are ways in which you are tempted in your ministry to draw the love of the Bride to yourself and not to Christ?

3. How might your preaching and service reveal the primacy of Christ to the Church, His Bride?

4. How have you experienced the Bride calling forth from you the greater love of total self-gift?

NOTES

1. We build on the important work of Laurent Touze in his dissertation Célibat sacerdotal et théologie nuptiale de l'ordre, Thesis ad Doctoratum in Theologia totaliter edita (Roma: Pontificia Universitas Sanctae Crucis, 2002). For a detailed study of the uses of the nuptial image in the tradition, see chapter IV: "Dossier sur la nuptialité sacerdotale," 119-184.

2. Including recent Magisterial teaching, we could add that the image is used to defend the reservation of the Sacrament of Holy Orders to males, see below.

3. Several important studies in the last three decades have argued that perpetual continence for married clergy was widespread in the Church even before the fourth century when the legislation becomes clear; see Christian Cochini, S.J., *The Apostolic Origins of Priestly Celibacy*, trans. Nelly Marans (San Francisco: Ignatius Press, 1990); Stefan Heid, *Celibacy in the Early Church: The Beginnings of a Discipline of Obligatory Celibacy for Clerics in the East and West*, trans. Michael Miller (San Francisco: Ignatius Press, 2000); Alfons Maria Stickler, S.D.B., *The Case for Clerical Celibacy*, trans. Brian Ferme (San Francisco: Ignatius Press, 1995). Also important is the work of Roman Cholij (*Clerical Celibacy in East and West* [Herefordshire, UK: fowler Wright Books, 1989]), who argues that the current eastern discipline of allowing married clergy developed out of the council of Trullo (691) and that before that, the eastern Churches also required almost universally clerical continence for their married clergy (see also Stefan Heid, *Celibacy in the Early Church: the Beginnings of a Discipline of Obligatory Celibacy for Clerics in the East and West*, trans. Michael Miller [San Francisco: Ignatius Press, 2000], 296-350). Even more controversial is Cholij's argument that the Trullan Fathers altered the meaning of an earlier canon apparently to justify their legitimation of married clerics. One Orthodox scholar summarizes Cholij's research: "The Trullan Fathers seem to have, as Cholij shows, an inconsistent approach to the law of continence. On the one hand they are on record favoring a celibacy discipline for bishops (Canons 12 and 48) and even allow for married priests in 'barbarian churches' to practice total continence in keeping with local custom (Canon 30); while on the other hand, with Canon 13 the practice is eschewed. Canon 13 is one of the anti-Roman canons specifically rejected in the past by several popes because it opposes the discipline of absolute continence of the Roman Church with what it claims to be the ancient rule of temporal continence only with a view to the handling of the sacred species. The Council Fathers explicitly appeal to the Council of Carthage (419) as the prime source for their teaching. Cholij decisively demonstrates, through parallel textual criticism, that the Trullan Fathers use the *Codex canonum Ecclesiae Africanae* in such a partial and selective way as to alter the meaning

and intent of the Carthaginian canons entirely" (Robert Slesinski, "Lex Continentia: The Need for an Orthodox Response," St. Vladimir's Theological Quarterly, 37 [1993]: 93-94). Even if the validity of this research is upheld, it must be stated, as Vatican II (*Presbyterorum Ordinis*, sec. 16) did, that the practice of ordaining married men to the priesthood in the East is legitimate, especially given the long history of the acceptance of married clergy in their tradition. However, some scholars argue that even in the eastern Church, celibacy is considered the ideal for the priesthood; and ordination of married men is allowed by way of exception. A famous speech given by a Russian Orthodox bishop of the Patriarchate of Moscow in the immediate post-conciliar period argues this point: "For us Orthodox, the priesthood is a sacred function. For this reason we are convinced that you, Westerners, you Latins, are not on the right path when you allow the question of ecclesiastical celibacy to be debated in public, in the forum of public opinion. In our Oriental tradition, it has been possible to authorize the ordination of a handful of married men, as in any case you have done and go on doing in certain regions. But take care: in the West, *if you separate the priesthood from celibacy, a very swift decadence will set in.* The West is not mystical enough to tolerate the marriage of its clergy without degenerating. The Church of Rome (and this is to her glory) has preserved this ecclesiastical *ascesis* for a whole millennium. Beware of compromising it" (quoted in, Crescenzio Sepe, "The Relevance of Priestly Celibacy Today," in *For Love Alone: Reflections on Priestly Celibacy*, trans. Alan Neame. Maynooth, Ireland: St. Pauls, 1993], 80-81). Even without the complicated history of celibacy and continence in the priesthood, some authors argue, based on the consistent tradition in both East and West, to ordain only celibate men to the episcopacy that there is here an essential connection between the fullness of the priesthood and celibacy (see Touze, 40-42).

   4.   "The Biblical Foundation of Priestly Celibacy," in *For Love Alone: Reflections on Priestly Celibacy* (Maynooth, Ireland: St. Pauls, 1993), 15, emphasis in original.

   5.   For a thorough overview of how modern Scripture scholars understand this phrase, see Sydney Page, "Marital Expectations of Church Leaders in the Pastoral Epistles," *Journal for the Study of the New Testament* 50 (1993):105-120. We will explain de la Potterie's position, which takes into consideration these other modern accounts while proposing a solution that surpasses them and is rooted in the tradition; see "Mari d'une seule femme. Le sens théologique d'une formule paulinienne," in *Paul de Tarse, apôtre de notre temps,* ed. by L. De Lorenzi (Roma: Abbaye de S. Paul, 1979), 619-638.

   6.   Stickler, *The Case for Clerical Celibacy*, 91.

   7.   The interpretation of *unius uxoris vir* as a pre-ordination demonstration of an ability to live continence may be more convincing when it

is seen in the light of the only similar scriptural formula, *unius viri uxor*, "woman of one man" (1 Tm 5:9), which St. Paul places as a condition for one entering the order of widows. This injunction is given in the context of Paul's expressing his concern that the widow will be able to live continently (1 Tm 5:11- 12). Stefan Heid develops this exegesis by connecting it with 1 Corinthians 7 where St. Paul counsels marriage for those who are unable to live continently. According to Heid, "behind the '*unius uxoris vir*' stands the thought: If someone as a widower believed himself unable to resist sexual desire and therefore remarried, how would he ever be able to practice together with his wife this total abstinence, which a widower without a spouse must also practice?" (49; for the complete exegesis, see Ibid., 40-55).

8. As Jerome Quinn says, "The phrase in the Pastoral Epistles always described persons with a public ministerial role among believers. In every instance it qualifies a man or woman in his or her marital status and thus implies some manifest form of sexual control" (*The Letter to Titus*, The Anchor Bible, vol. 35 [New York: Doubleday, 1990], 85).

9. La Potterie, "Mari d'une seule femme," 629, emphasis in original.

10. La Potterie, "Struttura di Alleanza," 105.

11. Ibid., "Mari d'une seule femme," 632. Jerome Quinn agrees with this opinion about the origin of *unius uxoris vir*. "The most convincing suggestion to date is that of Ignace de la Potterie, who has noted the way in which Paul, in 2 Cor 11:2, reminds his congregation, 'I promised you in marriage to one husband, to present you as a chaste virgin to Christ'" (Quinn, *The Letter to Titus*, 86).

12. The Greek words are also the same, just in a different case: 2 Cor 11:2: e`ni. avndri. and 1 Tim 5:9: e`no.j avndro.j.

13. De la Potterie notes ("Mari d'une seule femme," 633) that the formulas both put the same numeric adjective in the emphatic position.

14. "The Biblical Foundation of Priestly Celibacy," 23, emphasis in original.

15. La Potterie, "Mari d'une seule femme," 633.

16. La Potterie, "The Biblical Foundation of Priestly Celibacy," 23.

17. Ibid., 6.

18. See La Potterie, "The Biblical Foundation of Priestly Celibacy," 23-25.

19. Wilhelm A. Schulze, "Ein Bischoff sei eines Weibes Mann . . . Zur Exeges von 1. Tim. 3,2 und Tit. 1,6" *Kerygma und Dogma*, vol. 4 (1958): 287-300.

20. "Note sur un texte de Saint Paul," *Revue Apolgétique* 39 [1924-25]: 19).

21. La Potterie, "Mari d'une seule femme," 634, emphasis in original.

22.   As Touze comments about de la Potterie's exegesis: "This exegesis seems therefore to be the echo of a large tradition of understanding the formula *unius uxoris vir*, only interrupted for the last 2 centuries" (123).

23.   *Commentaria in I Epist. Ad Timotheum*, III, 2, in *Commentarii in Scripturam Sanctam*, Tomus 15 (Antwerp: Apud Henricum & Cornelium Verdussen, 1705), 720.

24.   While some authors see examples of the nuptial image in the *Didaché* (*Didaché. La Doctrine des douze apôtres*. In *Les Sources Chrétiennes*. Vol. 248. edited by Willy Rordorf [Paris: Les Éditions du Cerf, 1998], esp. 186-187), the earliest clear examples are from Tertullian. However, the majority of Tertullian's examples come from his Montanist period. This makes his examples worth noting but not rooted in the heart of the tradition. See *De Monogamia*, 8, 4 (*Sources Chrétiennes* 343, 164-167); Ibid., 11,4 (*Sources Chrétiennes* 343, 180-183); *De exhortatione castitatis*, 11, 2 (*Sources Chrétiennes* 319, 106-107).

25.   Nisibene Hymns 19,1 (English Translation: Nicene and Post-Nicene Fathers, Series II, Vol. XIII, 188). See also Ibid., 19, 13, (Nicene and Post-Nicene Fathers, Series II, Vol. XIII, 190).

26.   Nisibene Hymns 20, 1-2 (Nicene and Post-Nicene Fathers, Series II, Vol. XIII, 190).

27.   Ibid.

28.   Robert Murray, *Symbols of Church and Kingdom: A Study in Early Syriac Tradition* (London: Cambridge University Press, 1975), 151.

29.   *Adversus Jovinianum*, I, 34 (*Patrologiae Cursus Completus, Series Latina* [PL] 23, 257).

30.   See *Epistola LXIX: Ad Oceanum*, 5 (*Corpus Christianorum Series Latina* [CSEL] 54, 686-689). It is interesting to note that a few centuries after St. Jerome, the penitential books of the eighth century will list the sin of incontinence for a cleric under the category of "*adulterium*." Stickler lists several examples in his essay "The Evolution of the Discipline of Celibacy in the Western Church from the End of the Patristic Era to the Council of Trent," in *Priesthood and Celibacy*, ed. Joseph Coppens (Roma: Editrice Ancora, 1972), 515.

31.   *De bono coniugali*, 18, 21 (CSEL 41, 214-215).

32.   It is worth noting that Augustine, who was present at the Councils of Carthage (both in 401 and 419) and the Council of Hippo (393) gatherings, which all affirmed the mandatory continence of clerics (deacons, priests, and bishops), would have presumed that the bishop who was "man of one wife" also lived continently with his wife (See Cochini, 266-268).

33.   *Epistula 12: Ad Episcopos Africanos Mauritaniae*, c. 3 (PL 54, 648). The whole response is instructive: "The same law of continence applies to ministers of the altar, whether bishops or priests, who when they were laity or lectors, it was licit for them to take wives and have children.

But when they reach the aforementioned positions, that which was licit begin to be not licit. From that point, the marriage which was of the flesh should become spiritual, it is not necessary that they dismiss their wives, and though they may not have they have in another way, by which the charity of the marriage may be saved, as the works of the marriage cease" (Ibid.).

34.   Epostola CLXVII: Ad Rusticum Narbonensem Episcopum. Inquisitio III: De his qui altario ministrant et conjuges habent, utrum eis licito misceantur? (PL 54, 1204).

35.   *Liber Dominus vobiscum,c. XII* (PL 145, 241).

36.   *Super Epistolam ad Timotheum,* c. III, Lect. I, n. 96, ed. Raphael Cai, O.P. (Roma: Marietti, 1953), 232.

37.   *In IV Sent.* d. 27, q. 3, a.1, sol. 1. St. Thomas admits in the same passage that the candidate who has been married more than once also could demonstrate incontinence, which would not be appropriate to his state, but he says the main reason for the injunction of St. Paul is the symbolic meaning.

38.   St. Thomas says a similar thing in his commentary on Titus: "But there is a higher reason signified, namely that he is a dispenser of the sacraments, and for that reason there should be in him no defect of the sacraments. But the sacrament of marriage signifies the union of Christ and the Church. Now, in order that the sign may correspond to the thing signified, just as Christ is one, and the Church is one, so also it should be here with the bishop, which certainly would fail if the bishop would have had many wives" (*Super Epistolam ad Titum*, c. I, lect. II, n 14, ed. Raffaele Cai, O.P. [Roma: Marietti, 1953], 306).

39.   ΑΠΟΛΟΓΗΤΙΚΟΣ ΚΑΤΑ ΑΡΕΙΑΝΩΝ, 6 (*Patrologiae Cursus Completus, Series Graeca* [PG] 25, 260). At times, the Fathers also apply the phrase "husband of one wife" to mean that the bishop should be totally dedicated to his one diocese, as when Pope St. Hillary commented in his letter to Bishop Ascanius and the other bishops of the Iberian peninsula that no one should presume to be transferred from one diocese to another (*Epistola, II* [PL 58, 18]). Then, he added that this is because St. Paul taught that a bishop should be husband of one wife and for this reason also they should only be assigned one diocese (*Epistola IV* [PG 58, 19]). In addition, the Council of Nicea (325) forbade the practice of a bishop's transferring from one diocese to another (See *First Council of Nicea,* can. 15., in *Decrees of the Ecumenical Councils,* vol. I, ed. Norman Tanner, S.J. [Washington, D.C.: Georgtown University Press, 1990], 13).

40.   *Cum de Expulsione,* 4 (PG 52, 433).

41.   See Genesis 12:12-19.

42.   ΤΟΥ ΑΥΤΟΥ ΕΠΑΝΕΔΘΟΝΤΟΣ, 2 (PG 52, 444). St. John Damascene repeats this same image in a homily praising St. John Chrysostom. Referring to Chrysostom's exile, the Damascene says "the bridegroom

was thrust out of the bridal chamber" (ΕΙΣ ΤΟΝ ΑΓΙΟΝ ΙΩΑΝΝΟΥ ΤΟΥ ΧΡΥΣΟΣΤΟΜΟΝ), 18 (PG 96, 780). He continues praising Chrysostom's undying love in refusing to abandon his bride (See PG 96, 781).

43.   See 2 Corinthians 11:2.

44.   For a history of the use of this metaphor to prevent transfer of bishops, see Leo Ober, "Die Translation der Bischöfe im Altertum," *Archiv für katholisches Kirchenrecht* 88 (1908): 209-229, 401-465, 625-648, and 89 (1909): 3-33. There is also within the Tradition resistance to this strict application of the marriage image to the bishop and his diocese. For example, St. Jerome, although aware of Nicea's canon, believes that linking the bishop too closely to the diocese so that he can never be transferred is a forced application of the marriage image (see *Epistula LXIX: Ad Oceanum*, 5 (CSEL 54, 686-689).

45.   *Acta et Documenta Concilio Oecumenico Vaticano II Apparando*, Series II, vol. II, pars III, 650. This understanding was proposed again in the discussion in *Aula* on the schema *de episcopis et de dioeceseon regimine*, 7 November 1963, by Bishop Joseph Attipetty of Verapoly, India, when he argued that the marital image applied to the bishop and his diocese still has great value: "That mystical union of marriage with a bishop and his Church, which is dissolved only by death, has the highest value in diocesan life." (*Acta Synodalia Sacrosancti Concilii Oecumenici Vaticani Secundi*, vol. II, pars 4, 602). Leon Joseph Suenens (Cardinal Archbishop of Mechelen-Brussels) responded the following week (with tongue in cheek!), saying that if they would consider literally the bishop's bond with his diocese as an indissoluble marriage "then this council hall is filled by divorced bishops, many of them two or three times" (*Acta Synodalia*, vol. II, pars 5, 10).

46.   Antonio Miralles says that "the ecclesial conscience has seen in this prohibition not a necessary norm, but a contingent one" ("La dimensione universale e particolare dell'episcopato," in *I Vescovi e il loro ministero*, ed. Philip Goyret [Vatican City: Pontificia Università della Santa Croce- Libreria Editrice Vatican, 2000], 51).

47.   Paul VI, *Lumen Gentium* (1964), sec. 23.

48.   Miralles, "La dimensione universale e particolare dell'episcopato," 151. Miralles adds, "If a diocesan bishop is transferred to become the head of another particular Church, it is not that he leaves one bride to take another, rather he is always the bridegroom of the Church, from the moment of his consecration, precisely because from that moment he is a sacramental *representation*, in the highest degree, of Christ the shepherd and spouse of the Church" (Ibid., emphasis in original).

49.   *Rites of Ordination of a Bishop, of Priests, and of Deacons*, n. 87.

50.   See Antonio Santantoni, *L'Ordinazione episcopale: Storia e teologia dei riti dell'Ordinazione nelle antiche Liturgie dell'Occidente, Studia Anselmiana* 69 (Roma: Editrice Anselmiana, 1976), 161. The use of the ring is well established by the seventh century but at first is associated with the dignity

and authority of the bishop as the band that holds the bishop's seal; only in the tenth century does the meaning become nuptial in some ordination rites, especially in Rome. Most theorize the nuptial meaning came into the ordination Liturgy from the rings exchanged in the marriage ritual. The Roman theology of the ring eventually replaced the others (Ibid., 150-155, and 161-162). See also Michel Andrieu "Le sacre Episcopal d'après Hincmar de reims," *Revue d'Histoire Ecclésiastique* 48 (1953): 55.

51. Aurillac Pontifical, at the end of the ninth century beginning of the tenth, cited in Santantoni, 277.

52. Cited in Santantoni, 277.

53. *De sacramento Christianae fidei*, II, IV, XV (PL 176, 438).

54. It is noteworthy that in this context, St. Bernard says that St. Malachi was fulfilling the Levirate Law (see below) and appointing a brother to raise up offspring: "But lest someone leave behind something incomplete, begin to treat this as *He should raise up a seed for the deceased brother* (Deut 25:5)" (*Vita Sancti Malachiae Episcopi*, c. I, XV, 34 [*Sources Chrétiennes* 367, 266]).

55. Ibid., 268. Touze points out that this is a rare citation in St. Bernard where he directly calls the bishop the bridegroom. More often, he prefers the term *amicus sponsi* (friend of the bridegroom) in reference to the bishop; see Touze, 200-201; see also our explanation of the term *amicus sponsi* below.

56. *De baptismo*, VI, 3 (Source Chrétiennes 410:158).

57. ΠΕΡΙ ΙΕΡΩΣΥΝΗΣ, III, 6 (*Sources Chrétiennes* 272, 150-152). English Translation: St. John Chrysostom, *Six Books on the Priesthood*, trans. Graham Neville (Crestwood, NY: St. Vladimir's Seminary Press, 1996), 73.

58. ΕΝ ΤΩ ΠΡΩΤΩ ΕΥΓΓΡΑΜΑΤΙ ΤΗΣ ΕΥΑΓΓΕΛΙΚΗΣ ΤΟΥ ΕΩΤΗΡΟΣ ΗΜΩΝ ΑΠΟΔΕΙΘΕΩΣ, I, 9, 14-15 (PG 22, 81).

59. See John 1:27 and parallels.

60. *Contra Faustum*, 32,10 (CSEL 25, 768-769).

61. *De octo quaestionibus ex Veteri Testamento*, 7 (CCSL 33, 471). See other examples in *En. in ps.*, 44, 23 (CCSL 38, 510-511); *Sermo.* 380,8 (PL 39, 1682-83).

62. *De rubo et corrigia calciamenti*, 4 (CCSL 103, 394-395).

63. "Hinc Petro ait: *Simon Ioannis, amas me? Qui cum se amare protinus* respondisset, audivit: *Si diligis me, pasce oves meas* (Jn 21: 15-17). Si ergo dilectionis est testimonium cura pastionis, quisquis virtutibus pollens gregem Dei rennuit pascere, pastorem summum convincitur non amare. . . . Hinc Moyses ait, ut uxorem fratris sine filiis defuncti superstes frater accipiat, atque ad nomen fratris filium gignat; quam si accipere forte rennuerit, huic in facie mulier exspuat, unumque ei pedem propinquus discalciet. . . . Frater quippe defuncti ille est, qui post resurrectionis apparens gloriam, dixit: *Ite, nuntiate fratribus meis* (Mt 28:10). Qui quasi sine filiis obiit,

quia adhuc electorum suorum numerum non implevit" (*Regula pastoralis*, I, 5 [*Sources Chrétiennes* 381, 146]).

64.   For example, Venerable Bede, (*Quaestiones super Deuteronomium*, 14 [PL 93, 413]); Bl. Rabanus Maurus (*Enarratio super Deuteronomium*, III, 20 [PL 108, 944]); Innocent III (1216) (*De quadripartite specie nuptiarum* [PL 217,961]).

65.   ΟΜΙΛΙΑΙ ΕΙΣ ΤΟΝ ΑΓΙΟΝ ΙΩΑΝΝΗΝ, 29, 3 (*Corona Patrum Salesiana, Series Graeca*, 11, 145-146). Similarly, in his work on the priesthood, St. John, at times, speaks of the priest as the role of the friend or the guardian who has the responsibility to prepare the bride of Christ (ΠΕΡΙ ΙΕΡΩΣΥΝΗΣ, III, 6 [*Sources Chrétiennes* 272, 156]). See also Ibid., IV, 7 (ibid., 274).

66.   "*Regula Pastoralis*, II, 8 (*Sources Chrétiennes* 381,232).

67.   *In Ioh. Evang.*, 13,12 (CCSL 36, 137).

68.   See 2 Corinthians 11:2.

69.   *In Ioh. Evang.*, 13,12 (CCSL 36, 137).

70.   Michael Sherwin studied the title *amicus sponsi* in the writings of St. Augustine, and he shows that "during his conflicts with the Donatists, Augustine became especially interested in this title. He began to employ it not only in reference to John the Baptist, but also as a description of the ideal Catholic bishop" ("'The Friend of the Bridegroom Stands and Listens': An Analysis of the Term *Amicus Sponsi* in Augustine's Account of Divine Friendship and the Ministry of Bishops," *Augustinianum* 38 (1998): 197). According to Sherwin, Augustine uses the term *amicus sponsi* as a critique of the Donatist view. The Donatists, relying on St. Cyprian of Carthage, argued that baptism is valid only when it is done by someone who is connected to the true bride of Christ, the Church (Ibid., 204). Sherwin explains: "In Augustine's view, the core of their argument is still valid: the Church is Christ's sole bride, and those who separate from it are adulterers and do not give life. From Augustine's perspective, however, this fact does not support the earlier tradition's conclusions concerning rebaptism. Instead, it supports his position that baptism administered by heretics and schismatics is valid but not life-giving. Heretics and schismatics validly confer the sacrament of baptism, but for it to give life the recipient must be reconciled to full communion with the Catholic Church" (Ibid., 205-206).

71.   Ibid., 206.

72.   *Sermo.* 292, 8 (PL 38, 1526). See also *In Ioh. Evang.*, 13, 14 (CCSL 36, 138-139). As Sherwin says, "He is concerned about the infidelity of the friends of the bridegroom who lead the bride to themselves instead of leading her to Christ. In Augustine's view, the Donatists are adulterers because they seek to usurp the place of the bridegroom. Instead of leading the bride as a chaste virgin to her spouse, they seek to take the bridegroom's place and to bring forth children in their own name" (208).

73. *Sermo.* 268,4 (PL 38, 1233).

74. *Sermo.* 268.4 (PL 38, 1234).

75. St. Augustine, *In Ioh. Evang.*, 13, 18 (CCSL 36, 140). Augustine says the same, using the example of St. John the Baptist: "And this humble friend of the bridegroom, the zealous bridegroom, does not propose himself as an adulterous bridegroom, but offers testimony to his friend, and entrusts the bride to him who was the true bridegroom: that he may be loved in him, he hates himself to be loved in place of him." (*Sermo.* 288.2 [PL 38, 1302]).

76. See Touze's synthesis, 202 ff.

77. In the 2004 *Directory for the Pastoral Ministry of Bishops*, the Congregation for Bishops mentioned specifically the nuptial aspect of the episcopacy, but also included priests: "The Bishop's spirituality also has its own specific quality: being shepherd, servant of the Gospel and bridegroom of the Church, he must relive, *together with his priests*, the spousal love of Christ for his bride the Church, in intimate prayer and in self-giving to his brothers and sisters, so that he may love the Church with a renewed heart, and through his love may preserve her unity in charity" (*Apostolorum Successores* [Vatican City: Libreria Editrice Vaticana, 2004], 34, emphasis added).

78. Thomas McGovern summarizes the tradition this way: "Because bishops are ordained with the fullness of the priesthood, they image Christ the Bridegroom in a paramount way. This is why they wear a wedding ring and are always celibate in both East and West." (Thomas J. McGovern, *Priestly Identity* [Dublin: Four Courts Press, 2002] 114-115) Based on this, Laurent Touze argues that celibacy or continence for bishops is traditional in the strict sense: "There is a necessary continuity and universality, defended by the Church over the course of centuries with a constancy and energy that are signs of *formalitas*; that is to say, of the clarity with which the truth is recognized as revealed by the magisterium or declared necessary in order to safeguard and interpret the tradition" (Touze, 40). He cites Cochini (380-381) and Cholij (42-43) who both argue that a man who refused continence was never ordained a bishop except in heretical or schismatic communities. Touze argues in his conclusion that this tradition of celibacy for bishops is because of the Church's sense that the bishop must represent clearly her bridegroom (Touze, 237).

79. St. Thomas died before he was able to finish the *Summa*, and most scholars think the "Supplement" to the *Summa Theologiae* was written by Reginaldo da Piperno, O.P., who was Thomas's companion and friend. It was mainly gathered from Thomas's commentary on the *Sentences*. For this reason, its theological conclusions are sometimes not held as sure as the rest of the *Summa*, as the *Summa* represents Thomas's mature thought but the *Sentences* were among his first works, written about 1256. In fact, it is clear in other parts of the *Summa* that Thomas even contradicts his own writings in the *Sentences* (see "Editor's Note," in *Summa Theologica of St.*

Thomas Aquinas, vol. 5., trans. Fathers of the English Dominican Province, Westminster, Maryland: Christian Classics, 1981).

80. ST Suppl., 40, a. 4, ad 3.

81. See *In IV Sent.*, d. 24, q. 3, a.2, sol. 1, ad. 3.

82. d. 20, q. 1, a. 4, sol. 1.

83. *Contra impugnantes*, 4, 14, ad. 4.

84. Ibid. Thomas notes that this does not mean the Church has many bridegrooms, that because they all act in the place of only one bridegroom, they are thought of as one: "But it does not follow from these words that there is in one church a plurality of spouses. For priests assist their bishop in his work, and bishops cooperate with the Pope; he finally is the direct minister to Christ. Thus, Christ, the Pope, the bishops, and the priests are but the one spouse of the Church" (Ibid.). It is worth remembering here the distinction between an analogy and a metaphor that we made in the first chapter of this book. Saying the priest is a bridegroom by analogy is saying that in some way, he is a real bridegroom because he represents the true bridegroom, Christ.

85. Question 184 of the *Summa Theologiae* outlines the traditional teaching on the "state of perfection." As St. Thomas explains: "one is said to be in the state of perfection, not through having the act of perfect love, but through binding himself in perpetuity with a certain solemnity to those things that pertain to perfection. Moreover it happens that some persons bind themselves to that which they do not keep and some fulfill that to which they have not bound themselves. . . . Wherefore nothing hinders some from being perfect without being in the state of perfection, and some in the state of perfection without being perfect" (ST II-II, 184, a. 4, corpus).

86. ST II-II, 184, a. 5, corpus.

87. Ibid.

88. ST II-II, 185, a. 4, corpus.

89. ST II-II, 186, a. 7, corpus.

90. *Cursus Theologiae Moralis*, t. VI, tr. XXVIII, appendix *De beneficiis ecclesiasticis*, c. unicum, punctum VIII, ∫ IX, n. 384 (Venice: Apud Nicolaum Pezzan, 1724), 256.

91. ST II-II, 184, a. 8, corpus.

92. ST II-II, 184, a. 6, corpus.

93. ST II-II, 184, a. 8, corpus.

94. John Paul II, *Pastores Dabo Vobis* (1992), sec. 22.

95. The Dominican theologian Jean Hevre Nicolas (*Synthèse Dogmatique*, 1114) argues that Thomas's interpretation of the priest as not being especially obliged to the state of perfection was a consequence of the time in which he was writing, and that the Church's current understanding, at least in the West, seems to demand the same total self-gift of the priest as it does of the bishop.

96. Authors who proposed similar views include Hans Küng (*Why Priests?: A Proposal for a New Church Ministry*, trans. Robert C. Collins, S.J. [Garden City, New York: Doubleday, 1972], 63-64, see also 88-95); Edward Schillebeeckx, O.P., (*Ministry: Leadership in the Community of Jesus Christ* [New York: Crossroads, 1981], 138-139; see also 72-73; Ibid., *The Church with a Human Face: A New and Expanded Theology of Ministry*, trans. John Bowden [London: SCM Press, 1985], 120). Leonardo Boff argues in a similar vein when he proposes that in exceptional circumstances, an ordained priest is not necessary for the Eucharist. See *Ecclesiogenesis: The Base Communities Reinvent the Church*, trans. Robert R. Barr [Maryknoll, New York: Orbis Books, 1986], 70-75.

97. Some scholars have called this approach a kind of "functionalism" because of the focus that what makes the priest unique is his function and not his ontology. For a summary and critique of these functionalist views of priesthood, see Greshake, 25-30, or Toups, 99-100.

98. (23). He points out that this perspective has some strengths: "This theological interpretation of ministry can illustrate the basic idea, already expressed in the Second Vatican Council, that ministry is above all a service to the community of believers" (Ibid.).

99. Schillebeeckx argued that ministry in the Apostolic Church could not be traced directly to a power coming from Jesus but rather rose up from the community and then was confirmed by the Holy Spirit (*Ministry: Leadership in the Community of Jesus Christ*, 13 ff.). Several scholars critique this view as being both historically and theologically inaccurate, e.g., Henri Cruouzel, S.J., "Témoignanges de l'Église ancienne," *Nouvelle Revue Théologique* 104 (1982): 738-748; Kasper, "Ministry in the Church,"; Albert Vanhoye, S.J., "Le Ministère dans l'Eglise: Les données du nouveau testament," *Nouvelle Revue Théologique* 104 (1982): 720-738.

100. Gisbert Greshake, *The Meaning of Christian Priesthood*, trans. Peadar MacSeumais, S.J. (Westminster, MD: Christian Classics, 1989), 26.

101. "Letter to the Bishops of the Catholic Church on Certain Questions Concerning the Minister of the Eucharist," *Origins* 13 (15 September 1983): 229-33.

102. Walter Kasper, *Leadership in the Church: How Traditional Roles Can Serve the Christian Community*, trans. Brian McNeil (New York: Crossroad Publishing Co., 2003), 57. Greshake adds that when this distinction is forgotten, there is a danger that the essential mission of the Church will be lost: "Where this distinction is overlooked, or is not recalled and demonstrated with sufficient clarity, there is the danger of a church which in its basic activity does no more than celebrate its own unity, and which merely brings into play the abilities of its faithful (even though there be much talk of the Holy Spirit). The task of the official Church is to witness that Christ is and remains prior to his Church, and to make that priority effective in the center of the Church's life—since it does not regard its

office as derived *exclusively* from the community, or as one charisma among others, but separate from them, in this way, with power given by Christ and symbolically pointing to him, church office makes the foundation of the Church, Christ himself, effectively present" (27-28).

103.   Lawrence J. Welch, "Priestly Identity Reconsidered: A Reply to Susan Wood," *Worship* 70 (1996): 317.

104.   *Pastores Dabo Vobis*, sec. 16.

105.   Ibid., 22.

106.   Miralles, *"Pascete il gregge di Dio,"* 61.

107.   *Directory on the Ministry and Life of Priests*, 13.

108.   Gustave Martelet, S.J., "The Mystery of the Covenant and its Connections with the Nature of the Ministerial Priesthood," *L'Osservatore Romano*, English Edition (17 Mar. 1977): 7.

109.   "The Priest as Icon of Christ," *The Priest* 50.11 (1994): 43.

110.   Martelet, "The Mystery of the Covenant," 7, emphasis in original.

111.   Congar, "Les ministères," 641-42, emphasis in original.

112.   John Paul II, *Mulieris Dignitatem* (1988), sec. 26, emphasis in original. In this context, St. John Paul II cites *Inter Insigniores* which also makes the argument that the priest must be male in order to represent the bridegroom at the Eucharist. In that document, the Congregation for the Doctrine of the Faith explained how Christ's Incarnation as a male "is, indeed, in harmony with the entirety of God's plan as God himself has revealed it, and of which the mystery of the Covenant is the nucleus" (5). Then, they explain how the covenant always takes "the privileged form of a nuptial mystery" (Ibid.). As a result, they argue that "we can never ignore the fact that Christ is a man. And therefore, unless one is to disregard the importance of this symbolism for the economy of Revelation, it must be admitted that, in actions which demand the character of ordination and in which Christ himself, the author of the Covenant, the Bridegroom and Head of the Church, is represented, exercising his ministry of salvation which is in the highest degree the case of the Eucharist—his role (this is the original sense of the word 'persona') must be taken by a man" (Ibid.). An important explanation of how the priest represents the bridegroom is male is found in the works of Hans Urs von Balthasar who frequently addresses the nuptial nature of creation and redemption and argues that based on the symbolic value of the priesthood, it can only be exercised by a man. This argument, spread throughout the works of Balthasar, was the subject of the doctoral dissertation by Robert Pesarchick, *The Trinitarian Foundation of Human Sexuality as Revealed by Christ According to Hans Urs von Balthasar: The Revelatory Significance of the Male Christ and the Male Ministerial Priesthood*, in Tesi Gregoriana Serie Teologia, vol. 63 (Roma: Gregorian University, 2000). Pesarchick explains that the priest represents the bridegroom at the Eucharist: "In the Eucharist, the priest 'represents' and 'acts' in the person of Christ in relation to his Bride the Church. In this

case, both priestly ordination and the natural symbolism of gender are required, for the gender symbolism serves as part of the sacramental sign. In the Eucharist, when he acts *in persona Christi capitis et sponsi*, the gender symbolism of the person of the priest enters directly into the sacramental symbolism and action" (264: note 31). A short summary of Balthasar's position can be found in his article "Thoughts on the Priesthood of Women," *Communio* 23 (Winter 1996): 701-709.

113.　Sara Butler, M.S.B.T., "Priest as Sacrament of Christ the Bridegroom," *Worship* 66 (1992): 517, emphasis in original.

114.　Dermot Power, *A Spiritual Theology of the Priesthood: The Mystery of Christ and the Mission of the Priest* (Washington, DC: Catholic University of America Press, 1998),119.

115.　Brom, *Relatio in Aulam*, 2.

116.　*Pastores Dabo Vobis*, sec. 3.

117.　Ibid., sec. 22.

118.　*Directory*, 14.

119.　Ibid., the internal quote is from *Pastores Dabo Vobis*, sec. 3. Later, the *Directory* says that celibacy is "the sign of that spousal reality coming to be in sacramental Ordination" (80).

120.　Ibid, 14.

121.　Touze states this: "One could even write that in Christ, the priesthood and nuptiality in a certain way come together: all participation in the priesthood of Christ, also as a result the common priesthood, includes a spousal dimension, which is not unique to the ministerial priesthood." (77).

122.　See *Pastores Dabo Vobis*, sec. 16.

123.　Touze, 226.

124.　*Pastores Dabo Vobis*, sec. 12.

125.　Ibid.

126.　Ibid.

127.　Ibid.

128.　Stafford, 215.

129.　*Pastores Dabo Vobis*, sec. 23.

130.　Ibid. Cole and Connor also make clear this same careful synthesis of the priesthood in the spousal relationship of Christ with the Church when they comment on *Pastores Dabo Vobis*, sec. 23: "The compound imagery of bridegroom-head-shepherd takes an interesting turn when the pontiff applies it to the life of the ordained priest. The pope shows how the priest's spousal love for the Church is directly connected to his love for Christ himself, that is, how the priests love for the bride depends upon his love for the bridegroom. In this regard, the Holy Father recalls the Gospel text in which Jesus commissions Peter. Jesus 'entrusted to Peter the ministry of shepherding the flock only after his threefold affirmation of love [for Jesus].' It was in consequence of Peter's affirmative answer to the question 'Do you love me?' that Jesus said, 'Feed my lambs. Feed my sheep'" (322-23).

131.   *Pastores Dabo Vobis*, sec. 23.

132.   *Friend of the Bridegroom*, 214. Pope Benedict XVI spoke similarly at the ordination of priests for the diocese of Rome when he spoke of how the priest is properly close to his people: "However, it is only possible to do this properly if the Lord has opened our hearts; if our knowing does not bind people to our own small, private self, to our own small heart, but rather makes them aware of the Heart of Jesus, the Heart of the Lord. It must be knowing with the Heart of Jesus, oriented to him, a way of knowing that does not bind the person to me but guides him or her to Jesus, thereby making one free and open. And in this way we too will become close to men and women" ("Ordination Mass, St. Peter's Basilica: Sunday, 7 May 2006," in *L'Osservatore Romano*, English Edition [10 May 2006]: 3).

133.   McGovern, *Priestly Identity*, 63.

CHAPTER 7

BECOMING A LIVING IMAGE OF CHRIST THE BRIDEGROOM OF THE CHURCH THROUGH THE EVANGELICAL COUNSELS

The life of the priest must flow from the truth of his identity—that is, who he is called to be from his ordination. Only living rooted in this truth will lead to fulfillment and joy in his vocation, living his priesthood in proper relation with Christ and the Church. The purpose of our study has been to root the truth of the priestly way of life in the nuptial nature of the priesthood. We have now seen exactly how through ordination the priest is made "a living image of Jesus Christ the Bridegroom of the Church."[1] We must now see, then, how the priest is called to embrace Christ's own nuptial way of life, a life that is sacrificial, self-emptying, and fruitful. A life that He expressed through His own living of the evangelical counsels. Having seen clearly that the priest must seek to become a living image of this spousal love in pastoral charity, we must now see how this is most fittingly done through the evangelical counsels.

First, it must be acknowledged that there is an obstacle that one must face when speaking about the evangelical counsels to priests. Teaching about the evangelical counsels is often done in a predominately negative way. The focus is on what one must give up to follow Christ. Most priests have already given up a lot to follow their vocation: they have given up marriage, career plans, and a lot of freedom as they pursue very busy lives of service. They may be tempted to ask, "What else does Christ or the Church want to take from me?" It is good to begin by acknowledging the struggle to accept this teaching and try to see it in a different way, a way that leads to deeper union and fulfillment in priestly life.

In Christ's life, the counsels are not a restriction as much as they are a freedom. Through the counsels, Christ is free to be given to the Father and for us. Just as a hot-air balloon throws off weight in order to rise to God and be led by the wind where it needs to go, so also when we leave behind what God asks us to give up, we become free to fly and be led by the Spirit. We are more like Christ, more completely given. Most importantly, the counsels, like everything in the Christian life, must be seen as relational, not only functional. Christ's living of the counsels was not only practical—that is, for His mission—it was His way of living in union with the Father. So, also, the priest, through the counsels, makes a gift himself; this is not only for the salvation of the people but also for union with the heart of Christ. Here is the main reason for living the counsels—so that I might have Christ's heart, His pastoral charity.

Why the Profession of the Evangelical Counsels Is Not Required for Priests as for Religious

The evangelical counsels are co-natural with the priesthood—that is to say, they are so well adapted to the priesthood as to illuminate its very nature. However, as we know, the Tradition has not absolutely required the evangelical counsels of the priest, as it has for the religious. This is certainly true of evangelical poverty for diocesan priests, but even celibacy is not required in many Churches in the East; and the West admits of exceptions to the rule. If the evangelical counsels are co-natural with the priesthood, one might wonder why it is that they are not *absolutely* required.

In an article explaining the relationship of the priesthood and celibacy, Jean Galot gives us the answer, which is found in the nature of the priestly consecration:

In fact, the sacerdotal character effects a consecration in principle without however entailing the expressed, concrete determinations which would manifest this consecration in the life of the priest. A virginal life is the normal extension of this consecration, its most suitable application; but it is not strictly required to the point of being absolutely necessary. Although the character effects a fundamental resemblance to Christ to the point that the priest is made the representative of the Savior, this resemblance is not, nevertheless, so precise that it requires the practice of virginity as Jesus lived it. The character tends to this ideal but is not sufficient in itself to impose it. . . . Considered in themselves, the priestly functions are not incompatible with the married state—although their most suitable and fecund exercise are better assured by the renouncement of it.[2]

In its "essence," the Sacrament of Holy Orders is an objective consecration of the priest through which the sacramental character is imprinted on the soul. The evangelical counsels are not required for this objective consecration because they are, in fact, not in the domain of objective consecration; they are part of the subjective response to the consecration. No subjective response is *required* for the validity of sacrament except the intention. It is also true, as we saw in chapter 5, that no subjective response is *adequate* to the gift of this office. Only Christ offered the perfect personal response adequate to the divine consecration His human nature received. For every other ministerial priest, there will remain an infinite imparity between his office and his person, which no degree of human perfection can overcome. However, the objective excellence of the office (i.e., its essence) will always call the minister toward ever more perfect subjective consecration. And even though he will never live this consecration perfectly, the priest must seek to ever more perfectly configure his life. The evangelical counsels are, in fact, the best subjective response to this objective consecration because they are the way of total self-gift. It is true that they are not necessary to the sacrament, but neither is any other specific, limited, human response on the part of an ordained minister. However, to say they are not necessary does not allow us to dismiss them, lest we dismiss the importance of a subjective response at all. The Tradition has never been satisfied with priesthood only as an office. Christ Himself strongly criticized a priesthood that was seen only as a cultic office that focused on the externals without real love, charity.[3] The Tradition has always seen priesthood as a way of life, a way of life that clings deeply to Christ. The priesthood always calls for a subjective response; and, as we saw in the introduction, this response has tended toward the total self-gift of the counsels.[4]

The Unique Call of the Priest to Live the Evangelical Counsels

When *Lumen Gentium* speaks of the universal call to holiness, it makes clear that at least the spirit of the evangelical counsels is required for all Christians on their path to holiness:

> However, this holiness of the Church is unceasingly manifested, and must be manifested, in the fruits of grace which the Spirit produces in the faithful; it is expressed in many ways in individuals, who in their walk of life, tend toward the perfection of charity, thus causing the edification of others; in a very special way this (holiness) appears in the practice of the counsels, customarily called "evangelical."[5]

This universality of the counsels follows from the fact that all Christians are called to the perfection of charity.[6] We have already seen how poverty, chastity, and obedience are the greatest aids to perfect charity.[7] As St. John Paul II said, "whoever attains such a love, even if he does not live in an institutionalized 'state of perfection,' reaches the perfection that flows from love *through faithfulness to the spirit of those counsels*."[8] Thus, all Christians are called to the practice of the evangelical counsels according to their state in life.

Of course, there is an important distinction between the counsels as part of the universal call to holiness and the explicit call given by Christ to some to embrace a life of following Jesus concretely in poverty, chastity, and obedience.[9]

Some are called to a more radical conformation to the life of Christ in their special vocation. As Ghirlanda says:

> For all the baptized, conforming to the diverse conditions of life, there is a real demand of poverty, but not up to the liberation from every earthly good; of chastity, but not as far as the renunciation of marriage; of obedience, but not all the way to the complete stripping away of one's own will before those that take the place of God. In the consecrated life the precepts and evangelical values valid for all come to be lived, in a more profound insertion into the mystery of the cross of the Lord and of his resurrection, as a more close and more radical following of Jesus, in order to represent in the Church, in a permanent and visible way, the form of life that Jesus embraced and proposed to his disciples.[10]

Priests are called to this more radical following of Jesus in the form of life He lived, what Galot calls the way of greater love:

> However beautiful and holy the marriage state may be, a better way has been traced by Christ himself, one where charity can develop even more freely. The option is not between selfishness and love, nor between carnal passion and the spiritual life, but between love and a greater love. It is in virtue of greater love that the priesthood calls for celibacy.[11]

We can see this more radical call given to some beginning in the Scriptures. We already noted in chapter 4 that the origins of the evangelical counsels can be seen in Jesus' special command, "follow me."[12] The invitation "follow me" in the

Gospels invites one to a total response, leaving behind one's
former life and joining a new way of life in the company of
Jesus. This is the response that we see almost every time the
call is given: the one called immediately leaves everything to
follow Jesus. The only exception to this was already mentioned in chapter 4, the rich young man.[13] Every other time
the call is given, the one who hears it leaves everything and
begins a new way of life with Jesus:

> By his calls, Jesus does not only demand that a person
> believes in him; he invites them to radicalize this faith
> to the point of taking the risk of leaving all other goods
> and to place their trust completely in him. He is not
> content only with a love which consists in the practice
> of the commandments. He wants a love which consents
> to live for him and with him, in celibacy and poverty, the
> renunciation of family and other material goods.[14]

When Christ gives the command "follow me," the person
is asked to give up the things that are most profound in his
life—family relationships, life plans, earthly inheritance—all
this is left behind in order to be with Jesus and follow Him
wherever He goes. All this is left behind to receive the "hun-
dred-fold" that comes from following Jesus.

Of course, not everyone could be called to this kind
of renunciation in following Jesus; the call to this complete
following of Jesus is to a unique relationship with Him. As
Jesus says, "Not all can accept [this] word, but only those to
whom that is granted" (Mt 19:11). St. John Paul II explains
this when commenting on the call of the Apostles:

> Here we note the difference in vocations. Jesus did not
> demand this radical renunciation of family life from

all his disciples, although he did require the first place in their hearts, when he said: "Whoever loves father or mother more than me is not worthy of me . . ." (Mt 10:37). The demand for practical renunciation is proper to the apostolic life or the life of special consecration.[15]

Jesus invites some to be with Him always, to follow Him, which means sharing in His own way of life. This call is the origin of life according to the evangelical counsels. As St. John Paul II says:

> The evangelical basis of consecrated life is to be sought in the special relationship which Jesus, in his earthly life, established with some of his disciples. He called them not only to welcome the Kingdom of God into their own lives, but also to put their lives at its service, leaving everything behind and closely imitating his own *way of life*.[16]

It must be noted that the purpose of having these two categories of Christians is not for the sake of privilege but for service. Some are called to this more radical way of following in order to witness to the Gospel and to serve it with their whole lives: "They have freed themselves from the 'spirit of the world' that they may be totally at the disposal of God's mission to the world in his Son."[17]

We can already begin to see from what we have described that the priesthood finds its origin among those who were called by Jesus to follow His way of life. Those whom the Scriptures portray as called most closely to share Jesus' state of life are His Twelve Apostles. This is why, as John Paul II points out, the consecrated life is often called the "apostolic form of life":

This is the path marked out from the beginning by the Apostles, as testified to in the Christian tradition of the East and the West: "Those who now follow Jesus, leaving everything for his sake, remind us of the Apostles who, in answer to his invitation, gave up everything. As a result, it has become traditional to speak of religious life as *apostolica vivendi forma*."[18]

It is to these same Apostles that Jesus will give the authority of pastoral office. As we noted in chapter 5, in the act of Jesus' sending His Apostles with His own authority,[19] we can see the beginning of the representational priesthood. In fact, in the moment after His Resurrection when Jesus solemnly commands Peter to carry out His pastoral ministry,[20] Jesus also reissues the very first call: "follow me." It is a relational call, a call to share His own way of life in caring for His sheep. As Galot comments, the Lord mentions the same relational call when He speaks to His disciples about the authority of their office:

> By the call to follow him, Jesus has begun a state of life where the whole person is consecrated to him. He wanted this state for his disciples and especially for the 12, those to whom he has entrusted the priestly ministry of the Church. At the moment when he communicates to his apostles the power over the kingdom, the supreme pastoral authority, he also underlines the link which exists between the fact that they have followed him, that they have part of his destiny, and the assignment of this authority (Mt 19:28; Lk 22:28-29).[21]

Raymond Brown argues that this special call of Jesus for His Twelve Apostles has always affected the Church's ideals for the priesthood. He says, "the fact that Jesus chose from among his followers Twelve to be with him more intimately set up a pattern wherein Christians designated to the special ministry have been thought to be obliged to the closer discipleship of the Twelve."[22] What we see is that those who would share Jesus' mission through their office are also called to share His way of life, the way of life that allowed Him to be given to all.

The Evangelical Counsels in Consecrated Life and the Priesthood: Two Distinct Motivations

Theologically, both the consecrated life and the priesthood have their common origin in the call of Jesus to "follow me" which establishes a new state of life in the Church, a sharing in Jesus' own way of life.[23] Over many centuries, the consecrated life and the priesthood develop in distinct but related ways in order to serve different purposes in the Church. The consecrated life develops precisely around the subjective consecration of the counsels, marked by the desire to give all in love. The priesthood will have a different motivation for living the evangelical counsels, which will lead to living the evangelical counsels in different ways.

The difference is found in the different purposes for the Church of the priesthood and the consecrated life. The consecrated vocation is fundamentally rooted in baptism. For the religious, it is the desire to live radically the Sacrament of Baptism that motivates them to seek union with Christ through a life of the evangelical counsels. Through this radical living of baptism, they become a witness to the way of greater love that all Christians are called to imitate and which all will live in heaven. The priest finds his main motivation in the Sacrament of Holy Orders. Since he has been objectively configured to Christ in a way distinct from the baptismal configuration, he must subjectively conform his life to Christ's life so that he might be more true to his office. Dermot Power explains the distinction:

> The Evangelical Counsels provide an intensification of the baptismal character of the holy people of God; religious life is understood primarily, therefore, as an expression of the priesthood of all the baptized. The subjective holiness (*das Sollen*) and the consecration of those in the Evangelical state is of a qualitatively different character than those in the ordained ministry whose pastoral office constitutes a particular form of the participation in the Priesthood of Christ and his continuing service of the baptized. The holiness, therefore, of the Christian priest derives not from his baptismal character but from his ordained identity and from the subjective configuration with Christ which flows from this.[24]

As we have seen, the objective configuration to Christ happens through the sacramental character. Thus, as Galot writes, it is possible to find in the character itself a reason for the priest to live the evangelical counsels:

> Both in the priesthood as in the religious life there is a demand of the total gift of the person, conformed to the call to follow Christ; but for the priesthood the demand is written in the individual, through the priestly character, and belongs to the external structure of the Church; while for the religious life this demand is developed

in a more free charism toward such a structure, more spontaneous and more various in its manifestations.[25]

This is connected to the teaching of Vatican II about the consecration and mission of the priest. Both the religious and the priest are consecrated, set apart from the people for a special purpose. The religious is consecrated by his or her vows, set apart by this act of love, received by the Church, to witness the living of total self-gift within the radicalization of the baptismal call. The priest is consecrated by his ordination in order to be given as a sacrifice for the people. He is set apart for his office, so that he can be totally dedicated to the salvation of the people. As Vatican II stated: "By their vocation and ordination, [priests] are in a certain sense set apart in the bosom of the People of God. However, they are not to be separated from the People of God or from any person; but they are to be totally dedicated to the work for which the Lord has chosen them (Acts 13:2)."[26] Just as Christ was consecrated and sent into the world for our salvation,[27] so also the priest.[28] The objective consecration in the Sacrament of Holy Orders, demands a subjective complement, a placing of oneself completely at the disposal of Christ and His mission. Just as Christ's subjective consecration happened through His living of the evangelical counsels, so also the priest's. Through living the evangelical counsels, the priest seeks to imitate the self-gift of Christ:

> Already by reason of the baptismal consecration, the priest, like every other Christian, is required to live according to the spirit of the beatitudes, that is, to lead a holy life (PO 12a; CIC. 210); but by reason of the ministerial consecration, he must tend towards perfection

in the observance of the evangelical counsels, precisely
for a more faithful and worthy exercise of the ministry, in
which his personal consecration acts as a response to the
gift of love received from God the Father (PO 12).[29]

The evangelical counsels are the signs that the priest's
life has been totally consecrated, totally given. Through his
interior self-denial in living these counsels, his life becomes
inserted into the Paschal Mystery; he, too, embraces the daily
subjective self-gift that Christ embraced through poverty,
chastity, and obedience.

Another way to explain the difference in motivation
between the evangelical counsels as lived by religious and in
the priesthood is to use the nuptial image. Those in religious
life are drawn to union with Christ after the example of Mary,
who, as we saw in chapter 2, most perfectly represents the
bride in her response to Christ. In a concrete way, through
the vows, the consecrated person represents in his or her self-
gift this bridal response of the Church to Christ. As St. John
Paul II said, "The consecrated life thus becomes a particularly profound expression of the Church as the Bride who,
prompted by the Spirit to imitate her Spouse, stands before
him 'in splendour, without spot or wrinkle or any such thing,
that she might be holy and without blemish' (Eph 5:27)."[30]
The priest's motivation to live the counsels is also spousal,
but not primarily as a representative of the bride. By virtue of
his ordination, he stands in the forefront of the Church and
represents through his office the gift of the Bridegroom. As
Bishop Brom said in commenting on *Pastores Dabo Vobis*, the
priest must live the counsels in order to imitate the love of
the groom:

Diocesan priests, as well as religious order priests, are
exhorted to follow and imitate Christ, the "*vir evangelicus*,"
because they are not only "in" the Church, but also
"in the forefront" (PDV 16) of the Church, by virtue
of their configuration to Christ, Head and Spouse,
and their anointing for ordained ministry in his name.
Consequently, the pastoral poverty, celibate chastity and
priestly obedience become evangelical ways for priests to
be like the Bridegroom in behalf of his Bride. It is the
Bridegroom who, out of love for the Bride, "emptied
himself taking the nature of a slave" (Phil 2:7) and "being
rich, made himself poor" (2 Cor 8:9); it is the Bridegroom
who gave himself to the Bride with undivided love and
"delivered himself up to make her holy" (Eph 5:25-26);
it is the Bridegroom who "humbled himself, obediently
accepting even death, death on a cross" (Phil 2:9), in
order to show the depth of his love for the Bride and that
she might be his spotless spouse "without stain or wrinkle
or anything of that sort" (Eph 5:27).[31]

The priest's motivation for the total self-gift of the counsels is imitation of Christ's spousal love as a representative of
the bridegroom. As Power said, "if the Church's instinct is to
remain that the priest is configured to Christ in his pastoral
and spousal identity, then the existential life form of the
priesthood needs to correspond to the Form of Christ the
Shepherd and Spouse of the Church."[32]

The Unity of the Evangelical Counsels in the Life of the Priest

One of the central points of our argument for the priest
to live the evangelical counsels is their essential unity. As
we saw in the life of Christ, when one fully understands the

nuptial gift of the Cross, one sees that it was a total self-gift
for the bride and it included all three evangelical counsels.
Not only is Christ's celibacy a nuptial self-gift for the Church,
but also His obedience and His poverty. Because it was a total
self-gift, it must include all three evangelical counsels, as only
together do they include all there is to give.

The Church upholds the value of celibacy for the priest
because it powerfully affords him the chance to be given to
Christ with an "undivided heart," and allows the priest to
be more completely given, in Christ and with Christ, to the
Church. As *Presbyterorum Ordinis* expresses:

> Through virginity, then, or celibacy observed for the
> Kingdom of Heaven, priests are consecrated to Christ by
> a new and exceptional reason. They adhere to him more
> easily with an undivided heart, they dedicate themselves
> more freely in him and through him to the service of
> God and men.[33]

Celibacy opens up the priest to this total dedication with
an undivided heart so that he can live more completely for
the sake of the kingdom. But for celibacy to fully accomplish
this purpose, it *must* also include obedience and poverty. It
is certainly possible for someone to give up the intimacy of
marriage but allow one's heart to be divided from total service
to the kingdom by possessions or inordinate self-will. Truly
to cling to Christ with an undivided heart, and for the sake of
the eschatological witness, the gift of self must also include
obedience and poverty: "In order to be a total gift, it requires
poverty and obedience as complementary elements: without
these other two counsels, the gift would not be the total one

of an undivided heart."[34] This point was made strongly by St. Teresa of Calcutta in a talk she gave to priests:

> Priestly celibacy is not just not getting married, not to have a family. It is *undivided love of Christ in chastity.* Nothing and nobody will separate me from the love of Christ. It is not simply a list of don'ts, it is love. Freedom to love and to be all things to all people. And for that we need the freedom of poverty and simplicity of life. Jesus could have everything but he chose to have nothing. We too must choose not to have or to use certain luxuries. For the less we have for ourselves, the more of Jesus we can give, and the more we have for ourselves, the less of Jesus we can give. As priests, you must all be able to experience the joy of that freedom, having nothing, having no one, you can then love Christ with undivided love in chastity.[35]

We noted in chapter 3 the unity of the counsels, and how only all three together make a total self-gift. As St. Thomas noted, there is a big difference between the one who lives all three counsels and the one who only lives only one. It is the difference between a particular gift and a total gift, the difference between a sacrifice and a holocaust.[36] Christ's pastoral charity demands the latter, not merely the former. This means that the priest is also called to the total self-gift of the counsels; only in this light does his celibacy makes sense. As Balthasar says:

> Virginity in the Church can never be anything but a partial aspect of the one and only state that exists in the Church along with marriage—the state that Christ on the Cross brought into the world as a new form of divine

fecundity through the unity of poverty, virginity and obedience. Only this state can surpass all the perfection of a marriage that is at once natural and supernatural and, at the same time, fulfill and perfect it by a new spirit from above.[37]

This lack of understanding the unity of all three evangelical counsels has contributed greatly to the common confusion about celibacy in today's Church. Gisbert Greshake, in his book *The Meaning of Christian Priesthood*, points out that the isolation of celibacy from the other counsels has made it lose its true meaning:

> Celibacy is only *one* side of an indivisible whole. Is it then surprising if its practice as an isolated fragment cannot be convincing? Where a man does not devote himself to the whole call of the Gospel to follow Christ, his celibacy is like a foreign body in his life plan. Since, then, the Church for adequate reasons demands from the priest celibacy for the sake of God's kingdom, and that he should in this point live "according to the Gospel," this is not possible without somehow putting the other counsels into practice. If this is not done, celibacy cannot be a convincing sign or be lived in that joy which is the mark of Christ's disciples. Instead, it will be only a burden and consequently a matter of continual personal and ecclesial "reconsideration."[38]

It is only when the priestly life is seen as a completely given life that a priest's celibacy makes sense. If he has basically the same possessions as every other parishioner, and he determines his own schedule according to his desires, why should he not have his own wife? But if he is living his priesthood fully, placing everything at the service of his union with Christ for the sake of the people, in this light, his celibacy makes perfect sense:

> When celibacy is integrated in a life of following Christ, it is even today a convincing and respected sign. I have, for example, never heard that anyone has found the celibacy of Mother Teresa (can anyone imagine her as a married woman?) to be a problem, or the celibacy of the Brothers of Taizé. Here one can feel that celibacy has a harmonious place in the whole of their lives. For the priest also, it must be an important objective that his celibacy fits harmoniously into the whole of his life. But his effort cannot be successful except when he practices the other two forms of imitation of Christ—obedience and poverty.[39]

The priest is called through pastoral charity to make a gift of his life. This is why the Church has seen celibacy as so fitting for the priesthood. However, when the nuptial nature of Christ's pastoral charity is understood, and when the evangelical counsels are understood as the means of this unified self-gift of Christ, then we see that for the priest to live pastoral charity, he must live all three counsels.

The Priest's Spousal Love: Self-Sacrificing, Self-Emptying, and Fruitful

We saw how Christ's living of the evangelical counsels fulfilled these aspects of His spousal love. The same will be true for the priest. It is through living total self-gift of the evangelical counsels that his love will become self-sacrificing, self-emptying, and fruitful.

The office of priesthood is self-emptying of its very nature. The priest is not his own. This follows from the distinction we saw between the person and the office of the priest. The priest must allow his subjective person to be given for the office. He becomes, through ordination, what he was not, an official representative of Christ; and this office must take control of his whole life. He must allow his mission to take possession of him, as it did when the Apostles had to leave behind everything to follow Jesus.

With ordination, he is no longer the man he was. Now, he is a man of the Church, a man for others, a representative of Christ the Shepherd—and so, his life is completely given over to serve and not be served, after the model of Jesus, whom he makes present. Through ordination, the priest is "dispossessed" of himself and gives over his life to God for service of God's people, the flock, the body of Christ.[40]

This dispossession of self is what some theologians call expropriation. Just as Christ surrendered Himself completely to the Father, becoming a transparent image of the Father, so the priest surrenders himself to his mission, laying down his own personal identity so that he can become a transparent image of Christ. This is where the priest's mission, like Christ's, involves a personal kenosis: "This fidelity requires of the priest a *kenosis*, an emptying of all merely personal hopes and projects, all vanity and ambition, as the classic writings on the spirituality of priesthood have constantly insisted."[41] The priest who embraces this expropriation of himself follows the example of John the Baptist, "He must increase; I must decrease" (Jn 3:30). This expropriation will become practical in the day-to-day self-denial of the priest who dedicates his whole life to fulfilling his office. He will analyze everything he does in terms of his mission, even his free time and essential recreation. Pope Emeritus Benedict XVI encourages priests to determine how they spend their lives solely in light of their mission, so that Christ can work through them:

> Dear friends, let us pray ever anew for this intention, let us strive precisely for this: in other words, for Christ to grow within us and for our union with him to become ever deeper, so that through us it is Christ himself who tends the flock. . . . Day after day it is necessary to learn that I do not possess my life for myself. Day by day I must learn to abandon myself; to keep myself available for whatever he, the Lord, needs of me at a given moment, even if other things seem more appealing and more important to me: it means giving life, not taking it.[42]

Hans Urs von Balthasar built his argument that priests should live the evangelical counsels mainly upon this idea of the expropriation required by the office of the priest. It was for him in the very nature of priestly representation; since the priest represents Christ and not himself, he has to embrace self-effacement and self-emptying.[43] There is no better way to do this than through the evangelical counsels. By living obedience, celibacy, and poverty, the priest is able to place his person completely at the disposal of his mission. As Balthasar wrote, "the essence of this pure state of being always prepared, by virtue of their office, for whatever God or the church may require of them cannot be other than the *spirit* of poverty, chastity and obedience, although it will have the distinctive coloring of their office."[44] Balthasar spoke quite strongly about how important the evangelical counsels were for the life of the priest based on this need to subjectively, interiorly unite oneself to the mission that one has been given by Christ:

Intrinsic to the priesthood as an objective function in
the service of the priesthood of Christ is the demand
for a subjective complement, that is, for the priest's
unconditional gift of self that includes the vow in which
all love has its source—the renunciation of all one
possesses. The priest who by reason of his office is the
bearer of Christ's grace, can find no other and no better
answer to this grace than to be subjectively the kind of
priest Christ wants him to be, that is, as we have seen,
a priest who offers his whole life as a holocaust in the
service of God and man. No priestly ethic can have
any other basic content than the total expropriation of
one's own private interests and inclinations so that one
may be a pure instrument for the accomplishment of
Christ's designs for the Church. Such a gift is intrinsically
contained in the decision to become a priest and the
grace to make it is conferred on the priest with the
gift of sacramental grace and the indelible mark of his
priesthood. It is no less demanded and expected of him
than of one bound by the irrevocability of the vows.
It is in no way correct to say that, of itself, the priestly
function demands of the individual a less great and less
perfect gift of self than does the grace of election to
the state of the counsels. The opposite would be more
true: the greatness of the priestly vocation demands of
the one called to it the fullest gift of which he is capable.
Only when he has given literally all he possesses will he
be able to say that he is a useless, but nonetheless usable,
servant. Whether or not he takes explicit vows, he must,
in any event, respond to the Lord's grace by subjecting all
that he has to the Lord's command. Consequently, he will
seek his "perfection," that is, the proper conduct of his

service, only where one called to the state of the counsels
seeks his, namely, in poverty, chastity and obedience,
although, in his case, the manner of self-emptying,
of renunciation of what has hitherto constituted his
life and work, will have points of resemblance to the
special anonymity inherent in the functional aspect of
his office.[45]

The office demands a total self-gift, a holocaust. This self-
gift must be sought in the same way a religious seeks his total
self-gift, in the same way that Christ made His spousal self-
gift for His bride, through the evangelical counsels. The priest
who has become a representative of Christ by his office subjectively places himself completely at the disposal of Christ
through living the self-emptying of the evangelical counsels.
This is the meaning and purpose of the evangelical counsels:
"They mean precisely and centrally our total offering of ourselves to be disposed of by the Lord, just as he puts himself
totally at the disposition of the Father's will."[46]

We noted in chapter 5 that the sin of clericalism comes
from the priest's appropriating his office to his own person,
rather than allowing his person to be expropriated by his
office. The priest who seeks to live his office in imitation of
Christ's obedience, celibacy, and poverty will not become
a clericalist. Especially through humble obedience, he will
become like the Lord who came to serve and not be served.
Here is another reason that the evangelical counsels are so
important for the priest. He must preserve the authority of
Jesus, authority for service and not for himself:

The spirit of the counsels guarantees the radical reversal
of authority and power that Jesus specifically refers to

as the pattern of those who are called to leadership and community. It is a pattern that completely undermines relationships of domination and control which have characterized every human society. The paradox of the institution and of the office of priesthood is precisely that it is to exemplify only the pattern of Christ who was sent as a servant (cf. Lk 22:24-27).[47]

The evangelical counsels help to guarantee that the priest's ministry will not be about himself but about Christ. This is St. Paul's attitude when he speaks about his own ministry in 2 Corinthians 4. St. Paul makes it clear that the ministry is not about him, rather he has placed his whole life at the service of his mission: "For we do not preach ourselves but Jesus Christ as Lord, and ourselves as your slaves for the sake of Jesus" (2 Cor 4:5).

The constant struggle for the priest, however, is that even though he strives through obedience, celibacy, and poverty to become more and more like Christ, to allow himself to be expropriated, he will never achieve unity between his office and his person. As St. Paul also says, in the same passage, "But we hold this treasure in earthen vessels, that the surpassing power may be of God and not from us" (2 Cor 4:7). For the priest, there will always be a tension between who he is and who he is called to be. Feeling this tension will humble him and allow him to realize that he cannot attribute his ministry to himself. Again, Balthasar explains:

> However much he may strive, the priest's subjective commitment [*Sollen*] will never be the equivalent of his official ministry [*Sein*]. Indeed, the secular priest who, to achieve a more perfect gift of himself, adopts in whole or

in part the form of life proper to the counsels will never be tempted to believe that, in doing so, he has "done everything" (Luke 17:10). He will always see in the mirror of the "perfect life" of the saints who followed the Lord in poverty, chastity and obedience the unattainable ideal of his own striving. Even if he were himself a saint, he would not know it, but would be all the more aware of the holiness incorporated in his brethren.[48]

The humility that comes from living in this tension becomes a source of self-emptying that allows him to be more transparent to Christ. As he fully embraces the self-emptying life of the evangelical counsels and the humility of his own human poverty in the office, he will find that Christ is present working through him and in him because he is able to get himself out of the way. Through this self-emptying, he will discover an incredible fruitfulness in his ministry, a power that is far beyond him. He will be able to say with St. Paul: "I have been crucified with Christ; yet I live, no longer I, but Christ lives in me" (Gal 2:19-20). Thus, it is through the counsels that the priest becomes more and more what he is called to be by ordination: alter Christus.

It is also through the counsels the priest lives the sacrificial nature of Christ's spousal love. The divine marriage of Christ is fulfilled on the Cross. If the priest must be a living image of Christ the Bridegroom of the Church, as St. John Paul II has said, then this means that the priest must share in the manner of priesthood that Christ Himself lived. In the tradition this has often been expressed with the idea that the priest is both priest and victim; as St. John Paul II said: "The priest, among all the faithful, is especially called to identify himself mystically—as well as sacramentally—with Christ in order to be himself in some way *Sacerdos et Hostia,* according to the beautiful expression of St. Thomas Aquinas."[49] We might add that to understand fully Christ's gift of Himself on the Cross, one could say Christ was priest, victim, and bridegroom, since His gift was not only a sacrifice to the Father but also for His bride.[50] The priest imitates Christ's spousal love through his embracing of the Cross in a sacrificial way of life, on behalf of the bride and to the bride. Cardinal Godfreid Danneels pointed out that since Vatican II, the identity of the priesthood has been too often identified in its ecclesiological dimensions and not enough in its Christological dimension. We must remember the Cross in the life of the priest:

> Since Vatican II, *the identity of the priest* is defined above all under the ecclesiological aspect: the priest is the servant of the community. This view is correct. But, all the same one cannot pass over in silence the Christological dimension of the priest. We too often pass in silence the fact that the priest is defined also by his configuration to Christ. Even the interiority of the priest is defined as well by his configuration to Christ. We speak too little of his participation in the passion of Christ, of his agony in the garden, of the tragedy of the cosmic battle between good and evil which passes through the soul of the priest and of his solidarity with sinners . . . The priest is not only the servant of the community, he is placed on the cross with Christ."[51]

Here is where our synthesis of the priestly life can be applied. The bridegroom image helps to situate the priest in his relationship with Christ and the Church; it helps us see both the Christological dimension and the ecclesiological dimension. The ordained priest shares in Christ's mode of priestly life by incarnating in himself Christ's spousal love for the Church. Through his daily sacrificial living on behalf of the Church, he is united to Christ and the Church as the representative of the bridegroom. As the *Directory for the Life and Ministry of Priests* says, priests "must be faithful to the Bride and, much akin to living icons of Christ the Spouse, render fruitful the multi-form donation of Christ to his Church."[52] Thus, in his own life, the priest shares in Christ's mode of living, imitating Christ's spousal love, becoming in his self-gift priest, victim, and bridegroom for the people. The evangelical counsels are essential for this sacrificial self-offering. On the Cross, Christ lived obedience, celibacy, and poverty to the full.[53] The counsels were part of the internal sacrificial offering He made to the Father on behalf of the bride. They were at the heart of the true worship that He made to the Father on the Cross. Ghirlanda says that the priest also seeks to worship God with his whole life through living the counsels. Through this daily sacrificial self-offering, he joins his life to the perfect worship Christ offered to the Father on the Cross:

> Living the spirit of the beatitudes in the exercise of his ministry, the priest arrives at the perfection of charity and offers God true worship . . . As Christ offered to the Father the perfect worship in the offering of his life, thus also the priest must offer the true worship to God in the offering of his life. In this way the priest becomes a testimony of the cross of Christ and a living sign of the future world. In fact, Christ consummated on the cross his virginal chastity as universal love, in a perfect and

radical way; on the cross Christ adhered obediently to the
will of the Father in highest poverty and humility.[54]

In this way, the priest becomes a living image of the
bridegroom by becoming priest and victim with Christ
through the counsels. As St. Paul described his own ministry,
"Now I rejoice in my sufferings for your sake, and in my flesh
I am filling up what is lacking in the afflictions of Christ on
behalf of his body, which is the church" (Col 1:24). This is St.
Paul incarnating the spousal love of Christ through embracing his suffering. In the last chapter of this book, we will
see how this daily self-offering of the priest is done through
each of the evangelical counsels. Now, we must see how this
kenotic and self-sacrificing love is fruitful.

We noted in chapter 6 that the spiritual fruitfulness of the
priest is often seen in his celebration of the sacraments or his
preaching of the Word. But we can also see how this fruitfulness comes from his self-sacrificing, self-emptying love. Here,
we connect the fruitfulness of the priest to the fruitfulness
of Christ, who became fruitful through His Death: "unless
a grain of wheat falls to the ground and dies, it remains just
a grain of wheat; but if it dies, it produces much fruit" (Jn
12:24). Real fruitfulness in priestly ministry comes in the same
way it did for Christ, who gave His life for the salvation of
the world. St. John Paul II explains how the priest learns this
fruitfulness from his daily celebration of the Eucharist:

> It is Eucharistic love that daily renews [the priest's]
> fatherhood and makes it fruitful, transforming him ever
> more into Christ and, like Christ, makes him become
> the bread of souls, their priest, yes, but also their victim,

because for them he is gladly consumed in imitation of him who gave his life for the salvation of the world.[55]

Understanding this Eucharistic love as the heart of the priesthood helps to give a proper focus to the priest's ministry. It is easy for a priest to judge ministerial success by secular standards, believing that his ministry is a success only if it is being effective.[56] Cardinal Ratzinger pointed out in a homily to priests that this was also a temptation for Jesus' Apostles. Just when Jesus' preaching seemed to be the most effective, He began to teach about the Cross and to cease His preaching. Gradually, the crowds became smaller and smaller as He prepared to embrace the Cross. Ratzinger says the Twelve must have asked themselves how Jesus was going to succeed:

> How is Israel's salvation to come about if all he does is to preach, to spin words, and here and there occasionally heal some person of no influence or significance; if the little flock of those who stand by him is continually being reduced, if he meets with failure in the form of a message that is rejected ever more clearly and in the form of increasing opposition among influential circles?[57]

Yet Jesus was not embracing a worldly vision of success; His mission was not seeking the most effective means of influencing people. Jesus' success would come through the fruitfulness of His hidden sacrifice, like the small seed that falls to the ground and dies:

> All truly fruitful things in this world begin with what is small and hidden. And God himself conformed to this law with his work in the world. God himself entered this age incognito, in the form of wretchedness, of

powerlessness. And the realities of God—truth, justice, love—are small and downtrodden realities in this world.[58]

In fact, the real ability to be effective in Christianity cannot come outside of the mystery of the Cross. Just as Christ's mission required Him to be both priest and victim, so also the priest must understand that his ministry is under the sign of the Cross:

> Having been entrusted with pastoral office, priests, therefore are required to give their lives away in configuration to the Priesthood and Person of Christ himself. . . . pastoral love takes on the Form of the Cross. Acquiring this Form of Life requires a wholehearted surrender. . . . The mysteries of the Lord's Eucharistic self-giving love unfold in the life of his ministers: like him, they are to be taken and blessed, broken and given, not only in terms of liturgical gesture, but in the praxis of loving the community following the example of Jesus when he washes the disciples' feet on Holy Thursday (Jn 13:1). Such profound self-giving precedes any action or programme, and the seemingly passive life of interior identification with the Lord's passion is in fact the expression of a most highly active willingness for self-sacrifice.[59]

Thus, the priest's ministry will only be truly fruitful if he embraces the Cross in his daily life, making his life and ministry an offering just as Jesus' was. One can see here the importance of the priestly life of prayer, which could seem a very ineffective use of time but, in fact, is essential for his work to be fruitful. In fact, his prayer may be the most fruitful part of his work, as that work is the most empty of the self:

The hidden life of contemplation, prayerful intercession and interior self-giving are [sic] therefore understood as not simply the condition for greater pastoral effectiveness or availability although these might well be the secondary fruits of living so deeply in the Lord. . . . they are in themselves the most powerful actualization of pastoral love, for it is through prayer that the priest is drawn into the mystery of Triune love, and it is in loving Christ above all things that he brings forth spiritual fruitfulness in the life of the Church.[60]

We see this mystery of fruitfulness coming through the Cross so clearly in St. Paul's description of his own ministry. He describes how, even more than his preaching or teachings, his own daily dying with Christ brought life to the people he served:

We are afflicted in every way, but not constrained; perplexed, but not driven to despair; persecuted, but not abandoned; struck down, but not destroyed; always carrying about in the body the dying of Jesus, so that the life of Jesus may also be manifested in our body. For we who live are constantly being given up to death for the sake of Jesus, so that the life of Jesus may be manifested in our mortal flesh. So death is at work in us, but life in you (2 Cor 4:8-12).

St. Paul learned to see his daily disappointments and failures, his daily sufferings and sacrifices as participation in Christ's Paschal Mystery and, therefore, life-giving. How important is this way of seeing for the life of the priest? Through this way of seeing, the evangelical counsels become not a negative limitation but a way of self-giving love in the daily life of the priest. Life according to the evangelical counsels keeps the priest from being merely a professional teacher or an executive leader of the community, rather he is priest and victim. The life of the evangelical counsels becomes a protection against activism, which is usually only a disguised pursuit of pride and building up one's self in ministry. Balthasar points out that this is one of the great temptations in ministry today; and obedience, chastity, and poverty provide a protection against it because they make the priest radically available to whatever Christ wants from him:

> Against all the activism in the world and in Christianity today, we must absolutely hold fast to the fact—which is one of the most essential aspects of the Church—that nothing can be more welcome or more readily useful to the Lord for the purposes of his salvific providence than the pure gift of self that renounces every calculation and assessment of its own fruits and looks only to him, listens to him, perseveres in availability to him, and finds satisfaction only in him.[61]

This is the picture of the true representative and friend of the bridegroom, not drawing the bride to himself through his activism, but surrendering himself completely through his daily life to serve the mission of the true bridegroom. The choice that a priest makes to be chaste or poor will often not be seen by others and will be part of the hidden sacrifice only seen by Christ. The choice to be chaste when alone and tempted at night, the choice to go without what one does not really need, the personal cost of his little obediences to his prayer life, these things will not appear to the eyes of the world. But these choices are the seeds that are buried and bear much fruit. They are the way he comes to deep union with Christ in His Paschal Mystery. These are the ways he gives life to his bride.

In the humility of obedience, the priest contributes to the expansion of the Church, to the conversion of men to the Gospel, to the spiritual enrichment of humanity. Never does an act of submission, a gesture of dependence done in faith remain useless. The difficulty is to believe in the hidden fruits of obedience, but the example of Jesus sheds upon these fruits a decisive light.[62]

Through these sacrifices, the priest can say with St. Paul, "death is at work in us, but life in you" (2 Cor 4:12). Through faith, he knows that his hidden self-offering is actually more important than the talents and skills for which he receives attention. In fact, it will be in the failure of his talents that often the mystery of hidden fruitfulness is revealed:

> The fact that the one who lives according to the counsels of Jesus is no more able to demonstrate his successes than Jesus the Crucified himself could do belongs to the essence of the Cross, to its humiliation and shame, and thereby once again to the hidden fruitfulness of love's self-gift.[63]

One thinks of some of the great "failures" in the Christian tradition, such as St. John Henry Newman, who wrote in his spiritual biography the *Apologia Pro Vita Sua* that his life had been filled with much failure, or St. John of the Cross, who died without being able to see the fruitfulness of his attempted reform of Carmel. The consolation that the saints have in these "failures," this sacrificial self-emptying, is their union with Christ. Through faith, they know that Christ's self-emptying, sacrificial love was fruitful; and with Christ, they abandon in absolute trust that their lives given completely for Him will also be fruitful. This is the only consolation they seek.

Thus, through the living of the evangelical counsels, the priest gives concrete expression to the spousal love of Christ, often in hidden ways. Through embracing the counsels as a way of life, he seeks to transform his whole life into a way of spiritual fruitfulness through self-emptying, sacrificial, self-giving love.

The Evangelical Counsels Strengthen the Pastoral Charity of the Priest

As we have seen, this spousal love of Christ is pastoral charity. Pastoral charity is, according to St. John Paul II, both the love of the shepherd who lays down his life for his sheep,[64] and the love of the bridegroom who lays down his life for his bride.[65] The priest loves the Church with Christ's own spousal love and for this reason, embraces the evangelical counsels so that his love might be more and more a transparent image of Christ's love for the Church. The counsels allow the priest to make the total surrender of love for the sake of the Church that the priesthood calls for. As St. John Paul II said:

> The only fitting response to this gift is nothing other than total surrender: an act of complete love. The voluntary acceptance of the divine call to the priesthood was, without doubt an act of love which makes each of us a lover. . . . Christ Crucified shows us the measure of that surrender, since he tells us of obedient love to the Father for the salvation of all (Phil 2:6 ff.). The priest, attempting to identify totally with Christ, the Eternal

Priest, must manifest this love and obedience on the altar and in his life.[66]

The heart of the priest brings together two loves: an undivided love of Christ and, as a result, the desire to love the Church as Christ loved His bride. The same two loves are in heart of Christ who, on the Cross, gave Himself in undivided love to the Father for the sake of His bride, which is the Church. It is because the priest loves Christ that he wants to give himself in love for the Church as Christ did. Power explains how this personal love of Christ and communal love of the Church are united:

> The priesthood finds its own truth, that it is not an end in itself, but crystallizes, rather, the love of Christ for his church, the Body and Bride to whom and for whose sake he gives himself away. A strong ecclesial identity includes both a sense of living wholly only for service and a willingness to lose one's own identity to the absolute demands of ecclesial love. This is made possible only by a profoundly personal surrender to the radical call of Christ and of his gospel.[67]

This is the synthesis we explained at the end of the last chapter. The priest is not the true bridegroom; his goal is not ultimately union with the bride. However, it is through his self-gift to the bride that the priest acting *in the person of Christ the Bridegroom of the Church* draws close to Christ. It was through obedience, celibacy, and poverty that Christ allowed Himself to be completely given to the mission of the Father for the bride. The priest imitates Christ's total "yes" to the Father, a gift for the sake of the Church. Having placed his life in the hands of Christ through these three counsels, he removes impediments to his pastoral charity. Through the counsels, he unite himself to God with an undivided heart; this allows him to make a complete gift of himself to Christ's bride:

> By his vocation, the priest is called to unite himself to God, without dividing his heart or giving himself to other loves . . . with the goal of giving himself entirely to the service of others, separating from himself, in an act of renunciation which is joyful and full of fruitfulness, everything which, in his case, would be an impediment to the total availability and handing over of himself which pastoral charity demands.[68]

This is another aspect of the nuptial nature of the Sacrament of Holy Orders. Because the priest stands in the person of the bridegroom, he, in a certain way, belongs to the Church as well as to Christ. The bride has rights to the exclusive love of her bridegroom. As St. John Paul II said, "the Church, as the spouse of Jesus Christ, wishes to be loved by the priest in the total and exclusive manner in which Jesus Christ her head and spouse loved her."[69] Cardinal Wyszynski, the famous primate of Poland and the mentor of St. John Paul II, made this point clear in a letter he wrote to his priests:

> Commissioned as we are by God for the service of the People of God, we have become their property. All the energies of our soul and body ought to serve the people who have the right to our life, to our eyes and to our priestly lips to our hands which offer the sacrifice, and to

our apostolic feet. So we must dedicate to them entirely our unceasing work, while it is still daylight.[70]

We will explore in the next chapter how the demands of the bride will provide for the priest a specific, pastoral way to live the evangelical counsels. The more the priest lives obedience, chastity, and poverty, the freer he is to be given for Christ's bride and the more he incarnates Christ's own pastoral charity. In fact, filled with the spousal love of Christ for His Church, the priest wants to sacrifice everything for the sake of the Bride. As the famous motto of Don Bosco says, *"da mihi animas cetera tolle."*[71]

Since the Cross is the moment of the marriage between Christ and the Church, it must be seen as the supreme model of all nuptial love. On the Cross, Christ models "that love in which the human person becomes a gift and—through this gift—fulfills the very meaning of his being and existence."[72] Therefore, the Cross is also the model of pastoral charity. Pastoral charity is a love that is willing to give all. Christ's pastoral charity "attains its fullest expression in his death on the cross, that is, in his total gift of self in humility and love."[73] Thus, we can summarize all the reasons for the priest to live the evangelical counsels by saying the priest is called to live pastoral charity, the nuptial self-gift of the Cross. St. John Paul II explains how this self-gift of the Cross is rooted in the evangelical counsels:

> Jesus Christ, who brought his pastoral charity to
> perfection on the cross with a complete exterior and
> interior emptying of self, is both the model and source
> of the virtues of obedience, chastity and poverty which
> the priest is called to live out as an expression of his

pastoral charity for his brothers and sisters. In accordance with St. Paul's words to the Christians at Philippi, the priest should have "the mind which was in Christ Jesus," emptying himself of his own "self," so as to discover, in a charity which is obedient, chaste and poor, the royal road of union with God and unity with his brothers and sisters (cf. Phil. 2:5).[74]

Priestly obedience, celibacy, and poverty are the "expression of his pastoral charity for his brothers and sisters." They are, therefore, the main way the priest incarnates Christ's own spousal love. The evangelical counsels are the "the royal road of union with God and unity with his brothers and sisters"—that is, they are the way that the priest fulfills his call to be a living image of the bridegroom.

Questions for Discussion, Reflection, and Prayer

1. What do I know when Christ looks at me with love, inviting me each day to be with Him by saying, "Follow me"?

2. How is Christ inviting me to deeper union with Him through the evangelical counsels? What is He asking me to change?

3. How have I experienced Gospel fruitfulness, which comes through self-emptying, sacrificial love?

4. How does a spirit of activism affect my priestly ministry, and what are practical ways I am being called to renounce it to enter into the spiritual fruitfulness of the Gospel?

5. When do I experience the fire of love that makes
    me want to give myself for Christ and His Bride?
    When do I say with St. John Bosco: *"Da mihi animas,
    cetera tolle"*?

NOTES

1. John Paul II, *Pastores Dabo Vobis* (1992), sec. 22.

2. Jean Galot, S.J., "The Priesthood and Celibacy," *Review for Religious* 24 (1965): 950.

3. This is clearly the point of the parable of the Good Samaritan where the priest and the Levite put their cultic official duties ahead of charity (Luke 10:29-37); but it is also implicit in the cleansing of the temple, especially in the Gospel of John (John 2:13-22) where we find Christ expressing His broader critique of the Old Testament system of worship.

4. This does not rule out the possibility of some ways in which married priests may be called to incarnate in their lives the spirit of the evangelical counsels. As we noted in the introduction, our work is aimed at explaining the western tradition, which has tended toward celibacy, at least from the fourth century, and which, we have argued, is more true to the nature of the priesthood. But a married priest, legitimately ordained through the tradition of his Church, or by way of exception in the West, must still find ways to let his priestly consecration be expressed through self-sacrifice. In some way, this must include the spirit of the evangelical counsels, even the living of the virtue of chastity, as the Eastern Code of Canon Law says: "Clerics, celibate or married, are to excel in the virtue of chastity; it is for the particular law to establish suitable means for pursuing this end" (Canon 374).

5. Paul VI, *Lumen Gentium* (1964), sec. 39.

6. See Matthew 5:48; *Lumen Gentium*, sec. 40.

7. Thomas Aquinas, *Summa Theologiae* II-II, 184, a. 3. According to Jan G. J. van den Eijnden, St. Thomas considered the counsels "to be aids for perfection, given to all the faithful." (Jan G. J. van den Eijnden, O.F.M., *Poverty on the Way to God: Thomas Aquinas on Evangelical Poverty* [Louvain: Peeters, 1994], 41)

8. John Paul II, *Man and Woman He Created Them: A Theology of the Body* (Boston: Pauline Books and Media, 2006), 431, emphasis in original.

9. The distinction between living the spirit of the counsels and living them in fact is most clear in the counsel of chastity: "It would not be good to blur the distinction between the 'spirit' and the concrete living out of the counsels. This becomes clearest—once again—in the case of the second counsel. Its very name—whether one calls it 'virginity' or 'celibacy'—unequivocally contradicts the sacramental vocation called 'marriage.'" (Jörg Splett, "Evangelical Counsels in Marriage?" *Communio* 31 [2004]: 410)

10. Ghirlanda, *Il diritto nella Chiesa: mistero di communione* (Milan: San Paolo, 1993), 181.

11. Galot, "The Priesthood and Celibacy," 948.

12.   The imperative command is seen in all four Gospels and always with the same meaning: Mt 4:19; Mt 8:22; Mt 9:9; Mt 19:21; Mk 1:17; Mk 2:14; Mk 10:21; Lk 5:27; Lk 9:59; Lk 18:22; Jn 1:43; Jn 21:19, 22.

13.   See Mark 10:17-22 and parallels.

14.   Jean Galot, S.J., *Vivre avec le Christ: La vie consacrée selon l'Évangile* (Louvain: Sintal, 1986), 23-24.

15.   John Paul II, "Priests: Consecrated to Christ through Celibacy," General Audience, 17 July 1993, in *Priesthood in the Third Millenium*, 81-82.

16.   John Paul II, *Vita Consecrata* (1996), 14, emphasis in original.

17.   Hans Urs von Balthasar, *The Christian State of Life*, trans. Sister Mary Frances McCarthy (San Francisco: Ignatius Press, 1983), 349.

18.   *Vita Consecrata*, sec. 93, the internal quote is from John Paul II, "General Audience Address, Feb. 8, 1995," *L'Osservatore Romano*, English ed. (Feb. 15, 1995), 11. Galot will argue that in the Scriptures, we can also see that some women, although not apostles, seemed to be part of this closer following of Jesus: "However, this is not to limit this state of consecrated life to those who were called to the priestly functions. There were women who following, who did not receive sacerdotal powers, yet they had access, as the disciples did, to a life of union with him" (*Vivre avec le Christ*, 30).

19.   See John 20:21.

20.   See John 21:15-22.

21.   Galot, *Vivre avec le Christ*, 30.

22.   Raymond Brown, Priest and Bishop: Biblical Reflections (New York: Paulist Press, 1970), 22. Brown says the Gospels make clear that those who will be priests are called to the special kind of discipleship to which not all Christians are called: "We cannot read the Gospels in a way that would water down the specific fidelity and generosity required of those chosen from the wider group of followers to be Jesus' special disciples so that they may worthily represent him to others. In short we cannot discount the a fortiori implications of the discipleship of the Twelve for the ideals of the priesthood" (Priest and Bishop, 24, emphasis in original). Of course, the married state of most of the Apostles is unknown, and there is the scriptural mention of Peter's mother-in-law. Galot ("Lo stato di vita degli Apostoli," in Civiltà Cattolica 140.4 (1989): 327-340) has done a study of the question including a study of the opinions of all the Fathers. Although one finds diverse opinions about the married state of the Apostles among the Fathers, one finds no other real evidence to support marriage among the Apostles than what one finds in the Scriptures themselves (Ibid., 331). Galot argues that: "nowhere is there made mention for the apostles of a wife or of children. This fact is verified even in the case of Peter; one could add that, in the account in which the mother-in-law of Simon appears, the silence regarding his wife is even stronger evidence. Much more positive instead are the implicit indications

in the abandoning of all required from Jesus for those who he called to follow him: this involved the renunciation of family and marriage" (Ibid). Albert Descamps concurs with Galot that the renunciation of marriage and family was required by all the Apostles ("Aux origines du ministère, La pensée de Jésus," Revue Théologique de louvain 2 [1970]: 22). He points out that Peter reveals the totality of the abandonment made by the Apostles to follow Jesus when Peter says, "we have given up everything and followed you" (Mt 19:27). As we noted in chapter 4, the response of Jesus that "everyone who has given up houses or brothers or sisters or father or mother or children or lands for the sake of my name will receive a hundred times more, and will inherit eternal life" (Mt 19:29), seems to imply the renunciation of marriage rather than the abandonment of children. This would also be true of Luke's version 18:29, which actually mentions having left a wife. Galot argues Luke's version represents the more original words of Jesus, and Galot also underlines the impossibility of Jesus' inviting the Apostles to leave behind current wives by contrasting Jesus' teaching about the indissolubility of marriage with His teaching on celibacy in Matthew 19 (See "Stato di vita degli Apostoli," 332-33). According to Galot, then, "Jesus called to follow him only those who were free from a marriage bond" (Ibid., 335). Nicolas agrees that the New Testament gives us a picture of the Apostles as free from bonds of marriage and family: "That the apostles were married or not—one can only respond in the affirmative for Peter, because of the episode where there is the question of his mother-in-law—it is clear in the Gospels, in the Acts of the Apostles, and in the other apostolic writings, that they were free of all obligation and of all charge of families" (Jean-Hervé Nicolas, "Sacerdoce, célibat et sacraments," Nova et Vetera 53 [1978]: 127). Galot also takes up the unique reference where St. Paul speaks about apostles having a woman who accompanies them: "Do we not have the right to take along a Christian wife, as do the rest of the apostles, and the brothers of the Lord, and Cephas?" (1 Cor 9:5). The words often translated "believing wife" in Greek are "άdelfhv ganaika" (literally, a "sister woman"). After looking at the possible meanings of these words, Galot says: "it refers to a woman who is treated as a sister. The intention of the expression seems rightly to distinguish this woman from a wife and to evoke an exceptional situation" (Ibid., 337). He compares this woman to the women that followed Jesus and took care of His needs (Mk 15:41; Mt 27:55). He proposes that the Apostles had the same special privilege to have along a "sister woman" that would care for their needs (Galot, "Stato di vita degli Apostoli," 338-39).

23. "Calling men and women to follow him, Christ has founded a state of consecration which for some pertains to the priesthood, but for others has a destination independent of the priestly institution: this state constitutes the first origin of the religious life, as well as the priesthood" (Galot,

"Vita consacrata—vita carismatica alla luce del Nuovo Testamento" *Vita Consecrata* 15 [1979]: 374-5).

24.   Dermot Power, *A Spiritual Theology of the Priesthood: The Mystery of Christ and the Mission of the Priest* (Washington, DC: Catholic University of America Press, 1998), 95.

25.   Galot, "Vita consacrata—vita carismatica," 374.

26.   Paul VI, *Presbyterorum Ordinis* (1965), sec. 3.

27.   See John 10:36.

28.   *Presbyterorum Ordinis*, sec. 12

29.   Ghirlanda, "Formazione del prete al carisma della paternità," 4. This personal consecration would include not only the evangelical counsels, but also the other obligations of the office as Ghirlanda makes clear elsewhere: "This service, which is the content of the same consecration of ministry (PO 12b), must be lived in the forgetfulness of self, in dependence upon God, in universal charity, and it must manifest itself in a simple and modest life, in a spirit of poverty (PO 17; CIC. 282), in the observance of perfect and perpetual continence for the kingdom of god, that is in celibacy (PO 16; CIC 277, #1), in the full respect and obedience to the Supreme Pontif and to the Bishop (CIC. 273), and in all the other proper obligations of the clerical state (CIC. 273-289)" (*Diritto nella Chiesa*, 125).

30.   *Vita Consecrata*, 19.

31.   Robert Brom, "Consecration, Ministry and Life Give Priests an Ecclesial Identity," *L'Osservatore Romano*, English Edition (5 August 1992): 7.

32.   Power, 88.

33.   *Presbyterorum Ordinis*, sec. 16.

34.   Jean Beyer, S.J., "Life Consecrated by the Evangelical Counsels: Conciliar Teaching and Later Developments," in *Vatican II Assessment and Perspectives: Twenty-five Years After (1962-1987)*, vol. 3, ed. René Latourelle, S.J. (New York: Paulist Press, 1989), 68.

35.   St. Theresa of Calcutta, "Priestly Celibacy: Sign of the Charity of Christ," in *For Love Alone: Reflections on Priestly Celibacy* (Maynooth, Ireland: St. Pauls, 1993), 212-213, emphasis in emphasis.

36.   As we saw in chapter 6, according to St. Thomas, those who give up one aspect of their lives make a sacrifice; those who give up their whole lives make a holocaust (ST II-II, 184, a.8, corpus).

37.   Balthasar, *Christian State of Life*, 236.

38.   Gisbert Greshake, *The Meaning of Christian Priesthood*, trans. Peadar MacSeumais, S.J. (Westminster, Md.: Christian Classics, 1989), 131-132, emphasis in original. Balthasar quotes Adrian Van Speyr on this topic: "Priesthood without the life of the counsels is really a concession on the part of the Church. Every priest should be in the life of the counsels. As things are now . . . both the rule and the wife are missing. For the secular

priest, the parish is the focus of his vocation; apart from that in a sense he is free. The secular clergy have almost completely dispensed themselves from poverty: Why shouldn't a secular priest be a millionaire? Celibacy means that you sacrifice having a family for the sake of the parish. The end is external. The main motive for the sacrifice is the priest's professional work: as a celibate, he has more time at his disposal. . . . Obedience to the bishop has become very meager. You say 'Yes' or 'No' to him, according to your need. You explain things to him" (Hans Urs von Balthasar, *Our Task: A Report and a Plan,* trans. John Saward [San Francisco: Ignatius Press, 1994], 153).

39. Greshake, 132.

40. Mark O'Keefe, *In Persona Christi: Reflections on Priestly Identity and Holiness* (Saint Meinrad, IN: Saint Meinrad School of Theology, 1998), 24.

41. Benedict Ashley, O.P., *Justice in the Church: Gender and Participation* (Washington, D.C.: Catholic University of America, 1996), 88.

42. Benedict XVI, "Holy Mass for the Ordination to the Priesthood of 15 Deacons of the Diocese of Rome," (7 May 2006), available from: http://www.vatican.va/holy_father/benedict_xvi/homilies/2006/documents/hf_ben-xvi_hom_20060507_priestly-ordination_en.html, accessed 11 May 2006.

43. "Anonymity required of the secular priest is . . . the assimilation of the individual to a function that is itself anonymous. Priests are, for the most part, interchangeable in the functions they perform. The more transparent their spiritual substance, the more effectively the Spirit can work through them; the less they dim the presence of the divine that is revealed through them by the colossal proportions of their own so-called 'individuality' (or even their 'ideal self-image'), the more ideal they will be as priests" (*Christian State of Life,* 276).

44. Balthasar, *Christian State of Life,* 276, emphasis in original.

45. Ibid., 275. As Power says in his writings on Balthasar's understanding of the priesthood: "In Balthasar's view it is the spirit and life of the Evangelical Counsels that guarantee the 'emptiness' within the priesthood for its full meaning of service and pastoral love to be realized. This form of emptying out is the Form of Christ, the state of life of Jesus himself in his person and in his mission. It is in New Testament terms the 'having the mind that was in Christ Jesus.' Therefore in connecting so closely the ministerial priesthood with the life of the Counsels, Balthasar is being radically biblical, and it is this radicalism that characterizes his whole emphasis on the priesthood as the state of life. The state of life of the Christian priest, because it participates in the eternal priesthood of Christ and its continuation in the Church for the sake of all, is shaped within the obediential love, the poverty of kenosis and the chaste fruitfulness of the Son" (Power 98).

46. Balthasar, *Elucidations,* 142.

47. Power, 98.

48. Balthasar, *Christian State of Life*, 375.

49. "Priests, Ordained to Celebrate Mass," *General Audience*, 12 May 1993, in *Priesthood in the Third Millennium: Addresses of Pope John Pual II, 1993* (Princeton, NJ: Scepter Publishers, 1994), 40. See ST III, 83, a.1, ad. 3.

50. See Ephesians 5:25.

51. "Le petit nombre des vocations sacerdotales," *Relatio in Aulam*, Eighth Ordinary Synod of Bishops (5 October 1990), private collection, emphasis in original. Published summary is available in Italian: "Card. Godfried Danneels, Arcivesc. di Malines-Bruxelles," in Giovanni Caprile, S.J., "Il Sinodo dei Vescovi 1990," 203-204 (Roma: *La Civiltà Cattolica*, 1990).

52. *Directory for the Life and Ministry of Priests*, 14.

53. We remember how John Paul II described the Cross in terms of the evangelical counsels: "There his virginal love for the Father and for all mankind will attain its highest expression. His poverty will reach complete self-emptying, his obedience the giving of his life" (Vita Consecrata 23).

54. Ghirlanda, "Formazione del prete al carisma della paternità," 4, See *Presbyterorum Ordinis*, sec. 16.

55. John Paul II, "Address to Italian Clergy," in *L'Osservatore Romano* English edition (5 March 1984): 8.

56. See the discussion of "Avoidance of Functionalism" and "Supernatural Sensitivity" in David Toups, *Reclaiming Our Priestly Character* (Omaha, NE: IPF Publications, 2010),175-181.

57. Joseph Ratzinger, *Ministers of Your Joy: Scriptural Meditations on Priestly Spirituality*, trans. Robert Nowell (Ann Arbor, MI: Servant Publications, 1989): 12.

58. Ibid., 14.

59. Power, 47-48.

60. Ibid., 129.

61. Balthasar, *Laity and the Life of the Counsels*, 209.

62. Galot, *Vivre avec le Christ*, 178.

63. Ibid., 190.

64. See John 10:11.

65. See Ephesians 5:25.

66. "Address to Chilean Clergy" in *L'Osservatore Romano*, English edition, (13 April 1987): 7-8.

67. Power, 80.

68. Alvaro del Portillo, "Espiritualidad del Sacerdote," in *Render amabile la verità: Raccolta di scritti di Mons. Alvaro del Portillo, Pastorali-Teologici-Cononistici-Vari* (Vatican City: Ateneo Romano della Santa Croce- Libreria Editrice Vaticana, 1995), 290.

69. *Pastores Dabo Vobis*, sec. 29.

70.   Cardinal S. Wyszynski, *List do moich kaplanow* [Letter to my Priests], III, (Paris 1969), 162, 63; quoted by John Paul II in "Homily", 13 April 1987, in *L'Osservatore Romano*, English ed., (10 June 1987), 3.

71.   Give me souls, take everything else.

72.   John Paul II, *Man and Woman He Created Them*, 186.

73.   *Pastores Dabo Vobis*, sec. 21.

74.   Ibid., sec. 30.

CHAPTER 8

LIVING IN THE SPOUSAL LOVE OF CHRIST

More than a manual about how to live the evangelical counsels, this book is intended to be an inspiration about why a priest should want to live them. One only has to look at the different rules of religious communities to see many different ways to live the counsels. Especially for the diocesan priest, who, for good reason, lives in the midst of the world, the how of living the counsels will involve wisdom and prudence particular to different situations in his life. We can, however, serve the life of priests who desire to live this call if we begin to point to some of the principles about how the counsels can be lived, even though the practicalities will have to be worked out by individual priests or groups of priests. This is especially true since we are distinguishing between the priestly call to the counsels and the religious call. The priestly call to live the counsels is different than the religious motivation. The priest, by virtue of his ordination, must represent the spousal self-gift of Christ to His Church, his living of the counsels will have a specifically pastoral character; it will be at the service of the mission of his office.

In this chapter, we will look at each of the counsels to see its particular importance for the priest to become a living image of the bridegroom.

Living the Evangelical Counsels in the Midst of the World

Because of the priest's office in the Church, and the need to be a living image of the bridegroom for the people, the priest cannot live completely separate from the world. Many times, for the religious, the embracing of the counsels means embracing a life that is marked by separation from the secular sphere. The life of the diocesan priest does not permit this, and it makes living the evangelical counsels both more difficult and more necessary. To fulfill his office, in some ways, the priest must be like those in the religious state; and in other ways, he must be close to those in the lay state:

> The priest, through celibacy and obedience to the Bishop, shares to some extent in that separation from the world for the cause of Christ that characterizes the religious life. Through the relative personal autonomy required by the demands of the pastoral vocation and by close involvement with the life of the parish, its orientation to family needs, to the formation of the laity and to a freedom regarding material possessions, the priest seems to have a kind of "organic unity" with the lay state.[1]

This "in between" place is where Christ lived His life. Christ was not of the world; He did not live a secular life, no career and no personal property. He lived a life completely given to the Father. Yet Christ lived in the world. He taught the crowds; He visited homes; He ate and drank with others, living in the midst of the people. He drew close to them without compromising His own holiness in order to save them and show them the way to live His life of charity. The priest must seek to live in the same way as Christ, embracing fully his mission to live holiness of life through the evangelical counsels, even as he lives in the midst of his people. The more he is completely given for the sake of his mission, the more he will be like Christ and the more he will be able to lead his people to holiness.

Balthasar calls this position of the priest "medial" because it is in between the religious state and the lay state. He warns that this medial position has advantages but also dangers:

> This medial position of the priesthood has its advantages ... the advantage of immediate pastoral contact with the lay congregation; the even greater one of sharing with those in the evangelical state the privilege of the personal following of Christ. The priest, can in fact, assimilate his personal life as closely as he chooses to the spirit, and indeed to the reality, of the evangelical life. But there are also dangers attached to his medial position: The priest can fall prey to mediocrity and colorlessness, or even, in human weakness, extract from each way of life all that is pleasant in it while avoiding the radicality of "losing his soul" (in marriage or in the evangelical state).[2]

There is a big difference between being a bachelor and being a bridegroom. The relative independence in which the priest lives could make it easy for him to avoid the real sacrifice of self-gift that a wife or a community rule would demand of him. The priest often, because he lives alone, can live as he wants. Who really notices if he is obedient to all the hours of the Divine Office, or what he chooses to watch for entertainment? Living in the world amidst the laity will present constant temptations to live for oneself. Thus, in order to be true to his vocation, he has to interiorize the desire for a total self-gift. The evangelical counsels are his sure protection from the dangers of the world that would seek to divide his heart. Only living in total availability to Christ through obedience, celibacy, and poverty will he be able to avoid becoming mediocre and lukewarm, which will rob his vocation of its spousal fruitfulness. The daily choice to live the evangelical counsels will ensure that he does not live for himself, but for the sake of Christ and the Church—that is, he is a bridegroom not a bachelor.

The priest normally does not have to look far for the means to live self-giving love. He will find right within his ministry a sacrificial way of life that flows from his office. He mainly needs to prayerfully surrender to what the Lord asks of him in his pastoral mission. As Cardinal Ratzinger said:

> The ascetic discipline of the priest is not to be set alongside the pastoral activity, as an additional burden and an extra program that overloads my day still further. In my work itself, I am learning to overcome myself, to let my life go and give it up to others. . . . There is no doubt that this asceticism of service or ministry, seeing ministry itself as the actual ascetic discipline in my life, is a most important theme, which does of course demand repeated and conscious practice, an inner ordering of my activity on the basis of who I am.[3]

The living of the evangelical counsels is part of this inner ordering of one's activity. They ensure that the priestly way of life is ordered toward the bride in self-giving love. Thus, for the priest, his living of the evangelical counsels will have a particularly pastoral character. He must be obedient to the needs of his people in addition to his bishop; his celibacy will allow for self-gift as a spiritual father; his poverty will be in placing all his possessions at the service of his mission so he can live close to all, especially the poor. The counsels remove the obstacles for his union with Christ; and the more he embraces them, the more he will be free to be given with Christ in laying down his life for the bride. This is why, for the priest, the evangelical counsels are connected with his pastoral charity. Pastoral charity is the particular nuptial way of living the counsels for the priest.

The Nuptial Obedience of the Priest

Obedience is the heart of the counsels because it the most essential and decisive in the gift of self. It is especially important for the priest since "obedience to the Father is at the very heart of the Priesthood of Christ."[4] To be a priest is to be given for Christ's mission, the mission that continues today in the Church. This is why obedience is "intrinsically requested by the sacrament and by the hierarchical structure of the Church."[5] When the priest lives obedience, he knows he is not serving himself but Christ.

The call of obedience comes to the priest in many differ-ent ways. St. John Paul II explains in *Pastores Dabo Vobis* that priestly obedience is apostolic, communal, and pastoral.[6] It is apostolic in that it is obedience to the Pope and bishops as successors of the Apostles; this includes obedience to their teaching authority as well as their governing authority. This means the priest does not get to choose how he will serve in the mission simply based on his own gifts. Through obedience, he places his gifts at the service of the Church as discerned by his bishop. Of course, many times, this discernment rightly involves mutual conversation; but ultimately, the priest must learn to trust in the grace given for the leadership of the Church.[7] This obedience can become quite difficult when one sees the weaknesses of one's superiors, or when one receives an assignment that is in any way less than ideal. It is even worse when one feels one is being rejected in the process of assignments or simply thought of as a someone needed to fill a hole. Yet, even in these situations where human weakness and sin have an effect on an assignment, the fruitfulness of obedience is real. The priest should remember the Lord's promise to St. Peter: "Amen, amen, I say to you, when you were younger, you used to dress yourself and go where you wanted; but when you grow old, you will stretch out your hands, and someone else will dress you and lead you where you do not want to go" (Jn 21:18). This is the way of spiritual fruitfulness for one who bears the office of an Apostle. The priest who, having prudentially shared all his struggles with his superior, does not refuse a difficult or humbling assignment learns to see the power of God's grace, which is always sufficient.[8] Many faithful priests can testify that oftentimes, it was in accepting an assignment that at first seemed very difficult that they came to see the fruitfulness of the Cross.

Priestly obedience is also communal. It is communal because the priest never acts alone but always as a member of a presbyterate. Working together with his brother priests in a presbyterate can, depending on the circumstances, be one of the most difficult aspects of priestly ministry. It requires setting aside all jealousy, rivalry, not becoming "too bound up in one's own preferences or points of view" and taking "co-responsibility regarding directions to be taken and choices to be made."[9] Perhaps the most difficult part of this obedience is accepting the weaknesses of his brother priests. A priest should consider it part of his ministry to reach out and support his brothers, especially those who are weak. This is often difficult when his brothers can be hard to be around, or eccentric; but part of his obedience is being called to live in and support this particular presbyterate. The Lord said clearly to his Apostles, "This is how all will know that you are my disciples, if you have love for one another" (Jn 13:35). Fraternal charity should be the mark of a presbyterate, and it has to begin with someone. Choosing to support his brother priests and to work together with them, in obedience to the presbyterate, will require at times the embrace of the Cross.

Perhaps most central to the life of the priest is the pastoral nature of priestly obedience. Pastoral obedience is where the priest incarnates most clearly Christ's spousal love:

> Priestly obedience has a particular "pastoral" character. It is lived in an atmosphere of constant readiness to allow oneself to be taken up, as it were "consumed," by the needs and demands of the flock. These last ought to be truly reasonable and at times they need to be evaluated and tested to see how genuine they are. But it is undeniable that the priest's life is fully "taken up" by the hunger for the Gospel and for faith, hope and love for God and his mystery, a hunger which is more or less consciously present in the people of God entrusted to him.[10]

It is very easy for the demands of pastoral ministry to be seen, at times, as something being taken from the priest. My time is taken; my desires are taken, and it does not always seem to be worthwhile. Anyone who has served in the pastoral field knows how easily these demands can lead to exhaustion, frustration, and even bitterness. The call of Christ will mean that the priest tries to look at these constant sacrifices differently, that he learns to see in them a chance to be given, in union with Christ for the sake of Christ's bride, often in poor and humble ways. If he is able to see the way Christ sees, he can find joy in being given in obedience, the joy of surrendering all.

What is needed is an internalization of obedience, a way of seeing the sacrifices that obedience offers in union with Christ's way of seeing. This is how Vatican II described priestly obedience: "a frame of mind and soul whereby they are always ready to know and do the will of him who sent them and not their own will."[11] The priest must learn to surrender his own desires—here is the "cost" of obedience—to the desires of Christ. He wants to learn in his daily life to model Christ's own total humility before the Father: "because I came down from heaven not to do my own will but the will of the one who sent me" (Jn 6:38). How does he do this, especially when he feels so overwhelmed by daily demands? It can happen only if he is a man of prayer. He will find the prayer of total surrender that Christ prayed to the Father in the Garden of Gethsemane often on his lips: "not my will but yours be done" (Lk 22:42). He will learn to relate to Christ the moments when his own desires must die so that he can serve in joy. Through learning in prayer to live deep surrender, he will also be freed of false burdens, things that he thought the Lord required of him, but he realizes now were his own false expectations. Gradually, as he learns—over time and struggle—to see how the love of Jesus Christ is inviting this particular difficult surrender, he will also experience the deep peace in his heart that only Christ can give. The peace "that surpasses all understanding" (Phil 4:7) that comes from doing God's will.

If a priest is faithful in seeking to be obedient every day, he gradually learns to love obedience. He sees it as freeing him to become a transparent image of Christ. He finds that Christ is working through him in ways he could not have imagined. He seeks to be obedient not only to the external demands of his office, fulfilling his duty, but to the internal prompting of the Holy Spirit throughout the day. He desires to be truly led by Christ in all things. As he does this, he finds that God is directing all his ministry. As Raniero Cantalamessa says in speaking on Christian obedience:

> When God finds a person determined to obey him, he takes the life of that person in his hands like the helm of a boat or the reins of a horse. Minute by minute God begins to define the gestures and words of that person, his way of making use of his time, everything.[12]

Here is a picture of the priest who is a living image of the Bridegroom. He has learned to surrender his will to Christ at every moment and finds his whole life led by Christ. This kind of obedience comes to the priest only through death, just as it did for Christ, the spiritual death of surrendering all his desires to Christ, which leads to living a resurrected life with Christ. This death in obedience will always also be fruitful, as we see in St. Paul "So death is at work in us, but life in you" (2 Cor. 4:12).

The Nuptial Celibacy of the Priest

As noted in the introduction of this book, much has been written on the nuptial nature of priestly celibacy. St. John Paul II clearly articulated how the priest incarnates Christ's spousal love through his celibacy in *Pastores Dabo Vobis*:

> The Church, as the spouse of Jesus Christ, wishes to be loved by the priest in the total and exclusive manner in which Jesus Christ her head and spouse loved her. Priestly celibacy, then, is the gift of self in and with Christ to his Church and expresses the priest's service to the Church in and with the Lord.[13]

Here, one can see the synthesis of how the priest as a living image of the bridegroom must love the Church in and through Christ. St. John Paul II builds these insights upon his own theology of the body, where he explains that celibacy is not a denial of human sexuality but, in fact, a supernatural way to fulfill it. Human sexuality, or what he sometimes calls the nuptial meaning of the body, reveals that human persons find their fulfillment in making a gift of themselves. In celibacy, the priest is able to make a gift of himself in and with Christ to his bride:

> In virginity and celibacy, chastity retains its original meaning, that is, of human sexuality lived as a genuine sign of and precious service to the love of communion and gift of self to others. This meaning is fully found in virginity which makes evident, even in the renunciation of marriage, the "nuptial meaning" of the body through

a communion and a personal gift to Jesus Christ and his Church which prefigures and anticipates the perfect and final communion and self-giving of the world to come.[14]

In some ways, the gift of celibacy can be seen as a more complete self-gift than that in marriage. When one lives in chastity, one is more freely able to give without expecting return. As St. John Paul II said: "When he chooses continence for the kingdom of heaven, man has the awareness that in this way he can realize himself 'differently,' and in some sense 'more' than in marriage, by becoming 'a sincere gift for others' (Gaudium et Spes 24:3)."[15] Celibacy seen in this way is much more than "giving up marriage." Rather, it is a different way of living what is at the heart of human sexuality, self-gift. As Cardinal George once said:

> For a diocesan priest, celibacy is the practical and real way that he lives his existence as a sexual being. If sexuality involves connection, celibacy is a path of communion. If sexuality involves generativity, celibacy is a path of giving spiritual life. If sexuality is sacramental in the sense of being disclosive of the divine, celibacy is a path par excellence of revealing Jesus and the Father who sent him. Celibacy is a way of being married: in the case of priests, being married to the Church. It is not a way of life which would leave us ecclesiastical bachelors.[16]

Priestly celibacy seen in this light is not a lonely way of life; it is a path to deeper communion through self-giving love. The celibate priest is not a stoic who has learned how to live alone without intimacy. Rather, his heart has been captured by the love of Christ and filled with a desire to give himself for Christ's bride. This is the burning love of

which St. Paul speaks when he says, "For his sake I have
accepted the loss of all things and I consider them so much
rubbish, that I may gain Christ" (Phil 3:8). Here is a love of
communion that desires to give itself, "to know him and the
power of his resurrection and [the] sharing of his sufferings
by being conformed to his death, if somehow I may attain
the resurrection from the dead" (Phil 3:10-11). The more the
celibate priest receives this special call, having been chosen
by Christ to live in intimacy with the Trinity, the more he will
find joy in his celibacy, which makes this intimacy possible.

Indeed, the priest's heart is more and more conformed
to that of the Bridegroom; he will find himself burning with
a love that is open to all. The priest's celibacy properly lived
will not make him cold or distant from others. Instead, as
the celibacy lived by Christ, it will make him more able to
love the Church freely and generously. As Jean Galot says:
"Thanks to his celibacy the priest can be the man of charity,
full of sympathy and attention for all. The ideal of being all
things to all men is realized by means of the spiritual liberty
which virginity provides."[17] This kind of celibacy, as we noted
above, allows the sacrificial life of the priest to become fruitful. Thus, through his giving of himself in celibacy, the priest
truly becomes a father as well as a bridegroom. This is an
important theme for St. John Paul II's theology of the body:

> On the other hand, spousal love that finds its expression
> in continence 'for the kingdom of heaven' must lead in
> its normal development to 'fatherhood' or 'motherhood'
> in the spiritual sense (that is, precisely to that 'fruitfulness
> of the Holy Spirit' we have already spoken about), in a
> way analogous to conjugal love, which matures in physical

fatherhood and motherhood and is confirmed in them precisely as spousal love.[18]

The priest who lives this spiritual paternity truly will find in his relationships with his spiritual children a depth that can even surpass natural familial relationships. After all, very often spiritual children share with their spiritual fathers things they would never share with their own parents. They trust these spiritual fathers to help them work through the most intimate struggles of their lives, and they truly receive the gift of new life through the ministry of these priests who have become experts in the spiritual life.

It must be stated, as the Fathers of the Church often did, that the priest who is seeking to be a living image of the Bridegroom will always reverence this privileged relationship he has as a spiritual father and never use this relationship to draw others to himself. As St. Gregory the Great reminded us in chapter 6:

> For he is an enemy of the savior, the man who, through the good works he does, desires to be loved by the Church in the place of [Christ]. For a servant, through whom the bridegroom transmits his gifts, is guilty of adultery in his intentions, if he seeks pleasure in the eyes of the bride.[19]

Yet, the priest knows that if it were not for his celibacy, he could not be the same kind of spiritual father. It is because of his total self-gift to the bride that the children have freedom to come to him. It is because he has embraced the undivided heart of celibacy, seeking union with Christ, that he is free to be open to so many and lives as Christ did, to form a spiritual family and not a particular human family. Yes, this undivided heart has a sacrifice involved. There are certainly times when it is experienced as a death. Yet, ultimately, it leads to deep communion with the Trinity, and in that communion is found the greatest joys of the spiritual life. The celibacy of the priest provides an openness to union with Christ that could not be found if he were married.[20] It can allow him to become a truly spiritual man who not only delights to be an instrument of the creation of spiritual life through the sacraments, but also knows how to lead his spiritual children deeper into the mysteries of God because of his own experience in dwelling in communion with Him. Celibacy lived in union with Christ, laying down one's life with Him for the bride, can be deeply fulfilling and filled with the joy of spiritual fruitfulness.

The Nuptial Poverty of the Priest

Pastores Dabo Vobis stipulates three reasons for the poverty of the priest: poverty is part of the pastoral charity for the flock; poverty leads to interior freedom, and poverty is prophetic. As we have seen, pastoral charity is the desire to be given for the flock. When the priest renounces things of this world to live in poverty, he is better able to be completely given. The priest has been called, as the Apostles were, to leave all for the sake of following Christ. Through poverty, he places all his earthly possessions at the service of his mission:

> Poverty alone ensures that the priest remains available to be sent wherever his work will be most useful and needed even at the cost of personal sacrifice. It is a condition and essential premise of the apostle's docility to the Spirit, making him ready to "go forth," without traveling bag or

personalities, following only the will of the Master (cf. Lk. 9:57-62; Mk. 10:17-22).[21]

By not having exterior things, the priest is free to follow wherever the Lord needs to send him. But the goal of poverty is not simply an external freedom, rather the real goal is an internal freedom. The whole spiritual tradition speaks with one accord about the beauty of poverty, which leads to an interior freedom that opens one up to union with God. As *Presbyterorum Ordinis* says: "By using the world as those who do not use it (1 Cor 7:31), let them achieve that freedom whereby they are free from every inordinate concern and become docile to the voice of God in their daily life."[22] This is the freedom and joy that the saints found in letting go of the things of this world to live completely for God. It is what the Gospel calls poverty of spirit, a total dependence upon God in the joy of living only for God's kingdom:

> No one can serve two masters; for either he will hate the one and love the other, or he will be devoted to the one and despise the other. You cannot serve God and mammon. Therefore I tell you, do not be anxious about your life, what you shall eat or what you shall drink, nor about your body, what you shall put on. Is not life more than food, and the body more than clothing? Look at the birds of the air: they neither sow nor reap nor gather into barns, and yet your heavenly Father feeds them. Are you not of more value than they? . . . Therefore do not be anxious, saying, "What shall we eat?" or "What shall we drink?" or "What shall we wear?" For the Gentiles seek all these things; and your heavenly Father knows that you need them all. But seek first his kingdom and his

righteousness, and all these things shall be yours as well. (Mt 6:24-26, 31-33)[23]

It is important to realize that just as is the case in obedience and celibacy, poverty is not only practical but is part of the spiritual path to union with Christ, the undivided heart Christ asks for from His priests. As the priest lets go of things of this world, he finds his heart is more open to receive the true treasures that Christ offers, to have his "treasure in heaven" (Mt 19:21). As the *Directory for the Ministry and the Life of Priests* says:

> The example of Christ poor should lead the priest to conform himself to Him, with interior detachment regarding all the world's goods and riches (PO 17). The Lord teaches us that the true good is God and that true richness is attaining eternal life: "For what does it profit a man if he gain the whole world, but suffers the loss of his soul? Or what will a man give in exchange for his soul? (Mk 8:36-37)[24]

When Pope Francis speaks about poverty, as he does frequently, he speaks about it both as a means to achieve union with God and as an essential prophetic witness. Pope Francis, like the founder of his order, St. Ignatius, has clearly fallen in love with the beauty and gift of poverty and reveals to us its deep value:

> For Ignatius, and these are two key words that he uses, poverty is both mother and bulwark. Poverty nurtures, mothers, generates spiritual life, a life of holiness, apostolic life. And it is a wall, it defends. How many ecclesial disasters began because of a lack of poverty,

including outside the Society, I mean in the whole
Church in general. How many of the scandals which
I, unfortunately, have to find out about, are born
of money.[25]

One of the things Pope Francis speaks consistently
against is the sin of clericalism, which we have defined as
appropriating the privileges that belong to the Bridegroom
to oneself. This is especially dangerous in the area of wealth,
as the priest will often have access to much greater wealth
because of his position. This can be one way he lives for himself and not for Christ:

> Clericalism, which is one of the most serious illnesses
> that the Church has, distances itself from poverty.
> Clericalism is rich. If it is not rich in money, it is rich in
> pride. But it is rich: there is in clericalism an attachment
> to possession. It does not allow itself to be nurtured by
> mother poverty, it does not allow itself to be guarded by
> the wall of poverty.[26]

Since Christ Himself refused a life of privilege in favor
of the freedom and beauty of poverty, when the priest allows
himself to be seduced by the wealth offered him, it becomes
a serious counter witness to the beauty of the Gospel: "The
poor Church for the poor is the Church of the Gospel,
the Sermon on the Mount of the Gospel of Matthew, and
the Sermon on the Plain of the Gospel of Luke."[27] Pope
Francis's own love of the beauty of poverty and his personal
witness of living it can be a great source of inspiration for
the priest.

Although all the documents on priesthood since Vatican II are explicit in the need for priests to live poverty, they tend to avoid mandatory rules. Rather, the documents make clear that priests ought to live a "simple and austere lifestyle,"[28] and the priest ought to "deny himself those worldly activities which are not in keeping with his ministry."[29] As the *Directory for the Life and Ministry of Priests* says, "In all aspects (living quarters, means of transportation, vacations, etc.), the priest is to eliminate any kind of affectation and luxury."[30] The priest should also be known for his generosity:

> Remembering, moreover, that the gift he has received is gratuitous, he must be disposed to give in like manner (Mt 10:8; Acts 8:18-25), and to use what he receives from the exercise of his office for the good of the Church and works of charity, after having provided for his honest sustenance.[31]

For poverty to be lived well, it must be more than simply a discipline one takes on, but like Christ, it must involve a love for the poor and a desire to be close to them. As Vatican II made clear when speaking about poverty to priests:

> Led by the Spirit of the Lord, who anointed the Savior and sent him to evangelize the poor, priests, therefore, and also bishops, should avoid everything which in any way could turn the poor away. Before the other followers of Christ, let priests set aside every appearance of vanity in their possessions. Let them arrange their homes so that they might not appear unapproachable to anyone, lest anyone, even the most humble, fear to visit them.[32]

Again, Pope Francis provides a powerful witness here in his consistent calls for a poor Church that is close to the poor. "A poor Church is a Church that practices voluntary simplicity in her life—in her very institutions, in the lifestyle of her members—to break down every dividing wall, especially to the poor."[33]

What the Tradition also shows us is that there is a very close relationship between poverty in fact and poverty of spirit. The interior freedom of spiritual poverty, true dependence upon God, cannot be accomplished without poverty of fact—a real lack of material possessions. As Basil Cole, O.P., and Paul Connor, O.P., teach, the "authentic spirit of poverty cannot exist, [without] some degree of poverty in fact."[34] Poverty, to be real, must cost the priest something. As Gisbert Greshake says, "When does he renounce something which he could quite properly have, in order that Paul's words about Jesus could also apply to him: 'he was rich, yet for our sake he became poor, that through his poverty we might become rich' (2 Cor 8:9)."[35] The goal is seeking to become more and more a transparent image of Christ, to conform himself to the example of Christ. And as the priest imitates Christ's poverty, he becomes an important witness to the world of today: "A truly poor priest is indeed a specific sign of separation from, disavowal of and non-submission to the tyranny of a contemporary world which puts all its trust in money and in material security."[36] And this freedom also increases his pastoral charity. Because he has let go of the tyranny of things and learns to love poverty, he is easily able to be generous with others. As St. John Paul II said:

Poverty for the priest, by virtue of his sacramental configuration to Christ, the head and shepherd, takes on specific "pastoral" connotations . . . "Priests, following the example of Christ, who, rich though he was, became poor for love of us (cf. 2 Cor 8:9)—should consider the poor and the weakest as people entrusted in a special way to them, and they should be capable of witnessing to poverty with a simple and austere lifestyle, having learned the generous renunciation of superfluous things (cf. OT 9; CIC 282).[37]

When poverty is lived well by the priest, it gives a powerful weight to his message because it proves that he is truly living for the kingdom of heaven. As Greshake says: "In the preacher who is poor, needy, unpretentious, the claim of the message itself can appear unadulterated and without distortion."[38] Especially in the materialistic culture of the west, this witness is very important today and sometimes just as shocking as the priest's celibacy.

Poverty is part of the priest's self-gift, part of his self-emptying, sacrificial love for the bride. Priests in different situations may live poverty differently, but the self-denial of poverty is essential to making a total self-gift. The priest must be willing to place all his possessions at the service of his mission. He must seek to become a transparent image of the poor Christ. In this way, just as in obedience and celibacy, when the priest lives poverty, he also takes part in Christ's redemptive sacrifice. He makes his own life an offering, becoming both priest and victim. As St. John Vianney expressed in his deep desire to be totally given in imitation of Christ: "My secret is easy to learn. It can be summed up in these few words: give everything away and keep nothing for yourself."[39]

Questions for Discussion, Reflection, and Prayer

1. Do I welcome the obedience I promised my bishop, searching for its fruitfulness in my life, even when that obedience becomes difficult? Can I give thanks for seeing the hand of God in that suffering?

2. Do I seek to listen for God's voice to help me discern how to spend my time? How might I do that?

3. When do I experience loneliness in celibacy, and how is Christ inviting me there to deeper communion?

4. Who are my spiritual children, and how have I seen that my celibacy is fruitful for the kingdom?

5. Have I tasted the freedom and joy of poverty? How, practically, is Christ inviting me to live more poorly?

6. When do I spend time with Christ in the poor, and do they see me as close to them?

7. How might I grow more in the image of Christ the Bridegroom through my prayers?

NOTES

1.   Dermot Power, *A Spiritual Theology of the Priesthood: The Mystery of Christ and the Mission of the Priest* (Washington, DC: Catholic University of America Press, 1998), 96.

2.   Hans Urs von Balthasar, *The Christian State of Life*, trans. Sister Mary Frances McCarthy (San Francisco: Ignatius Press, 1983), 367.

3.   Joseph Cardinal Ratzinger, *Pilgrim Fellowship of Faith: The Church as Communion*, ed. Stephan Otto Horn and Vinzenz Pfnür, trans. Henry Taylor (San Franciscio: Ignatius Press, 2005), 170. Section 13 of *Presbyterorum Ordinis* points out that the priest does not have to look for the means to holiness outside of his duties but rather in his duties of preaching, sanctifying, and governing the Church, he will find the necessary means to his own sanctification.

4.   *Directory for the Life and Ministry of Priests*, 56. We note that in *Presbyterorum Ordinis* and *Pastores Dabo Vobis*, obedience is the first counsel discussed for the priest.

5.   *Directory*, 56.

6.   See *Pastores Dabo Vobis*, sec. 28; *Presbyterorum Ordinis*, sec. 15 and *Directory* 57.

7.   As section 28 of *Pastores Dabo Vobis* emphasizes: "This 'submission' to those invested with ecclesial authority is in no way a kind of humiliation. It flows instead from the responsible freedom of the priest who accepts not only the demands of an organized and organic ecclesial life, but also that grace of discernment and responsibility in ecclesial decisions which was assured by Jesus to his apostles and their successors for the sake of faithfully safeguarding the mystery of the Church and serving the structure of the Christian community among its common path toward salvation."

8.   This does not mean that he may never have to reveal to his bishop the interior struggle he is having. He may even have to ask in humble obedience to be relieved of an assignment for the sake of his emotional and spiritual health. All this is part of the trustful surrender in the Lord that he exercises when receiving the bishop's assignment as coming from the Lord.

9.   *Pastores Dabo Vobis*, sec. 28.

10.   Ibid.

11.   *Presbyterorum Ordinis*, sec. 15.

12.   Raniero Cantalamessa, O.F.M. Cap., *Obedience: The Authority of the Word*, trans. Frances Lonergan Villa (Middlegreen, England: St. Paul Publications, 1989), 55.

13.   *Pastores Dabo Vobis*, sec. 29.

14.   Ibid.

15. John Paul II, *Man and Woman He Created Them: A Theology of the Body* (Boston: Pauline Books and Media, 2006), 427.

16. Francis George, O.M.I., "Self-Gift in Generative Love: Priests Continue Jesus' Mission to Reveal the Father," in *Spiritual Fatherhood: Living Christ's Own Revelation of the Father,* March 13-16, 2003, by the Institute for Priestly Formation and Mount Saint Mary's Seminary, ed. Edward G. Matthews, Jr. (Omaha, Nebr.: privately printed, 2003): 18.

17. Jean Galot, "The Priesthood and Celibacy," *Review for Religious* 24 (1965): 946.

18. *Man and Woman He Created Them,* 432, emphasis in original.

19. "Regula Pastoralis," II, 8 (Sources Chrétiennes 381, 232).

20. See 1 Corinthians 7:34.

21. *Pastores Dabo Vobis,* sec. 30.

22. *Presbyterorum Ordinis,* sec. 17.

23. Pope Francis spoke of the joy that comes from relationship with Christ that material things cannot provide when he warned seminarians and novices in 2013 not to seek their happiness in the things of this world: "Some will say: joy is born from the things one has, and so, the search for the latest model of the smartphone, the fastest scooter, the car that attracts attention . . . Some will say: joy is born from possessions, so they go in quest of the latest model of the smartphone, the fastest scooter, the showy car. . . . but I tell you, it truly grieves me to see a priest or a sister with the latest model of a car: but this can't be! . . . True joy does not come from things or from possessing, no! It is born from the encounter, from the relationship with others. . . . In calling you God says to you: 'You are important to me, I love you, I am counting on you'. Jesus says this to each one of us! Joy is born from that! The joy of the moment in which Jesus looked at me. Understanding and hearing this is the secret of our joy. Feeling loved by God, feeling that for him we are not numbers but people; and hearing him calling us." ("Meeting with Seminarians and Novices," July 6, 2013, https://w2.vatican.va/content/francesco/en/speeches/2013/july/documents/papa-francesco_20130706_incontro-seminaristi.html.

24. *Directory,* 83.

25. "'To Have Courage and Prophetic Audacity' Dialogue of Pope Francis with the Jesuits gathered in the 36th General Congregation," *La Civilta Cattolica,* Oct. 24, 2016, http://jesuits.org/Assets/Publications/File/GC36-Dialogue_of_Pope_Francis_ENGLISH.PDF, accessed 10-4-18.

26. Ibid.

27. Ibid.

28. *Pastores Dabo Vobis,* sec. 30; *Optatam Totius,* sec. 9; *Codex Iuris Canonici,* 282).

29. *Directory,* 67. See *Codex Iuris Canonici* 286 and 1392.

30.   *Directory*, 83. See also *Presbyterorum Ordinis*, sec. 17.

31.   *Directory*, 83. See *Codex Iuris Canonici* 282; 222, sec. 2; 529, sec. 1.

32.   *Presbyterorum Ordinis*, sec. 17.

33.   Pope Francis, "General Audience," June 3 2015, https://w2.vatican.va/content/francesco/en/audiences/2015/documents/papa-francesco_20150603_udienza-generale.html.

34.   Basil Cole, O.P., and Paul Conner, O.P., *Christian Totality: Theology of the Consecrated Life*, revised edition (Mumbai, India: St. Paul's, 1997), 161, emphasis in original.

35.   Gisbert Greshake, *The Meaning of Christian Priesthood*, trans. Peadar MacSeumais, S.J. (Westminster, MD: Christian Classics, 1989), 140.

36.   *Pastores Dabo Vobis*, sec. 30.

37.   Ibid., sec. 30. The Internal quote is from Proposition 10 of the unpublished propositions from the synod fathers of the 1990 Synod on priestly formation.

38.   Greshake, 139. He continues: "[T]his is frequently pointed out in the Pauline writings also. In Philippians (1:17) St. Paul says that many who are preaching Christ are motivated by self-interest. On the contrary, Paul's glory is to have accepted nothing from anyone, although—as he says expressly in 1 Cor. 9:4 ff.—he would have had a just claim to be maintained by the community. 'Nevertheless, we did not make use of this right, but we endure all things, so as not to cause in a hindrance to the Gospels Christ' (9:12). 'Because I was not dependent on anyone, I made myself a slave to all, in order to win this many as possible' (9:19). . . . The first epistle of Peter makes a similar call to the presbyters not to shepherd the flock entrusted to them with a view to sordid gain. The poverty of the preacher helps the unhindered exposition of the gospel, and his own credibility."

39.   Quoted in John XXIII, *Sacerdotii Nostri Primordia*, (1 August 1959) in *Acta Apostolicae Sedis* 51(1959), 14.

CONCLUSION

The goal of this book has been to help priests embrace more deeply the way of life they are called to by virtue of their identity *in persona Christi Sponsi Ecclesia*. St. John Paul II introduced the nuptial image to the understanding of pastoral charity in order to inspire priests to make a more profound gift of themselves. This book has tried to explain St. John Paul II's insight and investigate the nuptial image of priesthood in the Tradition to see how this gift of self happens through the evangelical counsels. Alongside the whole work has been another consistent desire, to inspire the prayer life of priests. This has been the purpose of the questions at the end of each chapter. It is clear from this book that if priests are to live their identity fully, they need to be reminded of who they are and deeply rooted in this identity. This is the purpose of the prayer life of the priest. In prayer, the priest keeps before him the image of Christ the Bridegroom, not just as an ideal, but as a living person. The Apostles left everything because of a personal invitation to "be with" with Christ (Mk 3:14). Only in this "being with" that comes from prayer will the priest be able to experience the deeper freedom that comes from the evangelical counsels. Without this life of prayer, the counsels will remain as burdens to be carried, not joys that set free. In fact, it is normal that sometimes obedience, celibacy, and poverty are experienced as burdens. When this happens, the priest must bring these weights to prayer and learn to see these demands of his ministry as Christ sees them. Just as the Jesus in His agony presented honestly the weight of the Cross before His Father, so the priest must not be afraid to acknowledge the heaviness of the Cross in his daily life. Yet, also as in Christ, if he honestly brings these struggles to prayer, he will see that in every sacrifice his vocation asks of him is found an invitation to deeper union with the Trinity. This union happens the way it happened for Christ—through the self-emptying, sacrificial, fruitful love of the Paschal Mystery. Gradually, through his daily time in prayer, the priest will begin to see his life and ministry the way St. Paul saw his, in terms of the Paschal Mystery. A very important Scripture passage for the priest to understand his sacrificial way of life as an image of the Bridegroom is 2 Corinthians 4:7-12. We have already referred to this passage in several places, but here we offer it as summary of the life of pastoral charity of the priest:

> But we hold this treasure in earthen vessels, that the surpassing power may be of God and not from us. We are afflicted in every way, but not constrained; perplexed, but not driven to despair; persecuted, but not abandoned; struck down, but not destroyed; always carrying about in the body the dying of Jesus, so that the life of Jesus may also be manifested in our body. For we who live are constantly being given up to death for the sake of Jesus, so that the life of Jesus may be manifested in our mortal flesh. So death is at work in us, but life in you.

In light of the insights gained, it is easy to see the nuptial connotations of this passage. The Cross is the place of the marriage, the place of Christ's self-gift. Every time the priest experiences the Cross in his life, every time he embraces obedience, celibacy, and poverty in sacrificial and self-emptying love, his death is fruitful for the bride. The priest knows through faith that in Christ, death brings life: "death is at work in us, but life in you" (2 Cor 4:12).

If the priest is able to bring these deaths to Christ in prayer and embrace them as gifts from the Bridegroom for the bride, then he will find that his pastoral charity grows. We might offer as an aid to this prayer the Orthodox icon of Christ the Bridegroom. Here, in the image of Bridegroom prepared for the Passion, the priest discovers that "Jesus Christ, who brought his pastoral charity to perfection on the cross with a complete exterior and interior emptying of self, is both the model and source of the virtues of obedience, chastity and poverty which the priest is called to live." By spending time with Christ the Bridegroom, by learning to see His daily life in light of the self-gift of Christ the Bridegroom, the priest will find burning in his own heart the fire of love that burned in the heart of Christ. This is what allowed the great priest saints to spend themselves completely for the love of Christ. Through obedience, celibacy, and poverty, they made a total gift of themselves to Christ; and they found their lives filled with the pastoral charity of Christ. Their life became filled with one desire—to love Christ's bride with His own love. *"Da mihi animas, cetera tolle."*

CPSIA information can be obtained
at www.ICGtesting.com
Printed in the USA
FSHW010652131120
75800FS